ALL DRESSED UP

Irish Studies

James MacKillop, *Series Editor*

OTHER TITLES FROM IRISH STUDIES

A Chastened Communion: Modern Irish Poetry and Catholicism
ANDREW J. AUGE

Collaborative Dubliners: Joyce in Dialogue
VICKI MAHAFFEY, *ed.*

*The Irish Bridget: Irish Immigrant Women
in Domestic Service in America, 1840–1930*
MARGARET LYNCH-BRENNAN

Irish Theater in America: Essays on Irish Theatrical Diaspora
JOHN P. HARRINGTON, *ed.*

Joyce, Imperialism, and Postcolonialism
LEONARD ORR, *ed.*

*Making Ireland Irish: Tourism and National
Identity since the Irish Civil War*
ERIC G. E. ZUELOW

Memory Ireland: Vol. 1, *History and Modernity*; Vol. 2, *Diaspora
and Memory Practices*; Vol. 3, *The Famine and the Troubles*;
Vol. 4, *James Joyce and Cultural Memory*
OONA FRAWLEY, *ed.*

Modern Irish Drama: W. B. Yeats to Marina Carr, Second Edition
SANFORD STERNLICHT

*Rethinking Occupied Ireland: Gender and Incarceration
in Contemporary Irish Film*
JESSICA SCARLATA

JOAN FITZPATRICK DEAN

ALL DRESSED UP

Modern
Irish
Historical
Pageantry

Syracuse University Press

Syracuse University Press

Syracuse, New York 13244-5290

All Rights Reserved

First Edition 2014

14   15   16   17   18   19   6   5   4   3   2   1

∞ The paper used in this publication meets the minimum requirements
of the American National Standard for Information Sciences—Permanence
of Paper for Printed Library Materials, ANSI Z39.48-1992.

For a listing of books published and distributed by Syracuse University Press,
visit www.SyracuseUniversityPress.syr.edu.

ISBN: 978-0-8156-3374-7 (cloth)   978-0-8156-5284-7 (ebook)

Library of Congress Cataloging-in-Publication Data

Dean, Joan Fitzpatrick, 1949–

All dressed up : modern Irish historical pageantry / Joan FitzPatrick Dean. — First edition.

pages cm. — (Irish studies)

Includes bibliographical references and index.

ISBN 978-0-8156-3374-7 (cloth : alk. paper) — ISBN 978-0-8156-5284-7 (ebook)

1. English drama—20th century—History and criticism   2. English drama—Irish authors—
History and criticism.   3. Irish drama—20th century—History and criticism.   4. Historical
drama, English—History and criticism.   5. Pageants—Ireland—History—20th century.
6. Literature and society—Ireland—History—20th century.   I. Pearse, Padraic, 1879–1916.
Macghníomhartha Chúchulainn. English.   II. Macghníomhartha Chúchulainn.   III. Title.

PR8789.D43 2014

822'.0514099415—dc23   2014029521

Manufactured in the United States of America

For Phoebe Cashill Davis and all her kin

While it is not within the province of the Theatre to enter into matters political, it is its duty to present to the public at large in an easily assimilated form the great and stirring events which have helped in moulding the destiny of a nation. There is scarcely any country in the world with such a proud and noble past, so crowded with memorable epics as Ireland. For centuries our forefathers have fought and died that our country might be free. The stories of their unselfish deeds, deathless sacrifices, and heroic battles are more exhilarating than fictions [*sic*] greatest libraries.

—"On Guard Again!," *Signal Fires* program, 1942

JOAN FITZPATRICK DEAN
is Curators Teaching Professor at the University of Missouri–Kansas City where she teaches drama and film. She was Fulbright Scholar at University College Galway (1992–93) and Fulbright Lecturer at the Université de Nancy (1982–83). She is the author of *Riot and Great Anger: Stage Censorship in Twentieth-Century Ireland*, the Irish Film Institute/Cork University Press study of Friel's *Dancing at Lughnasa*, books on Tom Stoppard and David Hare, and articles in *Modern Drama*, *New Hibernia Review*, *Irish University Review*, *Theatre Journal*, and *Theatre Survey*.

Contents

Illustrations

COLOR PLATES

Following page 130

Acknowledgments

The University of Missouri–Kansas City generously supported my research for this project over many years. I am particularly indebted to the University of Missouri Research Board. My thanks to Tom Stroik, Jeff Rydberg-Cox, Virginia Blanton, and Jennifer Phegley for the often-thankless task of chairing the Department of English.

I enjoyed as much as I benefited from a Moore Institute fellowship at the National University of Ireland, Galway, in 2012. The historians, several of whom, including Nicholas Canny and Dáithí O Cronin, spoke with me about G. A. Hayes-McCoy, were ever generous. To my colleagues in English at NUI Galway, I owe an abiding debt. Special thanks to Riana O'Dwyer, who shared her office with me in 2012 and her friendship over a much longer period. I had the good fortune to speak with several people, including Barry Cassin, Gearóid Ó Tuathaigh, and Paraic Breathnach, who kindly shared their direct experience with historical pageants. Maurice MacMahon, son of Bryan, very kindly provided access to his father's extensive and carefully preserved papers. In Wexford, Eithne Scallan, daughter of Seamus MacCall, offered hospitality and encouragement as well as permissions and access. Thanks, too, to MacCall's great-nephew Oisin Creagh for generating high-resolution scans.

My debt to librarians and archivists is profound. Sincere thanks to Stuart Hinds, Scott Gipson, Teresa Gipson, and Kelley Martin in the Kenneth J. LaBudde Special Collections and the other staff in the Libraries at the University of Missouri–Kansas City; the helpful personnel at the National Library of Ireland, including Glenn Dunne, Honora Faul, Elizabeth Harford, and Katherine McSharry; Scott

Krafft, Sigrid Perry, Nicholas Munagian, and the late Ellen Howe at the Dublin Gate Theatre Archive in the Charles Deering McCormick Library of Special Collections at Northwestern University; Marie Boran, Kieran Hoare, Barry Houlihan, and Margaret Hughes in Special Collections in the James Hardiman Library at the National University of Ireland, Galway; Hugh Beckett, Lisa O'Dwyer, and Commandant Padraic Kennedy at the Military Archives of Ireland in Dublin; Deirdre Wildy and Ursula Mitchel in Special Collections in the McClay Library at Queen's University Belfast; Susan Hood at the Reorganized Church Body Library in Dublin; Marilyn Carbonell at the Nelson-Atkins Library in Kansas City, Missouri; Karen Wall at the Irish Film Institute; Lar Joye at the Collins Barracks of the National Museum of Ireland; Sharon Sutton at Trinity College Dublin; and Vera Orschel, now archivist for the Irish Jesuits. Sincere thanks to those in Special Collections in the Kenneth Spencer Research Library at the University of Kansas, especially Karen Cook, Elspeth Healey, and Kathy Lafferty, who balance the paradoxical demands of providing access to and preserving the splendid collection of P. S. O'Hegarty, the sine qua non of my research.

I enjoyed many opportunities to present phases of this research at the conferences of the American Conference for Irish Studies and the International Association for the Study of Irish Literatures. To my colleagues in those organizations, particularly the conference organizers, my enduring gratitude. At the Command and General Staff College in Fort Leavenworth, Kansas W. H. Kautt and my Mindszenty classmate, Richard V. Barbuto, patiently responded to many questions. Chris Le Beau at the Miller Nichols Library provided heroic assistance with intricacies of copyright. Special thanks to Barry Cassin, Donnacha O Briain, Seán Farrell Moran at Oakland University, and James H. Murphy at DePaul University. Gareth Cox shared a trove of material on the Irish Army's musical heritage. Síghle Bhreathnach-Lynch proved a priceless resource. Thanks to Bruce Stewart for the wonderful ricorso.net. Many friends in Ireland, including Vinny Browne, Noreen Collins, Pat O'Dwyer, and Harry White, offered all sorts of clues and insights that proved invaluable. Thanks, too, to

Irene Stevenson, librarian for the *Irish Times*, and to Sharon Sutton at Trinity College Dublin.

An earlier version of chapter 2 appeared in the *New Hibernia Review* (13, no. 1, 21–40) under the congenial editorship of Jim Rogers. I am grateful for Lindsey Quinn Osman's help in formatting the manuscript. Thanks to Jennika Baines, Lisa Kuerbis, Kay Steinmetz, and Annette Wenda at Syracuse University Press as well as the outside readers who expressed confidence in the work and offered cogent suggestions.

I am especially grateful to Seán Ó Briain for his translation of Pearse's *Macghníomhartha Chúchulainn*, which discloses elements of the pageant submerged in Pearse's summary of the pageant.

Were it not for an eternity of Wednesdays at the Record Bar, I might never have completed this project. Rave on.

Many wonderful friends, who know who they are, encouraged me, not least by allowing me to share my enthusiasm for this project. I am blessed with amusing and generous relatives, especially my sister, Margaret; my brother, Christopher; and a bevy of in-laws. My daughters, Margaret and Flannery, may realize neither how much they, each in her own way, contributed to this project nor how deeply grateful I am to both of them. To Jack, my husband of forty-one years, let me say that it seems more like forty-one weeks, and a good forty-one weeks at that.

My sincere gratitude to the following for permission to reproduce copyrighted material:

A. P. Watt at United Agents, LLP, on behalf of the Executors of the Estate of Magdalen Perceval Maxwell [King-Hall] for excerpts from her *Pageant of Greyabbey*.

The Board of Trinity College Dublin for photographs of Denis Johnston's *The Pageant of Cuchulainn*.

Ciarán MacGonigal for the Estate of Maurice MacGonigal, RHA (1900–1979), for the cover image created by Maurice MacGonigal for the *Dublin Civic Week, 1929: Official Handbook*.

Eithne Scallan on behalf of the Estate of Seamus MacCall for excerpts from his essays, scrapbooks, pageant manuscripts, and costume designs for the 1927 Dublin Civic Week held in the Seamus MacCall Collection.

Felicity Hayes-McCoy for excerpts from G. A. Hayes-McCoy's *The Common People, Trumpet Call, The Pageant of St. Patrick*, scrapbooks, and correspondence held in the Hayes-McCoy Papers at NUI Galway's James Hardiman Library on permanent loan from Felicity Hayes-McCoy on behalf of the Hayes-McCoy family. The papers were preserved after G. A. Hayes-McCoy's death by his wife, Mary M. Hayes-McCoy, née O'Connor.

The *Irish Times* for images of *The Pageant of St. Patrick* and *The Pageant of Cuchulainn*.

Katy O'Kennedy for the Estate of Niel O'Kennedy (1923–2010) for his cartoon in *Dublin Opinion*.

Macnas and the Macnas Archive, James Hardiman Library, National University of Galway, for the program cover and photographs of *The Táin*.

Maurice MacMahon for excerpts from Bryan MacMahon's *Seachtar Fear, Seacht Lá*; *The Pageant of the Four Fields*; *The Pageant of Ireland*; and *A Pageant of Pearse*, held in the Papers of Bryan MacMahon.

Micheal Johnston for excerpts from Denis Johnston's *The Pageant of Cuchulainn*.

Michael Travers for the Estate of Edwards-macLíammóir for excerpts from Micheál macLíammóir's published works *All for Hecuba: An Irish Theatrical Autobiography* and *Theatre in Ireland*, macLíammóir's illustration of the cover of T. H. Nally's *Finn Varra Maa*, macLíammóir's costume designs for Owen Roe O'Neill and Dervogilla, the still from *The Ford of the Hurdles*, excerpts from the unpublished manuscripts of *The Ford of the Hurdles*, "The Narrative of *The Pageant of the Celt*," and *The Pageant of St. Patrick*; Hilton Edwards's essay "Historical Pageant"; and Edwards's correspondence.

The Military Archives of Ireland, Dublin, for excerpts from the correspondence and announcer's script for the Step Together pageants and 1945 Military Tattoo and for photographs from the Step Together Scrapbook.

The National Library of Ireland for the cover of *The Roll of the Drums* and excerpts from the program for *Signal Fires* held in the Joseph Holloway Ephemera Collection.

Rory Johnston for excerpts from Denis Johnston's program note for *The Pageant of Cuchulainn*.

Special Collections, Kenneth Spencer Research Library, University of Kansas Libraries, for images from the *World's Work: Irish Number*, program cover for *A Twelfth Century Pageant Play*, the Christian Brothers Pageant in the *Journal of the Ivernian Society*, and the *Grand Military Tattoo and Fireworks Display*.

Abbreviations

2RN	the first radio station in the Irish Free State
CIÉ	Córas Iompair Éireann (Irish Transport/Trains)
DFA	Department of Foreign Affairs
FÁS	Foras Áiseanna Saothair, the Irish Training and Employment Authority
FCA	An Fórsa Cosanta Áitiúil, army reserve
GAA	Gaelic Athletic Association
GPO	General Post Office, O'Connell Street, Dublin
IRA	Irish Republican Army
IWFL	Irish Women's Franchise League
NTS	National Theatre Society
LDF	Local Defence Forces
RDS	Royal Dublin Society
RTÉ	Radió Teilifís Éireann
TAOIS	Department of the Taoiseach
UCD	University College Dublin
ULT	Ulster Literary Theatre

ALL DRESSED UP

Introduction

Throughout the twentieth century, public spectacles portrayed the Irish past through the theatrical idiom of historical pageantry. Often involving the expenditure of public funds and resources, these historical pageants demonstrated the allegiances and affiliations of both performers and spectators through selective and sometimes highly imaginative treatments of Irish history. Historical pageants construct narratives that relate, impart, and perpetuate an interpretation of the past shaped less by empirical research or professional historians than by the appropriation of key events and figures to suit the immediate purposes of a community. Historical pageants are paratheatrical events in which performers impersonate figures from the past. Early in the twentieth century, the word "pageant" was synonymous with "spectacle." In 1910, for instance, the press routinely referred to the funeral of Edward VII as a pageant. Royal visits, vice-regal functions, military tournaments, Corpus Christi processions, and the 1932 Eucharistic Congress were all called pageants because they were public spectacles. Defined so broadly, pageants have existed at least as long as have population centers. Unlike conventional plays, performance takes precedence over text in such paratheatrical events. Commemorations, mass meetings, and religious ceremonies such as Christenings, marriages, and funerals form the very fabric of life yet are set off from quotidian reality by distinguishing theatrical elements. In *The Archive and the Repertoire*, Diane Taylor describes these performative paratheatricals as the repertoire: "The repertoire, whether in terms of verbal or nonverbal expression, transmits live, embodied actions. As such, traditions are stored in the body, through various mnemonic methods,

1

and transmitted 'live' in the here and now to a live audience. Forms handed down from the past are experienced as present. Although this may well describe the mechanics of spoken language, it also describes a dance recital or a religious festival."[1] The very act of personation of figures from Ireland's past, mythological as well as historical, carried affective, ludic, and cultural powers.

Paratheatrical events follow, in outline at least, a predetermined and rehearsed action, if not script. Highly choreographed, ritualized, or symbolic movement situates these events within local, religious, and national traditions but equally removes them from the workaday world. The liturgy and ceremonies of the Catholic Church may predispose its faithful to value such spectacles.[2] Whereas the Catholic Mass can be read as a reenactment of Christ's life, historical pageantry involves the personation of figures from the past, brought back and represented as ancestral. If one asks what theatrical experience was both routine and popular with ordinary Irish people in the twentieth century, pageantry surfaces as a likely candidate.

Irish paratheatrical traditions are especially rich for many reasons, including a long colonial history that marginalized performances of Irish identity, not least through a network of penal laws and the denial of franchise. Many Irish paratheatrical events aspired to reach the widest audience possible. Whereas a wedding or commemorative service would typically restrict access to a select, specially invited cadre, public spectacles like pageants sought as large an audience as possible and often moved into the open air to accommodate the thousands or even hundreds of thousands they attracted. Religious celebrations, monster meetings, civil rights marches, labor demonstrations, sporting events, and political rallies—all of them paratheatrical events—drew remarkably large audiences in nineteenth- and twentieth-century Ireland. The most famous and largest public spectacles since Irish Independence, the 1932 Eucharistic Congress and the 1979 visit of Pope John Paul II, both reflected the country's identity as a Catholic nation, but neither was a historical pageant since neither personated people from Ireland's history. Occasionally, Irish pageants used allegorical figures to represent, for example, the four provinces or Irish industries, and these too portrayed an Irish heritage.

Like conventional Irish history plays and commemorations, historical pageantry thrives on an appetite to imagine, understand, or recover the Irish past by dramatizing a narrative. While both history plays and historical pageants engage in a highly selective treatment of the past, pageantry overwhelmingly celebrates rather than interrogates the past. Contemporary historians, Pierre Nora among them, describe these manipulations of the past as *lieu de mémoire*: "If the expression *lieu de mémoire* must have an official definition, it should be this: a *lieu de mémoire* is any significant entity, whether material or non-material in nature, which by dint of human will or the work of time has become a symbolic element of the memorial heritage of any community."[3] Although historical pageants often aimed to entertain, they all incorporated symbolic elements and aspired to forge Ireland's heritage.

The overarching purpose of historical pageantry in and outside Ireland has been to legitimize, consolidate, and expand power. Throughout the nineteenth and early twentieth centuries in Ireland, public spectacle was associated with the colonial administration, aristocrats, and the monarchy. Pageants were typically royal, imperial, or vice-regal. James H. Murphy and Sean Connolly have studied the elaborate ceremonies that attended Queen Victoria's four official visits to Ireland in 1849, 1853, 1861, and 1900. Her great-granddaughter's visit in 2011 was likewise marked by ritual and symbolic action, perhaps most memorably Queen Elizabeth's use of the Irish language.

Although historical pageants aimed to attract and to entertain a vast audience, they all had a propagandist dimension. Most pageantry is hegemonic—state sponsored, supported, or subsidized—but there are in Ireland, especially before 1922, fascinating examples of counterhegemonic pageantry performed by nationalists, students, or suffragists. Patrick Pearse's pageants were neither the first nor the best attended, but they remain the best-known and best-studied Irish historical pageants. Pageants typically depend on mustering a larger

number of participants to create an epic mise en scène in hopes of
drawing a proportionately large audience; the epic scale to which
pageantry aspires is one of its defining characteristics. Pageantry
minimizes what Constantin Stanislavski and most theatre practitioners call acting and depends on a large cohort of performers, usually
amateurs with a small nucleus of experienced or professional actors,
to produce dramatic effects on a grand scale. Typically unpaid, perhaps employed by Defence Forces, the Garda Síochána, or even on
an Foras Áiseanna Saothair (FÁS) scheme, supernumeraries may be
drawn from a locality, a club, a student body, an army, a trade guild, a
parish, a craobh of the Gaelic League, or similar organization. Counterhegemonic pageants often drew together several such constitu-
encies, which otherwise operated with considerable independence.
Especially in the early decades of the twentieth century, pageantry
was an appealing theatrical idiom because it mobilized a large number
of amateurs to create impressive spectacles that could attract publicity, enlarge participation, and channel enthusiasm. In the twenty-first
century the idiom survives in the opening ceremonies of the Olympic
Games. In 2008 the opening ceremony of the Games in China celebrated four great inventions: paper, movable type, gunpowder, and
the compass. Four years later Danny Boyle developed an extravaganza
of British history in London, *Isles of Wonder*, that likewise aspired to
stage a nation's past.

The history is generally told in terms of text-based, published
plays; in common parlance, the words "theatre" and "stage" refer to
enclosed architectural spaces. Theatre historians and theoreticians like
Marvin Carlson endorse the analysis of theatre as performance based
rather than text centered.[4] Rarely published and usually performed
outside purpose-built theatres, Irish historical pageants appropriated
spaces, typically public and occasionally site-specific ones. Against a
natural landscape, in sporting arenas, or even in school halls, pageants
could attract spectators who might never attend a play in a conventional theatre, let alone Ireland's national theatre, the Abbey. When
performed in the open air and at night, pageants could employ the
spectacular effects of *son et lumière*: the use of powerful searchlights,

bonfires, torches (battery powered and incendiary), fireworks, and other illuminations. Performed in darkness, "torchlight evolutions," the mass, precision formations of supernumeraries with torches remain a regular feature of military tattoos. Even more spectacular pyrotechnics appeared in the 1935 reenactment of the Easter Rising when the Free State Army constructed and then set ablaze a half-scale replica of the General Post Office (GPO) in the Royal Dublin Society (RDS) every evening for five consecutive nights.

Through such intense, systematic auditory and visual stimulation, pageantry privileges the sensory over the cerebral, the affective over the intellectual. By creating a monumental mise en scène, pageants cast the action they represent as a defining moment: the salvation of mankind, the nobility of ancestors, the winner of the sweepstakes. Pageants avail of the widest array of auditory sensation possible: song, silence, chanting, gunfire, keening, instrumental music, shouting, and explosions play key affective roles. Perhaps even more important is the visual dimension: masks, exotic costumes, fire, weapons and implements, colorful flags and banners, and pyrotechnics still create populist spectacles that hope to thrill audiences, much as had sensation scenes on the nineteenth-century stage. Costumes, uniforms, and other distinctive clothing, often made of local fabrics such as tweed or linen, disclose the cultural if not political identity of those individuals who play central roles. Performers with supernumerary parts or spectators might also announce their affinity with the production through clothing and ornament. Saffron kilts, jewelry, the Orange sash, lapel accessories (including badges or sprigs of shamrock) all express an allegiance that might blur the barrier between actor and audience. Gunpowder, incense, or bonfires might evoke the olfactory sense. By creating sensory overload, pageants reclaim the theatricality that realism drained from drama. As spectacle comes to dominate, the spoken word or text recedes.

Historical pageants create a dynamic between spectator and spectacle quite unlike the relationship between audience and performance in conventional drama played in purpose-built theatres. A wholly different deportment is demanded of an audience ensconced in assigned seats in a playhouse than of one viewing an open-air pageant from a hillside.[5] In his 1903 lecture, "The Reform of the Theatre," William Butler Yeats told prospective audiences that "when truth and beauty open their mouths to speak . . . all other mouths should be . . . silent."[6] Yeats and his codirectors imposed a strict protocol on proceedings at the Abbey: in the darkened auditorium, the audience was expected to witness the performance in reverential silence and with respectful decorum.[7] Much of the fame of Abbey audiences rests on those occasions when the audience did not conform to Yeats's dicta.

In celebrating their enactors as well as the personages enacted and even the spectators witnessing the enactment, historical pageantry blurred the distinction between actor and audience. Like British stage plays that had been routinely playing or singing the national anthem at the end of theatre performances since 1745, a practice that proved controversial for the Lyric Players in Belfast after World War II, historical pageants almost invariably exploited the participatory possibilities of communal singing. For counterhegemonic pageants before 1922, singing nationalist anthems such as "The Rallying Song of the Gaelic League" or "A Nation Once Again" created a subversive solidarity in which spectator became performer.

Historical pageants did more than efface the distinction between spectator and spectacle: their reenactment of the past manipulated the audience's sense of time and place. Carefully selected historical episodes constructed a continuous past, a heritage that offered the pageant's audience a proud identity. In the first half of the century, the March of the Nation was a regular trope in historical pageants, especially the ones performed by the advanced nationalists before 1922 and by the Defence Forces after Independence. Historical pageants could also manipulate the audience's sense of time and place by reenacting specific historical events, particularly military engagements or political orations. In 1929 *The Ford of the Hurdles* presented an early instance of verbatim theatre: a reenactment of the trial of Robert Emmet that culminated in Paul Farrell's rendition of Emmet's famous speech from the dock. When Micheál macLíammóir revived the production and took the role for himself four years later, *Dublin Opinion*, the humor magazine whose stock in trade was irreverence and satire, wrote that in this scene, "the Masque broke suddenly from artistic competence to greatness . . . due entirely to macLíammóir's fine portrayal. . . . We should imagine that Emmet himself, could his shade come back from his disputed grave, would have been perfectly satisfied with the representation."[8]

MacLíammóir's revival of *The Ford of the Hurdles* is a rare instance of a historical pageant performed beyond a single run and in more than one venue. Very few pageant makers even attempted to create works that might be revived, let alone ones that aspired to the status of art. More often, the very ephemerality of a pageant was part of its attraction, its once-in-a-lifetime appeal. Although the texts of several pageants appeared in their programs, only two of the many Irish historical pageants, Patrick Pearse's *Macghníomhartha Chúchulainn* (*The Boyhood Deeds of Cúchulainn*)[9] and Denis Johnston's *The Pageant of Cuchulainn*, were published in book form after their performance, both in each author's collected works. Historical pageants typically leave only fugitive traces: programs, posters, photographs, costume designs, reportage. Written to suit the moment, most historical pageants were never intended for revival and, in fact, have a short shelf life, which only makes them more candid and especially revelatory about the cultural moment they address. In comparison to Irish history plays, the narratives of Irish historical pageants are cruder, more simplistic and propagandistic, but they are also more expansive and unabashed in presenting a *grand récit* of the Irish past. Historical pageants are dated in two senses: in retrospect, they may indeed appear passé, but they are also deeply rooted in their historical context.

Historical pageants were sometimes connected with or occasioned by larger events such as civic weeks, industrial exhibitions, language processions, or national festivals. In reckless disregard of meteorological history, pageants were usually but not necessarily performed outdoors. In the early years of the twentieth century, the Abbey Theatre closed for a summer break: in 1908, for instance, productions wound down in June, with the new season not beginning until October. Advanced nationalists, the many actor-activists and activist-actors, turned their energies to outdoor pageants, including the Gaelic League's aeridhearcht or its annual Language Week Procession.

The most venerable pageants are intimately connected with religious observance and festivals. The medieval mystery cycles that date from the late thirteenth century offered their audiences a history of the world—beginning with the expulsion of Adam and Eve from Eden, through Noah's survival of the flood, to the birth, life, crucifixion, and resurrection of Christ. Myles V. Ronan asserts that "the most imposing plays, or *pageants*, were those ordered in 1498 by the Mayor and Commons of Dublin on the feasts of Corpus Christi and St. George. . . . The various Craft Gilds [sic] of the city were directed to enact the plays assigned to them, any Gild failing to fulfil its part of the pageant to be fined 30s. (about £45 present [1939] value)."[10] Governed in regulations codified in the "Chaine Book," so-called because it was chained to the Guildhall for ease of consultation, these pageants were performed by craft guilds in Dublin.[11] Similarly, Corpus Christi processions have their origin in medieval religious celebrations. Still held in many parishes in Ireland, these processions bring the Eucharist, which Catholics believe to be the body of Christ, out of the sacred space of the church's tabernacle and parade it through secular space. In contemporary Ireland, Corpus Christi processions are characterized not only by ornamental canopies and colorful clerical vestments, but also by a second display of the children's often-elaborate First Communion costumes. Of course, not all public spectacles in Ireland were religious. Even into the twentieth century, the most extensive records of historical pageantry in Dublin document hegemonic exhibitions of political power. The Riding of the Franchises, for instance, a symbolic journey in which the lord mayor and other officials asserted dominion by traveling the borders of the city, was performed triennially until 1772.[12]

Daniel O'Connell and his Repeal Association used another form of public spectacle, the monster meeting, to demand an end to the penal laws and the Act of Union in highly theatrical fashion. In Gary Owens's formulation, "Every monster meeting was nothing less than a performance in three acts whose players and audiences shifted with

each change of scenery."[13] O'Connell said that the astonishing turnout of 750,000 at Tara on Lady's Day, August 15, 1843, would instill
fear and pride; it did exactly that. As in 1825, when the success of
O'Connell's Catholic Association occasioned legislation that crimi-
nalized the organization, monster meetings were banned as felonious
treason. Unlike the traditional pageantry of the monarchy and aris-
tocracy, such nationalist spectacle was demotic pageantry: the demos
in question still did not have the vote, but by the 1840s they had
well-defined political aspirations and unprecedented mobility. Two
legislative events in the mid-1880s shaped the mass public spectacles
for at least the next three decades. The first was the passage of the
Third Reform Act in 1884, which increased the number of registered
voters threefold. The expansion of the franchise not only drew new
voters into public demonstration of their affiliations, but also, especially in the United States, prompted pageants designed to educate
the electorate. A second key legislative act, the narrow defeat of the
First Home Rule bill in the House of Commons in 1886, gave, as Ian
McBride observes, new life to a siege mentality in Protestant Ulster.[14]
Throughout the second half of the nineteenth century and into the
twentieth, the development of historical pageantry was hastened and
reinforced by cycles of sectarian action and reaction: in response to
nationalist activities, the Orange Order underwent a renaissance that
in turn intensified the nationalist campaign, and so on. Stephen Howe
observes, "Unionist historical narratives in modern Ireland have
evolved in parallel—and, increasingly though still too incompletely, in
dialogue—with nationalist versions."[15] Sean Farrell's analysis of William Johnston's campaign to repeal the Party Processions Act between
1860 and 1872 plainly shows that nationalists were not the only Irish
given to mass public protest: "The turbulent sectarianism of militant
plebian processionists and the sectarian riots that loyalist exhibitions often provoked were a constant source of acute embarrassment
for aristocratic Orange leaders."[16] After O'Connell, Irish nationalists
eagerly sought out occasions for counterhegemonic spectacles and
found them in the appropriation and elaboration of republican funerals. As Thomas J. Brophy demonstrates, the funerals of Terence Bellew

McManus (1861), the Manchester Martyrs (1867), John O'Mahony (1877), Charles McCarthy (1878), Charles Stewart Parnell (1891), and, in the twentieth century, O'Donovan Rossa on August 1, 1915, evolved distinctive ceremonial patterns. Each funeral echoed and recalled its predecessors; ceremonial actions developed into symbol and ritual.

As the nineteenth century drew to a close, some of the most contentious civic spectacles were commemorative ones, notably the 1898 centenary of the 1798 Rising. Especially after 1886, the ostentation of royal visits and progresses triggered counterhegemonic displays by Irish nationalists. Nationalists answered the bombastic celebrations of hegemonic power—a royal visit, for instance—with gleefully subversive pageants of resistance. In response to the Children's Treat staged during Queen Victoria's visit to Ireland in 1900, Inghinidhe na hÉireann (the Daughters of Erin) sponsored a Patriotic Children's Treat that paraded some twenty thousand children through Dublin's streets.[17] Daniel Jackson documents cycles of massive public political rallies, increasingly paratheatrical in both Ireland and Britain, triggered by the prospect of Home Rule in Edwardian times.

Erika Fischer-Lichte's *Theatre, Sacrifice, Ritual: Exploring Forms of Political Theatre* traces the resurgence of pageantry in the late nineteenth century to philosophers, artists, and anthropologists who operated in the shadow (or the light) of Darwin, among them Friedrich Nietzsche, whose *Birth of Tragedy* (1872) located the origins of Western drama in the obliteration of the individual, and James Frazer, author of *The Golden Bough* (first two volumes, 1890; through 1936), which was no less scandalous for stressing "the sameness of all societies and cultures."[18] Nietzsche, Frazer, and others looked back to the ritual origins of theatre, long before drama contracted into realism, the constrictive, narrowly defined dramaturgy of ordinary language in a reassuringly recognizable environment. That box created by the fourth wall of realistic stagecraft was so rigid, so confining, that it precluded and denied much that was, at root, theatrical. Brenna Katz Clarke described the naturalism of the peasant plays performed to reverential silence in the darkened Abbey auditorium: "It was the quality of seeing naturalness that differentiated the peasant style from the artificial style of the poetic plays [including Yeats's]. The very essence of a peasant play was to express the peasant in his 'natural state' in order to separate the real peasant from . . . the stage Irishman."[19] Dawson Byrne claims that before *The Playboy of the Western World* (1907), the Abbey cultivated an exclusive highbrow audience, one prepared to sit "through a play in an attitude of stony indifference."[20] In early-twentieth-century Ireland the contrast between realism and broader indigenous theatrical traditions might be seen by comparing the performance of a peasant play at the Abbey and a rousing political melodrama at the Queen's.[21]

Fischer-Lichte surveys the commonalities animating Richard Wagner's Bayreuth Festival (1876), Pierre de Coubertin's revitalization of the Olympic Games, Max Reinhardt's Theatre of the Five Thousand, the Nazi rallies documented by Leni Riefenstahl in the 1930s, and American Zionist pageantry.[22] Outside the narrow, elitist, and prescriptive limits of realism, these disparate paratheatrical events staged a popular and populist pageantry that created community through what Fischer-Lichte elsewhere calls "the retheatricalization of theatre."[23] There were striking examples of historical pageants in the folk spectacles of the nineteenth century, particularly in Germany. In *Imperial Culture in Germany, 1871–1918*, Matthew Jefferies chronicles the popularity of historical drama and historical pageants, especially concerning the *gründerseit* (the age of the founders). In 1884, for the six hundredth anniversary of the Pied Piper of Hamlin, "a large proportion of the town's inhabitants donned thirteenth century outfits."[24] By the 1930s such participatory public spectacles assumed far more menacing dimensions when performed in Nazi Germany.

In the nineteenth and early twentieth centuries, the most conspicuous public spectacles in Dublin were functions of the vice-regal court, including the ceremonial appearances of the lord lieutenant, visits from royalty, and other assertions of British power in Ireland. In Dublin the annual Lord Mayor's Parade, closely allied to its London counterpart, fell into this category until early in the twentieth century, when, as John Hutchinson points out, the Gaelic League took it over.[25] Language Week Processions appropriated a dramatic idiom that was once the domain of the sacred, the royal, or the aristocratic. Timothy

G. McMahon in *Grand Opportunity* documents that the political as well as cultural and historical messages of these processions were unmistakable. Forerunners and prototypes of historical pageantry in twentieth-century Ireland appeared not only in Dublin but also in the Gaelic League celebrations orchestrated and documented by Francis Joseph Bigger. In 1902 Bigger recalled the technological innovations in a Kilkenny production of *Hugh Roe O'Donnell*: "The scenery was shown by a lantern [slide projector] from behind a huge screen, surrounded by a high ruined arch. Each picture was from a photograph or drawing of the actual place referred to in the play, coloured to life."[26] O'Grady's play ends with the recitation of a genealogy tracing Hugh Roe O'Donnell's direct lineage back through, inter alia, Niall of the nine hostages; Milesius, king of Spain; Magog; Noah; to Adam, "the son of God."[27] Joseph McBrinn details the procession, banners, exhibits, and craftworks that drew five thousand to one of Bigger's most successful ventures, the Feis na nGleann (Festival of the Nine Glens in Antrim and Rathlin Island) on June 30, 1904.[28] Similarly, Alan Gailey records an analogous development in the Wexford mummer plays: "Early in the twentieth century their popularity gave way to a new set of rhymes including the same number of performers, twelve in all, but each one representing Irish patriots and heroes. . . . The sole function of the rhymes was to recall for the audience past glories and present aspirations, and to introduce a sort of sword-dance or stick-dance. However, in preserving this choreographic connection, the 'patriot' rhymes must be considered as an extension of the older tradition."[29] In the very first years of the twentieth century, a sharpened political edge appeared in these processions, festivals, and performances.

Beginning with the Language Week Processions, Irish historical pageants sought and often found large audiences throughout the twentieth century. The notion that these or any theatre audiences are randomly composed is dubious, since there is inevitably an element of self-selection. Those spectators who attended historical pageants brought with them an especially well-defined horizon of expectations that predisposed them to find merit in the performance. Advanced nationalists, past pupils, and parents attending Irish historical pageants sponsored by Castleknock College, St. Enda's, or the Gaelic League were naturally more receptive to and less critical than they would have been of other theatre events. By their very scale and the inclusions of supernumeraries, pageants expanded the prospective, well-defined, sympathetic audience: the friends and families of the performers, people who might rarely or never frequent theatres such as the Abbey. Because children, especially adolescents, were often included both as supernumeraries and in this expanded audience base and because pageants were so often performed in open-air venues, several historical pageants attracted audiences in excess of one hundred thousand over several performances.

Pageants had the potential not only to display power and allegiance, to entertain and to educate, but also to make money. Most historical pageants, especially before the Tóstals in the 1950s, benefited a charity. In March 1907 the Irish Industries Pageant, performed under the patronage of Lady Aberdeen, devoted its proceeds to one of the many organizations she founded: the Women's National Health Association. Eva Jellett wrote *A Pageant of Early Irish Saints*, performed in 1921, 1924, and, subsequently, specifically as a fund-raiser for the Dublin University mission in Chota Nagpur, India. Simply naming a charity—the St. Peter's Church Organ Fund, the Gaelic League, the Army Benevolent Fund—might attract a ready-made audience. Nationalist "evenings," those fund-raisers that typically included song, recitations, and perhaps dance, routinely drew comparably self-selecting audiences.[30]

The reluctance of most theatre historians to consider pageantry as a distinct theatrical idiom owes largely to the fact that pageants often left no script. Worse, there may never have been a definitive script at all. Even if a script might have existed, a "stage direction" would inadequately express the highly choreographed movements involving hundreds and sometimes thousands of participants. A surprising number of scripts do survive in the archive as programs, manuscripts, or periodical articles, but the visual record of historical pageants is perhaps even more compelling: emblematic program covers, production photographs, publicity stills, costume designs, and other illustrations.

Like conventional plays, historical pageants typically advertised in the public press where intriguing, exotic visual images sought the largest audience possible. Newsreel makers and filmmakers as well as photographers occasionally documented Irish historical pageantry, in large measure precisely because it privileged the visual, affective, and sensory over the literary, the image over the word. When the press covered pageants, rarely did theatre critics review them; more often, journalists focused on crowd size and novelty.

The vogue for historical pageantry in Ireland at the beginning of the twentieth century was neither unique nor wholly autochthonous. In Europe and North America, Robert Withington reports that "pageants swept the land. . . . [P]eople went pageant-mad."[31] David Glassberg's *American Historical Pageantry: The Uses of Tradition in the Early Twentieth Century* examines the proliferation of pageants that represented the American past to a young nation with a rapidly expanding electorate. As during other periods and as in other places, pageantry proved especially useful in introducing the recently enfranchised to their political responsibilities. Moreover, pageantry allowed new voters (or those individuals seeking the vote) to display their political engagement and allegiance through public performativity. Throughout the English-speaking world, this heyday of historical pageantry was intimately related to the expansion of the franchise. In *The New Citizenship: A Civic Ritual Devised for Places of Public Meeting in America* (1915), Percy MacKaye, high priest of American pageantry, hoped "to create an appropriate national ritual of American Citizenship."[32] His pageantry of naturalization featured Liberty (a man), America (a woman), representatives of the (then) forty-eight states, the thirteen original colonies, Thomas Jefferson, fifty-six signers of the Declaration of Independence, Alexander Hamilton, Benjamin Franklin, George Washington, Abraham Lincoln, and scores of "new citizens" (25). The pageant aspired to encapsulate the democratic ideals of American government and history specifically for use at citizenship ceremonies. MacKaye's appendix revealed how deeply concerned with immigration he was: "[The 1910 census shows] there are at the very least 3,000,000 unnaturalized males over 21 years of age in the United

States. . . . Since 1910 more than 5,000,0000 immigrants have been added to the population of the United States" (91). When he realized the importance of educating new voters, MacKaye had not even reckoned with the expansion of the franchise to women. Naturalization ceremonies retain their affective powers: a century after MacKaye's pageant, on February 2, 2012, both Taoiseach Enda Kenny and Minister for Justice Alan Shatter officiated at a moving ceremony to welcome twenty-two hundred new Irish citizens.

In Ireland an especially rich vein of historical scholarship focuses on the role of public spectacle in sectarian struggle in Ulster. Marching season, counterprotests, civil rights marches, royal visits, and other nationalist and unionist forms of pageantry have attracted insightful scholarly interest. Owens's analysis of nineteenth-century mass meetings, Farrell's work on political order and disorder in nineteenth-century Ulster, and Brophy's studies on republican funerals all document the accretion of ritualized, formal actions that created the traditions of sectarian public spectacle in Ireland. Mary Helen Thuente chronicles the abiding influence of the ballad traditions whose reach profoundly shaped popular attitudes toward the past. Work by Dominic Bryan, Neil Jarman, Ruth Dudley Edwards, and Brian Walker interrogates the meaning and importance of populist spectacles in modern Ulster. Lawrence W. McBride's 1999 landmark study, *Images, Icons, and the Irish Nationalist Imagination*, undertook a significantly interdisciplinary approach that brought together historians, art historians, and literary historians. More recently, Marie Coleman and Mike Cronin focus on the spectacles that attended the Irish Sweepstakes and sporting events. Guy Beiner, Gillian McIntosh, and Anne Dolan consider the ways in which commemoration, although it only rarely involves the personation of historical figures fundamental to pageants, recovers and rewrites the Irish past. In both tone and scope, moreover, most commemoration is strikingly unlike Irish historical pageants. Whereas commemoration is, as Dolan underscores, often contentious and almost inevitably solemn, historical pageantry is festive, celebratory, even carnivalesque. And whereas commemoration targets an individual, event, or date, historical pageantry sweeps through decades, centuries, even millennia. Its sense of the past is characteristically anodyne, inoffensive, aspirational, inviting.

Specific Irish pageants figure in several recent studies of Irish culture. Elaine Sisson's *Pearse's Patriots: St Enda's and the Cult of Boyhood* (2004) considers the historical pageants staged by Pearse as intrinsic to the school's ethos especially in fostering its cult of masculinity. Paige Reynolds's *Modernism, Drama, and the Audience for Irish Spectacle* (2007) examines pageantry in the context of the Aonach Tailteann. James Moran's *Staging the Rising* as well as Roisín Higgins and Anthony Roche in *1916 in 1966: Commemorating the Easter Rising* survey depictions of the Easter Rising. Christie Fox's *Breaking Forms: The Shift to Performance in Late Twentieth-Century Irish Drama* locates the Macnas pageants in the larger theatrical context of performance-based plays in contemporary Ireland. A range of recent scholarship from Fischer-Lichte's analysis of events as diverse as the Olympic Games and Nazi rallies to Tracey Hill's study of the Lord Mayor's Parades provides a foundation for the study of the theatre of historical pageantry in Ireland.

Art historian Nicola Gordon Bowe recognizes pageant production as a distinct phenomenon, one she links directly with Irish Arts and Crafts. In *The Arts and Crafts Movements in Dublin and Edinburgh, 1885–1925*, Bowe groups an intriguing and eclectic selection of six productions under the separate heading "Pageants": the 1906 open-air production of Standish O'Grady's *Finn and His Companions* at the Vice-Regal Lodge,[33] the 1899 tableaux production of Yeats's *The Countess Cathleen* at the Chief Secretary's Lodge, the 1902 performance of AE's *Deirdre* in George Coffey's garden to celebrate his son's twelfth birthday, the 1909 *Irish Industries Pageant*, Pearse's St. Enda's pageants, and the 1917 *Finn Varra Maa*. Bowe points to engagement of personnel allied with the Irish Arts and Crafts movement at this time: George Coffey (first keeper of Irish antiquities of the National Museum), sisters Ella and Elizabeth Young, AE, Beatrice Elvery, and dozens of other artists, actors, and craftspeople who contributed to pageant production.[34] What bound these people together was not simply the possible coincidence of working in a popular theatrical idiom, but the further potent combination of nationalist sympathies and visual acuity. Indeed, in the first three or four decades of the twentieth century, Irish historical pageants were in dialogue with the Irish Arts and Crafts movement.

As Bowe's selection of pageants also suggests, pageantry is closely related to other theatrical forms that flourished in the late nineteenth century. McBrinn, Beiner, and others explore the extensive use of colorful banners depicting historical scenes and personages often carried in nineteenth-century processions. Diarmuid Ó Giolláin documents the Irish pattern, those celebrations of a parish's patron saint, which "included religious devotions at the holy site followed by amusements of an often riotous nature."[35] Tableaux vivants, "living pictures," might construct a symbolic narrative that would constitute an entire dramatic presentation; a tableau might be struck at the end of a conventional stage scene; several tableaux might be included on a bill with musical performances, lectures, and dancing. By the 1880s the use of tableaux and processions in pageants had become commonplace. For the tercentenary of the defeat of the Spanish Armada, a pageant in Plymouth depicted "celebrated characters of the Elizabethan and Victorian eras [and] historical tableaux representing all the sovereigns of England from William the Conqueror to her Majesty the Queen."[36] Historical pageants were also in evidence at the one thousandth anniversary of the incorporation of Ripon, where *The Pageant at Fountains Abbey* "was illustrative of twelve great epochs in English history from Bodicea [*sic*] to Victoria."[37] The tableaux staged on the Isle of Wight for Queen Victoria in early January 1891[38] were utterly unlike the ones performed at the National Theatre of Varieties in Dublin at the very same time. Whether command performance or music hall entertainment, played by professionals or amateurs, as chronicle or comedy, tableaux proliferated in the 1890s in England as well as Ireland. Because a large number of ordinary people—amateur actors, seamstresses, set dressers, et al.—could contribute to these painterly, symbolic configurations, tableaux vivants were popular across wide spectra of class and political affiliation. As Maria Tymoczko observes, the tableaux vivants were "clearly used to excite and intensify emotion."[39] Performed on platforms moving through the Dublin streets, at the Vice-Regal Lodge, or in conventional theatre spaces, tableaux vivants circumvented patent and copyright law and were often staged as benefits or fund-raisers. The tableaux staged by Inghinidhe na hÉireann (the Daughters of Erin) were advanced nationalist productions, but Yeats's *The Countess Cathleen* was first performed as a series of tableaux vivants at the Chief Secretary's Lodge with the Countess of Fingall in the title role (whom Yeats advised, "You can't be too thin for this part!").[40] Herr documents the incorporation of allegorical tableaux of Irish figures, specifically ones incarnating Ireland Free, the Dark Rosaleen, et al., in the productions staged at the Queen's Theatre in the 1890s.[41] In May 1898 the Belfast Gaelic League in association with the Belfast Arts Society presented a series of tableaux that incorporated narration along with music, song, and dances. The program in Irish outlines seven tableaux from Red Branch legends (including Medb, Fedelm, Cúchulainn, Ferdiad, Fergus mac Róich, Finnabair, and charioteers) and several from Fenian tales featuring Diarmuid and Grainne, King Cormac Mac Airt, Ossian, Oscar, a druid, and finally, at the court of Queen Elizabeth, Grace O'Malley. The *Belfast Newsletter* ascribed "the credit for the conception of the tableaux" to Alice Milligan.[42] Catherine Morris describes Milligan's 1898 tableaux vivants, produced in collaboration with the Belfast Arts Society, as "a very self-aware part of a highly sophisticated visual culture,"[43] yet sometimes hastily improvised, with a rocking chair made to serve as a horse. In parish halls nativity plays and other traditional religious productions might employ similar representations precisely because of their accessibility.

A lineal descendant of the tableaux vivants was the Irish mythological play that dramatized episodes from Irish mythology. Milligan's *The Last Feast of the Fianna* (1899), George Moore and Yeats's *Diarmuid and Grania* (1901), Padraic Colum's *The Children of Lir* (1902), AE's *Deirdre* (1902), and a score of other plays adapted specifically Irish myth for the stage. Christopher Morash rightly argues that "the Irish mythological play was something of a *cul de sac*," yet outside purpose-built theatres, myth and legend enticed visual artists, directors, actors, designers, and writers to create confections of Irish historical pageantry for decades to come.[44]

The accelerant for Irish historical pageantry after 1905 was Louis Napoleon Parker's pageantry in English towns. In 1905 Parker organized a pageant for Sherborne School, where he taught music for a decade. Parker, who trained at the Royal Academy of Music in London, incorporated music, song, and dance in a spectacle that covered the Dorset town's history from 705 to 1593. The *Sherborne Pageant* was so well received that it begot five other town pageants in other towns and cities written by "pageant-master" Parker. His was a distinctly antimodernist project. He was horrified when "confronted with the latest steel-frame six or seven storied Emporium, the basement of which is all plate-glass and ginger bread, covered with horrible advertisements of monstrous comestibles, quack nostrums, foods for the fat, pale pills for pink people, all labeled with hideous outrages on the English language in the shape of new words—clenol for a soap, quicklite for a match, ritefast for an ink." Only months after his success at Sherborne, in December 1905, he had already formulated highly prescriptive rules to govern historical pageants. In an address to the Society of Arts in London, Parker took credit for "the invention of what to all intents and purposes is a new form of drama."[45] He called for "a narrative chorus of men's voices only," a full symphony orchestra, and no intermission. He stipulated performance at a site of historical consequence and meaning. All props, costumes, and accoutrements were to be locally sourced and manufactured. He proscribed professional actors ("Nobody is too good to be in a Pageant and almost everybody is good enough"), scenery of any description, and the representation of incidents from recent centuries. Pageants ended, Parker declared, with the communal singing of the national anthem. Parker wrote that pageants were "absolutely democratic," but that the master of the pageant "must exercise absolute authority."[46] Commentators note the contradictions between the celebration of the pageant's communal spirit and the autocratic control of Parker and his fellow pageant masters, among them F. R. Benson, Frank Lascelles, and Parker in Britain as well as

Percy MacKaye, Thomas Wood Stevens, and William Chauncey Langdon in America.

Of course, Parker had not invented a new form of drama. He recuperated elements from multiple dramatic genres and idioms and recycled them in ways suited to the civic needs of English cities and villages in the Edwardian era. Reaching back to Greek drama, he appropriated the chorus and tapped what Victor Turner describes as the ritual origins of theatre.[47] He drew on traditions that attended royal processions and progresses, the City of London's Lord Mayor's Parades (which Parker organized from 1907 to 1913), local celebrations and commemorations. Withington describes Parker's pageants as the "resurrection of the old chronicle-history of Elizabethan drama."[48] Whatever the exact nature of Parker's intervention in theatre history, historical pageants flourished in the English-speaking world after 1905. In representing episodes that might span decades or centuries, even millennia, historical pageants characteristically claimed authenticity and accuracy in even the smallest archaeological detail of costume, armaments, and implements. Meghan Lau notes that political activists soon adopted the theatrical idiom of pageantry: "In the years leading up to World War I, pageantry became a powerful tool for political protest: the NAACP [National Association for the Advancement of Colored People], British and American suffragettes, and striking workers in Paterson, New Jersey performed scenes from their respective histories in large-scale outdoor performances."[49] The potential for theatre events was no less keenly felt by Irish nationalists. In 1906 Arthur Griffith's *Sinn Féin* claimed that "drama is the greatest nationalising force we have in our possession."[50]

Unlike Parker's and other English pageants, Irish historical pageants addressed the emergent or young nation rather than a village or town to suggest a venerable native history that had been long suppressed by a colonial power. They freely mingled mythological and historical personages. They were less spectacular and often integrated into larger events. Bergeron and Hill describe the use of tableaux in the London lord mayor's shows where distinguished parties moved from one platform to another,[51] but the Gaelic League Processions moved the tableaux past an audience rendered classless in the streets. For all of the similarities that exist in the historical pageants in Ireland and the pageants in other English-speaking countries, ruptures unique to the Irish experience profoundly shaped not only the narratives of historical pageantry but also when it flourished. At the beginning of the twentieth century, Irish historical pageants often created aspirational narratives in which a young man came to lead a weary, oppressed people. Much of the pageantry in the first decades of the twentieth century is what Eric Hobsbawm describes as a distinctly modern phenomenon: "the invention of tradition"—the construction of symbolic and ceremonial actions to which are imputed venerable histories.[52]

In his essay on Tomas Mac Anna's pageant *Aiseirí*, which commemorated the fiftieth anniversary of the Easter Rising in 1966, Anthony Roche notes, "The script is composed of extracts from existing literary and popular sources."[53] That observation applies to pageantry throughout the twentieth century that used well-known ballads, familiar melodies, iconic images, and popular poetry to tap affective chords in their audiences. Only rarely did historical pageants build or develop characters; instead, music, spoken word, and spectacle played into the affective responses to which their audiences were predisposed.

A chronological approach to Irish historical pageants reveals parallels and repetitions, as well as discontinuities and innovations. As for the Fenian funerals Brophy describes, an accretion of symbolic action may ritualize elements of the pageant. To paraphrase Turner's comment on pilgrimages, all of this reinforces the need to study any particular pageant as part of a *field* of pageants, rather than as an isolate.[54] This survey of historical pageants is not comprehensive. Marie Coleman documents the pageants staged for the draw in the Irish Sweepstakes, including the 1932 spectacle that focused "on 'Old Gaelic legend' . . . in which the employees were dressed as ladies at Tara's court, galloglasses and elves."[55] The Girls' Friendly Society staged several pageants, including *The Picture* in 1927; the Christian Brothers O'Connell Street School staged *Iona*, in which "the early Christian age of Ireland is linked with Emancipation days and modern times," in 1928;[56] on May 3, 1953, Cashel hosted a *Historical Processional Pageant.*[57] Other pageants may exist in the archive; many more may survive only in human memory; still others have left no trace. Nor can this survey fully contextualize events that were not only collaborative but also dependent upon myriad factors as diverse as funding, publicity, amateur acting, musical accompaniment, equestrian deportment, and the weather. Certainly one, perhaps sometimes the, decisive factor was access to the costumes and artifacts from an earlier iteration, as was the case for the Defence Forces after 1935.

In twentieth-century Ireland, four periods stand out as dedicating considerable resources to create historical and mythological pageantry. The first and most intense mania for historical pageantry, 1907–14, not only capitalized on the vogue for Parker's pageants but also reacted against "the rise of the realists" at the Abbey and its claim to the status of national theatre.[58] The popularity of pageantry during this period also owed much to an increasingly vibrant visual culture. Not only did a vernacular Irish Arts and Crafts tradition flourish, but the visual representation of figures from Irish current events, history, and mythology in inexpensive publications did as well. As those individualized in graphic representations, such as Brian Boru or Owen Roe O'Neill in booklets published by the *Irish Messenger*, became national icons, the opportunity to replicate them in pageantry proved irresistible. With producers as diverse as Lord Iveagh, Patrick Pearse, the vice-regentrix, Sinn Féin, the Gaelic League, and the Irish Women's Franchise League, historical pageants flourished across class lines and political affiliations between 1907 and 1914. The exigencies that followed the Dublin Lockout in 1913–14, the Easter 1916 Rising, the Anglo-Irish War of Independence, and the Irish Civil War all but extinguished historical pageantry between 1914 and 1924.

A second flurry of pageantry occurred in the decade following Independence, between 1924 and 1932, when the new Irish Free State deployed pageantry to reinforce its legitimacy, to instill pride in its citizens, and to offer the popular imagination an alternative to an oppressive colonial history. After Independence, the Irish state played the central role in funding and supporting historical pageantry through direct funding, aid in kind, and the support of the Defence Forces, the Garda Síochána, the Irish Tourist Board (and its later iterations), and a range of cooperative schemes providing transport. Irish historical pageants were often doubly public: first, in their expenditure of public funds and, second, in their mobilization of a large number of citizens to perform an Irish identity. By the 1920s professionals, including theatre practitioners, academic historians, career army officers, accomplished artists, and trained actors, would write, design, act, and produce historical pageants. In the Aonach Tailteann and the Dublin Civic Weeks of 1927 and 1929, the historical pageantry of newly independent Ireland imbricated theatre, the Irish Arts and Crafts movement, nationalist commemoration, and nation building.

Pageantry endured in surprising ways in the 1930s and '40s. The grandest pageant in Ireland, the 1932 Eucharistic Congress, begot a spate of religiously oriented Protestant pageants of Irish history in Northern Ireland. The appetite for pageantry in the Irish Free State was fed by lavish military tattoos and Dublin stage extravaganzas as well as more modest Step Together pageants, all sponsored and performed by the Defence Forces.

In the fourth period, the mid-1950s, the early Tóstal festivals featured St. Patrick and then Cúchulainn as the focus of national pageants that aspired to attract international tourists. After the national pageants of the mid-1950s and 1966, historical pageantry faded. Pageants might be performed at halftime at a Gaelic Athletic Association (GAA) event, as part of a larger commemoration, or as an after-dinner entertainment, but the heyday of pageantry had passed. Only by returning to its autochthonous roots did companies such as Macnas recover the potential of historical pageantry at the end of the twentieth century.

1

Drama-Mad, Cúchulainn-Mad, Pageant-Mad

The flurry of Irish historical pageantry early in the twentieth century has both national and international contexts. Roy Foster, among many others, observes, "Certainly the period between 1880 and 1914 was a great age of jubilees and commemorations."[1] Between 1907 and 1914, historical pageants served what many saw as the imperative of providing the public with a narrative of an Irish past distinct from an English one. Like many Irish historians, Eoin McNeill, professor of history at University College Dublin (UCD) and future Free State minister for education, saw the need to present an Irish historical perspective to Irish people as compelling: "Irish history is not taught to them [the people of Ireland] during their youth. They read accounts of the Armada and of the Battle of Waterloo, but they don't hear a word about the Battle of the Yellow Ford or about the deeds of King Dáithí."[2] The Gaelic League Language Week Processions and pageants, Lord Iveagh's *A Twelfth Century Pageant Play*, and the pageants of Castleknock, St. Enda's, and Cork's North Monastery all instilled a sense of the Irish past, although their vision of the past was as highly selective as it was heroic. These historical pageants did not depict centuries of victimization, oppression, and failure; rather, they constructed, often imaginatively, a glorious and noble Irish past. The often-breathtaking liberties taken with history, the suspect claims to archaeological accuracy and integrity, the effacement of the English presence in Ireland, and the emphasis on the nobility of Irish heroes were the hallmarks of the twentieth century's most intense era of pageant production.[3]

The turn of the twentieth century was an especially tumultuous period for public entertainment in much of Europe. Not only did the nature of theatregoing and of the audience change, but entertainment did as well. Populist spectacles like national expositions and world's fairs or Pierre de Coubertin's revival of the Olympic Games in 1894 mark the late nineteenth century's appeal to newly enfranchised citizens who had not only the vote, but also leisure time and the price of a ticket. In theatre, reactions against the narrow and, for many, elitist confines of realistic drama took many forms. From Richard Wagner's Beyreuth Festival in 1876 or the symbolism of Maurice Maeterlinck and Paul Claudel to avant-garde affronts such as Jarry's *Ubu Roi* (1895), a swarm of heretics subverted theatre orthodoxy.[4]

The Irish stage underwent seismic change in the twentieth century's first decade. The Irish Literary Theatre, founded in 1899, morphed into the Irish National Theatre Society (NTS). The controversies over Yeats's *The Countess Cathleen* in 1899 and Synge's *In the Shadow of the Glen* in 1903 were not only prelude to the protests against Synge's *Playboy* in January 1907, but intrinsic to the larger debate over Irish identity and a national theatre. Adrian Frazier enumerates more than "seven definitions of an Irish national theatre, all put on the table for discussion in Dublin, 1900–1905."[5] The second half of the decade was no less contentious; as Karen Vandevelde observes, "The following years [1906 and beyond] marked a difficult time for the NTS at the Abbey Theatre. The nationalist press attacked the company and its plays with even more vigour than before. In the *Leader*, D. P. Moran kept a watchful eye on the Abbey Theatre, and in his new radical *Sinn Féin* Arthur Griffith gave full rein to his antipathy for the society he had originally supported."[6] The repercussions of the Fay brothers' departure from the Abbey were felt throughout 1908. Upstart nationalist theatre groups like the Cumann na nGaedheal or the National Players (1903), the Theatre of Ireland (1906), and the Ulster Literary Theatre (ULT, 1902, as the Ulster Branch of the Irish Literary Theatre) openly competed with the fledgling Abbey, not only for the theatregoing public but also for recognition as Ireland's national theatre. Many of the personnel from these alternative theatres, especially the more politically active among them, moonlit in pageant production. So "drama-mad," in the phrase of Mary Colum,[7] was Ireland at this time that the lure of enacting Irish tales was irresistible. For ordinary Irishmen and -women who had no instrumental training and lacked vocal and dance skills, pageantry offered especially appealing performative opportunities to express affiliation with the nationalist cause.

No single year in Irish theatre history has attracted more critical attention than 1907 and no single production more commentary than the premiere of Synge's *The Playboy of the Western World*. New plays by George Fitzmaurice, Padraic Colum, Lewis Purcell (David Parkhill) and Gerald MacNamara (Harry Morrow), Lady Gregory, W. B. Yeats, Seumas O'Kelly, and a half dozen others appeared in Dublin in 1907. The Ulster Literary Theatre was active in Belfast and, as in earlier years, made a December visit to Dublin. Splits in what became the Abbey Theatre had begotten the Theatre of Ireland and the National Players. But much, perhaps even the majority, of that commentary on the Irish theatre in 1907, especially the scholarly analysis, focuses on the premiere of Synge's *The Playboy of the Western World* at the Abbey during the last week of January.

Although controversy over *The Playboy* persisted over months, even years, by spring 1907 much of Dublin's attention turned to the preparations for the Irish International Exhibition, the Great White Fair, at Herbert Park. The landmark in the exhibition movement, sometimes credited with triggering the vogue for world's fairs, remains the Great Exhibition of Britain in 1851, for which the Crystal Palace was constructed in Hyde Park. More modest exhibitions in Ireland dated back to 1734 when the RDS began to hold triennial exhibits "in a one-acre site in Kildare Street."[8] Exclusively Irish goods were featured at exhibitions in 1834 and 1847. In Ireland forerunners of the 1907 Great White Fair were the International Industrial Exhibitions held in Dublin in 1850, 1853, 1865, and 1872; the 1882 Irish National Exposition; the 1883 Cork Industrial and Fine Arts Exhibition; and the 1902 Cork International Exhibition.[9]

In 1899 the industrial exposition and world's fair movement created its own publication: the *World's Work*. In its May 1907 issue on

Dublin's Great White Fair, the editors sensed that support in Ireland for the exhibition was less than consensual: "After a brief visit to Ireland, and even briefer meetings with leaders of various movements, one has a general idea of a smooth cushion stuffed with thorns, of pressing upon a fair and inviting exterior only to find the pointed thrust beneath."[10] Editors sought out Irish natives for explanations and solicited those of Bram Stoker and Emily Lawless. Stoker situated the exhibition in the historical and geographical context of Donnybrook Fair: "Perhaps there has been some joy of living and much humour lost with the passing of the country fair, its merry-makings, its rows and its shillalahs; but there has come in its place a strenuous industrial spirit."[11] Stoker obligingly embraced the editorial line of the *World's Work*, a simple and simplistic solution to Ireland's problems: "Ireland's salvation must be accomplished by means of her industrial regeneration."[12] The Irish International Exposition at Herbert Park ran for more than six months, from May 4 until November 9, 1907, and featured two of the staples of advanced nationalist gatherings: displays of Irish-made goods and prominent use of the new Irish trademark. Advanced nationalist groups such as Sinn Féin and the Gaelic League, however, were having none of it. They railed against the Great White Fair as a pernicious commercial import, employing foreign workers using imported goods to serve up yet another fraudulent version of the Irish. Griffith denounced it as "an Anglo-Jewish bazaar"; the Gaelic League threatened to expel members who attended the exhibition.[13] In August Éamon Ceannt reminded readers of the *Leader* that "two pipers and one woman-fiddler were hissed off the Oireachtas stage by a small section of the audience because the fiddler and one of the pipers (Harrison) had previously been playing for fees at the International Exhibition."[14] Looking back in 1911, D. P. Moran recalled it as "an expensive and wasteful fiasco."[15]

Against the prestige and vice-regal patronage fawning over the Irish International Exposition, the Gaelic League staged its annual Language Week Procession on Sunday, June 9, 1907. Early in the century, the Gaelic League "took over the traditional Lord Mayor's Procession in Dublin, mobilizing up to 500,000 people . . . to participate in

1. *World's Work: Irish Number* (1907). Courtesy of Special Collections, Kenneth Spencer Research Library, University of Kansas Libraries.

symbolic tableaux that portrayed the moral lessons of Irish history."[16] The Gaelic League experienced enormous growth between 1901 and 1904: 43 branches in 1897 grew to 227 in 1902–3 to then 600 branches with fifty thousand members in 1904, but by 1906 membership began to decline.[17] The league's growth owed much to its conspicuous presence in the public eye: the feiseanna, the annual Language Week Processions in Dublin, and the Oireachtas were popular attractions, well publicized and supported in the burgeoning nationalist press. The Gaelic League encouraged its members, including children and young people, to seize performative opportunities in areas as diverse as athletics, singing, dancing, reciting, and writing. The annual Gaelic League procession drew together individual craobh (branch or chapter) as well as a wider constituency of sympathetic organizations. In May 1907, for instance, *Sinn Féin* advertised: "Coisde Cenntan Bhaile-Atha-Cliath invites the co-operation of the various trades bodies, schools, colleges and other educational establishments, temperance associations, the Gaelic Athletic Association clubs, city bands, and public bodies and organisation."[18] As Mary Colum recalled, "Everybody I knew was working in one or several causes, some people were working in all of them. Any public meeting by any organization for any movement would very likely be addressed by a selection of people prominent in all the other movements."[19]

The Gaelic League Language Week Processions included bands, marchers, commercial and industrial displays, and tableaux staged on horse-drawn wagons. Like the craft guilds in the production of the medieval mystery cycles, when the shipbuilders' rendition of Noah would vie with the goldsmiths' presentation of the three kings in the York cycle, a healthy degree of competition among Gaelic League branches emerged in creating their entries in the annual Language Week Procession. One of the most intriguing aspects of the development of the Gaelic League Language Week Processions was that the reliance on visuals and music elided the need for any language, Irish or English. Despite all the animated debates among advanced nationalists about the Irish language, the Gaelic League provided thousands of ordinary people with performative opportunities, including pageantry, whatever their fluency or interest in the Irish language.

By 1907 the Language Week Processions were well established and essential to the league's finances, as collections were taken outside churches and during the procession itself. In 1907 *Sinn Féin* and *An Claidheamh Soluis* reported the meetings of a special subcommittee on the tableaux: "The tableaux committee are keeping in close touch with the Gaelic League branches, advising as to correct and suitable costumes for the periods to be illustrated, and generally rendering willing assistance in the arrangement of the tableaux. The effect of the historical series illustrating periods of Irish history, from the earliest records down to most recent times, is sure to be extremely picturesque."[20] Among the subcommittee members was Fred Morrow, one of a surprisingly large number of writers, activists, and artists from Northern Ireland who migrated to Dublin between 1906 and 1914. His enthusiasm for historical pageantry would resurface over the coming years.

Timothy G. McMahon's analysis of the Language Week Processions in the first decade of the century suggests three categories for the tableaux: historical, historical with contemporary relevance, and allegorical. The historical tableaux in the Language Week Processions were, McMahon writes, "often anachronistic hodgepodges constructed from popular histories or the lectures prepared for League branches by autodidact members."[21] A month before the 1907 procession, James Stephens wrote in *Sinn Féin*: "They [Irish heroes] should to us be symbolic of the Irish race and all that the Irish race stands for. It is not on the ruins, but on the foundations of the past that the pinnacles of the future can be erected with any degree of solidity, and only by conserving the bravery, the energy, the poetry, and the worth of our ancestors can ourselves and our posterity be other than a nation of illiterates, quacks, and barbarians."[22] Heeding Stephens's charge, the subjects of the nationalist historical pageants in the first decade of the new century were often legendary and mythological as well as historical heroes. The 1907 Language Week Procession was no exception.

The 1907 procession, held in June rather than March, as it had been the previous year, left from St. Stephen's Green at 3:00 p.m. under fair skies. The "exceptionally large" crowds of spectators saw tableaux that "represented in chronological order some of the most striking scenes in Irish history and literature" as well as other tableaux addressing contemporary issues, including the Great White Fair.[23] The day before the procession, *Sinn Féin* previewed eleven tableaux that offered a history of Ireland from the "Mythological or De Danaan Period" to the time of Patrick Sarsfield:

1 Mythological or De Danaan Period: Manannan Mac Lir restoring her arts, industries, and commerce to Eire
2 Red Branches or Cuchulainn Period
    Meeting of Cuchulainn and Emer
3 Oilioll, King of Connacht, and Queen Maeve comparing possessions
4 Fenian or Ossianic Period
    Ossian and Niamh in Tir na nOg
5 Christian Period: Dialogue between Oisin and St. Patrick
6 Danish Period
    Brian Boruimhe meets Mahon and his brother
7 Norman Period
    Marriage of Eva and Strongbow
8 Lorcan Ua Tuathaill appeals to chiefs for unity against the invader
9 O'Neill and O'Donnell Period
    Reception of Red Hugh O'Donnell at Glenmalure
10 Confederation Period: Geoffrey Keating hiding in Aherlow from English Soldiers
11 Patrick Sarsfield "discussing with Ginkel the Treaty of Limerick."[24]

The chronological progression offered no distinction whatsoever between mythological figures and persons from recorded history; this version of the Irish past subsumes them equally.

McMahon notes that the 1907 tableaux focused on "the intellectual and spiritual attainments of Gaelic-speakers of the distant past."[25] Most of the historical vignettes contrived to represent moments of peace and stability. The first tableau, showing the restoration of Eire's arts, industries, and commerce, featured distinctive Irish work by twelve artisans from Evelyn Gleeson's Dun Emer industries: "The great sea god was represented as introducing figures symbolic of artistic metal work, stone work, and illuminating . . . agriculture and spinning."[26] The second tableau, sponsored by the Star of the Sea branch from Sandymount and led by its president, George A. Moonan (Seoirse O Muanain),[27] represented the Meeting of Cúchulainn and Emer with "Emer engaged at embroidery." Brian Boru is seen with his brother Mahon at Limerick, supposedly, that is, in 969 after the defeat of the Norse in Limerick. Whereas Brian was frequently depicted in full armor and identified as the victor of the Battle of Clontarf (1014), here he appeared as a younger man with battles yet to win.[28] Similarly, the marriage of Strongbow and Eva suggested peace between the Normans and the Irish, just as Sarsfield's negotiations with Ginkel for the Treaty of Limerick were prelude to a period of stability. Spiritual virtue was celebrated in representation of Lorcan Ua Tuathaill (Archbishop Laurence O'Toole). Although Geoffrey Keating was seen at work writing his history while pursued by red-coated soldiers, what were celebrated were typically occasions of reconciliation, accomplishment, victory, stability, and peace. Rather than depicting Cúchulainn or Brian Boru in battle, the tableaux configured them in peaceful domestic situations—wooing Emer or celebrating with his brother, respectively. In addition to the chronologically presented tableaux from the Irish past, the National Players created a symbolic tableau with contemporary relevance, "Driving Back the Demon of Anglicisation": "In the industrial section the National Players are arranging tableaux representing the importation of foreign wares and the deportation of the population."[29] Now in dialogue with the Irish International Exhibition at Herbert Park, the tableaux showed "the demon offering numerous foreign wares—plays, songs, language, and games—to Erin, but Erin is protected by a Gael armed with a stout caman."[30]

Although the *Irish Times* acclaimed the 1907 procession "the most successful demonstration of its kind ever held under the auspices of the Gaelic League," *Sinn Féin* lamented historical inaccuracies in the tableaux: "In some instances the costuming was historically wrong. This is a serious blemish on what is intended to be an educational feature, and should not be repeated."[31] Whatever inaccuracies crept in, the participation of visual artists is especially noteworthy. Pageantry is only one strand of a burgeoning visual culture in the early years of the twentieth century, an especially fertile period in the history of art and visual design. In the second half of the nineteenth century, a distinctive Irish iconography emerged and flourished. Jeanne Sheehy observes, "The Celtic Revival affected costume in interesting and amusing ways. It was a period when people were attracted to fancy dress, and pageants were popular. These required people to invent Irish costume, based on what was known of medieval dress from illustrated sources and from ancient Irish literature."[32] As Bowe, McBrinn, and others suggest, pageantry was fueled by an increasingly vibrant Arts and Crafts movement, with which it was closely intertwined. The authenticity of ancient Irish costume was a concern not just in 1907 but earlier in and throughout the twentieth century.

The eleven tableaux representing Ireland's history in 1907 formed what came to be commonly known as the March of the Nation.[33] Nationalist historical pageantry, leaping from mythic periods to and over centuries of recorded and unrecorded history, was marked by chronological discontinuities and ended its narrative centuries ago, here in 1691. With the exception of the final symbolic tableau of a contemporary Erin resisting the anglicization threatened by the Great White Fair, the recent past was too painful to be represented so frivolously. Reluctance to represent recent centuries, especially the nineteenth century, was a distinguishing feature of nationalist pageantry for decades. The March of the Nation in the 1907 Language Week Procession was neither unique nor groundbreaking. Moreover, the diaries of Cecilia Saunders Gallagher, kept while she was imprisoned in 1923, record that on August 20, women from B Wing attended a similar historical procession in A Wing in Kilmainham Jail: "All the costumes were prepared in a day. We had Brian Boru, St. Patrick, Maeve, Deirdre, Cuchullain, Conor Mac Neasa, Turlough, Strongbow, Mac Murrough, Eva, Owen Roe, Hugh O'Neill, Silken Thomas, (myself), Robert Emmet, Pamela, John Philpot Curran, (Miss Breen), Sarah Curran, Lord Edward Fitzgerald, (Miss Brown), Mangan (Bridie O'Mullane), and everyone you could think of. The costumes were great and were made up out of prison blankets and sheets, brown paper, nighties, petticoats, dressing gowns, frocks, and other materials. They were really wonderful."[34] Similar historical arrays figured in earlier processions and appeared in the lavish spectacles in the Dublin Civic Weeks in 1927 and 1929 and in the Military Tattoos of 1935 and 1945. The March of the Nation not only endured in the tattoos and stage shows devised by the Defence Forces long after Independence; it became the default version of the Irish past that appeared even in the 1966 commemorative pageant *Aiseirí.*

A TWELFTH CENTURY PAGEANT PLAY (1907)

Later that same month, Lord Iveagh presented a pageant of twelfth-century history at St. Stephen's Green for seven performances (afternoon and evening) on June 25–28, 1907. Edward Cecil Guinness, Lord Iveagh, who served as sheriff of Dublin and as chief executive of Guinness until 1889, was well known for his philanthropy. On May 2, 1907, the *Irish Times* referred to "the great munificence of Lord Iveagh" in developing the Iveagh markets on Francis Street, one of his many urban renewal projects to benefit Dublin.[35] The text of this pageant contains not only the dialogue, but also some of the musical selections and footnotes that provide historical background and document sources (including Giraldus Cambrensis).

The cover illustration of *A Twelfth Century Pageant Play* features a young page in tights, his tunic emblazoned with a lion rampant, borrowed from the royal standard of England, holding a flagstaff adorned with the victors' laurels and wearing the plumed tricorne traditionally associated with the City of London's Lord Mayor's Parade. Written by Percival Aungier,[36] *A Twelfth Century Pageant Play* was performed "under the patronage of the Lord Lieutenant and Countess of Aberdeen, the Commander-in Chief of the Forces in Ireland and Lady Grenfell, and the Viscount and Viscountess Iveagh," which suggests that many of the supernumeraries were drawn from the ranks of the military or the Guinness brewery. Seated on the lawn tennis grounds, the pageant audience braved sometimes rainy weather to watch nearly a hundred performers, "many well-known amateurs," including William Lane-Joynt Jr. as Diarmuid, who had been stage managed by Captain Stamer O'Grady.[37] Like many of the civic events that Ishbel Aberdeen supported, *A Twelfth Century Pageant Play* was staged to benefit charities—here, the St. Peter's Church Organ Fund and the National Children's Hospital. Reserved seats were available at three or five shillings, unreserved seats at one shilling. Both an orchestra, "supplied by members of the Royal Irish Academy of Music," and the band of the Dublin Metropolitan Police provided music. The involvement of the military and police would swell the ranks of performers to epic scale and mark the Iveagh pageant as hegemonic.

In six acts the pageant covers the time from Diarmuid's founding of All Hallows' Priory on the site that became Trinity College to 1172, when Henry II celebrates Christmas in Dublin with Aoife and Strongbow. Each of the pageant's six acts is prefaced by an eight-line verse sung by a chorus of bards (a quartet of boys) and incorporates tableaux as well as other songs. The first act recounts Diarmuid's fulfillment of his promise to God that if he recovered from illness, "rich lands and revenues will he bestow, and there shall pious Augustinians dwell, and ever bless their princely founder's name" (2).[38] This site, "the lands of Baldoyle" (3), of All Hallows' Priory subsequently became the site of Trinity College. This Diarmuid is "to learning such a friend, that he bade gather in from far and near the legends of our ancestors and tales already old ere St. Patrick raised the cross within our lands. These in a mighty tome were written down—the Leinster Book, the glory of thy reign" (3). Not only is Diarmuid remembered for granting the land on which Trinity stands, but he is also portrayed as patronizing the arts. By the second act, a year later (1167), Diarmuid's fortunes have turned as "with cruel wrong / [he] has won himself deadly hate" (4). Dual

Price 6ᵈ.

Dramatic Pageant

JUNE
25th,
26th,
27th
and
28th,
1907.

EACH DAY

4 o'c Afternoon,

8 o'c Evening.
(Except 25th June)

IN THE GROUNDS OF

80
St. Stephen's
Green,
Dublin

2. Program cover for *A Twelfth Century Pageant Play*, 1907. Courtesy of Special Collections, Kenneth Spencer Research Library, University of Kansas Libraries.

narrators, The Scribe and Storyteller, offer competing accounts. The Scribe's more sympathetic version presents him as a man betrayed: Diarmuid's "under-chiefs, who long have chafed beneath too stern a rule, have risen now against their lord. . . . Without friend he stands" (5). The Storyteller counters that Diarmuid had treated his underlings cruelly: "Has he not pressed a heavy hand on all? Blinded, loaded with fetters and in dungeons held. Lands hath he plundered; treaties hath he broke" (5). The Scribe replies that others did just the same. Diarmuid describes himself as banished (7), forced into exile in France: to "the Norman Henry's Court I will, and beg his aid against the traitors who deposed me" (6). The Scribe introduces a second recurrent theme, the internecine wars that pit Irish against Irish—"Alas! That we, who dwell on Irish soil, have never learned to love our country as one whole, but ever one with another war" (6)—and prophesies that "not upon Judas's self shall heavier curses fall than on the head of Diarmuid of the strangers, great Leinster's King."

In the third act, Diarmuid arrives at Henry II's crowded court where, after Crusaders depart on their "pious pilgrimage" (8), he learns of Pope Hadrian's bull placing Ireland under Henry's control so that "we to this distracted isle may bring peace" (9). Henry addresses Diarmuid warmly, "Brother of Leinster" (9), and authorizes him to recruit "our barons," especially those adventure seekers and the border lords who are in "constant strife" (9) against the Welsh. Only then does Henry insert his terms: if Diarmuid succeeds, the Irish will "pay us homage, and [I will] hold thy land in vassalage." Caught off guard by these conditions, Diarmuid nevertheless agrees: "Pay what I may, my revenge I will have" (9). In the fourth act, the Chorus of Bards announces that Diarmuid "giveth to Strongbow his daughter fair" (10) to gain support in his bid to reclaim power in Ireland. Strongbow, too, has terms: after Diarmuid's death, power will pass to Strongbow and his heirs. Diarmuid acknowledges that this violates Irish tradition, but cravenly he does not care who rules after his death. "Before the ruined walls of Waterford, August, 1170," the point of view in the fifth act shifts to the laments of an Irish Harper and Soldier. Diarmuid and the Normans celebrate their victory and the marriage of Aoife and

Strongbow. The act culminates in a "Tableau of Marriage Scene" that replicates Daniel Maclise's painting *The Marriage of Aoife and Strongbow*, which had been a centerpiece of the National Gallery of Ireland historical painting collection for nearly thirty years.[39]

The final act, set during the Christmas season in 1172, finds Henry II celebrating in Dublin: the once-free Irish all now "shall bow at his feet by the Liffey's wave, / And own him their king and lord" (14). One of the Normans mocks the Irish, but others praise their illuminated manuscripts, their bravery, their pleasant land. Henry speaks of Diarmuid's death and demands (and, with Strongbow's acquiescence, receives) the lands from Aoife. Laurence O'Toole declines the invitation to feast with the English king and asks to be excused from the revelry ("Sad at heart these troublous times have made me, too sad a guest to join in a Royal feast" [16]), but before he leaves Strongbow offers that three of Henry's knights will bear the cost of rebuilding sacred sites, specifically, as a footnote explains, the choir, steeple, and three chapels (16) of Dublin's Christ Church Cathedral.

The pageant plainly celebrates the Irish landscape and laments the pain of exile: "Store are her streams with fish, her woods with game; her golden corn-fields ripen in the sun. So fair is she that each day passed in exile seems bitter till I see her cliffs again" (11). Not only is the physical landscape idealized, but so is its cultural landscape. Ireland is "a land worth fighting for" where "every clansman must have a voice to say who is king" (11). By positing a democratic tradition in Ireland, however ahistorical, the pageant appeals to its audience's twentieth-century sensibilities. The pageant honors Diarmuid's and Strongbow's philanthropy, which has obvious resonance in Lord Iveagh's life: a year after this pageant, Lord Iveagh was elected chancellor of Trinity College and donated Iveagh Gardens to University College. But for a pageant, and perhaps for any Irish play in 1907, *A Twelfth Century Pageant Play* is uncommonly nuanced, toying with both unionist and nationalist pieties. Diarmuid MacMurrough is not simply the original sinner that advanced nationalists vilified for the English presence in Ireland, but a benefactor celebrated for his largesse. Nor is Diarmuid merely a traitor, but a man betrayed by the people closest to him. Although generous or least capable of keeping his promises, he grows increasingly callow, vengeful, and selfish. Henry II is a conniving opportunist, inserting his demand for vassalage and homage only after allowing Diarmuid to raise an army among the English. The sardonic wit of the king's Court Fool undercuts Henry's generosity: "These gifts cost Henry nought, in such he most delights" (15). At times Henry's Fool echoes King Lear's: "Nothing for nothing, such is Henry's rule" (9). In the final scene, the Normans now resident in Dublin ridicule the Irish as "Barbarian chieftains, but few of them can speak a Christian tongue," to which the Court Fool rejoins, "Forsooth, no tongue doth fit a Christian but our Norman French" (14). Diarmuid's daughter Aoife hopes to "prove a faithful and submissive wife" (13) to Strongbow, but recoils at the prospect of marrying the Norman who has slaughtered so many of her countrymen. *A Twelfth Century Pageant Play* celebrates the English coming into Ireland for their philanthropy and enlightenment of their descendants. Lord Iveagh's philanthropy[40] appears as a continuation of a centuries-old tradition. Like the pageants of Louis Napoleon Parker, an unquestionable influence,[41] *A Twelfth Century Pageant Play* was site specific, but rather than celebrating a community as did Parker's pageants, it was primarily a tribute to the largesse of British aristocrats in general and Lord Iveagh in particular. At its heart, the pageant affirmed the status quo and suggested that there was no need for Ireland to pursue Home Rule, let alone independence from Britain; after all, Ireland had enjoyed the largesse of generations of generous donors. *A Twelfth Century Pageant Play* offered a narrative of the past congenial to Lord Iveagh's unionism and its Ascendancy audiences and entirely unlike the colonial oppression seen in the nationalist tableaux of the 1907 Language Week Procession only days earlier. Not surprisingly, the nationalist press roundly ignored the production.

Despite the weather, the pageant was reported a success. It was an ambitious undertaking during an eventful summer that included the attractions of the Irish Industrial Exhibition. The *Irish Times* welcomed *A Twelfth Century Pageant Play* as "the first function of the kind that has been attempted in Dublin."[42] Press reports praised the costumes and singled out Herbert Lumley, who served as Narrator, for his "fine voice and accurate singing [that] helped on the action of the Pageant incalculably."[43] There would be other historical pageants generated and patronized by the Ascendancy, but more provocative and more memorable were the pageants staged at two elite Catholic colleges in Dublin.

THE BATTLE OF CASTLEKNOCK (1908)

Ignoring the unionist pageant in Lord Iveagh's gardens the previous year, the *College Chronicle*, the journal of the Castleknock union (or alumni association), claimed that *The Battle of Castleknock* was "the first Pageant Play ever produced in Ireland."[44] Castleknock, also known as St. Vincent's College, had a well-established tradition of "theatricals" and "a theatre and stage apparatus second to none."[45] For Shrovetide (Fat Tuesday) in the mid-1890s, Castleknock students performed a Shakespeare tragedy—*Julius Caesar* in 1894, *Hamlet* in 1895—followed by a farce as well as program of music. At least two graduates of Castleknock, Joseph Holloway and D. P. Moran, played key roles in recording and reporting Irish theatre history early in the twentieth century; both avidly followed Castleknock's pageants.

Between 1908 and 1914, Castleknock College premiered three original historical pageants: *The Battle of Cnucha* (Castleknock) in 1908, *St. Patrick at Castleknock* in 1910, and *King Niall at Castleknock* in 1914. These pageants were revived on several occasions, including the college's centenary in 1935 when the three pageants were compressed into a single portmanteau, *The Pageant of Castleknock*. In 1914 the *College Chronicle* published a "Special Pageant Number" with the texts of all three pageants as well as numerous photographs that document the scale and staging of the productions. Scores, perhaps hundreds, of students in elaborate costumes were outfitted with wigs, tunics, banners, shields, swords, pikes, flags, and other accoutrements and properties. As printed, these scripts include footnotes explaining the legendary and folkloric background as well as the sources of various songs, odes, and recitations. Although student productions, the

pageants at Castleknock College drew on the talents of theatre professionals, including Fred Morrow, who earlier worked with the ULT
and the Theatre of Ireland and who served on the 1907 Language
Week Procession tableaux subcommittee.

The pageants were staged at a critical moment in the history of
Castleknock College, especially in its negotiation of a relationship
with the Irish Revival. When in 1907 Paul Cullen[46] became president
of Castleknock College, he found himself at odds with D. P. Moran,
alumnus and editor of the *Leader*, who advocated a Gaelic Catholic
"Irish Ireland." As James H. Murphy notes, May 1908 "saw the climax
of Cullen's major response to Irish Ireland. At the end of the month
there were three performances of an elaborate historical pageant entitled 'The Battle of Castleknock,' staged in the open air on the castle
mound in front of audiences of invited guests."[47] Holloway and the
nationalist press delighted in the Castleknock pageants.

St. Vincent's College, Castleknock: Centenary Record attributes the
inspiration for the pageants at Castleknock to Parker's pageants in
England.[48] The first of the Castleknock pageants, *The Battle of Castleknock* draws on the association of the college's location with Fionn.
Even today the Castleknock College website features this association:

> The association of Fionn with the area that encompasses the Col-
> lege lies in the story of his father Cumhall's death. The Fianna were
> organised in clan, or family groups. The two leading clans being
> Clann Baoiscne, the family of Cumhall, and Clann Morna lead by
> the hero Goll. This rivalry reached its climax when Goll challenged
> Cumhall for the leadership and the rival clans met in battle at Cnu-
> cha. Goll slew his rival and assumed the leadership. This caused those
> who were Fionn's guardians to send him into hiding for fear of Goll's
> vengeance. It was while Fionn was in hiding that he famously burnt
> his thumb while cooking the salmon of knowledge, and thus gained
> the gift of foreknowledge. Fionn rarely used this gift as it necessitated
> his biting his thumb down to the bone, causing him great pain.[49]

A distinguishing feature of *The Battle of Castleknock* is its claim to
being "reproduced, on the very spot, where it is recorded to have taken

place—the grounds of the old Castle."[50] *The Battle of Castleknock* was staged on the evenings of May 28, 29, and 30, 1908, "on the splendid natural stage of the slopes of the Castle hill, the actual spot where the real events took place," thus satisfying one of Parker's well-publicized criteria for pageant production.

The Battle of Castleknock begins with a chorus's recitation of lines from Charlotte Brooke's "Moira Borb," from her *Reliques of Irish Poetry* (1789), the refrain of which intones: "Never again shall two such chiefs contend."[51] Coohal; his wife, Murinda; their sons, Fionn and Tolcha; and their defenders learn of Goll's imminent attack. After Fionn rejects his mother's bid to flee to safety, The Bard, almost metatheatrically, foretells, "The brave deeds of noble Coohal and his renowned son shall be sung amongst us in all ages to come" (7). In the second scene Goll allies with the forces of Connaught and Ulster, while Coohal leads his Leinstermen, the "brave Fianna" (7), into battle with war pipes. In a brief third scene, Conn the Ard Ree (High King), Criffin, and their Bard, all on horseback, relish the opportunity to defeat "this haughty rebel Coohal" (7). The war cries and clashing swords quiet when Fergus, the Bard of Connaught, "shakes 'the Chain of Silence'"[52] and recites the "War Ode of Goll McMorna" (8). Goll defeats and kills Coohal, but Murinda and their sons escape, leaving Goll to fear that "the son of Coohal lives and may yet avenge his father" (10). The first act ends with a caoine performed in Irish, as was the War Ode.[53]

The second act, "The Return of Peace," set twenty-five years later, opens with the chorus's recitation of another ode from Brooke's *Reliques*, this one calling for peace. Fionn will take possession of his father's realm but hopes to make peace with Goll and asks to marry his daughter, Finn-dealbh McMorna. After "the happy re-union of [Fionn] and Goll McMorna" (13), *The Battle of Castleknock* ends as Fionn uses the prophetic gifts of the Salmon of Knowledge: "(*putting his thumb between his teeth) prophesies*—From this day forth, O Goll, and valiant Fianna, the glory of Erinn [*sic*] shall increase. I foresee and foretell great peace and splendour in coming years. There shall shortly be amongst us a Tailcenn from over the raging sea, with his holy garment and crooked-headed staff. He will unite all the provinces of Erinn in worship and in one true belief, until the Galls come to separate them" (13–14). Not only does *The Battle of Castleknock* end with peace, reconciliation, and marriage, but it also anticipates the coming of Christianity.

By portraying Fionn and Tolcha, the sons of Coohal, as children and, in the second act, having the same actor who played Coohal now play his son, *The Battle of Castleknock* reminded even the youngest students of their responsibility and projected a future of service to Ireland. *The Battle of Castleknock* featured students who were quite young, under the age of twelve in the case of Coohal's sons, Tolcha and Fionn (played by Frank Clinch and Patrick Butterly); Queen Murinda was played by a fourteen-year-old Cecil Lavery.[54] Castleknock students were invited to imagine themselves as powerful men who could avenge the wrongs of the past, act with mercy and generosity, and inherit a noble past. In this regard, the message of the pageant was wholly consonant with the lessons of the Gaelic League Language Week Processions, the many Revival history texts, and other representations of a glorious Celtic past that proliferated in stage productions and the advanced nationalist press. But perhaps most strikingly, and unlike Standish O'Grady's *The Return of Fionn*, the Castleknock Fionn does not insist on fighting, let alone killing, Goll; instead, Fionn negotiates peace with him. And Fionn's gift of prophecy enables him to foresee what would make this pageant of pagan myth so acceptable at an elite Catholic school: the conversion of Ireland to Christianity.

The interpolation of existing texts was intrinsic to the integrity of all three Castleknock pageants and, in fact, the claim to authenticity by most historical pageants. Over the next century, the creation of a pageant through bricolage, the assemblage of existing, and often well-known, texts, became the dominant strategy in pageant production. The use of existing texts was not merely acknowledged, but carefully documented in footnotes: "*The Rosg Catha, or Martial Ode of Cnucha,* is said to have been composed by Fergus, poet of Connacht and countryman of Goll. The original poems is very ancient and was transcribed and read before the members of the Royal Irish Academy by Sylvester O'Halloran in 1789. Vide *Transaction R.I.A.*, Vol. ii, from which the ode and translation given above are copied, and also MSS. copy of Battle of Cnucha."[55] Such scholarly citations were not mere antiquarian fancies, but the foundation of the pageant's authenticity. The pageants were worthy undertakings for impressionable young men not despite but precisely because of drawing on these Irish texts. The *College Chronicle* identifies the author as Father John P. Campbell, CM, a Vincentian priest who not only attended Castleknock, but also served on the college faculty, between 1899 and 1917 and from 1929 to 1947.[56]

In 1914 the *College Chronicle* captioned its photograph of Fred Morrow "Director of Pageant." No one was more immersed in production of historical pageants in Ireland between 1907 and 1914. Fred Morrow (1875–1949) was one of eight brothers from Belfast, including Albert (1863–1927, illustrator), George (1869–1955, dramatist who wrote under the name Gerard MacNamara), Jack (1872–1926, theatre and costume designer, cartoonist), Edwin (1877–1952, portrait, landscape, and commercial artist), and Norman (1879–1917, illustrator and cartoonist).[57] J. W. Good's 1905 account of the Ulster Literary Theatre singles out his contribution: "To Mr. Fred Morrow in particular the members of the society [ULT] wish to record their indebtedness, for they recognise that it is to him, in the first instance, that they owe whatever measure of success has been gained."[58] Similarly, of the ULT Seosamh de Paor wrote, "If they have not Mr. W. G. Fay, they have Mr. Fred Morrow, than whom a better stage-manager for their purpose could not be desired. Under his care each successive performance has marked a distinct improvement."[59] Sam Hanna Bell believed that "no account of the [Ulster Literary] Theatre can ignore the work of Fred Morrow who was its producer for thirty years."[60] In his retrospective on the Castleknock pageants, George Moonan identified Fred Morrow as the director of all three pageants. Over the next five years, Fred Morrow's enthusiasm for Irish historical pageantry crossed disciplinary lines between theatre and the visual arts, the political no-man's-land between Ascendancy and advanced nationalists, and the religious divide between Protestants and Catholics.

Fred's brother signed his illustration for the 1908 pageant both as Jack Morrow and as Seaghan Mac Murchada (Plate 1).[61] As the cover of the 1935 program for the portmanteau *The Pageant of Castleknock*, the illustration shows a young barefoot boy whose hand rests on the wrist of a powerful Celtic warrior who holds a sword in his right hand and a shield in his left. Both boy and man, seen in profile looking at Castleknock mount, wear tunics decorated with Celtic motifs. The image suggests that both look to the past for inspiration and that the boy, guided by the man, will follow in his footsteps.

A detailed one-thousand-word review in the *Leader* of the 1908 production of *The Battle of Castleknock* was ecstatic: a "great success . . . an inspiring work. We learn by its means that we have a country to be proud of, with an ancient history that tells of heroes as distinguished as those of any other nation. Such a way of teaching history cannot be surpassed. It is, indeed, a work of real culture." Castleknock College had been brought into the nationalist fold and satisfied even D. P. Moran: "The old College seems to have taken a new lease of life, and to have adapted itself thoroughly to realise the ideals of Irish Ireland."[62] The *Freeman's Journal* noted that "as Castleknock College set the example in Ireland for College Unions [alumni associations], so it has taken the lead in Irish historical plays."[63] A more substantial measure of the success of *The Battle of Castleknock* was the other historical pageants that followed at St. Enda's and the Christian Brothers North Monastery in Cork.

THE FATE OF THE CHILDREN OF TUIREANN (1908)

Only weeks after the first Castleknock pageant, *An Claidheamh Soluis*, urging readers to attend the aeridhearcht of the Gaelic League's Craobh na gCúig gCúigí held on June 29, 1908, recommended pageantry as appropriate for such nationalist gatherings: "Pageants such as that being arranged for the above Aeridhearcht, might well form a feature at many others. Numerous legends, scenes, and incidents of the past could thus be illustrated in a pleasing manner and prove very instructive as well as entertaining."[64] The *Freeman's Journal* reported "glorious weather" for the "highly enjoyable" aeridhearcht[65] performed on a platform erected on the grounds of St. Ann's in Donnybrook, offered by J. A. Trench, LL.D. For admission of 1/6, which included tea, the audience saw a program of Irish song, dance, and recitations followed by a performance of what the *Freeman's Journal* advertised as the legendary pageant of *The Fate of the Children of Tuireann*. Many of this pageant's performers were connected with the renegade Theatre of Ireland: Pronsias Mac Shiubhlaigh (Frank Walker, brother to Maire), Honor Lavelle (Helen Laird), Ambrose Power, Seamus O'Connolly (James Connolly), and Eibhlin (Eileen) O'Doherty. Like *The Battle of Castleknock* and many of the productions of the Theatre of Ireland[66] and the ULT to come, Fred Morrow served as stage manager and, in this instance, also performed a small role. The narration of W. F. Stockley, professor at Queen's College Cork, provided a synopsis of the action. The aeridhearcht concluded with performers and audiences joined in singing "The Rallying Song of the Gaelic League."[67]

By early next year, the *Leader* not only enthusiastically reported on specific pageants but ran two articles on pageantry: "Open Air Drama," by L. P. B. (possibly Andrew E. Malone, pseudonym of Laurence P. Byrne) and "Irish Drama in the Open Air," by Cuan Dor. Citing Castleknock's pageant, Craobh na gCúig gCúigí's 1908 *The Fate of the Children of Tuireann*, and the Gaelic League tableaux, L. P. B. argued that open-air performance offered a solution to the problem of the dearth of suitable theatres in rural Ireland. Avoiding the obvious reference to Parker's English pageants, he adduced two French theatre venues, Bussang and Aulnay, where "village plays, dealing with the traditions and customs of the people who would witness their production, would bring to the minds of the older population some manners and customs which had perhaps long been out of use and forgotten."[68] Cuan Dor was enthusiastic about the potential for open-air performances by nonprofessional players. "It would be advisable," he wrote, "that one great distinctive National pageant should be annually held in one fixed place. The Hill of Tara, of course, has prior claim here."[69] The *Leader*'s editor, D. P. Moran, perennially railed against what he called "rowdyism," especially when it made its way into the nationalist events, as it did in 1905 when he was nearly roughed up at the Language Week Procession.[70] The previous year Moran himself expressed grave reservations about the procession:

> Let me say at the outset that, to me, processions in connection with such serious movements as this of ours are, at best, but necessary evils. They proclaim, of course, the Faith that is in us, nerve and cheer our friends, correspondingly depress and weaken the enemy, and so on. In a word, they are a big advertisement for us, and an indispensable. I don't care to be too often reminded of the fact that a very great number of our young men and women are ready and willing to do anything in their power for the language except—learn it.[71]

Cuan Dor, like Moran himself, urged the Gaelic League to undertake pageantry as an alternative to the "absurdly slip-shod style" of some Irish "evenings": "If [the Gaelic League] has a care for the teaching of Irish history, as history ought to be taught, if it wants to fire again the (in many cases) dying, indifferent spirit of the people, let it take the pageant movement under its wing, and nurse it into strength."[72]

IRISH INDUSTRIES PAGEANT (1909)

In 1909 the lord lieutenant, the Earl of Aberdeen, John Campbell Hamilton-Gordon, celebrated March 17 with a formal state occasion: the *Irish Industries Pageant*. Even in 1886 during his brief first term as lord lieutenant, Aberdeen supported Home Rule. When Lord and Lady Aberdeen returned to Ireland for a second term between 1905 and 1915, their support for Home Rule was already "well known."[73] Lady Aberdeen's aggressive agenda included public campaigns to support home industries, to educate girls and women, and to eradicate tuberculosis (TB).[74] She founded the Women's National Health Association in 1907 and throughout her second vice-regency promoted a series of civic spectacles: the 1907 Irish International Exhibition, the 1909 *Irish Industries Pageant*, the 1911 Ui Breasail (Isle of the Blest) with its children's pageant *Slainte*,[75] a 1913 Pageant of Nursing (a series of tableaux staged at the Abbey),[76] and the 1914 civic exhibition at Dublin's Linenhall.

The 1909 *Irish Industries Pageant* was an occasion of state, not open to the public, held at the Concert Hall (the forerunner of the National Concert Hall later built on the same site). Some nationalists might have seen the event as an improvement over recent observances of March 17; eight years earlier, the then lord lieutenant, the Earl Cadogan, celebrated St. Patrick's Day by reviewing a military parade. The *Irish Industries Pageant* drew inspiration from the 1907 Irish Industries Exhibition. Early in the century industrial displays and pageants were ubiquitous, a regular feature of the civic weeks, such as Ui Breasail in 1911 and the Gaelic League feiseanna. In the 1930s industrial pageants, as Marie Coleman shows, figured in the Irish Sweepstake draws; in the 1950s the National Agricultural and Industrial Development Association would again stage industrial pageants in connection with St. Patrick's Day.[77]

The *Irish Industries Pageant* promoted native industries, such as agriculture, milling, shipbuilding, textiles, and the like. The Aberdeens' memoir recalls the pageant: "Different quadrilles and other dances being organised by various leaders to represent Irish Industries . . . all the dancers passing in an imposing and picturesque procession preceded by heralds, the chief lady of each section walking in front carrying symbols of her industry."[78] The pageant's participants included Margaret Mary, Lady Pirrie (who fifteen years later would succeed her husband as the president of Harland and Wolff shipbuilders), and members of the Arnott, Pim, and Palles families, all prosperous, recognized for philanthropy, and entrenched in the Ascendancy. Although there is nothing in the *Irish Industries Pageant* to suggest dialogue, character (beyond, of course, a narrow metonymy), plot, development, or setting, the event was called a pageant, not least to suggest that it was au courant. The *Irish Industries Pageant* closely resembles the pageant style that remains the most familiar today: the beauty pageant. The intention is to display beauty, specifically in the person of an attractive young woman, adorned in a symbolic fashion and exposed to the public gaze: "Miss Molly Nutting, for instance, represented Beekeeping, in a gown of yellow satin, with brown stripes painted on it, bodice of brown velvet and gold gauze wings; brown gloves and bronze shoes and a bumblebee in her hair."[79] Commenting on Ireland's agriculture, for instance, the program echoes the vision of the 1907 Irish Industrial Exhibition: "the flowers and fruits which Ireland may hope to reap such a golden harvest when her people, and the people of England, realize that certain districts can easily compete with the Channel Islands and Continental Countries, when these Industries are organized, and methods of transit are improved and cheapened."[80] The Ascendancy identity permeates this pageant, not only as a formal occasion of state but also in the future it projects.

In banners, costumes, and its program, the pageant prominently displayed the recently designed trademark logo created by the Irish Industrial Development Association in 1906. The trademark, which uses a distinctively Celtic iconography incorporating interlocking scrollwork with Gaelic typeface and the words "Déanta i nÉirinn" (Made in Ireland), appeared on the pageant flag and tunic of the chief page featured on the program cover. In 1907 Griffith conspicuously displayed the Irish trademark on his front page between the words "Sinn" and "Féin" in the newspaper's masthead; it could frequently be seen in advertisements and illustrations throughout *Sinn Féin*. For Griffith, the Irish trademark was both an emblem of authenticity and a statement of Sinn Féin's politics.[81] The pageants associated with the Aberdeens expose how unpopular the couple was with nationalists. Displays of Irish industries were a routine feature of Gaelic League events, but when associated with the vice-regal court, the advanced nationalist press mocked them and the Gaelic League forbade them. The 1909 *Irish Industries Pageant*, like *Sinn Féin*, prominently featured the Irish trademark but doing so did not diminish the nationalist animus against the Aberdeens. Lady Aberdeen was accused of profiting from her antituberculosis campaign; Griffith referred to her TB sanitariums as concentration camps; Brian O'Higgins mercilessly lampooned her as Lady Microbe. No other health advocate was as badly treated in Ireland until Noel Browne. Even the fact that the Aberdeens

MILLING
(FLOUR)

White dress, black and grey stencilled
design. Powdered hair. Small sack of
flour carried in the hand.

3. "Milling" from the *Irish Industries Pageant*, 1909. The Irish trademark, resembling a lower-case *e*, appears in the center of the gown's bodice.

produced Standish O'Grady's *The Coming of Finn*, the very same play as Pearse chose for his inaugural dramatic program at St. Enda's, could not provide even the shakiest common ground between the Aberdeens and the nationalists. The Aberdeens' memoir recalls the production of "an open-air Irish play, *Finn and His Companions*, by Mr. Standish O'Grady, at a garden party at the Viceregal Lodge," where "Lord Farnham made a splendid presentation of Finn, and the grounds lent themselves to a very pretty spectacle."[82] Press accounts report two performances of *The Coming of Finn* on August 31, 1906, at the Vice-Regal Lodge, three years before it appeared at St. Enda's.[83]

The visual dimension of the 1909 *Irish Industries Pageant*, especially its banners and costumes, offers yet another instance of the engagement personnel working in the Irish Arts and Crafts movement in pageantry. "Practically all the dresses," reported the *Irish Times*, "were designed by students of the Metropolitan School of Art, with the co-operation of the principal, Mr. J. Ward, and Miss [Alice] Jacobs."[84] Nicola Gordon Bowe records that Alice Jacobs, "the gifted Teacher of Design and Ornament at the Dublin School of Art," appointed in 1899, was one of the artists who "could achieve the desired fusion of national and artistic expression through technical skill and originality." Bowe also reproduces a photograph of "revivalist dress for a Dun Emer guild pageant, 1903," for which no script has been sourced.[85] Pageantry offered a vehicle to display in striking visual fashion vernacular nationalism outside the privileged spaces of museums and galleries.

While no historical characters appear, *Slainte* (Health), a pageant performed for and by children, sponsored by the Howth and Baldoyle branch of the Women's National Health Association, and directed by Fred Morrow, provides yet another measure of the vogue for pageantry in 1911. Performed twice at "Sheep Hall" as part of the Ui Breasail festival, the pageant depicts "the banishment of the microbes from Ireland by the new goddess of health 'Slainte.'" Its costumes, designed by another of the Morrow brothers, Norman, included singlets for younger children, more elaborate Irish costumes for the older girls, and imposing, grotesque Shrek-like masks covering the heads

and shoulders of Ma and Pa Microbe.[86] Photographs of Morrow's pageant in the *Irish Times* show a cast that included Bay Jellett, future
violinist and musical director at the Abbey, along with one of her older
sisters, possibly Mainie, and an Irish piper.

ST. ENDA'S PAGEANTS

Desmond Ryan traces Patrick Pearse's long-standing affinity for the
stage to 1890 when "at the age of eleven he commenced to interest
himself in the stage, acting in a play dealing with the battle of Clontarf," written by Pearse himself.[87] While editor of *An Claidheamh Soluis*,
Pearse frequently wrote about drama and, after the 1899 production
of Yeats's *The Countess Cathleen*, memorably inveighed against the Irish
Literary Theatre: "Let us," he urged, "strangle it at its birth."[88] Pearse
was, of course, involved in the Gaelic League Language Week Processions. His experience of pageantry dates from at least 1899 when, still
only nineteen years old, he traveled as an official delegate of the Gaelic
League, then riven over the possibility of an international affiliation
with Pan-Celtic organizations, to the annual Eisteddfod in Cardiff.
Already a venerable institution, the Eisteddfod was, in fact, marking
its centenary. On Friday, November 26, 1899, Pearse was inducted
as a member of the Gorsedd of Bards, prophetically selecting Are-
ithiwr (Orator) as his bardic name.[89] Indeed, it was as the orator at
O'Donovan Rossa's funeral that Pearse would utter his most famous
words. An early biographer, Louis N. LeRoux, claims that Pearse also
attended the Welsh National Pageant in the summer of 1908.[90]

If Pearse did not attend *The Battle of Castleknock* in May 1908, he
was certainly aware of the rival school's foray into nationalist pageantry
from the glowing accounts that appeared in the *Leader*, *An Claidheamh
Soluis*, and the *Freeman's Journal*. Not only was Pearse positioning
St. Enda's, which opened in the fall of 1908, in competition with and
recruiting students away from other elite Catholic schools in Dublin,
but St. Enda's drew on the talents of some of the same artists and theatre practitioners as the Castleknock pageants. The Morrow brothers designed and directed *The Battle of Castleknock* and were among

the artists and craftsmen recruited by Pearse in 1908 to renovate and decorate Cullenswood House as an Irish-Ireland school. Jack, who designed the program cover for *The Battle of Castleknock*, and George Morrow executed the image of Cúchulainn and the uncial lettering of Cúchulainn's and the school's motto: "It means little to me were I to live but one day and one night but that tidings of me and my deeds would endure after me."[91] In March 1909 Holloway described it as "a beautiful room newly decorated by the Morrows of the Ulster Literary Theatre + Theatre of Ireland fame."[92] The son and brother of sculptors, Pearse devoted precious resources to artworks and decor at St. Enda's. Finola O'Kane notes, "At Cullenswood the artworks had included pictures, friezes and sculptures by Jack B. Yeats, George Russell, Edwin and Jack Morrow, Sarah Purser, and William Pearse."[93] The value Pearse placed on Irish visual elements is evident not only in the school's physical environment, but also in the mise en scène of the St. Enda productions.

Pearse recognized the affective potential of offering young students performative opportunities as did the Gaelic League's feisanna. Shortly after Pearse's death, Cathaoir O'Braonain observed that "the boys who were to take part in the Cuchulainn Pageant, and in the Irish Passion-Play, were not likely to forget the great lessons taught by the characters they personated, and the parts they played."[94] Pearse himself famously wrote that "the spirit of Fionn and his heroic comrades had been instilled into their [students'] minds but those for the noble old-time love had a vivid and ever-active and effective meaning. Fionn and Cúchulainn and their high-heroic kin had become part of the mental life of the teachers and the taught."[95] Through the act of personation, pageantry provided the opportunity to inhabit the physical being as well as the mental life of ancient heroes.

Pearse's pageants attracted both contemporary press coverage and some of the best scholarly commentary on early-twentieth-century Irish pageantry. Philip O'Leary offers an invaluable analysis of Pearse's sources and excisions in creating St. Enda's first pageant, the *Macghníomhartha Chúchulainn (The Boyhood Deeds of Cúchulainn)*,[96] here translated by Seán Ó Briain in the appendix. Elaine Sisson structures her analysis of the ethos and progress of Pearse's schools and politics around the plays and pageants performed by St. Enda's students. More recently, Brendan Walsh's *Boy Republic: Patrick Pearse and Radical Education* and Pádraic Frehan's *Education and Celtic Myth* examine the St. Enda pageants in the context of Pearse's educational philosophy and the Revival's understanding of Celticism, respectively.

The first performances at St. Enda's were held only six months after the school's opening in its first premises, Cullenswood House in Ranelagh. Pearse wrote neither of the first two plays performed on a double bill on March 20–22, 1909, in celebration of St. Enda's feast day (March 21): Douglas Hyde's *An Naomh as Iarraidh* (The Lost Saint, performed in Irish) and O'Grady's *The Coming Of Fionn* (given in English). Both O'Grady's *The Coming of Finn* and his *Hugh Roe O'Donnell* "were performed outdoors initially, and O'Grady seems to have felt that the open-air was the appropriate place for drama, as well as all life-giving human activity,"[97] but in March 1909 the Hyde and O'Grady plays were performed in the St. Enda's gymnasium, "a little corrugated iron shed in the grounds"[98] at Cullenswood House. Holloway, a theatre architect, praised the design of the makeshift theatre: "The proscenium was excellently and ingeniously worked into the shape of the hall and the opening of semicircular shape, with a head forming the key + festooned curtains falling in graceful folds."[99] With an audience of about one hundred, Holloway recalled that "when the company squeezed in they certainly were a tight fit."[100]

The double bill of *An Naomh as Iarraidh* and *The Coming Of Fionn* negotiates the Irish and English languages, the religious and the heroic, the Christian and the Celtic. Surviving photographs document the famous costumes, but an even more arresting visual image created in these first productions might well have come in the climax of O'Grady's play when only on "the last day of the last year, and this the last hour of the last day,"[101] does Fionn arrive with his father's satchel to display the severed head of Luchat Mael. Unlike the Fionn of Father Campbell's Castleknock pageant, O'Grady's did not negotiate.

Like Pearse's own *An Ri*, *The Coming of Fionn* offers the possibility to include a variable number of supernumeraries, but might be performed with a cast of only ten. The program began with a violin solo, and then moved to Hyde's play, a harp performance, O'Grady's *The Coming of Fionn*, and finished with the players and audience singing "The Rallying Song of the Gaelic League." Holloway discovered "a strange fascination about their crude boyish playing that I cannot account for. . . . The boys who played Crimall, Fionn + others though they chanted their words in a style outside nature created an impression not easily forgotten. The torches gave an element of danger to the scene not wholly peaceful to the needs of the spectators. . . . Each + all [the audience] felt as they left the hall that they had witnessed a unique and inspiring show + one that promises great hope for the Ireland of the near future."[102] Even among the most jaded spectators, torches wielded by boys in a crowded corrugated shed might create a keenly attentive audience.

In reviewing the Hyde-O'Grady bill in March 1909, the *Irish Independent* wrote, "It is not easy to overestimate the educational and nationalizing influences of such plays on the youthful mind."[103] *An Claidheamh Soluis* hoped to see similar school productions "repeated all over Ireland."[104] Pearse commissioned staff and parents to place reviews and articles on this initial theatrical program in the nationalist press. W. P. Ryan wrote in the *Irish Nation* that unlike most student productions, in *The Coming of Fionn*, "the boys for the time were a part of heroic antiquity." These articles were unqualified not only in their praise of the productions, but in their enthusiasm for St. Enda's, "that ideal Irish school."[105] Pearse recycled these stellar accounts in *The Story of a Success*: "Mr. Colum wrote very generously of us in *Sinn Féin*, Mr. Ryan in the *Irish Nation*, and Mr. Bulfin [writing as Che Buono] in *An Claidheamh Soluis*."[106]

Pearse created the first of his own St. Enda pageants, *The Boyhood Deeds of Cúchulainn*, expressly for performance by his students and apparently after the success of the first dramatic performances in March. Recognizing the limits of a proscenium stage in a corrugated shed, Pearse staged *The Boyhood Deeds of Cúchulainn* in the open air at the school's annual garden party in Irish before "over five hundred guests"[107] only three months after the Hyde-O'Grady double bill. In

1909 there was no shortage of representations of Cúchulainn available to Pearse. Standish O'Grady's *The Coming of Cuculain* appeared in 1894, Lady Gregory's *Cuchulain of Muirthemne* in 1902, Winifred Faraday's *The Cattle-Raid of Cualnge* in 1904. Maunsel published Mary Hutton's translation of *The Tain* in 1907. Yeats's third Cúchulainn play, *The Golden Helmet*, first appeared on the Abbey stage and in print in 1908. Described as a "heroic farce," *The Golden Helmet* sees Cúchulainn crowned with "a cat-headed helmet" in the only of Yeats's seven Cúchulainn plays to portray the young hero. Desmond Ryan recalls Pearse's well-read copy of the *Cattle Spoil of Cúailnge*. By 1908 much of the English-speaking world was pageant-mad; Ireland was not only drama-mad but Cúchulainn-mad as well. After all, Cúchulainn, not St. Enda, appeared on the school's crest.

Like *The Battle of Castleknock*, *The Boyhood Deeds of Cúchulainn* was an equestrian pageant staged in the open air. Structurally, both follow a similar format: a chorus to provide background, the incorporation of song and musical interludes, simple dialogue that celebrates the landscape and Irish nationalism. Like Rev. John Campbell at Castleknock, Pearse took care to underscore the integrity of and his fidelity to his sources: "I have extracted the story and a great part of the dialogue from the *Táin*, merely modernising (but altering as little as possible) the Magnificent phrase of the epic." His account of the pageant in *The Story of a Success* claims authenticity not only about the text and language, but also for the staging, the music by Thomas MacDonnell, and the songs ("kindly checked" by Tadhg O Donnchadha). Pearse credited his brother Willie as "responsible for the costumes, grouping and general production of the Pageant" and his nephew Alfred McGloughlin with construction of the properties, including Cúchulainn's chariot.[108] These elements of pageant production were no less important than Pearse's script. Indeed, Sisson argues that it "was performed in Irish but it was primarily a visual, not a textual, piece."[109]

The Boyhood Deeds emphasizes Cúchulainn's youth: he is a "little lad," "a small sad black-haired boy."[110] Indeed, the fascinating, widely circulated image of Frank Dowling shows a ten-year-old boy in Celtic dress exuding determination. The cultural revival sought to provide exemplars that boys as young as Dowling might emulate to counter both the proliferation of popular, inexpensive reworkings of Arthurian legend and the emergence of Boys Brigade and, later, the Boy Scouts, all of which targeted young British subjects. The *Leader* routinely featured unflattering images of a pudgy, West Briton boy as an effeminate "shoneen." The Fianna Éireann, founded in 1903 in West Belfast by Bulmer Hobson and, in cooperation with Constance Markievicz, Helen Moloney, and Sean McGarry, as a national organization in 1909, offered young Irish boys an affiliation with a vigorous Irish cohort, one imbued with a nationalist ethos. Philip O'Leary documents an array of nationalist projects—essay contests, historical plays in Irish, and the like—to engage young people in the study of Irish history.[111] These Irish nationalist interventions were hardly isolated developments. Throughout much of Europe, inculcating values and beliefs that would produce dutiful, responsible citizens had become a priority.[112] The specific deeds that Pearse selects for his young hero model not only the "heroic masculinity" that Sisson describes, but also assertiveness, even aggression, and a propensity for brinksmanship. These qualities are, of course, hardly uncommon attributes in epic heroes, but, set as ambitions for young boys, they cultivate an ambivalent attitude toward authority that is largely consonant with the ethos of Pearse's educational philosophy (and his future as a rebel leader). Perhaps more surprising is the boy Cúchulainn's unalloyed desire for fame.

Before earning the name Cúchulainn (hound of Culann), the young Setanta is simply an outsider who distinguishes himself on the playing field, despite the fact that he violates the rules, the prevailing mores, to do so. Although Setanta will soon reveal his lineage, he appears uncredentialed. Power, valor, and vigor are the qualities attributed to him in the opening choral verses. By the end of the first brief episode, he emerges as a savior to provide the leadership that the Boy Corps willingly and very quickly embraces. He is fearless, strong, skilled, and "beauteous." In the first two episodes, Cúchulainn twice approaches a community sealed off to him. Twice, he enters an inhospitable space unwelcomed. Twice, he triumphs and is carried aloft on the shoulder of the warrior Fearghas, raised above the others in victory.

King Conchobar, the "noble artisan" Culann, and the druid Cafach are figures of authority who command respect and wield great power. In three instances in this brief pageant, Cúchulainn must face and, to varying extents, challenge their authority. When Conchobar tells him that Cúchulainn must end his quarrel with the Boy Corps because "it's obvious that you're not playing fair with them," Cúchulainn, rather than apologizing, answers that he did not receive hospitality ("a fair welcome") from them. In the second episode, he again chooses not to apologize for killing Culann's vicious dog but instead offers to take the place of the loyal hound. In the third episode, moreover, once selected to be the only one to receive arms that day, Cúchulainn twice refuses the weapons presented to him as unworthy of him until Conchobar gives the boy his own weapons. No less remarkable is Cúchulainn's brinksmanship. In the first episode, all the boys attack him with "ferocious vengeance," and Conchobar might well punish him; in the second, he is presumed dead, mauled by the hound of Culann. Likewise, his battle with Ulster's enemies has a David-and-Goliath quality about it. But the most striking quality in Pearse's boy Cúchulainn is his lust for fame. From the outset he believes and announces that his mission is to lead the Boy Corps: "If they do not come under my patronage, I will not stay my hand against them." He initially protests that he does not want to change his name, Seatanta, and accepts his new name, Cúchulainn, only after the druid Cafach prophesies that the new name will bring him fame. In the next episode, Cafach announces that whoever accepts arms that day "shall be illustrious and renowned, but his life will be short and impermanent." Fame and with it early death are what Cúchulainn seeks. In the final episode, he insists on being saluted by the other youths for his decision to take weapons. When Conchobar asks Cúchulainn if he lied about Cafach's encouraging him to take weapons, Cúchulainn does not deny that he did, but utters the words that appeared in Irish on St. Enda's crest: "It means little to me were I to live but one day and one night but that tidings of me and my deeds would endure after me."

The wider fame for *The Boyhood Deeds of Cúchulainn* came through the press, specifically in a daily paper with a large circulation. Stephen MacKenna's article "Pageants" in the *Freeman's Journal* celebrated *The Boyhood Deeds* as "noble work to help to make the race owner again of its own best possessions, the memories of its old-time chivalry, recorded in beauty, and ringing Irish still after two thousand years."[113] MacKenna posited a native tradition of Irish pageantry: he adduced references by John (Eoin) MacNeill and William Hone and attributed to George Sigerson's *Bards of the Gael and the Gall* the suggestion that "the Gael had miracle-plays and dramas. He [Sigerson] discovers an ancient drama concealed under the romance of the Sorrows of the Sons of Usnach. . . . [It] may therefore be the first tragedy, outside the classic languages, in the literatures of Europe."[114] The cumulative record of St. Enda's performances was reiterated in midsummer 1909 in the first issue of *An Macaomh* (The Student), where Mac-Kenna's ringing endorsement of pageantry as a native Irish form again appeared in full.

Pearse's inspired next move was to present the heroic macaomh and his loyal Boy Corps to a wider audience by remounting the productions outside the school. Walsh asserts that Pearse arranged for the St. Enda pupils to perform Hyde's *An Naomh as Iarraidh* at the Dublin Feis in April 1909.[115] Four of the one-act plays—Hyde's *An Naomh as Iarraidh* (The Lost Saint) and O'Grady's *The Coming of Finn* as well as the two (Pearse's *Iosagan* [The Child Jesus] and Colum's *The Destruction of the Hostel*) performed at Cullenswood House on February 5, 6, and 7, 1910—were performed at the Abbey on April 9, 1910. In early June 1910, Pearse set an ambitious touring schedule for the St. Enda's plays. *Iosagan* was presented as the finale of the Frankfort Feis held at Mrs. Clarke's residence in Blackrock, where Douglas Hyde, Agnes O'Farrelly, and Mary Hayden spoke.[116] Two weeks later, in June 1910, *The Boyhood Deeds of Cúchulainn* was played outdoors at the Castlebellingham Feis in Dundalk in arrangement with William Tempest, whose Dundalgan Press "designed, printed & published" the Irish-language Cúchulainn Teaching Charts in use at St. Enda's.[117] In April 1911 Pearse took *The Passion Play* to the Abbey. Within two years the St. Enda performances had become a valuable asset in the school's capital. From the outset Pearse cultivated an elite audience for performances at St. Enda's.[118] For the March 1909 performances, Holloway "noted what a distinguished company had come—Stephen Gwynn (who by the way has his son at St. Enda's), Edward Martyn, P Colum, John McNeill, Mary Hayden, Mr and Mrs Donn Piatt, the Count and Countess [Markievicz], Mr + Mrs Standish O'Grady, Miss Agnes O'Farrely [sic] and her brother and sister, W B Yeats."[119] Standing on a chair after the final performance of *The Coming of Fionn* on March 22, 1909, O'Grady, a frequent visitor at St. Enda's, delivered "a delightful speech" to the audience and performers.[120]

Over the summer in 1911, the upper school for boys was relocated to the Hermitage in Rathfarnham, and at the end of the school year, on June 15, 1912, Pearse's *An Rí*, "A Morality in Irish," was staged in the open air in pageant fashion at the annual garden party. By now the St. Enda performances were favorably reviewed not only in the nationalist press but also in the *Irish Times*: "The play was enacted an ivied archway forming a perfect background to a natural stage. . . . The play dealt with an historical episode in which a little boy wins freedom for the people after many failures by an unrighteous King. . . . [Performers] revealed a thorough knowledge of Irish pronunciation."[121] In April 1913 Pearse availed of Yeats's offer for the St. Enda production to appear at the Abbey with Rabindranath Tagore's *The Post Office*. That same month the *Irish Times* reported that Bulmer Hobson and Pearse were at work on a pageant of the *Táin* for St. Enda's,[122] which quite possibly became *The Defence of the Ford*. In June 1913, "the students of St. Enda's College assisted by a hundred other performers"[123] presented three pageants at Jones Road:[124] *The Defence of the Ford* on June 9, 11, and 14; *The Fianna of Fionn* on June 10 and 12; and *An Rí* on June 13. Sean O'Casey puffed the St. Enda weeklong fete in the *Irish Worker*: "Two hundred performers will take part in this pageant. Here you will be shown the Boy Corps of Ulster hurling on the field. The news of Cuchulainn's wounding; the march of the boys to defend the frontiers till the Hero recovers; the scene of the men of Ireland around their Camp Fires; the attack by the Boy Corps of Ulster; and, finally, in the last act, the 'Battle of the Ford' between the two Heroes, Cuchulain and Feardiadh."[125] Decades later O'Casey fondly recalled "Paudraic Pearse's lovely pageant done by night [that] showed, in fair language, patterned movements, and shining colours, the battle for the Brown Bull of Cooley between Ulster and the Men of Eireann; the defence of the ford on the way to the north by Cuchulainn."[126] In the day, Holloway lamented the fete's lack of dignity, perhaps owing to the "ceaseless rain every evening."[127]

The first two pageants staged at Jones Road in June 1913 do not survive, but *The Fianna of Fionn* may well have been performed the next year for the annual fete day in 1914. Of that production the *Irish Times* described teachers as well as students performing: "With a wondrous spear [Fionn] slays the Son of Modhna, who had come to burn down the royal city of Tara. . . . The principal part, that of Conn of the Hundred Battle, was admirably played by Mr. William Pearse, while David Sears as Fionn was also excellent."[128] On Friday evening, April 23, 1915, St. Enda students performed tableaux at the Brian Boru Centenary held in the Round Room at the Mansion House that featured recitations by Maire nic Shiubhlaigh, songs by Gerard Ua Croifte, harp solos, and a lecture on Boru by J. J. O'Kelly (Sceilg). Pearse's plays continued to be performed by the pupils of St. Enda's after his death. On St. Enda's day in 1917, *Iosagan* and *An Ri* were performed at the Mansion House, and on December 13 and 14, 1917, *Iosagan* was paired with *The Singer* at Foresters' Hall, with Maire nic Shiubhlaigh taking the role of MacDara's mother.[129]

Thematically and visually, the pageants at Castleknock and at St. Enda's had much in common: Both negotiated the Irish and English languages, the religious and the heroic, the Christian and the Celtic. Both used the same dramatic idiom, employed students of the same age, related some of the same legends. But the productions of the two schools also offered as much in contrast as in comparison. After St. Enda's moved from Cullenswood House to the Hermitage in Rathfarnham, it lost many of its day students, and its enrollment was fewer than one hundred. At the time of *The Boyhood Deeds of Cúchulainn*, the enrollment of St. Enda's was "70, exclusive of 24 girls, who are being

instructed in an auxiliary school."[130] Although smaller, involving only
a fraction of the pageant performers at the much-larger Castleknock,
the St. Enda's pageants were much more aesthetically conscious. St.
Enda's and Castleknock pursued different models of Catholic nationalism. Written by a Vincentian priest, the Castleknock pageants
depicted Fionn and the Fianna, despite their many virtues, as incom-
plete because they had yet to be enlightened and saved by Patrick's
religion. The Castleknock pageants were performed primarily, but not
exclusively, in English, whereas *The Boyhood Deeds* and other pageants
at St. Enda's were performed entirely in Irish. Pearse pursued a much
more well-publicized path for the St. Enda's pageants; Castleknock's
pageants, although they were better attended, never received the same
level of public exposure.

No less than in the decoration of his schools, when it came to the
plays and pageants, Pearse fully recognized the power of images and
documented the St. Enda productions with the now-famous photographs of the boys in costume—some taken outdoors against striking
natural landscapes at the school, others more precisely posed, lit, and
modulated in studio photography by Lafayette. These images grace
the covers of several scholarly works on modern Irish drama, but the
photographs were taken neither for publicity nor for posterity. Along
with scenes of the grounds at the Hermitage, the images themselves
were part of much-needed fund-raising, as they were available for pur-
chase as postcards.

LUG LAMFADA: A PAGEANT IN SIX ACTS (1909)

No theatre event in 1909 was more hyped in Ireland than the Abbey's
production of George Bernard Shaw's worst play, *The Shewing-Up of
Blanco Posnet*. Even after Synge's death in March 1909, the Abbey was
still reaping the blowback of *The Playboy*'s productions in Dublin and
London: anemic attendance, incessant needling from the nationalist press, and challenges from rival companies. With summer loom-
ing and stage censorship much in the news, *Blanco Posnet* seemed an
inspired choice for Horse Show Week. Nearly everyone who saw it was

disappointed; some were angry to be so bored. Shaw knew the Lord Chamberlain would ban the play; he wrote it to be banned. The Abbey knew *Blanco Posnet* would cause controversy; they produced it to cause controversy.[131]

In August *Sinn Féin* tried to entice nationalists away from the Abbey and *Blanco Posnet*: "The National Council has arranged for the production of a National pageant in the grounds of Marino, Clontarf, which have been kindly lent for the occasion by Mr. James Walker. . . . We hope to see Marino Grounds crowded with thousands, and we can promise them delightful evenings." As late as four days before the first performance, on August 21, *Sinn Féin* sought additional supernumeraries ("Rehearsals for the pageant are taking place in the National Council Rooms, and any who desire to assist should apply to the secretary"), offered a detailed summary of the pageant's six acts, and reprinted Milligan's seventy-two-line poem. The next issue offered further tempting details: "Over a hundred persons will take part and the ensemble of heroic costumes, designed by the artistic Morrow family, will provide beautiful grooming effects. Prominent members of the Theatre of Ireland are taking the leading roles."[132] On the very evening that Shaw's Lord Chamberlain–banned *Blanco Posnet* premiered at the Abbey Theatre, *Lug Lamfada: A Pageant in Six Acts*, featuring Seumas O Conghaile as Lug, Sean MacGiobuin as Manaanán, and Austin Martyn as the Ard Ri, was performed in the open air (and rain) at night, with searchlights dramatically illuminating the players.[133]

Lug Lamfada was inspired by Alice Milligan's poem "The Return of Lugh Lamh-fada," which was collected in the Maunsel edition of her *Hero Lays* the previous year (1908). Frazier describes Milligan and James Cousins as "Griffith's staff writers for his weekly episodes of Irish Masterpiece Theatre,"[134] the agit-prop playlets that appeared in the nationalist press. Many of Milligan's poems drew, sometimes promiscuously, on tales from Celtic literature. Catherine Morris describes her creative process in 1892 as part of "her self re-education programme. She continued to construct historical ballads from the prose texts she read."[135] Published in the *United Irishman* on May 12, 1893,

Milligan's "The Return of Lugh Lamh-fada" responds specifically to
Hyde's *The Children of Tuireann*.[136] Both Milligan's poem and Hyde's
work, which he described as a "resume of the toils and difficulties
which the three brothers underwent,"[137] relate the battle between Lug
the Long-Handed and Balor of the Evil Eye. Whereas Hyde's preface
makes clear that his is only a redaction of a vastly more complicated
tale, Milligan's poem further reduces Hyde's treatment, eliminating
complications such as Nuadh's refusal to take up arms against the Formorians; the killing of Lug's father, Kian, by Brian and his brothers;
and the sorrows that befall the three children of Tuireann in rendering
the *eric* that Lug demands for the killing of his father. Hyde's *Children
of Tuireann* ends poignantly, tragically, with Lug denying Brian and
his dying brothers the lifesaving skin, thereby ensuring the extinction
of the children of Tuireann:

> Lugh listened cold and hard, unmoved as Fate,
> Nor ever once withdrew his steady gaze
> From Brian's quenching eyes. He answered him
> Slowly, and weighing well each word.
> "I will not give the skin. You slew my sire:
> Your brothers gave you aid in slaying him.
> If each of you possessed ten thousand lives,
> And by one word, I could preserve them all,
> I would not do it."[138]

Milligan's poem instead recounts the native Irish rising up against the
Formorians' colonial terror and vanquishing their oppressors. Without mention of the children of Tuireann, it ends on a triumphant note:

> And Lugh-Lamh-fada, the child of an immortal,
> Who came with the flame of the sunburst over sea,
> Leads on the host, both man and ghost, against the tyrant's portal.
> The stronghold shakes! The barrier breaks! His fatherland is free![139]

From the same material, Milligan and Hyde create virtually antitheti-
cal readings of Lug. Milligan positions Lug as a heroic Irish demigod,

a religious savior, and a rebel leader; for Hyde, Lug is a vastly more complex figure who bears responsibility for the extinction of the De Danaan. In its crude political allegory, Milligan's poem further simplified the complexities that Hyde regretted abridging; its allegory was ideally suited to the easily accessible, typically celebratory narratives that historical pageants demand.

Lug Lamfada: A Pageant in Six Acts, performed on Wednesday and Thursday, August 25 and 26, began at 8:00 p.m. with musical selections performed by the Celtic String Band followed by the Emmet Choir, the Dublin Pipers' Band, and, on Thursday, the Dublin Meister Singers. At 9:00 p.m. the pageant itself, which ran about an hour, began with a festive scene in Tir na nÓg where Manaanán, the Irish god of the sea, presents the child Lug who will save Ireland. With music and dancing, the Arts and Crafts process before Lug, the master of them all. In the second scene, Lug, now an adult, still basks in the Edenic Tir na nÓg, where "Ireland is as yet to him unknown. The appointed ones appear, and . . . tell him the story of the oppression under which his father's country and his father's people suffer under the Formorians."[140] The third scene shows the brutal tyranny of the Formorians: tax collectors extort their payment, and Balor's soldiers abuse the people. At the darkest moment, as women of Tara keen their kin slaughtered by the Formorians, Lug arrives and demands admittance to the palace. He is initially refused, but after he wins a game of chess against the king, Lug is acclaimed champion and organizes the men to fight the Formorians. In battle these newly militant forces defeat the Formorians; in the final battle, Lug defeats Balor of the Evil Eye and appears on horseback brandishing the iconic Sword of Light. The pageant concluded with performers and the audience all singing "A Nation Once Again."

One surviving illustration of the pageant appeared in *Sinn Féin* in early September. A drawing by Austin Molloy[141] depicts an equestrian scene of Lug on horseback, equipped with sword and shield, leading scores of followers, both male and female, arrayed in period costumes (laced footwear, tunics, pikes, shields, and so on), their arms uplifted in gestures of support. Surrounded by enthusiastic supporters, Lug carries the Sword of Light; he is the long-hoped-for savior who leads the people to victory against their oppressors, the Formorians.[142] The illustration's caption describes a "beautiful Pageant" and mentions plans "to reproduce it at an early date." On the same page, a poem by Theo. C. Henley, "The National Pageant," celebrates the performance. As if the pageant's allegory might be missed, *Sinn Féin* wrote, "The symbolism of the story is particularly applicable at this time, when Ireland is struggling to free itself from modern Formorians and their taxes."[143] Like the Castleknock and St. Enda pageants, *Lug Lamfada* conflates Celtic, Christian, and nationalist mythologies to advance the cause of Irish independence. There is no doubt that physical force is the way forward: Lucetmael must be beheaded; the tax collectors and then Balor must be killed.

Holloway was entranced by the pageant: "There was a spectacular beauty about many of the visions I beheld that could not be equaled inside the walls of a theatre. Nature touched the scene with its magic-+ the charm of fairyland was revealed. When all was over—the audience like a lot of conspirators wandered in the halfdark through the ground to the entrance—a swarm of shadowy forms fading into the shadows of the leafy trees as if they peopled a spirit world."[144] The centrality of a child figured as a coming messiah points to affinities between *Lug Lamfada* and the pageants at St. Enda's and Castleknock. Seán Farrell Moran writes that Pearse's attraction to Cúchulainn was to a hero who was "pure, guileless, and morally superior to his conquerors. He was defeated only because, like Jesus, he allowed himself to be defeated. In so doing, Cúchulainn, like Jesus, took on the role of the 'child-hero redeemer.'"[145] By the summer of 1909, a master narrative emerged in the historical pageants staged by Castleknock, St. Enda's, and Sinn Féin: the Irish people, in desperate circumstances, threatened by an oppressor (Formorians, Coohal, Ulster's enemies, Medb's invading armies), wait anxiously until a hero (Lug, Fionn, Cúchulainn) appears to lead and to liberate them. McMahon documents a tableau in the 1910 Language Week Procession in which "*Éire* laid 'despondent and hopeless' until a boy dressed in a 'national costume,' featuring a shield and spear, awakened her 'to energy, to hope and fearlessness.'"[146] In

THE NATIONAL PAGEANT.

A Scene from the beautiful Pageant, " The Return of Lugh Lamh-fada," which was given at Marino, Dublin, last week. It is hoped to reproduce it at an early date.

4. Austin Molloy's illustration of *Lug Lamfada: A Pageant in Six Acts* for *Sinn Féin* (1909).

Lug Lamfada, as in O'Grady's *The Coming of Fionn*, an exhausted people drift toward hopelessness as their oppressors grow ever crueler and more powerful. Despite claims of fidelity to original, authentic sources, the mining of Irish heroic literature for narratives that would conform to this pattern prioritized the extraction of suitable material over fidelity to the original texts; none of these pageants touches on Cúchulainn's eventual defeat and death. Indeed, throughout the Revival, for O'Grady as well as Pearse, Yeats as well as Milligan, fidelity to ancient tales was far less important than the ways in which the tales could be reshaped to suit the purposes of the artist or the perceived needs of Ireland in the early twentieth century. In historical pageants from the century's first decade, Celtic literature was reread

as nationalist propaganda advocating rebellion and physical force; at
midcentury Denis Johnston situated it in dialogue with classical and
Shakespearean tragedy; by century's end the Macnas *Táin* read it in
yet a completely different way.

ST. PATRICK AT CASTLEKNOCK (1910)
AND *KING NIALL OF CASTLEKNOCK* (1914)

Castleknock College celebrated its diamond jubilee in 1910 with three
performances of *St. Patrick at Castleknock.* An elaborate day of festivities on May 24, 1910, began with High Mass, followed by a series of
addresses by dignitaries including the lord mayor of Dublin, a lun-
cheon, musical performances, the *St. Patrick at Castleknock* pageant, a
gymnastics display, and fireworks. Again, the pageant was staged on
the grounds of Castleknock College, and, again, great importance was
assigned to the locale and authenticity of this second pageant: "*All* the
minor incidents are those actually recorded as happening in the battle
between Meath and Leinster, owing to the latter's resistance to paying
the Boru tribute. . . . It must be remembered they are still real descrip-
tions of actual facts, or at least of the customs of the time represented,
namely, the fifth century."[147] While the ending of *The Battle of Castleknock* anticipated St. Patrick, at least the title of Castleknock's second
pageant foregrounded the conversion of the Irish to Christianity.

The first act of *St. Patrick at Castleknock* addresses not the saint but
the impending war between Meath's King Laoghaire and Leinster's
King Criffan Mac Enna Kinsella. The choir celebrates a "Land of
heroes! Fruitful clime!" and calls upon the Clans of Leinster to resist
the payment of the Boru tribute, part of "proud Laeghaire's knavish
plans" (15) to extort the wealth of Meath. As Criffan and his sons,
Angus and Dathi, arrive on horseback, the men of Leinster unite in
opposition to Laoghaire. Just as Goll united Ulster and Connaught
against Leinster, Laoghaire again brings Ulster and Connaught
together, but nonetheless the Bards of Leinster foretell Laoghaire's
defeat. Criffan's spy, Rowan Kerr, who had disguised himself as a crip-
ple with a wooden leg in Laoghaire's camp, reports the approaching

armies, and, with war cries and war pipes, the Leinstermen march to battle. In the second scene Criffan's druids, Mael and Coplait, also predict Criffan's safe return and Leinster's victory. When the armies come in view of each other, Fergus, the Bard of Leinster, shakes the chain of silence and chants the bloodthirsty War Ode in Irish (given here in its English translation):

> Rise, might of Erinn, rise!
> O Criffan of the generous soul! . . .
> Wide around thy carnage spread!
> Heavy be the heaps of dead! . . .
> Aspect of beauty! Pride of praise!
> Summit of heroic fame!
> O theme of Erinn! Youth of matchless deeds
> Think of thy wrongs; now, now let vengeance raise
> Thy valiant arm and let destruction flame! (18, 20)

In single combat Criffan defeats and captures Laoghaire, while the Leinstermen rout the combined armies of Meath, Ulster, and Connaught. The scene ends with a caoine for fallen Leinstermen composed in Irish by Torna.

Only in the third scene, as the king's sons play chess and a Jester mocks the captured Laoghaire, does news surface of "a white-robed meek man, who would subdue our country, but not by arms." Rowan Kerr warns the Leinstermen against Patrick: "'Tis said Laoghaire and his followers have already listened to him, and therefore their martial valour has departed from them" (22). After extracting a vow that Laoghaire will never tax or raise arms against the Leinstermen, Criffan sets him free. The first act ends with a festival held in honor of the victory and reconciliation where bards sing and recite in Irish "The Praises of Mac Enna Cinnsellach" accompanied by a harpist: "Sweetest of all it is when the seven constant battalions of the Fianna assemble on our plains and raise their standards of chivalry above their heads" (22).[148] The final act, "The Coming of Patrick," stands in utter contrast to the boisterous return of Criffan and his men from hunting:

twelve white-robed monks, the young Benignus, and Patrick arrive in Castleknock. Criffan initially refuses to meet with Patrick, but when Patrick preaches his message of love before the king and court, he wins over Criffan, his family, and his followers. Once Criffan has embraced Christianity, St. Patrick foretells great victories for Criffan and the future renown of Cnucha (28–29).

The pageant's first act, filled with violent language and combat, is twice as long as the second act, which is dominated by Patrick's mildness and serenity. Footage from a 1931 production of *St. Patrick at Castleknock*, which survives in the British Pathé collection, offers the most likely explanation for why a pageant named for Ireland's patron saint is dominated by the bloody conflict between Criffan and Laoghaire: epic battle scenes. Scores of students, all outfitted in tunics and swords, do furious battle across the hillside.[149] The action is so frenetic, the students so enthusiastic in their rough sword fighting, "the whole hillside . . . aglow with life and bright costumes," as Holloway recalled it, that its appeal to performer and audience alike is unquestionable.

Joseph Holloway was often effusive about what he enjoyed; he gushed about his alma mater's second pageant:

As the day was gloriously fine everything passed off splendidly-the beautiful pageant on the hillside amongst the sun bathed trees particularly so. . . . The pageant was a splendid spectacle and most of the youthful performers spoke out clearly and with splendid enunciation. Master Thomas Austin as the Bard (Fergus) sang sweetly to his own harp accompaniment and also spoke nicely. The dressing and the grouping of warriors was beyond praise. The chief parts were St. Patrick (Thomas Donovan), Criffan, King of Leinster (Desmond O'Neill), Laegharie (King of Meath)-John Sheehy; and Messenger, Rowan Kerr (Angus Whitty). All were well impersonated. Not in the wide world could be found such another spot so naturally suit for a pageant as that at Castleknock.[150]

Holloway liked *St. Patrick at Castleknock* so much, he saw it twice. Casting Thomas Donovan as St. Patrick proved prophetic: in 1935, possibly the last time pageants were performed at Castleknock, Donovan was president of the college. Only a few press reports appeared, and most of the coverage focused on the jubilee celebrations rather than the 1910 pageant.[151] Whereas Pearse cultivated extensive coverage for the St. Enda's performances as theatrical events, the Castleknock pageants remained school plays and their audiences primarily families, alumni, and friends.

In 1914 the third of the Castleknock pageants, *King Niall of Castleknock*, set in the tenth century, depicts Niall Glenduff (or Glundub, d. 919), who battled the Danes and secured the "forty years' rest" for Dublin. The preface to this last pageant asserts a geographical link in that Castleknock was one of Niall's favorite residences and concludes with a quotation from O'Curry favorably comparing Niall Glenduff to Brian Boru. Moving out of mythic prehistory and into a far better-documented Christian era, *King Niall of Castleknock* begins in crisis, one now familiar to pageantgoers: a nation awaits salvation from a barbaric power. A chorus of bards sings of Erin's cry for deliverance:

> "Niall" (she cries) "behold my ruin'd land
> The prostrate shrine—the blood-stain'd fields
> Behold! My slaughtere'd sons and captive sires
> Thy vengeance imprecate, they aid demand
> From reeking swords and raging fire . . .
> Pluck! Pluck the fierce barbarian down
> And be triumphant vengeance all thy own." (32–33)

The opening procession sees Niall; his wife, Queen Gormley; and their company return from Tailtin, "*where King Niall has re-established the famous Fair after many years' lapse*," and learn of the Danes' "savage slaughter. . . . [They have] destroyed our churches and slain the inmates of our monasteries" (33); his people plead with Niall to save Ireland from the Danes. A Messenger warns of Danes landing in Dublin in "an immense fleet of their long dark dragon ships" (34). The Danes are especially fearsome warriors; their champion, Sitiric Gale, "a tall commanding dark-haired stranger, with flowing locks down to his

waist" (34), is encased in triple-plated armor. Despite Queen Gormley's misgivings, Niall promises to "stop their hostings against our
sacred shrines and monasteries" (33) and plans to attack immediately.

The second act begins with the choir chanting its war song,
adapted from T. D. Sullivan's *The Spirit of the Nation*, that uses familiar nationalist imagery:

> The Sun-burst that floats o'er us
> In banner'd pride, in banner'd pride,
> Has ever waved before us
> O'er Victory's tide, o'er Victory's tide! (36)

Amid war pipes and war cries, Niall evokes the proud tradition of the
forebears in his oration to his troops and urges them to remember the
women and children left behind at Castleknock and the Danes' cruelty
against the defenseless. Perhaps most important, he reminds his men
that the Danes "have come to plunder your shrines and destroy your
faith. They hate your God and seek to root out your holy religion."
To distract the queen from her anxiety and foreboding, the Bard sings
from Brooke's *Reliques of Irish Poetry*. After Niall dies by Aulaffe's
hand, Queen Gormley caoines over her husband's corpse, but his son
Murkertagh and others swear revenge.

The lyricism of the selections that address the beauty and the love
of the land is, throughout, at odds with the violence and villainy of
the Danes. The Danish leader, Aulaffe, exhorts his men: "Spare none
of these Christian dogs—seek out those white frocked monks we saw
on the battle-plain. Dye their garments with their blood, sacrifice
them to Odin for today's victory" (41). The Danes' sadistic violence
against the Irish delights in attacking the most vulnerable, specifically women, children, and the clergy. The greatest incitement to the
warriors and the pageant's purplest prose is reserved for the Danes'
blasphemy: ransacking the monasteries, mutilating priests, preying on
the defenseless.

Holloway's account of his experience of the pageant was predict-
able delight: "The effect on the picture was magical—all the beech

leaves overhead twinkling in yellowish sunkissed delight the while—
no limelight could have cast such a spell of splendour over the scene
as this all too fleeting burst of sunshine—birds caroled in the trees
and the caws of the rooks were heard as they flew over the tall tree
tops. . . . The grouping was always effective and the marching to and
fro impressive. The youthful actors spoke with rare distinction in
measured tones." Holloway encountered Jack Morrow at the pageant,
and they chatted about his creation of the costumes in bold primary
colors and of the wigs made from dyed flax at a cost of fifty pounds.
Morrow created "armor" by applying aluminum paint to crocheted
yarn. Holloway was duly impressed, noting, "What [Jack] Morrow
doesn't know about pageant costumes isn't worth knowing."[152] In the
press *King Niall of Castleknock* received even less coverage than *St. Patrick at Castleknock*, not least because the Ulster Covenant (1912) and
the Dublin Lockout (1913–14) had redirected the energies of advanced
nationalists.

A FEIS AT TARA (1911) AND
THE RETURN OF CÚCHULAINN (1911)

For the summer Oireachtas in 1911, the Gaelic League offered three
performances of what it advertised in *An Claidheamh Soluis* as a "Magnificent Pageant" in the Rotunda Gardens, *A Feis at Ancient Tara*:
"The people who will enter the Gardens of the Rotunda next week to
witness the historical pageant to be enacted there will find themselves
carried beyond the flight of nearly 1,700 years, to the days when Ireland was ruled over by King Cormac Mac Airt."[153]

Supported by a choir, an ensemble of dancers, and supernumerary
druids, ollaves (poets), seanachies (storytellers/historians), bards, and
court retainers, the principal action is the arrival of the Ard Ri (High
King) and his queen, who in turn welcome the kings and queens of the
four provinces. Closer to costume parade than play, *A Feis at Ancient
Tara* still billed itself as a pageant. For Holloway, the highlight of the
3:00 p.m. performance on Monday, August 7, 1911, was the arrival of
the king and queen of Ulster on horseback: "I noticed that Countess

Markievicz, who was allowed out bail this afternoon, was the Queen of Ulster. The audience recognizing her part set up applause."[154] Indeed, the countess had just made bail after her first arrest the previous day and awaited trial for throwing gravel in the face of a police constable at a demonstration protesting the visit of King George V.[155]

A week later the costumes and personnel from *A Feis at Ancient Tara* were recycled in another pageant, *The Return of Cúchulainn*, at Castle Bellingham, where in 1910 St. Enda's had performed *The Boyhood Deeds of Cúchulainn*. The County Louth Archaeological Society "advanced the sum of £200 to buy outright the fine old Dun or Fort of Cúchulainn at Dundalk," and the completion of restorations at what was called Cúchulainn's Fort occasioned another historical pageant. The *Irish Times* announced "an interesting programme arranged for Lady's Day, Tuesday, 15th inst. . . . including a pageant entitled 'The Return of Cuchulainn.' Sir Henry Bellingham will preside."[156] In his opening address Francis Joseph Bigger, antiquarian, Irish-language enthusiast, and longtime proponent of pageantry, told the crowd that "the Irish were the richest people in Europe: they had a past far beyond any banker's account, they had traditions that no ledger could make up, and they had a history to be proud of."[157] Bigger's obituary in the *Journal of the County Louth Archaeological Society* concludes by fondly recalling the festivities on August 15, 1911: "But first in our memory stands the great day at Dundealgan when he [Bigger] gave the Inaugural Address at the Society's dedication of the Dun as a shrine for the County's legends and a storehouse for the relics and emblems of the past, and when, before the Pageant of Cuchulainn, staged so beautifully by Mr. Morrow's talented troupe, he recalled in glowing phrase the romance of the heroic figures that haunt the spot."[158] Again, the Mr. Morrow in question was Fred, who organized "over fifty performers from the recent Oireachtas Pageant in Dublin."[159] The balance sheet for the Dun Dealgan Fund, which appeared in the *County Louth Archaeological Journal*, shows that the gate money for the opening ceremony and pageant (including the sale of postcards and booklets) was nearly thirty-two pounds, but costs exceeded thirty-seven pounds, most of which went to railway fares for the performers (twelve pounds) and two piper bands and the payment of a fee, train fare, and sundries to Fred Morrow.

The most ambitious pageant project staged without the support of the military or state in twentieth-century Ireland celebrated the centenary of the Christian Brothers in Cork in 1911. R. J. Ray documents three separate pageants dramatizing episodes from Red Branch mythology performed over a week.[160] Photographs of the Christian Brothers Cork pageants in the *Cork Examiner*, the *Cork Free Press*, and the *Irish Independent* show hundreds of pageant participants lavishly costumed in ornate tunics and robes, most armed with either pikes or ornamental shields. The students of the all-boy North Monastery performed all of the parts, including Medb, Deirdre, Iver, and other women characters. Ray set the number of participants at five hundred, but in *Faith and Fatherland* Coldrey writes that "800 of the boys were directly involved, 500 costumes had to be designed and manufactured."[161] The costumes, helmets, shields, spears, and chariots, praised for their accuracy, were all designed and made in Cork after careful study of Eugene O'Curry's *On the Manners and Customs of the Ancient Irish.* Many costumes were spectacular: "Charioteers wore costumes of skins, and their heads were surmounted by the gaping jaws of wild animals of the chase"; the druid Cathbad sported "a long, snow-white costume"; Queen Medb's chariot was adorned with "rich with bosses of gold and Celtic ornamentation; her daughter, Finovar, was borne on a palfrey."[162]

On September 3, 1911, after a Solemn High Mass at the cathedral, a huge parade of hundreds of pageant participants joined by numerous labor and trade groups, city bands, county councilors, the lord mayor and corporation, and harbor board and district council officers moved through the streets to city hall, where the lord mayor presented a resolution from the corporation to the Christian Brothers. The procession offered a spectacular preview of the pageants: the Herald of Ulster appeared on horseback; two horse-drawn chariots carried King Conchobar Mac Nessa and Queen Medb; the bardic choirs, dancers, and warriors from Connaught and Ulster arrayed in ancient costumes marched through Cork. Interspersed among the contingents were four tableaux from the pageants: the chess scene from *Deirdre*, a hunting scene from *Deirdre*, the battle of Cúchulainn and Ferdiad, and a representation of the young Seatanta. Photographs published in the *Cork Examiner* show thousands of people crowding the sidewalks and streets.

The Christian Brothers Centenary pageants covered a much wider range of legendary material than the pageants staged at Castleknock or St. Enda's. Over the course of the week, three pageants from the "semi-mythical age of Cúchulainn, the Red Branch Cycle,"[163] portrayed Cúchulainn, the Boy Hero of the Gael; "Deirdre and the Sons of Usneach"; and "Maeve the Warrior Queen." No single author is credited, although Coldrey attributes the pageants' scripts to Brother A. Walker. The pageants were performed on an elevated open-air stage constructed on Our Lady's Mount on the grounds of the North Monastery: "a central platform as wide as O'Connell Street," flanked by "the battlements of an ancient castle, brilliantly illuminated."[164] Photographs in the Cork papers show a large orchestra with three large harps positioned in front of stage right; in addition to the stage itself, a large arena for the equestrian episodes also served as a performance space. Configured with Connaught on one side of the huge stage and Ulster on the other, each pageant began with a prologue delivered by the herald of Ulster on horseback, verses sung by the bardic choir, an opening tableau, and a formal procession by the entire cast. The detailed account of the first installment, *The Boy Deeds of Cúchulainn*, in the *Cork Free Press* stresses the martial skills of the Boy Corps of King Conchobar, outfitted with shield, spear, and brightly colored trews, and of the chieftains and warriors who appeared in long-flowing cloaks with manly wigs and beards. The youthful Cúchulainn is portrayed in four episodes: his arrival as the unknown Seatanta who proves himself and appointment as leader of the Boy Corps by King Conchobar; his encounter with Culann and acceptance of a new name, the Hound of Ulster; his taking up arms; and finally his victory over

5. Christian Brothers Pageant in Cork, 1911, *Journal of the Ivernian Society* 4, no. 13 (1911). Courtesy of Special Collections, Kenneth Spencer Research Library, University of Kansas Libraries.

Ulster's enemies. By the end of the first pageant, Cúchulainn has ruthlessly vanquished his enemies: when he returns from battle, "the gory heads of Foll, Tuacall and Fandall dangled from [his chariot's] beam."[165]

In the second pageant, *Deirdre and the Sons of Usneach*, Fergus MacRoy brings the sons of Usneach and Deirdre back from Alba to fight Maeve and the Connaughtmen. Deirdre protests, but they do return to Ireland, where they are betrayed. Deirdre commits suicide by drinking poisoned wine. Fergus Mac Róich "called for fire that he might destroy the palace of the King, and there was then seen by the audience a truly remarkable piece of realism: into the night, dispelling the semi-darkness, shot tongues of flame, and so was the royal residence reduced to nothingness."[166]

The third pageant begins with the appearance of Medb in her war chariot, urging her troops to battle by recounting the insults she has endured from Ulster. A mature, very domestic Cúchulainn, seen parting sadly from his wife and child, is unable to rouse the Ulstermen afflicted by Macha's curse at the Gates of the North. Cúchulainn agrees to a series of single combats, and in the last of them he kills and laments his foster brother, Ferdiad. During the combat between Ferdiad and Cúchulainn, Ray recalls, "The spectators continuously applauded. . . . I cannot conceive anything more realistically clever than this mimic combat was."[167]

Good weather prevailed throughout that first week of September 1911, and the pageants proved extremely popular: an extra performance was added to meet audience demand. The centenary celebration involved a large segment of the Cork population; Ray described it "as notable in the history of the City,"[168] not just the school. "Between five and six thousand people attended each performance, and the combined attendances for the week were 32,000 people."[169] Given that the population of Cork was 76,673 in 1911, that attendance figure is all the more astonishing. Press coverage of the pageants was superlative in both Cork and Dublin. The *Leader* reported a great success: "Truly no spectacle, so elaborate and so beautiful beyond all description, has ever been witnessed in Cork or in Ireland."[170] As Coldrey notes, the unionist *Cork Constitution* praised the pageants for undertaking subjects that "few of the citizens knew anything about."[171]

The Christian Brothers pageants were the most ambitious of the decade, not only in the detail and variety of the episodes represented but in their equestrian and pyrotechnic effects. Like Castleknock and St. Enda's, the Cork pageants had to negotiate the contradictions between Catholic teaching and Celtic myth. The celebrations in Cork addressed the fact that the pageants dealt with pagans rather than Christians, beginning with the sermon preached at the opening Mass delivered by the Reverend P. A. Roche on Sunday, September 3, 1911: "Even before the coming of St. Patrick, religion and learning were esteemed. . . . So perfect were the brehon laws that St. Patrick had little change to make in them before accepting them as the most suitable code for the people." As at the end of *The Battle of Castleknock*,

6. Christian Brothers Pageant in Cork, 1911, *Journal of the Ivernian Society*
4, no. 13 (1911). Courtesy of Special Collections, Kenneth Spencer Research
Library, University of Kansas Libraries.

the coming of Christianity is anticipated, here even more explicitly
by the druid Cathbad. After Medb's army flees and night has fallen,
"The news of the Redemption is joyfully received by these well-dis-
posed Pagan ancestors of ours, and Cathbad continuing, foretells the
future renown of the Island of Saints and Scholars."[172] Ray recalls how
the final pyrotechnics displayed the Christian symbolism: "There
appeared against the black background a luminous Cross, signifying
the coming of a new day when all that was material and pantheistic in
the worship of the people should disappear and their thoughts should
quicken, and the spirit of Christianity permeate them."[173] The explicitly Christian dimension of the Cork and Castleknock pageants sets
Pearse's pageants apart. St. Enda's was a Catholic school; students did
attend Mass every morning,[174] but the warrior rather than the saint
appeared in the school's emblem. In comparison with the pageants at

the North Mon and Castleknock, St. Enda's plainly subordinated their Christian dimension to nationalist aspirations.

The passion for pageantry would soon wane, but the Irish Women's Franchise League (IWFL) staged the suffragist Daffodil Fete at Molesworth Hall on April 24 and 25, 1914. The fete included stalls offering work for sale (books, sweets, and so forth) and four performances (afternoon and evening) of a one-act play and *A Pageant of Great Women*. The theatrical program incorporated tableaux vivants, addresses, recitations by Una O'Connor, and musical interludes by women instrumentalists. Margaret Cousins, one of the founders of the IWFL, then living in Liverpool, was quoted in the *Irish Times* as saying that the performances "formed object lessons of what women had done in the past, and would act as an incentive to future deeds as great as those of earlier ages."[175] The two evening performances saw the premiere of Francis Sheehy-Skeffington's one-act comedy *The Prodigal Daughter*, in which Lily Considine, a "jailbird" suffragist imprisoned for breaking a window, returns to her small hometown. Undaunted by her family's shame and their belief that she is ruined, she defiantly announces her plans to sell newspapers like the IWFL's *Irish Citizen* and to stage a suffrage rally. The play ends as she defiantly unfurls a green and orange banner emblazoned with her message: "Votes for Women."[176] Francis Sheehy-Skeffington's text appeared in the suffrage newspaper the *Irish Citizen* and as a separate volume in 1915.

The pageant that followed derived from Cecily Mary Hamilton's popular *A Pageant of Great Women*, first performed in Britain in 1910. Hamilton's tableaux mingled historical personages and allegorical figures such as Justice and Prejudice. Whereas in England Lady Jane Grey, Jane Austen, and George Sand were among the women portrayed in tableaux vivants,[177] in Dublin the national figures represented were Maeve (Mrs. McDonagh), Deirdre (Elizabeth Young), St. Brigid (Mary Walker [Maire nic Shiubhlaigh]), and Anne Devlin (John

Brennan [Sidney Gifford Czira]). The *Freeman's Journal* reported that "the concluding tableau was 'Fight on and God will give the victory' (Irish Suffrage prisoners)."[178] Indeed, in the years between Countess Markievicz's first arrest in 1911 and her appearance in this pageant, her activism had only increased, as had the protests of the Irish suffragists caught up in the 1913 "Cat and Mouse" act.[179]

The *Irish Citizen* judged the four scenes featuring Joan of Arc, who had been beatified by the Catholic Church in 1909 and would be canonized in 1920, "the most successful" of the tableaux.[180] Surviving photographs document a tableau entitled "The Suffrage Prisoner" and show Constance Markievicz as Joan of Arc in full armor liberating the suffrage prisoner, played by Kathleen Houston.[181] The pageant producers did not want for ingenuity: the countess's impressive suit of armor was actually made of linoleum.[182] The *Irish Citizen* reported the event "a great financial success" and credited Markievicz, who "helped to arrange many of the pictures, . . . who drew in much dramatic talent to the service of Suffrage, and who supplied many beautiful costumes."[183]

The Daffodil Fete recalled the theatrical activism of the Daughter of Erin, not only in the use of tableaux vivants, but in the appearance of Markievicz and Maire nic Shiubhlaigh, the latter playing both Lily's mother in *A Prodigal Daughter* and St. Brigid in the pageant. Several participants, including Charles Power, who produced the play and served as stage manager, had close ties to the Theatre of Ireland. At least two of this pageant's performers, Desiree (Toto) Bannard-Cogley and Elizabeth Young, would be involved in Irish historical pageantry in the 1920s and 1930s. *The Pageant of Great Women* also underscores how marginalized women were in this first wave of historical pageantry. Although girls from St. Ita's appeared in some of the St. Enda plays, notably Mary Bulfin as Mary in *The Passion Play* in 1911, and despite boys at Castleknock and the North Monastery playing women characters such as Murinda, Queen Gormley, and Deirdre, the women characters in these historical pageants, with the notable exception of Medb, usually erred on the side of caution.

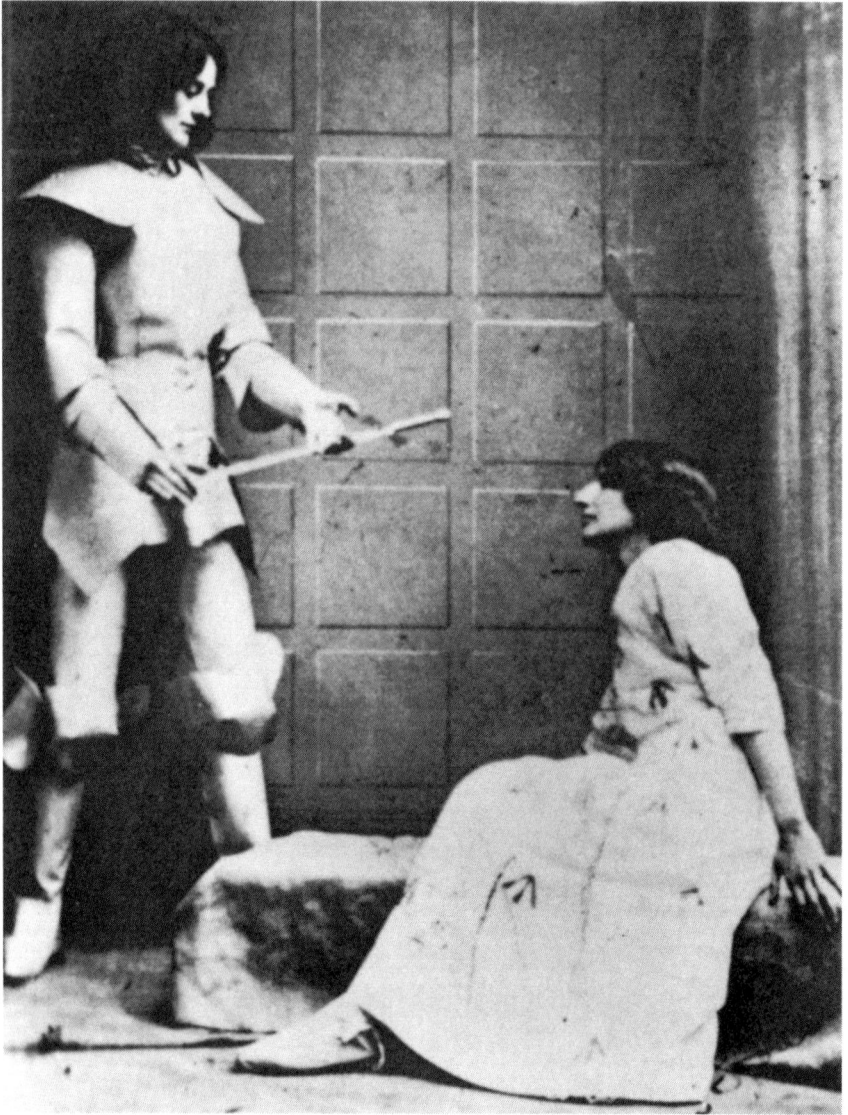

7. Joan of Arc (Constance Markievicz) liberating the Irish suffrage prisoner (Kathleen Houston), in *A Pageant of Great Women*, 1914, *Irish Citizen*.

PAGEANTRY ON THE WANE

By the time of *A Pageant of Great Women*, historical pageantry in Ireland was in precipitous decline, but in the United States the vogue for pageantry was still on the ascent when *An Dhord Fhiann: An Irish Historic Pageant* was performed on May 7 and 8, 1913, at the 69th Regiment Armory in New York, which, only a few weeks before, hosted the celebrated Armory Show. The pageant, attributed to Anna Throop Craig, was designed and directed by John P. Campbell, Joseph's brother. Paul Lamour convincingly argues that Campbell "supplied the ideas for the Irish Historic Pageant which took extremely well in New York: 'it is by far the best thing we have ever gotten up here [in New York]. His pictures have been reproduced in all the leading papers throughout the United States. Perhaps modesty has restrained him from sending any account of this.'"[184] Deborah Sugg Ryan documents two episodes, the first set in ancient times drawing on Fenian legend and the second after Ireland's conversion to Christianity, that were well received by sold-out audiences and very favorable press coverage.[185] *An Dhord Fhiann* is yet another example of the long-distance impact of the artists and craftsmen trained at the Belfast School of Arts in the late nineteenth and early twentieth centuries.

Twenty months after the Easter Rising, the Christmas pantomime *Finn Varra Maa*, staged at the Theatre Royal, proved at least mildly subversive. Presenting an entertainment "racy of the soil" that employed more than a hundred performers ("Leprachauns [*sic*], Banshees, Sheeogues, Sprites, Imps, Schoolboys, Schoolgirls, etc., etc."),[186] sophisticated technological gimmickry, and popular actors in Dublin's largest theatre spoke to the urgency that nationalists felt to reach young Irish audiences. With a full score by Geoffrey Molyneaux Palmer (1882–1957) and costumes designed by the Dun Emer Guild, *Finn Varra Maa* was a family-friendly extravaganza of Irish Ireland. Its central confrontation pits Caílte (Breffni O'Rorke), "the personification of Good as exemplified by Christian teaching," against "the evil fairy Aoibill" (Elizabeth Young). Fionn mac Cumhaill is now Finn Varra Maa, an advanced nationalist Irish Santa Claus. In one of his many disguises, here as a "travelling tinker," he laments the cultural condition of Ireland:

> They've stolen our Poetry, Music, and Stories
> Our Orators, Statesmen, our Letters and Art
> But they shall not rob us of our ancient glories.
> They're guarded too well in each true Irish heart.[187]

Initial response was so positive that excerpts from five newspaper reviews appeared in the play's advertising.

On January 8 the *Freeman's Journal* reported that the provost marshal had censored the play, banning lines found in contravention of the Defence of the Realm act. The lines in question appear in this exchange between Constable Keogh and Sheamus Pat:

CONSTABLE: Well, I'm not going to the war,
> If that is what you're hinting at;
> I'd see them hanged first, Sheumas Pat.
SHEUMAS PAT: You're in the "Force," God help you, Keogh
> And you'll be bound some day to go.
> They want to let the German see
> Our sable-belted R.I.C. [Royal Irish Constabulary] . . .
> 'Twill be a dreadful sight to see!
> 'Tis riddled like a sieve you'll be.
> Just lying in a heap, out there,
> Without a mother's son to care;
> And then the names all will tell
> How Keogh, the peeler, fought and fell.[188]

Whatever comment the provost marshal or his deputy made, what was irresistible was the impulse to inflate it, to transform it into an unprecedented imposition of theatrical censorship in Ireland, the absence of which was flaunted in the 1909 Abbey production of Shaw's *Blanco Posnet* and was distilled as a hallmark of Irish theatre since the 1907 controversy over *The Playboy*. Such an inflation promised what both *Blanco*

Posnet and *The Playboy* enjoyed, "the boom of the ban" that prevailed whenever Irish plays were linked to censorship. Indeed, years later the *Irish Independent* recalled that advertising the play in relationship to censorship caused "crowds [who] flocked to see *Finn Varra Maa* and . . . the committee who were financing it came out very substantially on the right side."[189]

Musicologist Axel Klein considers *Finn Varra Maa* an early operatic effort by Palmer and "wouldn't hesitate calling this print [the Talbot Press edition of 1917] a libretto."[190] Journalist Fintan O'Toole describes it as "a conscious attempt to repel the invasion of the alien Santa."[191] Links between *Finn Varra Maa* and Beatrice Elvery and Violet Russell engage the attention of art historian Nicola Gordon Bowe.[192] The exquisite illustration of Micheál macLíammóir on the publication's cover and Grace Gifford Plunkett's design for the souvenir program offer even more direct ties between *Finn Varra Maa* and the Irish Arts and Crafts movement.

Another exception to the decline of historical pageantry after 1914 was *A Pageant of Early Irish Saints*, which premiered in two open-air performances on June 10 and 11, 1921, in Iveagh Gardens. Eva Jellett, the first woman to take a degree in medicine from Trinity College Dublin, where her father served as provost, and aunt to painter Mainie Jellett, scripted a charity entertainment to raise funds for the Dublin University Mission to Chota Nagpur in India. The year after she graduated, 1906, Jellett went to work in the Dublin University Mission in Hazaribagh, rose to be head associate in the mission, and served in India until her retirement in 1924.[193] *A Pageant of Early Irish Saints* was hardly a subversive piece. Its goal, to raise funds, demanded a narrative with broad appeal, one directed to a Church of Ireland audience.

In its first iteration, Jellett's pageant treated three Irish saints: Patrick, Brigid, and Columba (or Colmcille). Summoned to Ireland by a vision, Patrick preaches the gospel of love, contends with Laoghaire's druids, wins over Laoghaire's daughters and bard, and finally blesses Ireland. The pageant's three acts rely heavily on narration by a "Prologist" as well as songs performed by a chorus accompanied by an orchestra. Like later pageants on St. Patrick, the action draws on

8. Micheál macLíammóir's cover illustration of T. H. Nally's *Finn Varra Maa* (Dublin: Talbot Press, 1917). Courtesy of the Edwards-macLíammóir estate.

familiar features of his life: his childhood in England, abduction, and captivity in Ireland; a spiritual vision directing his escape and flight; his return to Ireland, culminating with the confrontation with the evil powers of the druids at Slane; his success at King Laoghaire's court at Tara; and his death after a long career in converting the Irish people. The final scene in *A Pageant of Early Irish Saints* struck a time-transcending tableau depicting Patrick with his successors: Saints Brigid and Columba as well as Kieran, Columbanus, Gall, and Fin Barr. For the performances in 1924, the pageant ended with a "procession illustrating some of the work of the Mission."[194]

British Pathé newsreel footage of a rehearsal and performance in 1921 suggests a score of elaborately costumed amateurs, with children performing as supernumeraries.[195] Protestant clergymen took many of the male roles, including St. Patrick and St. Columba. Not only does Jellett's original script survive, but so do several photographs; newspaper accounts; a letter of congratulation from John, Archbishop of Dublin; and about two minutes of the Pathé film. A review praised it as "recall[ing] very realistically something of the atmosphere of early Irish Church life" but lamented the pronunciation of Irish words. With "Early" dropped from its title, *A Pageant of Irish Saints* was revived on at least two later occasions: for three performances on June 5, 6, and 7, 1924, and again in 1940.

The press noted that such an undertaking in June 1921 was "no common act of faith and courage to plan and carry out an outdoor pageant under present conditions of life in Dublin."[196] Undoubtedly, there were other, smaller, historical pageants. On April 11, 1914, *Sinn Féin* reported, "Dublin corporation has at length decided to organize a civic celebration of the ninth centenary of the battle which freed Ireland from a tyranny to which England and France succumbed," but if Dublin celebrated Boru's victory at the Battle of Clontarf, the press took little notice.

The historical pageants produced between 1907 and 1914 share an enthusiastic engagement with the distant past in order to shape history's narratives and the celebration of a neglected, submerged, or imagined heritage. Using a popular and often populist dramatic idiom, Irish historical pageants entertained and instructed large audiences by appealing to a more general public, including children and adolescents. Most of them depart significantly from the "Irish story," the grand narrative of so much of the nineteenth century. They suppress elements of abjection, defeat, and poverty by showing oppression overcome by physical force and bravery, often in uneasy combination with Christian virtue. These pageants were, in fact, "unmodern, ideal, breezy, springdayish, Cuchulainoid,"[197] just what Synge hoped to avoid in a national theatre. Ironically, the very person to whom Synge addressed those five oft-quoted adjectives, Stephen MacKenna, played a pivotal role in endorsing pageants as a native Irish form.

The sudden collapse of historical pageantry after 1914 suggests that as a theatrical idiom, it flourished only during times of relative stability. The turbulent period of the Dublin Lockout (1913–14), World War I (1914–18), the Easter Rising (1916), the Anglo-Irish War (1919–21), and the Irish Civil War (1922–23) saw no large-scale historical pageants in Ireland. The demise of pageantry after 1914 might likewise be attributed to the rise of cinemagoing and the accessibility of epic films whose scale could dwarf even the Christian Brothers' pageants in Cork. The vogue for historical pageantry in Ireland between 1908 and 1914 may also have been just that: a dramatic fad that left audiences sated with the sameness and participatory demands of such public spectacles. Like most appetites, the hunger for public spectacle would return after Independence.

2

Forging the Past
in the Irish Free State

On March 7, 2012, Minister for Tourism Leo Varadkar announced plans for the Gathering, a tourist initiative that would attract three hundred thousand additional diasporic visitors to Ireland and generate two hundred million euros in 2013.[1] The idea was hardly a new one. Similar plans had been suggested even before Irish Independence: at the 1922 Irish Race Congress, J. J. Walsh, the Free State's first minister for posts and telegraphs, proposed a national "Home Town Week." Like other key figures in the creation of public pageantry in the century, Walsh had been actively involved in the GAA.[2] He was an enthusiastic supporter of the two enterprises that featured civic pageantry in the first decade of the Free State: the Aonach Tailteann and the Dublin Civic Weeks of 1927 and 1929. Nor was the impulse to attract overseas visitors to spectacles of Irish history without precedence. In *Revolutionary Underground*, León Ó Broin records disappointment at the turnout for the centenary of the 1798 rising in 1898: "The absence of American visitors and the great lack of funds had knocked the bottom out of the celebrations."[3]

Until recently, the first decade of the Irish Free State has been characterized as, in Seamus Deane's formulation, a "provincial backwater."[4] Brian Fallon, Nicholas Allen, Frank Shovlin, and others have reanimated interest in this period through their examination of culture, fiction, and literary periodicals. Of a slightly longer period, Andrew Kincaid writes, "Far from being a moment of stagnation and isolation, the years between 1922 and 1945 were a time of cultural

89

gestation and expansion."[5] Despite John Turpin's observation that after "the British withdrawal in 1922, Ireland had been starved of spectacle. Gone were the regimental marching bands, displays with flags, cavalry formations, carriages of notables, festivities for the monarch's birthday and for royal visits,"[6] the Free State and its client government in the city of Dublin, a troika of city commissioners, embraced pageantry on a grand scale, not merely to compensate for the demise of British pageantry, but to impart a sense of the nation's identity and past and to consolidate its authority. In the period between 1922 and 1932, the Irish Free State undertook several attempts to "resurrect" the Aonach Tailteann[7] and supported the many historical pageants associated with the Dublin Civic Weeks in 1927 and 1929, all of which whetted the appetite to host the 1932 Eucharistic Congress in Ireland.

The early years of the Free State were so economically perilous that it implemented hugely unpopular, draconian measures, such as cutting the old-age pension by one shilling in September 1924. Financial exigencies compromised state funding for arts and cultural organizations, yet a point of consensus in the new Irish Free State was the importance of civic education and nation building. The Irish Free State did, perhaps surprisingly, invest in public spectacles to assert its identity and to unite a public divided by civil war in celebrating a positive, progressive image of the nation.[8] Paige Reynolds and Mike Cronin have surveyed the state-building intentions of Aonach Tailteann, including its cultural dimension such as its competitions in arts and crafts. Síghle Bhreathnach-Lynch has looked at the Free State's early efforts at public commemoration, the Garden of Remembrance in Parnell Square and the war memorial in Islandbridge in particular. Anne Dolan has considered the efforts of the Free State to affirm its power and legitimacy by commemorating Michael Collins, Arthur Griffith, and Kevin O'Higgins. As Bhreathnach-Lynch and Dolan demonstrate, the extremely problematic commemorative efforts in the 1920s may have done more to expose the divisions within rather than to unite the Irish public. Dolan's description of the contentious nature of the ceremony at the cenotaph that honored Collins and Griffith confirms the proximity of commemoration and historical pageantry:

"But as the curtain closed on this pageant, this gathering of pro-Treatyite players left a bitter postscript to the civil war; they left a legacy of triumphalism which could only serve to make the memory of the war even more divisive."[9] What proved vastly more palatable were the populist entertainments devised for the Dublin Civic Weeks. Drawing on the pageantry of the Aonach Tailteann, the Gaelic League Language Week Processions, native Irish traditions, and British military tattoos, the civic weeks made extensive use of pageantry in parades, military tattoos, tableaux vivants, stage shows, and other spectacles. Those representations of Irish history intended to be educational and inspirational, but also sought to affirm the legitimacy of the Dublin city commissioners and, perhaps more important, the Free State government and its army.

In January 1922, only weeks after the Treaty, the Irish Race Congress convened in Paris with an agenda to secure "International Recognition of the Irish Republic," to promote trade in Irish products, and to "establish a permanent Secretariat" in a neutral country to advance these objectives.[10] Variously described as a fiasco, a failure, or a debacle, the Irish Race Congress was probably doomed, not least because two separate delegations from Ireland competed with each other. As John Brannigan notes, "As a result of the split over the treaty, there was not one official delegation from Ireland, but two, nominated separately by Arthur Griffith and Eamon de Valera, funded separately."[11] Among the Griffith-appointed delegates attending the Irish Race Congress was J. J. Walsh, who reminded delegates of the pending Irish Race Olympic, planned for August 6–13, 1922, but not realized until the 1924 Aonach Tailteann. "Race" has long been recognized as a slippery term, but in 1922 both in the Irish Race Congress and in the title of the promotional brochure *Tailteann Games: Irish Race Olympic*, it referred to ethnic identity rather than athletic competition: an Olympic Games for the Irish race, including the diaspora.

As well as encouraging foreign students to study English in Ireland, advancing a "Back-to-Ireland Movement," and promoting Irish drama, music, and literature, the Irish Race Congress entertained a proposal from Walsh for "an Irish Home Town Week—a period during which the exiles would visit the motherland."[12] Brannigan notes that the Irish Race Congress employed "the rhetoric of racial destiny, and racial cohesion across the globe . . . and often takes this form of reconfiguring the diaspora not as a sign of historical trauma and colonial subjugation, but as a sign of the vitality and potency of a race."[13] The pageantry of the civic weeks employed a similar rhetoric: to reconfigure the Irish past, to efface the narrative of colonial subjugation, and to situate the government and army as not only lineal but also worthy descendants of mythic and historical heroes.

Not unlike historical pageants in their desire to promote civic engagement, civic weeks flourished in England after World War I. The *Irish Builder* had drawn Dublin's attention to Liverpool's 1926 Civic Week. Historical pageants and civic weeks pursued virtually identical goals: educate the public, instill pride in citizens, and stage a public history that celebrated a community's heritage. Lady Aberdeen sponsored two such celebrations: the 1911 Ui Breasail and the 1914 Civic Exhibition, "Ireland in Miniature," billed as "the first function of its kind to be held in these islands," which transformed a slum area around Dublin's Linenhall buildings into "a veritable fairyland of attractions."[14] Opened on July 15, the 1914 Civic Exhibition advertised "plenty of entertainment indoors. Outdoors, massed bands, torchlight tattoos, pipers." The *Irish Builder* was supportive and congratulatory of both these events, especially since the Ui Breasail featured a Town Planning Exhibition, but the advanced nationalist press saw both the 1911 and the 1914 events as opportunities for fresh assaults on Lady Microbe. In any case, the assassination of Archduke Franz Ferdinand in Sarajevo and the outbreak of world war less than two weeks after its opening stunted attendance at the midsummer 1914 Civic Exhibition.

The conception of the Aonach Tailteann owed much to civic week celebrations, but even more to the Olympic Games. The presentation of the Aonach Tailteann as a venerable and authentically Irish event obsessed its planners. In his 1923 book, *Aonach Tailteann*, T. H. Nally, the creator of *Finn Varra Maa*, claimed both artistic and physical greatness for the Irish: "This story of the historic games of Ancient Ireland has been compiled with a view to familiarizing the Irish people with knowledge, however imperfect, of their ancient greatness in the Athletic World. It is surely something to be proud of to know that our country has played a great and noble part in the Past, not merely in leading all the nations of Europe in intellectual culture and the higher arts of civilization, but also in the no less important province of physical development."[15] Nally traced the Aonach Tailteann back to 632 BC, when Lugh Lámfhota, here not the oppressor of the Irish people he was in the Sinn Féin pageant of 1909 but rather the dutiful foster son, held the games to honor his foster mother, Queen Tailte. Eighty years after the Famine, Nally offered another dimension to "the Revival," one in which the bodies of the Irish people, like the body politic of the newly independent Free State, had recovered the strength they once had. Like his 1917 Christmas pageant, *Finn Varra Maa*, Nally's imaginative account of the Tailteann Games was grounded more in the culture of modern rather than ancient Ireland.

Similarly, M. J. MacAuliffe's 1927 edition of his study of ancient Irish law, *The History of Aonach Tailteann and the Ancient Irish Laws*, first published in 1923, offered an analogous and wholly extraneous originary account of the Aonach Tailteann. MacAuliffe reported that the Tailteann Games arose during a golden age in the Celtic past when there were "no heavy rains in Ireland, the land being watered chiefly by nocturnal dews."[16] In reaching back to the second or seventh century before Christ to reclaim the ancient Irish Aonach Tailteann, Nally's and MacAuliffe's accounts reflect the nativist enthusiasm that informs many of the scholarly and popular histories that anticipated or addressed Irish Independence: Seamus MacManus's *The Story of the Irish Race: A Popular History of Ireland* (1921), Mary Teresa Hayden and George Moonan's *A Short History of the Irish People from Earliest Times to 1920* (1921), Francis Hackett's *The Story of the Irish Nation* (1922, revised for several editions through 1939), and Stephen Gwynn's 549-page *History of Ireland* (1923, condensed and revised in 1925 as the basis for *The Student's History of Ireland*). As their titles suggest, many are popular histories or student textbooks designed to construct a coherent narrative history. In general, they seek links between twentieth-century and pre-Union times to offer an alternative to the colonial status of Ireland by fashioning, sometimes from whole cloth, a master narrative of Irish achievement. The 1922 games were canceled because of the Civil War, but in 1924 the event was staged shortly after the Dublin Horse Show and the 1924 Paris Olympics. Mike Cronin quotes the *Irish Times* asserting that the 1924 games "may be the most important psychological moment in the history of the Free State" and observes that the Aonach Tailteann "offered a symbolic victory over the bitterness, division and destruction of a civil war that had drawn to a close only 13 months earlier."[17]

The signature graphic design that would appear in the 1924, 1928, and 1932 Tailteann Games was the striking profile of an athlete in a Celtic tunic, cape, and leggings poised to throw a spear (or javelin). Created by W. Victor Brown, the image appeared in 1922 on the cover of the *Tailteann Games: Irish Race Olympic* that announced the games' aspiration to "the unity of the whole Gaelic family."[18] The image, like the historical costumes and the Irish wolfhounds, one lent by Mrs. J. J. Walsh, at the opening ceremonies at Croke Park gestured toward the ancient heritage of the games, as did the personation of Queen Tailte in a stage pageant. During the second week of the games, on August 12 and 14, 1924, organizers arranged for the presentation of *The Story of the Games* at Dublin's Theatre Royal. Written by Major A. T. Lawlor, this pageant claimed to be "an absolutely original production in its form in that it is an attempt to construct a portrayal of the times of Queen Tailte, on forms drawn from Gaelic literature and the tradition of the old culture. . . . A narrator, Miss Elizabeth Young, recites the story of the Queen to the accompanying chant of the Cantora, Mr. M. J. Dolan and Mr. F. J. McCormick, both of the Abbey Theatre. The story is in the form of visions (aislingi) and after each narration the vision of majestic times of Ancient Ireland appears." Configured as a prelapsarian state, ancient Ireland was enacted by "rhythmical movement to the accompaniment of music."[19] As Reynolds observes, the production was not well received in 1924,[20] but it was revived and expanded in 1928 and by 1932 had "a supporting cast of some four or five hundred performers."[21] In an uneasy alliance of ancient heritage and modern technology, an immense image of Queen Tailte at Croke

Park was illuminated in fireworks. For the 1928 Tailteann Games, another short pageant, Seamus MacCall's *The Coming of Fionn*, was staged in Lord Iveagh's gardens as an entertainment at the Tailteann Games awards ceremony.

The Dublin Civic Weeks of 1927 and 1929 recognized the possibilities of building on the civic engagement offered by the Aonach Tailteann, problematic as Reynolds demonstrates they were. The civic weeks embraced historical pageantry to propagate an even grander narrative of the Irish past and to affirm the legitimacy of the city and national government in festive and even carnivalesque ways. Dominic Bryan records that by 1926, "the [Orange] Twelfth parades became rituals of state,"[22] and it seems likely that the Free State's games and the civic weeks were in dialogue with the resurgence of unionist pageantry in Northern Ireland. The Free State knew it needed such rituals of state, but as Dolan demonstrates the ceremonies at the Cenotaph were neither successful nor satisfying. The Aonach Tailteann paved an inclusive and populist direction for the civic weeks to portray a glorious heritage for the Free State, one that not only was much more venerable than loyalist commemoration of the seventeenth century, but reached much closer to the present day. Although the Free State government did not present itself as the sponsor of the Dublin Civic Weeks, it cooperated by facilitating transport, accommodations, and publicity; perhaps most important, it supplied personnel from the Irish Army and the Garda Síochána to provide security, to perform in the tattoos, and even to swell the ranks of the supernumeraries in other pageants.[23] In his creative autobiography, *All for Hecuba*, macLíam-móir, for instance, recalls "fifty oversized civic guards, who were to be Gaels, Vikings, Normans, and Volunteers" in his 1929 pageant, *The Ford of the Hurdles*.[24]

DUBLIN CIVIC WEEK (1927)

Like the Tóstal in the 1950s, the first Dublin Civic Week hoped to extend the tourist season beyond the summer months—into April for Tóstal and into September for the civic weeks—but the latter took as its principal audience the citizens of Dublin. The first civic week unfolded as the Free State entered an especially hard-line phase after the assassination of Minister for Justice Kevin O'Higgins only nine weeks earlier, on July 10, 1927. Cosgrave's "snap" election of September 22, 1927, would take place in the midst of the first Dublin Civic Week. In the context of theatre history, the historical pageantry of 1927 and especially of 1929 responds directly to Sean O'Casey's popular versions of recent Irish history in his Dublin trilogy: *The Shadow of a Gunman* (1923), *Juno and the Paycock* (1924), and *The Plough and the Stars* (1926). For O'Casey, the recent Irish past was shambolic and unheroic, an opportunity missed; the Irish characters in the Dublin trilogy are not only badly served by militant nationalism but sacrificed on its altar.

Programming for the 1927 Civic Week included lectures by UCD historians Mary Hayden and Eoin MacNeill, sporting events, concerts, dances, exhibitions, and a recital by John McCormack at the Theatre Royal. An ornate white arcade adorned the median of O'Connell Bridge.[25] Bulmer Hobson's publicity for the 1927 Civic Week produced an elegant handbook, posters, several programs, the prospectus for the Historical Costume Ball (where "historical costume must be worn"),[26] and a torrent of press releases. Like the 1924 Tailteann Games, the 1927 Dublin Civic Week enlisted the support and contributions of an impressive array of intellectuals, craftsmen, artists, and writers. The 1927 *Dublin Civic Week Handbook*, designed by the founder of the Three Candles Press, Colm O Lochlainn, was the first of several luxe publications edited by Hobson: *The Book of Dublin* (1929, with subsequent revised editions), *The Saorstát Eireann Official Handbook* (1932), and *The Gate Theatre Book* (1934) would follow.[27] The handbook collected essays on Dublin's history and its contributions to science and the arts by prominent intellectuals: Thomas Bodkin on the visual arts, John Larchet on music, C. P. Curran on literature, and Michael Tierney on scholarship. Perhaps more memorably, the 1927 *Dublin Civic Week Handbook* was lavishly illustrated by established as well as young Irish artists: Matthew Barry, Brendan Clinch, Harry Kernoff, William MacBride, Hilda Roberts, Estella Solomons,

Sean O'Sullivan, and George Monks. Paul Henry served as honorary director of the 1927 Civic Week art committee. Kathleen (Kitty)
McCormack created a poster specifically for the 1927 *Grand Pageant
of Dublin History*, manufactured by the Dun Emer guild, that depicts
a fleet of silhouetted Viking longships and their warriors, armed with
halberds and wearing horned helmets, sailing on a turbulent sea into
Dublin Harbor.[28] As Brian P. Kennedy observes, in the years after
Independence, "all manifestations of the pre-Norman period were
now in vogue."[29]

The even more beautiful 1929 *Civic Week Handbook*, illustrated by
intricate ornamental borders depicting Dublin's heritage and culture,
paid homage to Harry Clarke's exquisite *Ireland's Memorial Records,
1914–1918* (1922). Maurice MacGonigal's striking cover (Plate 4) depicts
a ship, its sail adorned by the three dual-towered gates of the Dublin
City Coat of Arms, on a turbulent sea against an image central to nationalist iconography: the rising sun. Paul Henry's poster for the 1929
Civic Week, an uncharacteristic representation of an urban landscape,
depicts a quayside stevedore against the backgrounds of the mast and
rigging of a sailing vessel, the Liffey, Dublin's Customs House, and a
sky laden with Henry's trademark billowing clouds.[30] The civic week
involvement of Irish artists, also including Kathleen Quigley, Austin
Molloy, Art O'Murnaghan, Francis Bowe, Micheál macLíammóir, and
Liam (William) Megahey, argues not only for a consciousness of the
power of the visual arts, but for the engagement of leading visual artists in creating distinctly Irish images for these civic weeks, ones that
skirted the visual clichés of the round tower, high cross, shamrock,
and harp. The representations of an urban Dublin environment in
civic week publications employed a recognizable Irish visual idiom
that is in many ways analogous to the celebration of Irish history in
the civic week pageantry.

The civic week handbooks were among several publishing ventures that appeared after Independence to project an image of Dublin
as a modern European capital with a venerable past. D. L. Kelleher
revised his book *The Glamour of Dublin*, first published in 1918, not
least so it could begin with a description of O'Connell Street, renamed

after Independence. However horrific the plight of Dublin slum dwellers or the Irish economy, these luxe publications bespoke a modern European society. As well as tapping the support of leading cultural figures, both civic weeks deliberately enlisted bright young things: Harry Kernoff was twenty-seven and Sean O'Sullivan only twenty-one when they contributed illustrations to the 1927 handbook. By the time of the 1929 week, Hilton Edwards was twenty-seven and Micheál macLíammóir was twenty-nine. No less important was the mobilization of thousands of participants—soldiers, artists, artisans, actors, seamstresses, designers, and spear carriers—bound in a common task. Reynolds's assessment of the Tailteann Games is equally applicable to the civic weeks: "Pro-Treaty artists and politicians asked citizens and tourists to ignore the reality of an Ireland hobbled by widespread poverty and ongoing political discord. Instead, audiences were encouraged to embrace the appearance of an affluent, cosmopolitan, and confident new nation."[31]

The chairman of the Dublin city commissioners, Seamus Murphy, announced that the Dublin Civic Week of 1927 would "tell of the history of Dublin, its past glories and triumphs, its present greatness and its promise for the future."[32] A proud, non-British history is at the heart of the pageantry of the 1927 Dublin Civic Week. Not only did the Dublin city commissioners construct a distinct Irish history, but they used the broad strokes of pageantry to justify their nonelectoral appointments. Indeed, the handbook's article on municipal government in Dublin served that interest precisely. The town clerk of Dublin, John J. Murphy, wrote, "As is generally known, in May, 1924, by a sealed order of the Minister for Local Government and Public Health made under statutory authority, the system of civic administration controlled by an elected Council was temporarily superseded by that of three Commissioners, Messrs. Seamus O Murchadha, P. J. Hernon and Dr. W. C. Dwyer. . . . [C]ertain advantages of the system of administration by City Commissioners had become generally recognized."[33] Murphy's use of passive voice masks who exactly recognized those advantages.

Historical pageantry suffused the 1927 Civic Week. The opening parade through Dublin's streets assembled all of the dramatis personae who would appear in the tableaux vivants, military tattoos, and pageants: costumes were recycled, historical incidents recirculated, and motifs reiterated throughout the week. Events were scheduled to take full advantage of the hundreds of historical costumes produced to represent the Irish past from Mesgedhra, first-century king of Leinster, to the Irish Volunteers of 1782. On Saturday, September 17, an opening parade featuring the full complement of historical costumes passed through the city center; another parade, the Pageant of Irish Industry, was held on Thursday, the twenty-second;[34] the Grand Pageant of Dublin History twice was staged outdoors in Trinity College Park, on Monday, the nineteenth, and Friday, the twenty-third; the Mansion House hosted *The Historical Pageant and Tableaux* performed on Tuesday, the twentieth, and Saturday afternoon, the twenty-fourth; three performances of the Grand Military Tattoo took place in the Lansdowne Road stadium on the evenings of Saturday, the seventeenth, Wednesday, the twenty-first, and Saturday, the twenty-fourth; and the gala Historical Costume Ball was held on Friday, the twenty-third. To accommodate its vision of Dublin's greatness, most of the pageantry excluded the past century and a quarter by prescribing, in the words of the announcement of costumes appropriate for the Historical Ball, "any epoch from 1000 B.C. to the end of the eighteenth century."[35] Featured lectures on Irish history considered Ireland before the Act of Union: one lecture by Mary Hayden focused on Ireland in the eighteenth century, and another by Eoin MacNeill examined early Irish historic sites in County Dublin. In 1927 the sole exception to the exclusion of the past century and a quarter was found in the military tattoo.

The opening parade featured hundreds of elaborately costumed participants as mythic, legendary, and historical figures from Ireland's past. They appeared in an imagined chronological order, the mythic freely conflated with the historical. Unlike many of the other events of the week, the opening parade was free and as such served as a "coming attraction" to entice audiences to other ticketed events. Led by the Bands of the Army and Civic Guard, the procession depicted Mesgedhra, king of Leinster; royal bodyguards and Leinster warriors; Queen Buan, his wife, attended by court ladies and Leinster maidens; Conall Cearnach; knights and warriors of the Red Branch; Fionn and the Fianna; hunters and warriors; the Norsemen; the Volva (Seeress of the Tribe); thingwomen and bondsmaids; Chief Viking and attendants; Vikings' wives and thingwomen; King Brian Boru; Irish chieftains and warriors; Brodir; Danish chiefs and warriors; Laurence O'Toole; twelfth-century Dubliners; Hasculph (the Dane); Strongbow and other Norman knights; Aoife and ladies-in-waiting; Diarmuid MacMurrough; Art MacMurrough Cavanagh; Hugh O'Neill with spearmen, kernes, and galloglasses; sixteenth-century Irish war pipers; O'Sullivan Beare; Owen Roe O'Neill; and Patrick Sarsfield. The parade ended with the Irish Volunteers—not Eoin MacNeill's 1913 militia, but volunteers from 1782. Norsemen, Vikings, Danes, and even the Normans were personated, the English ignored.

Two performances of *A Grand Pageant of Dublin History*, ranging from mythic times to the late eighteenth century and staged on a huge 200-by-200-foot platform in Trinity College Park, sold out by 5:00 p.m. the day they went on sale.[36] Advance publicity promised "a departure . . . from ordinary pageantry on this occasion with real acting by real actors. . . . Altogether 600 characters will be represented in various episodes."[37] An elaborate musical score for *A Grand Pageant of Dublin History* was composed and directed by Herbert Bailey. The program provided a detailed synopsis of the five episodes as well as lengthy notes on the costumes in the first two episodes. Set in "the heroic days of Conaire Mór, High King of all Erin, [when] the Province of Ulster was governed by an arrogant ruler, Conchobar, son of Nessa,"[38] the first episode, "Poet's Fee, and How Baile Atha Cliath Got Its Name," has Conchobar dispatch his poet, Aithurné the Importunate, to travel through Ireland provoking strife so that Conchobar can invade and expand his kingdom. "The sacred laws of hospitality and the respect of the people of ancient Ireland for their men of learning" demand that King Mesgedhra welcome Aithurné in Leinster. Having failed to

9. Seamus MacCall's costume design in pen and ink with watercolor for Norse thingmen, 1927 Dublin Civic Week. Courtesy of the Seamus Mac-Call Collection.

provoke the other kings, Aithurné extorts from Mesgedhra first material goods (gold and raiment) and livestock (seven hundred white cows and seven hundred white sheep), then women slaves, then the king's own wife, and finally safe passage, all under the pretext of collecting his "poet's fee" and the threat of composing satires of Leinster. When Aithurné finds he cannot ford the Liffey with his booty, he constructs a causeway of wicker hurdles, earning Dublin's epithet, the Ford of the Hurdles. As soon as Aithurné crosses the makeshift bridge, however, he leaves Leinster and his safe passage behind. The Leinstermen turn on him and whisk their women back across the bridge, but strand Queen Buan and her attendants. Ulster's Conall Cearnach, "one of their most distinguished heroes" (5), crosses the ford and, to avenge his brother's death, beheads Mesgedhra. When he displays the severed head of Mesgedhra, the queen swoons and dies. The venal, manipulative greed of Ulster is finally defeated by the cleverness and moral superiority of the Leinstermen, their druids, and councilors, but at a steep price. Fraught with graphic violence, the episode mocks the powers of and deference paid to the poet Aithurné.

The second episode, set about AD 600, shows invading Norsemen who because "the Celts of Europe had successfully dominated the more Northerly nations [display] evidence of Celtic influence both in costume and in religious observation" (8). The synopsis suggests that a pillar stone or dolmen was the focal point for the action as "the numbing chill of the North descended . . . those ferocious Norse raiding-parties."[39] The episode ends with the Viking annexation of Dublin: "The Northmen's ceremony of taking formal possession of the land . . . is symbolised in the casting of the three golden arrows—one before, and one to each side of them" (8). The third and fourth episodes, depicting Brian Boru's murder after his victory over the Danes at the Battle of Clontarf and Archbishop Laurence O'Toole's defense of Dublin against the forces of Diarmuid MacMurrough, show yet two more waves of invasion and resistance. The final and most unlikely episode traced the rise of the Irish Volunteers in 1778 by relocating the Battle of Flamborough Head from Yorkshire to Belfast Lough. The program offered this fanciful explanation: "Captain [John] Paul

Jones, an American privateer, had actually captured a vessel in Belfast Lough. An invasion was expected, and Ireland had no Military force with which to meet it. Out of this state of helplessness there grew the Irish Volunteers."[40]

The prominent thread running through all five episodes of *A Grand Pageant of Dublin History* is invasion by wave after wave of outsiders—Ulstermen, Vikings, Danes, Normans, and finally American pirates—all of whom encounter a thriving native culture. The British, however, are strikingly marginalized, excised. Dublin's history weathered these invasions to emerge as a city with a heritage as rich as it is complex. Although Boru's death meant that "all his work and plans for a restoration of Ireland to her ancient glory were ended" (9), the pageant, almost metatheatrically, offered its representation of a noble past as a step toward restoring that ancient glory. The very acts of personation for the performers and of spectation for the audience not only recalled but revived the Irish past. Here was an anodyne if imaginative version of Irish history that Treaty as well as anti-Treatyite partisans could tolerate, perhaps even embrace. The press certainly did. The *Irish Times* reported an enthusiastic audience of five thousand in Trinity College Park for the first performance of *A Grand Pageant of Dublin History* and praised it as providing "most interesting and picturesque glimpses of some outstanding episodes of Ireland's stormy past—in the days when marauders from countries far and near were attracted by her wealth."[41] The sensational, graphic representation of the arrival of the violent Norman invaders brought praise from the press: "Effect to the subsequent massacre and pillage within the city was added by the red flares lighted behind the gates."[42] *Honesty* recorded that "the historic pageant has been, to our mind, the outstanding feature of the Civic Week's display. It surpassed the anticipations of many and to those conversant with the history of the country it was such a splendid living picture of past periods and great personalities as would have greatly rejoiced the heart of a Davis, a Pearse or a Griffith."[43]

The personnel, costumes, and ethos of *A Grand Pageant of Dublin History* also appeared in *The Historical Pageant and Tableaux* staged in the Round Room of the Mansion House. Described as an "Illustrated

History from the time of Fionn and the Fianna down to the Irish Volunteers of 1782 . . . in thirty-five magnificent tableaux," *The Historical Pageant and Tableaux* employed songs, musical interludes, and tableaux in a pastiche of Irish history.[44] Attendance at the special children's matinee on Saturday, September 24, with "the greater portion of the House . . . reserved for the poor children of the City," was reported as twenty-five hundred. Tableaux were a prominent feature in historical plays such as Dion Boucicault's *Robert Emmet* (1884), and the tableaux vivants provided performative opportunities for the Ascendancy as well as nationalist groups such as the Gaelic League and the Daughters of Erin.[45] *The Historical Pageant and Tableaux* not only posed hundreds of elaborately costumed figures in dozens of historical tableaux, but also incorporated two dramatic episodes: MacCall's "The Feast's First Carving," described as an "ancient Irish interlude . . . when cantankerous bards and high-spirited warriors wrangled at a King's feast for the privilege of 'the first carving,' to be bewitched and soothed by the 'laughter spell' of the harper,"[46] and "A Country Ceilidhe," "a folk scene of modern Ireland arranged by Gearoid O'Lochlainn . . . an idealistic representation of modern country life among the real Irish of Connemara."[47] The *Irish Independent* reported that "in these tableaux one was taken through the pages of Irish history from the days of Fionn and the Fianna to the heyday of the Irish Volunteers in 1782. . . . It is difficult to realise that so much ground could be covered by thirty-six tableaux."[48] Like the opening parade, where Vikings and thingwomen marched with Irish patriots, the pageants appear at ease with the hybridity brought by waves of influences, invaders, and immigrants. What was excluded, both the past century and a quarter and virtually any detail of the English colonial presence, is as significant as the romanticization of the select mythic and historic figures that did appear.

Not only did Seamus MacCall script the five episodes of *A Grand Pageant of Dublin History* and "The Feast's First Carving" in *The Historical Pageant and Tableaux*, but he also designed hundreds of costumes as well as footwear, headgear, weapons, implements, and accoutrements for the parade, pageants, and tattoo (Plates 2 and 3).[49] Executed by

10. Photograph of participants wearing Seamus MacCall's costumes in the 1927 Dublin Civic Week. Courtesy of the Seamus MacCall Collection.

Irish workers under the supervision of Madame Daisy (Toto) Bannard-Cogley, now a cabaret impresaria[50] and soon to be a founding member of the Dublin Gate Theatre, MacCall's meticulous costume designs offered "a complete story of the evolution of Irish art."[51] MacCall was an intriguing choice for several reasons. Born at sea in 1892, he worked as a railway engineer in South America before enlisting in the British army and serving in World War I. He attended the Metropolitan School of Art where he met many of the artists and craftspeople who contributed to the civic weeks. Hardly a Free State apparatchik, Mac-Call was with de Valera when the latter was arrested in October 1924 for posing a threat to law and order in Northern Ireland by addressing a republican meeting in Newry.[52] Between 1926 and 1931, MacCall collaborated with Toto Cogley on pageants, cabarets, and the 1926 production of his play *Bealtaine*, which was performed at Molesworth Hall on a bill with Eimar O'Duffy's *Bricriu's Feast* and for which he not only designed the sets and costumes but also appeared as King Conchobar. In May 1926 MacCall was the key organizer in the Ancient Irish Nights' Entertainments sponsored by the Cabaret Committee of the Radical Club, a group of artists who earlier that month exhibited work by, inter alia, Harry Kernoff and Maurice MacGonigal. "The

general scheme of the festival," advised publicity for the Ancient Irish
Nights' Entertainments, "is based on the supposition that it is being
held in pre-Christian times." Like the merrymakers attending the
1927 Historical Costume Ball, patrons hoping to take part in the all-
night "dancing and other festivities must be attired in appropriate costumes of Ireland (from the earliest known times down to the Christian
era)." MacCall's designs were made available for consultation because
"visitors are also warned that, in connection with the special ceremonies of the Feast of Bealtaine, all who attend other than in the costume
of the period are liable to be regarded as 'foreigners' and therefore as
legitimate victims for the 'Druidical Rites.'"[53] A Mr. (Alec) Newman
of Trinity College Dublin as Cúchulainn and Dr. Isabel Speedy took
first prizes for their costumes.[54] *Honesty*, which attributed *The Historical Pageant and Tableaux* to the Studio Cabaret Company, praised the
authenticity of MacCall's "The Feast's First Carving," where "one did
not for instant doubt the characters that laughed or cheered, bickered,
sneered and fought, danced and sang."[55] Between the two Civic Weeks
of 1927 and 1929, MacCall delivered a series of 2RN radio broadcasts
on the Irish past. "The Feast's First Carving" as well as MacCall's "The
Coming of Fionn" were periodically performed over the next several
years—at the 1928 Tailteann Games and by the Free State Scouts at a
jamboree in Birkenhead in the summer of 1929, for instance. In July
1930 MacCall contributed to a historical pageant produced by Toto
Cogley and supported by the Irish Tourist Association in Bray and later
Dun Laoghaire, variously called *Erin through the Ages* or *The Colour of
History*. MacCall later became the arts editor at the *Irish Press* and, "in
charge of Army publicity during the emergency,"[56] created scores of
documentary films for the military. MacCall published several books,
including biographies of Thomas Moore and John Mitchel as well as
And So Began the Irish Nation (1931), which was illustrated by hundreds
of his own drawings. MacCall literally visualized the Irish past; his
pageants, cabarets, costume designs, and entertainments showed that
seeing was believing. Civic week organizers, like MacCall, stressed the
authenticity of the clothing, weapons, and accoutrements and the Irish
provenance of their design, materials, and manufacture. In all of the

civic weeks' historical pageantry, great pride was taken in the accuracy of period dress, artifacts, and implements, an accuracy that enhanced the personation of Irish ancestors for participants.

No matter how tragic the ends that these historical figures met—suicide, exile, execution, or death in battle or in a distant land—the Free State brought them back to the streets of Dublin in all their glory. History plays, from Shakespeare to Boucicault, have always taken such liberties.[57] No matter how deep the wounds from the Civil War or how perilous the economy or how unstable the government, the civic week served up an entertaining, celebratory, even festive history. The depth of those wounds, the perilousness of the economy, demanded no less. The opening parade and all the pageantry eradicated the English, but otherwise aspired to remarkable inclusivity. Rather than endorsing an essentialist view of Ireland's past and identity, one racy of the soil, the parade offered representative Vikings, Danes, and Normans often attended by their wives, partners, children, and exotic retainers.

As rosy, naive, or facile the historical perspective that informed McCall's 1927 pageants, they were staged by skilled artists and artisans and applauded by pro- and anti-Treaty commentators alike. The *Irish Times* referred to the tableaux staged at the Mansion House as "a brilliant success."[58] The *Irish Builder*, which had an abiding enthusiasm for civic spectacles, devoted extensive coverage to both civic weeks: "Dublin rose to the occasion and even surpassed itself. . . . To most people the whole thing was a revelation";[59] the organizers "appear to have devised just these attractions which appeal to the Dublin public. . . . People learned more than ever they knew before as to the scope and standard of native industries."[60] Although the anti-Cosgrave *Honesty* was critical of some staffing of the Dublin Civic Week committees (denounced as imperialist holdovers), it was unstinting in its praise for the historical pageantry:

> The costumes, which are not only wonderfully beautiful but absolutely authentic in every detail, were designed by Mr. Seamus McCall [*sic*]. . . . In order that there might not be the slightest inaccuracy in the carrying out of the designs, the work was directed by Madame

Annotations within the illustration:

IRISH 10th, 11th, 12th Centuries

metal frame only lined leather or cloth.

Short triangular cloak with hood.

with or without cloak short triangular.
To carry spear and axe ~or~ spear and sword

Tunic, close-fitting and much ornamented.
cloak as for Fianna.
Lana (generally white) reaching nearly to knees.

026
Ordinary Soldier

027
Chieftain.

also for Brian Boru

028
(add leg coverings)
Foot Soldier

Copyright
Seamus mac Cormac

10

11. Seamus MacCall's costume design in pen and ink with watercolor for Irish warriors in the tenth, eleventh, and twelfth centuries, 1927 Dublin Civic Week. Annotation indicates design on the left for an "ordinary soldier," the center costume "also for Brian Boru," and on the right for a "foot soldier." Courtesy of the Seamus MacCall Collection.

Bannard Cogley. . . . The properties are the work of Mr. Francis Bowe, and the extraordinary skill with which helmets, spears, and other armour have been fashioned is an artistic achievement in itself. The other artwork in connection with the Pageant has been carried out by Mr. Art O'Murnaghan. The scenery is by the young Dublin artist, Mr. Harry Kernoff.[61]

Perhaps more important than the enthusiastic press notices for the Dublin Civic Week was its popularity with audiences. Almost all of the events were commodified: tickets to the 1927 Historical Costume Ball, including supper, charged a very hefty guinea until September 19 and thereafter £1 and 5s.; the commemorative handbook, filled with commercial advertisements as well as the work of talented artists, sold for a very reasonable 1s. The parades, of course, promoted a carnivalesque atmosphere accessible and free to all. In several surviving informal photographs, the parade and pageant participants seem delighted with their performative postures. In contrast to the carefully posed soldiers in publicity stills from the Curragh, a compelling, although anecdotal, feature of these images is how festive the civic weeks seem. Photographs of the opening parade that appeared in the *Irish Independent* show Dublin's streets thronged with onlookers. The pageants staged at the Mansion House and even the one at the open-air venue in Trinity College Park sold out, but the appropriation of the colonizer's military tattoo attracted the biggest crowds of all.

TWO TATTOOS (1927 AND 1929)

Garrison theatricals and military tattoos were traditions of the British army reaching back to the seventeenth century. From the eighteenth to the twentieth centuries, Irish military personnel, perhaps most memorably Wolfe Tone,[62] were involved as actors both in military productions and in mainstream theatre productions. Garrison theatricals in Ireland can be seen in 1855: for instance, a "Fashionable Military Amateur Performance" of W. H. Murray's *Diamond Cut*

Diamond, *Bombastes Furioso*, and *Box and Cox* in Parsonstown (now Burr) that featured members of the 21st Fusiliers accompanied by the company's band. Eleven days later they performed *Don Cesar de Bazan* and *Slasher and Crasher*.[63]

Tattoos, a name derived from a Dutch phrase referring to the call for innkeepers to shut down their taps and for soldiers to return to their barracks, had been typically performed in Ireland in conjunction with the vice-regal court and predate the most famous surviving tattoo, held annually in Edinburgh. In 1879, for instance, military festivities at a Torch Light Tattoo in Dublin included an adaptation of the *Zapfenstreich*, the German military ceremony that dates to the late sixteenth century. By the 1890s Royal Irish Military Tournaments featured parades with musical accompaniment, mimic battles, and numerous competitions: "both with lances and swords, lemon-cutting . . . cleaving the Turk's head, fencing, boxing, sabre v sabre, mounted combats,"[64] tent-pegging, gymnastic displays, bareback riding and jumping, and tugs-of-war. Performed by the military at night by torch or artificial light, accompanied by fireworks, often attended by the lord lieutenant and lord mayor, the tournaments were popular displays often repeated for two or more performances. The term "tattoo" came into popular usage in Ireland by 1896, when the Royal Irish Military Tournament concluded with a "grand military tattoo," or parade. On June 29, 1906, *The Grand Military Tattoo* held on the Cork Football Ground was a comparatively modest affair, basically a military concert and equestrian display. The Imperial War Museum holds programs for several British tattoos staged after World War I that show several common features with the Irish tattoos, including the incorporation of a "mimic battle," typically a reenactment of a specific military engagement.

The Military Tattoo at the 1927 Dublin Civic Week took place only a month after a similar event, the *Northern Ireland Military Torchlight Tattoo*, was held for six performances in Belfast. The program cover for the Belfast event depicts a bearded warrior holding aloft a torch that illuminates four biplanes. In his other hand is an unsheathed scimitar; a similar, smaller, curved knife rests in his waistband. The warrior wears curled-toe shoes and stands silhouetted against a skyline with dome and minaret. Two graphic inserts on the cover depict modern British soldiers at war. These visual elements encapsulate the narrative of the pageants staged at the Northern Ireland Military Torchlight Tattoo: "An Incident from the Indian Mutiny of 1857: The Relief of Lucknow" (India) told in two scenes and "A Phase from the Great War," which ends as "the victorious British force" captures the enemy prisoners and machine guns.[65] No less remarkable than the representation of an extremely sanitized portrait of trench warfare and an episode in which British colonial forces vanquish a native uprising is the absence of even an Irish inflection to the musical selections, costuming, or presentation. Indeed, the 359 torchbearers of the finale, drawn from the 1st Battalion of the West Yorkshire Regiment, performed a British identity for England's faithful garrison.

Only a few years after the departure of the last British forces, the military tattoos staged at Lansdowne Road[66] were the most popular feature of both civic weeks.[67] As counterintuitive as it may be, these tattoos appropriated the colonizer's martial festivities to celebrate the Free State army by forging an unbroken line of direct descent from the Fianna through great Irish military men and their armies. The Free State army was no less in need of a facelift of its public image than the unelected Dublin city commissioners—perhaps in greater need. The military had been substantially downsized in funding and numbers. Eunan O'Halpin points out that

in March 1924 defence spending was over £11 million; the next year it was reduced by almost two-thirds to £4 million; by 1931 it was £1.5 million, which was spent on fewer than 7,000 men with virtually no equipment—and not a dog barked. . . . An American military attaché reported in 1928 that the minister for defense had informed him that "his idea is the biggest army possible for the least money," a suitably classic formula under which the defense forces were allowed to shrink to practically nothing. The exception to this frugal policy was "a very fine band. . . . The authorities feel that a good band and snappy turnout is a good political argument for maintaining the army."[68]

Many of the demobilized troops felt hard done if not cheated by the Cumann na Gaedheal government. But demoralization among the demobilized was hardly the only problem. Since Independence the army had been saddled with carrying out the executions after the reimposition of the death penalty.[69] One of the regular taunts hurled against the Cumann na Gaedheal government and its military was shouting out the number 77, a reference to the number of anti-Treaty executions carried out by the Free State. Even worse perhaps, a faction of the army mutinied in 1924 and brought about the resignation of two government ministers and a hundred officers in the Defence Forces.[70]

The Irish tattoos directly lifted elements from the British tattoos of the post–World War I era: spectacular lighting effects generated by searchlights, fireworks, and torches (incendiary or battery powered); massed physical displays to demonstrate the army's physical conditioning, discipline, and coordination; performances by bands and pipers; huge parades of military forces that included historically accurate costumes and uniforms; military reenactments; and the singing of the national anthem. Some of the British tattoos of the 1920s incorporated playful elements absent from their Irish counterparts. A Southern Command Searchlight Tattoo in the UK in the summer of 1927, for instance, featured young cadets with rouged red cheeks performing to "The March of the Tin Soldiers." Moreover, because the tattoos proved extremely popular with the public in both Ireland and Britain, they played a role in improving the military's esteem and raised tens of thousands of pounds and punts for military charities. Reporting on the Aldershot Tattoo in May 1928, the *Irish Times* editorialized in favor of tattoos: "Tattoos sometimes are deplored as an encouragement of belligerent feeling and as a bad incentive to the young. They ought to be regarded, more rightly, as an attempt to praise 'famous men' and to awaken an intelligent interest in the drama of history."[71] Even anti-Treaty publications would respond favorably, at least to the 1927 tattoo.

The Irish tattoos differed from the British by recuperating from the Language Week Processions the March of the Nation, the procession of Irish armies over the millennia. In 1927 and 1929, as they

12. Fionn and the Fianna, *Grand Military Tattoo and Fireworks Display* (program) (Dublin: Dublin Civic Week, 1927). Courtesy of Special Collections, Kenneth Spencer Research Library, University of Kansas Libraries.

would again in 1935 and 1945, Irish military tattoos constructed a heritage of Irish warriors that spanned the millennia. They aimed not only to enhance the reputation of the contemporary Defence Forces and to demonstrate the imperative for an army but to infuse an educative and affective understanding of a noble Irish past. The caption for a publicity still that appeared in the *Irish Independent* on September 3, 1929, captures the spirit of the military tattoos: "An ancient Irish Chieftain of the 4th century greets an Irish Citizen Army Captain of 1916." The former, in cape, tunic, and helmet, holds a sword and shield in his left hand and reaches across sixteen centuries to greet his direct descendant with his right.[72]

The aspirational title of the 1927 tattoo, *Eire: 1014 to 1927*, reveals the monumental ambition of the three-hour extravaganza. Both the 1927 and the 1929 Dublin tattoos featured fireworks, mass gymnastics, precision drilling, Colonel Fritz Brase's arrangements of Irish airs, the dramatization of an episode from Irish history, and the

March of the Nation. For each tattoo carefully rehearsed, costumed, and choreographed soldiers performed two variants of historical pageantry: first, a historical reenactment and, second, the March of the Nation. Detailed summaries in the programs for both tattoos guided audiences through dramatized historical reenactments from the seventeenth century. In 1927 "An Incident from the Jacobite Wars in Ireland: How Sergeant Custume Defended the Bridge at Athlone"[73] showed how a small band of brave Irishmen withstood the assault of twenty-five thousand men led by Godart Van Ginkle on May 30, 1691: "Wave after wave of Dutch, Danish, Scotch and English troops were hurled against them in vain. . . . When further defence was seen to be impossible, the rere [sic] files turned, and working like furies destroyed two arches of the bridge. . . . Under cover of darkness the enemy brought planks and beams and made a footway across the chasm. . . . Custume calls out 'Are there 10 men to die with me for Ireland?' . . . Two waves of Irishmen rush to demolish the makeshift bridge. Almost all perish, but 'Athlone was saved, for the time being, once again'" (21).

In 1929 the army produced an even more elaborate military tattoo at Lansdowne Road not just on three evenings as in 1927, but on five. The historical episode dramatized was the Siege of Clonmel, here dated over six rather than two months, from November 1649 to May 1650, when a small group of Irishmen held off Cromwell's forces. The program provided a detailed summary of the three scenes and epilogue to the "Incident," a fifteen-minute reenactment that began at 9:35.[74] In the first scene, "The Breach," a small group of warriors under Hugh Dubh O'Neill returns from a successful raid on the English camp with arms and equipment. The English bombardment of Clonmel hits and sets on fire a house sheltering the wounded who are rescued by fearless Irish soldiers. In the second scene, "The Trap," the Irish garrison and townsfolk build an enclosure ("the pound") around a breach in the defense lines that in the third scene traps so many advancing Cromwellian soldiers that "those within can scarcely raise their arms" (13). In the epilogue the mayor of Clonmel negotiates favorable terms of surrender to Cromwell. Although vastly outnumbered, armed mainly with swords, pikes, and only two pieces of artillery, the wily Irish forces inflict heavy losses on the British and secure the townspeople's safety.

The historical reenactment of the Siege of Clonmel was overseen by Major T. McKinney and Colonel J. J. (Ginger) O'Connell, who published and lectured widely on military history and was later director of the Military Archives. Herbert Bailey was thanked for his advice in staging the episode's music; MacCall was credited as historical adviser to the entire tattoo. Organizers invested considerable resources to construct a replica of Clonmel's West Gate as well as a house that could be set ablaze at each nighttime performance of the tattoo. As in 1927 the 1929 Siege of Clonmel showed that the defense and protection of the civilian population were the army's priorities. This same episode was restaged in a military tattoo twenty-one years later for the tercentenary of the Siege of Clonmel in 1950.[75]

The Athlone and Clonmel reenactments deployed hundreds of soldiers, all outfitted in period costume, in action-packed episodes, with towns bombarded, buildings set afire, bridges destroyed. Surviving photographs show the field littered with the bodies of soldiers enacting the many wounded and killed. Press accounts comment on the deafening noise of artillery and firelocks. Narrated by an announcer and staged to sensational effect, both reenactments showed the Irish forces vastly outnumbered by foreign invaders but dedicated to protecting a frighteningly vulnerable civilian population. In 1929 the staging of the Siege of Clonmel took place more than an hour after sunset, so the fiery English bombardment, the burning of the house, and the army's rescue of the survivors inside were carried off with sensational and "most realistic" effect. The *Irish Independent* commented on how the staging of the siege of Clonmel drew in the audience: "As soon as the battle began . . . we realized that we were supposed to be burgesses of Clonmel watching our defenders, and from that moment a child could follow the story."[76] Such reception pays tribute to both the educative and the affective power of the reenactment.

The March of the Nation, or "Military Pageant," in many ways resembled the opening parade in the civic week, but here the participants were all military men, costumed to represent, in 1927, the

Fianna, Brian Boru's soldiers, Art MacMurrough Kavanagh, Hugh O'Neill, O'Sullivan Beare, Owen Roe O'Neill, Patrick Sarsfield, the Irish Volunteers of 1782, the Volunteers of 1916–21, and finally "the Army of To-Day." Fully armed and colorfully arrayed parties, several on horseback, entered the darkened arena in dramatic fashion: "a single searchlight pouring its rays across the field, and each group of warriors passing in turn out of the darkness into the light and then returning to the darkness."[77] As each contingent came into view in the glare of a powerful searchlight, loudspeakers broadcast a descriptive narration. The 1929 tattoo reached back further into history to the early fourth century BC, when "Labhraidh Maen, an Irish exile . . . returned to Ireland to recover his kingdom" (19–20) and increased the number of representative proto-armies from ten to twelve by beginning with the Celts and the Red Branch knights and including the United Irish-men. The March of the Nation in both tattoos brought thousands of participants into the arena for the finale performed by the massed bands and buglers, followed by the communal singing of the national anthem and fireworks. Bringing the "Army of To-Day" on the pitch with its supposed progenitors positioned it as the modern incarnation of centuries of tradition. Were there any question of the historicity of the figures represented, the program reminded audiences that Fionn mac Cumhaill was "an undoubtedly historical personage" (20).

As fanciful as the array of personages from Irish history may now seem, analogous versions of this master narrative informed other Free State agencies. In October 1927 *An tOglach*, the journal of the Irish Army, began a new quarterly series. In its inaugural issue, the lead editorial traced the proud traditions of Irish Army back to the Fianna in terms nearly identical to the words that informed the 1927 Dublin Civic Week historical pageants:

Our Army has . . . popular traditions that preserve the exploits of the heroes of the dawn of our history, in the annals that narrate the actions of native princes and leaders in momentous military cri-ses. . . . Fionn, who perfected the organization of the country on a military basis, an organization begun when Suetonius Paulinus was butchering the Druids in Anglesea and threatening to advance the Roman Eagles across the Irish Sea, Brian, who broke the Dane at Clontarf, Owen Roe O'Neill of Benburb, Hugh O'Neill of the Yellow Ford, the Wild Geese of later years, and our recent noble dead afford an example and an inspiration.[78]

Like all of the historical pageantry of the civic weeks, the tattoos reaffirmed the legitimacy of the Free State and its army. Not only were army personnel prominent in the opening parade as themselves, but they also performed in the orchestras, bands, reenactments, and March of the Nation.

Many of the press reports of the tattoos were ecstatic. The *Irish Independent* wrote, "At times the sheer beauty of the scene almost exhausted ones [sic] powers of admiration."[79] The *Irish Times* was initially favorable but also editorialized against "astonishing and even ludicrous"[80] omissions in the tattoo, particularly the neglect of the Irish who fought in World War I for the British. Both of the tattoos were expensive, carefully orchestrated extravaganzas involving thousands of participants and tens of thousands of spectators. History lesson as well as visual spectacle, each performance created the sensory overload that evoked enthusiastic response from audiences at Lansdowne Road. The historical processions and the reenacted military encounters hammered home the need for a well-trained army whose principal concern was the welfare of the domestic populace. The strong emphasis on historical accuracy in depicting armaments, uniforms, banners, flags, weapons, and scenery by talented artists, craftsmen, and military men was widely admired as well as very popular. Tickets for the tattoos were not inexpensive. In 1927, for instance, seating in the reserve stands was on offer for between 2/6 and 5s. Suitable as family entertainment, the tattoos were especially successful in reaching a hitherto untapped audience: adolescents and children. People loved them. For the 1929 tattoo, the *Irish Independent* reported total attendance in excess of one hundred thousand.[81]

THE FORD OF THE HURDLES (1929)

Commissioner Seamus Murphy's goals for a second Dublin Civic Week in 1929 stressed providing citizens with "a more intelligent appreciation of the city's services" (such as water and electric supply), "afford[ing] a pleasant way of learning history," and seeing "a record of municipal enterprise." Murphy described the week's target audience as Dubliners and people up from the country, rather than foreign visitors. Unlike many of the subsequent events such as the Tóstals, the 1929 Dublin Civic Week was designed less to attract tourists from abroad than to educate the Free State population. As in 1927, "authentic" period costumes, epic battle sequences, extensive musical performances, and huge casts drew capacity crowds. The 1929 Dublin Civic Week was explicitly positioned as a carnival. Dublin "would be en fete, a novelty being introduced by way of a river ballroom. This was not being provided out of the resources of the municipality, but by the Civic Week Council."[82] The military tattoo expanded in 1929, but the week's other historical pageantry was consolidated and further professionalized. Gone were the tableaux vivants and the special children's matinee. In their place stood a single historical pageant by a newcomer hoping to make a name and a theatre for himself in Dublin.

Having recently re-created Alfie Willmore of North London as an Irish-speaking Corkman, few were as well situated to invent a national history as Micheál macLíammóir. In the twentieth century no one was more involved in creating, designing, and performing Irish historical pageantry. His impressive nationalist credentials included a childhood exile among the Sassenach (including Noel Coward) and the authorship of plays written in Irish and performed by Irish speakers at the Irish-language theatre, Galway's An Taibhdhearc, which he founded in 1928. The previous decade he illustrated several Talbot Press covers, including *Finn Varra Maa* in 1917. MacLíammóir wrote, directed, designed, and starred in some of the century's greatest public spectacles of Irish history. In a career that spanned seven decades—from the 1910s until the 1970s—he and his partner, Hilton Edwards, created (or assembled) three pageants that dramatized Irish history and identity:

The Ford of the Hurdles, The Pageant of the Celt (staged in Chicago's immense Soldier Field in 1934), and the second version of *The Pageant of St. Patrick* for the third Tóstal festival in 1954. MacLíammóir also created costumes for the 1935 Military Tattoo and narrated Tomás Mac Anna's *Aiseirí* in 1966.

Subtitled "A Masque of Dublin," *The Ford of the Hurdles* was macLíammóir's first theatre work written in English.[83] MacLíammóir was scrambling for all the publicity he could get. On offer were two thousand one-pound shares in the Gate Theatre Company that would capitalize the theatre company to challenge the Abbey. "If insufficient applications have been received the Dublin Gate Theatre will not re-open," warned an ad run in the *Irish Statesman*.[84] Moreover, macLíammóir needed to clarify public perception of his stance on Irish nationalism. Only three months earlier, the Dublin Gate Theatre production of *The Old Lady Says "No!,"* Denis Johnston's fantasy pastiche of Irish history, appeared at the Peacock Theatre. Both Johnston's play and macLíammóir's pageant were portraits of Dublin's history and heritage directed by Hilton Edwards that featured appearances by Robert Emmet (played by none other than macLíammóir in Johnston's play) and Sarah Curran (played by the same actress, Muriel Moore, in both). Both were expressionistic in style, although *The Ford of the Hurdles* confined its nonrepresentational dramaturgy to its first and final episodes. Whereas Johnston parodied nationalistic rhetoric and sentimentality, the final episode of macLíammóir's pageant, "Easter 1916: The City at Dawn," was a manifestly patriotic tribute to the Rising's nationalist martyrs.

The Ford of the Hurdles was more daring and coherent in its dramaturgy, structure, and message than the 1927 pageants.[85] A nineteen-piece orchestra, under the direction of John F. Larchet, professor of music at UCD, performed five interludes: an instrumental "Gavotte and Minuet," "Diarmuid's Lament,"[86] and three vocals sung by Eily Murnaghan. Throughout his pageant macLíammóir employs familiar nationalist tropes such as the betrayal of the Irish cause from within by a Judas figure and the contrast between the life-affirming Irish and the repressed and repressive English.

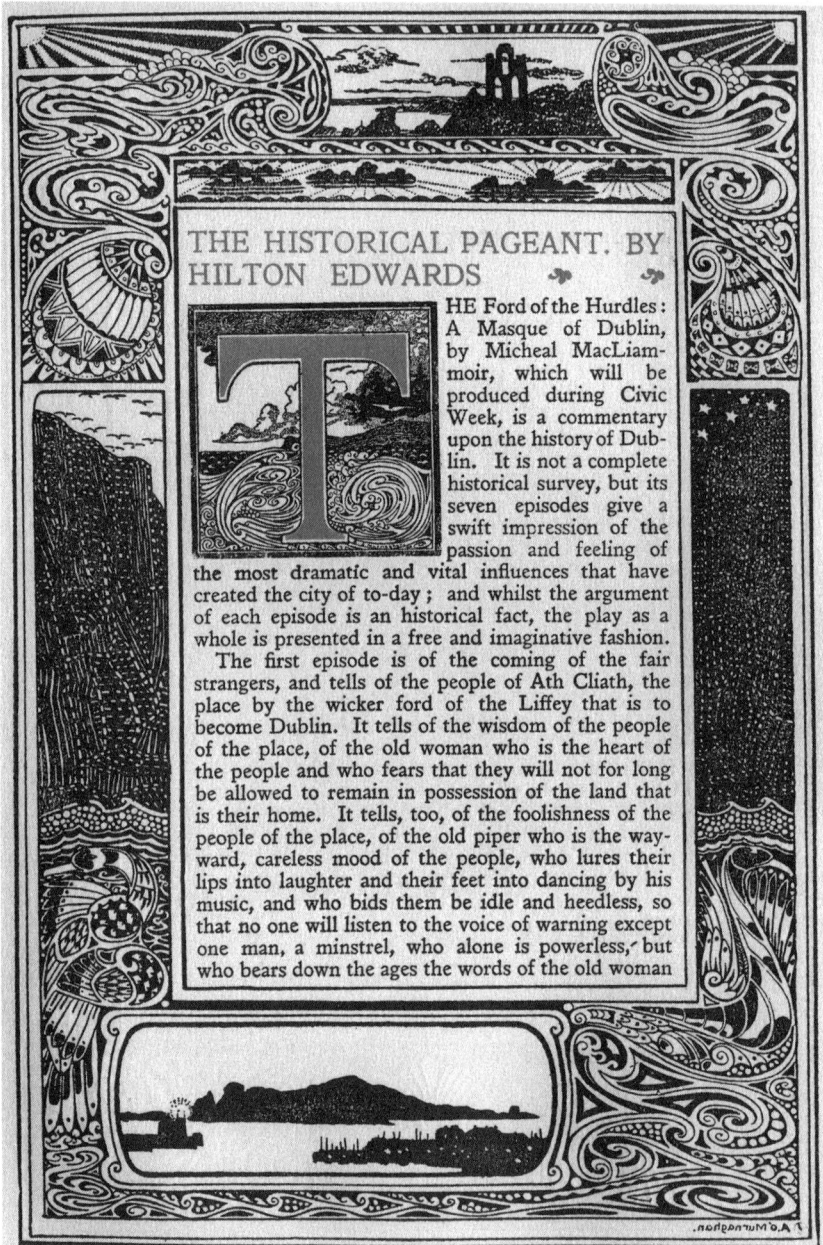

THE HISTORICAL PAGEANT. BY HILTON EDWARDS

THE Ford of the Hurdles: A Masque of Dublin, by Micheal MacLiammoir, which will be produced during Civic Week, is a commentary upon the history of Dublin. It is not a complete historical survey, but its seven episodes give a swift impression of the passion and feeling of the most dramatic and vital influences that have created the city of to-day; and whilst the argument of each episode is an historical fact, the play as a whole is presented in a free and imaginative fashion.

The first episode is of the coming of the fair strangers, and tells of the people of Ath Cliath, the place by the wicker ford of the Liffey that is to become Dublin. It tells of the wisdom of the people of the place, of the old woman who is the heart of the people and who fears that they will not for long be allowed to remain in possession of the land that is their home. It tells, too, of the foolishness of the people of the place, of the old piper who is the wayward, careless mood of the people, who lures their lips into laughter and their feet into dancing by his music, and who bids them be idle and heedless, so that no one will listen to the voice of warning except one man, a minstrel, who alone is powerless, but who bears down the ages the words of the old woman

13 and 14. "The Historical Pageant" by Hilton Edwards with borders by Art O'Murnaghan in the *Dublin Civic Week, 1929: Official Handbook*. Courtesy of the Edwards-macLíammóir estate.

THE HISTORICAL PAGEANT

of Ath Cliath, and who speaks in every hour of defeat and despair her message of patience and hope. It tells finally of the coming of the Fair Strangers in their long black ships from the " East of the North," their heads " plumed and horned like the heads of carrion birds and beasts " and " their hands full of fire and steel."

The Second Episode, which is called the " Rape of Dervogilla," shows the obscure origin of the expulsion from Ireland of Diarmuid MacMurchadha, King of Leinster and of the Danes; and the subsequent events that changed, not only the history of Dublin, but of all Ireland. It shows Dervogilla, the wife of Tiarnan O Ruairc, as a woman of harsh and vivid beauty, who bickers with her husband, and who persuades her brother Maoilsheachlainn to find her a means of release from Tiarnan's petty tyranny. It tells of Diarmuid MacMurchadha, and his attempt to seize Dervogilla and her dowry; of how she hesitates and is torn away at last by her lover in the red light of the flames that is all that he leaves of her husband's house; of Tiarnan's vow of vengeance against Diarmuid MacMurchadha; and it holds a prophecy of great evil for the Town of the Ford of the Hurdles that shall spring from the passions of this woman and of these two men.

Then is sung the Song of the Fate of Dervogilla, telling how she returned to her husband many years later, but how this failed to satisfy his hunger for revenge on his ancient enemy; and this is followed by the third episode, which is called " Diarmuid of the Gall," and which shows how the revenge of the husband of Dervogilla is fulfilled. The scene is

The Ford of the Hurdles takes as its starting point "The Coming of the Fair Stranger," macLíammóir's breathtakingly euphemistic description of the Viking invasions. An Old Woman, an incarnation of the Shan Van Vocht or Cathleen ni Houlihan, tries to rouse the sleeping citizens against the invaders, but more popular among the inhabitants of the ford is the seductive Piper, who repeatedly urges the people to "dance, dance and forget."[87] The Old Woman finds but a single disciple, the Minstrel (called the Messenger or Herald in later revisions), played by macLíammóir in 1929, who vows to carry her message through the ages. Along with music and recurrent images of fire, the Minstrel's commentaries provide continuity from episode to episode, from the ninth century through the Easter Rising.

The second, third, and fourth scenes, set between 1154 and 1171, focus on Diarmuid (Hilton Edwards), "the Judas of the Gael." The first of these three scenes, "The Rape of Dervogilla," featured Coralie Carmichael, arrayed in a daring saffron ensemble evocative of Jean-Paul Gauthier,[88] the unhappy wife of Tiarnan O Ruairc (Plate 5). When she mocks him as "no longer young" and otherwise impotent, he threatens her: "Shameless insolent woman, slut and drab of the street, I will tear your hair from your skull and your flesh from your bones. I will blind your eyes with red irons and pierce your heart with a thorn—I will—I will" (2/4). Just as Tiarnan is about to strike her, her brother Maoilseachlainn enters and, soon after, her lover, Diarmuid. Under Tiarnan's threatened domestic violence, Dervogilla runs off with Diarmuid. When she protests leaving her home in darkness, Diarmuid orders Tiarnan's castle to be burned to light the way. The scene ends with the stage illuminated only by the flames consuming the castle as Tiarnan, like all tragic cuckolds, vows to avenge himself. MacLíammóir's Dervogilla is very much a product of his time and challenges the sense of this period as sexless, repressed, and dull. Unlike her appearance as a sorrowful old woman in Lady Gregory's 1907 *Dervogilla* or as the contrite, masked Young Girl in Yeats's *Dreaming of the Bones* (set in 1916, written and published in 1919, but not performed until 1931), macLíammóir's Dervogilla, like Helen of Troy or Kitty O'Shea, is trapped in a loveless and abusive marriage. She emerges as equal parts of Celtic princess, flapper, and home wrecker. Although we learn that she eventually returned to Tiarnan, Dervogilla appears only in one scene, "The Rape of Dervogilla." Tiarnan is so humiliated by her infidelity that he goads Irishmen into killing other Irishmen and masterminds the banishment of Diarmuid, which will lead to the Norman and English invasions of Ireland. As the Irish fight among themselves, the Minstrel warns of "the cross of blood and of flame" (3/1), familiar to all as the cross of St. George on England's flag.

In the early twentieth century, nationalists positioned the Diarmuid-Dervogilla tryst as a, perhaps the, pivotal event in Irish history. D. L. Kelleher's 1929 publication for the Irish Tourist Association, *Ireland of the Welcomes*, offers a nearly identical representation of Diarmuid's central role in Irish history. Kelleher describes him as "Ireland's most notorious King," as responsible for betrayal of his country that marked "a turning point in the history of the world": "MacMurrough, having run off with the rival King's [Tiarnan's] wife [Dervogilla], resented the discarded husband's indignation and sent up the S.O.S. . . . When first the resident worms ate the royal gross ulcers off this King [MacMurrough] they took a feed of decorations that passion had put upon him. He was a dirty man, fit only for worms, when all is said and done."[89] Kelleher's graphic description of a chancroid Diarmuid appeared seven years after Joyce's *Ulysses* has Mr. Deasy target Dervogilla as a destructive vixen: "A faithless wife [who] first brought the strangers to our shore here, MacMurrough's wife and her leman O'Rourke, prince of Breffni. A woman too brought Parnell low." In the Cyclops episode of Joyce's *Ulysses*, the Citizen describes Dervogilla as the "dishonoured wife . . . the cause of all our misfortune. . . . The adulteress and her paramour brought the Saxon robbers here."[90] A photographic still from the end of the first act of *The Ford of the Hurdles* depicts Diarmuid's comprehensive revenge on the Irish. In abject submission, the Irish, broken, brought low, and humiliated, kneel with their hands clasped behind their backs before Strongbow and Diarmuid, who loom over them at center stage.

As *The Ford of the Hurdles* approached its own day, it tapped an increasingly emotive, patriotic chord in audiences. Eliding nearly five

15. Still from *The Ford of the Hurdles*. Courtesy of the Edwards-macLíam-móir estate and the Dublin Gate Theatre Archives in the Charles Deering McCormick Library of Special Collections at Northwestern University.

centuries during the intermission, the pageant picks up at Donnybrook Fair in 1653 where the dour English Roundheads contrast with the lively, ballad-singing Irish. In a moment of ahistorical schadenfreude, the Irish dunk the Cromwellian killjoys in a pond. In contrast to this lighthearted fantasy, the widely praised sixth scene, "Green Jackets and Pikes," was a brilliant instance of verbatim theatre replicating the trial of Robert Emmet.[91] With Lord Norbury (Hilton Edwards) and two other robed English judges at the bench stage right, the seven periwigged counsels for the defense and prosecution center stage, and a defiant Emmet stage left, three witnesses testify against Emmet, who defends himself in his celebrated speech from the dock. MacLíam-móir's treatment of Emmet offered a wholly different representation of the Irish patriot than audiences had seen in Johnston's *The Old Lady Says "No!"* MacLíammóir improves Emmet's speech from the dock by editing and reordering his language. For instance, Emmet's oration includes: "I have much to say why my reputation should be rescued from the load of false accusation and calumny which has been heaped upon it." Here is macLíammóir: "As to why my character should not be relieved from the imputations and calumnys [*sic*] thrown out against it, I have much to say" (6/3). In *The Ford of the Hurdles*, Emmet's rebellion prefigures the Easter Rising;[92] both are steps in undoing the betrayal of Diarmuid centuries earlier. MacLíammóir's deployment of a sustained typology, more often associated with biblical texts, provides internal unity, reinforces the narrative structure, and advances religious parallels in his rendition of Irish history. Moreover, the Rising's leaders as well as Emmet are presented as martyrs. *The Ford of the Hurdles*, like Shakespeare's *Henry V*, was an overtly nationalistic history play designed to legitimate the state and to instill pride in the nation's noble past.

James Moran points out that early representations of the Rising, most notably O'Casey's *The Plough and the Stars* and Yeats's *The Dreaming of the Bones*, neglected the key roles that women, homosexuals, and socialists played in the Rising.[93] Although macLíammóir's expressionistic presentation of the Rising accords with this pattern, in 1929 "Easter: The City at Dawn" made extensive use of quotations from Roger Casement and Patrick Pearse. Moreover, it was endorsed by extremely favorable reviews by impeccably credentialed republican women. The final episode of *The Ford of the Hurdles*, "Easter: The City at Dawn," became a Gate staple for the next few years, particularly for its patriotic Easter-week bills. In April 1930 it was paired with *Juggernaut*, written by a past pupil at St. Enda's, David Sears, and, in late March 1932, it appeared with a revival of Pearse's *The Singer*. In a casting coup, Maire nic Shiubhlaigh played MacDara's mother in Pearse's play and the Old Woman in macLíammóir's pageant. In April 1933 a revival of the entirety of *The Ford of the Hurdles* offered Dublin audiences yet a fourth opportunity to see macLíammóir's "Easter: The City at Dawn."

That final episode of *The Ford of the Hurdles* owes an intricate debt to Denis Johnston's *The Old Lady Says "No!"* as well as to continental expressionism and republican pieties. Here macLíammóir returns to the fluid, quasi-expressionistic style of the first scene of *The Ford of the Hurdles* as frenetic action envelops the stage in chaos, not in response to the Viking invasion, but over the occupation of the GPO. The events in Dublin on the morning of the Easter Rising are staged expressionistically—without much dialogue and little in the way of coherent plot or characters—to capture some sense of the confusion that morning. A chorus of modern voices bombards the audience with references to World War I, the Fairyhouse races, fires in O'Connell Street, and "Romantic Ireland." Newspaper boys calling out the names of their papers and shouts of "God save Ireland and the King" vie with the words of both Pearse ("I am Ireland. Older I am than the Beare" [7/3]; "One man can save a nation as one Man saved the world" [7/3]; "In the name of God and of the dead generations" [7/4]) and Roger Casement ("Ireland has outlived the failure of all her hopes and yet she hopes" [7/6]; "The government of Ireland by England rests on restraint and not on love" [7/6]).[94] In a brazen, full-blooded response to the second act of O'Casey's *The Plough and the Stars*, a "Strange Voice," not identified as Pearse, but given his lines, seen in silhouette against the Dublin skyline, just as he is in O'Casey's play, is struck down by a single shot. Of the 1932 revival, H. S., writing in *An Phoblacht*, offered this account: "The seven signatories, in silhouette, mount the steps to the Firing Squad—sturdy Tom Clarke, first, James Connolly last, borne wounded on his stretcher—that scene was indescribably gripping and poignant. In a few broad strokes, with mass effects, we are given as fine a representation of the spirit of 1916, as could be achieved."[95] The Minstrel offers macLíammóir's understanding of a hybrid Irish identity:

A thousand years ago the Dane
With raven banner swept the seas—
The Viking stock on Irish ground
Has grown, and strongly still shall grow—
The Norman took the Danish way
And Ireland's is the Norman sword—
The Dane and Norman force were held
To build the Irish race at length—
We Gael, we Dane, we Norman now
Have heard the word we waited long. (7/7)

The pageant ends with a recitation of Thomas MacDonagh's "The Marching Song of the Irish Volunteers," the singing of "Let Erin Remember," and one of macLíammóir's favorite sound effects: the chiming of bells.

Even after several revivals, reviewers grappled to find a language appropriate to the staging: *Dublin Opinion* called it "a rather extraordinary slice of good-class Impressionism" (May 1933); the *Irish Times* described the final episode as "one of the best examples of impressionist work that Dublin theatre-goers have ever seen" (April 26, 1933); the *Evening Herald* wrote, "We shall always maintain that this Toller-like sketch of the Rebellion of 1916 is a masterpiece, and the best thing in the expressionist style that has been written in Ireland."[96] In the *Irish Press*, Dorothy Macardle, "hagiographer royal to the Republic"[97] and anti-Treaty historian, offered a full-page rave entitled "An Artist's Tribute to the Men of 1916." Hers is an enthusiastic account of "Easter 1916: The City at Dawn":

> There is a confusion among those stark buildings, and in our minds is evoked a confused dream-like recreation of all the bewilderment of that time. Voices, sounds, rushing figures whirl about in the dim light—raucous voices of street women, chatter of holiday makers, sharp commands of Volunteer officers, phrases from the Proclamation read in a ringing voice, the rattle of machine-gun fire; under it all the throbbing of the music that has haunted the whole tragedy, and a murmur of distant voices complaining—"Why did you wake us? We were happier when we were asleep."

Writing as "M. G. MacB.," Maud Gonne offered an even more decisive endorsement: "It is not too much to say that Michael Mac Liammóir's play *The Ford of the Hurdles* is a national achievement. Not since W. B. Yeats' [*sic*] *Cathleen Ni Houlihan* has any Irish dramatist written so fine a play embodying the spirit of Ireland."[98] The mainstream press was likewise pleased. Con Curran favorably reviewed *The Ford of the Hurdles* for the *Irish Statesman*. The *Irish Times* called it a "truly a fine production and an undoubted success, to the achievement of which went three things—the beauty of the play itself, the beauty of the lighting, and the beauty of the incidental music."[99] MacLíammóir's pageant, never published and surviving only in the archives, was a triumph. Not only did the play receive stellar reviews, but he and Hilton Edwards succeeded in opening their Gate Theatre. *The Ford of the Hurdles* offered a radical alternative to O'Casey's *The Plough and the Stars*, an alternative that emblematizes the difference between the nascent Gate and the established Abbey, between a dramaturgically adventurous company and the more conservative national theatre. Moreover, in subsequent revivals, macLíammóir would play Emmet and advance himself as the premier Emmet interpreter of his day. Marianne Elliott demonstrates that many took Emmet's speech from the dock as their party piece; none, however, had such glowing endorsements from Macardle and Gonne. MacLíammóir and Edwards, moreover, succeeded on their own terms: expressionistic dramaturgy, stunning design, and sensuous nationalism.

The *Irish Independent* headlined "Triumph of the Carnival,"[100] but elsewhere the 1929 Dublin Civic Week was pilloried in the press. The *Honesty* denounced the showboat and condemned the historical element of the tattoo as "far more a parody than a stimulus to a sense of true citizenship."[101] In the regional press, the *Mayo News* condemned the 1929 Civic Week for fostering "an illusion of prosperity . . . so that the poor may forget their misery in renewed hope and the rich may enjoy playing at being somebody."[102] Worse, the 1929 Dublin Civic Week saw the city hobbled by a tramway strike, which often figured even in otherwise positive accounts. Perhaps the most embarrassing incident occurred when a group of the unemployed inserted themselves in an industrial pageant as it marched through the city streets: "In the midst of the Industrial Pageant . . . marched a number of unemployed men, who joined the procession as a protest against the display in view of the amount of unemployment in the city."[103]

The civic week pageantry is remarkable for its unabashed festivity and its projection of an untroubled image of Ireland at an especially tumultuous time. The Irish reinvention of the colonizer's tattoo was as popular as it was counterintuitive. The public enthusiasm for ancient Ireland not only survived Independence and the Civil War, but was, in fact, shared by Treatyites and anti-Treatyites alike. The exceptions to the erasure of the previous century and a quarter were the tattoos' linkage of the modern Defence Forces with ancient Irish fighting men and macLíammóir's 1929 "Easter: The City at Dawn," a unique instance of the integration of expressionistic techniques in pageantry's presentational dramaturgy. Perhaps what is most surprising about the civic week pageantry is its conscientious nonsectarianism.

After 1929 the Dublin Civic Weeks died out. Perhaps they did not survive because in at least one financial reckoning, they could be said to have lost rather than made money.[104] The restoration of the Dublin Corporation, an elected rather than appointed administration, and the election of Alfred (Alfie) Byrne as lord mayor cast the civic weeks as the enterprise of a nondemocratic regime best forgotten. The ascension of Fianna Fáil and the impending Eucharistic Congress would see Irish identity more narrowly prescribed and copper fastened with Catholicism. In comparison with what was to come, the civic weeks seem progressive, conciliatory, secular, even European. In retrospect, it is striking to see how negligible a role religious identity played, how risqué Dervogilla's costume was, how popular the appropriation of a British military tradition proved.

These civic celebrations challenge the widely received understanding of the cultural values endorsed and transmitted in the early years of the Irish Free State. The historical pageants focused not on the West, but on Dublin; they were secular rather than religious in their orientation; they did not privilege tradition over the modern, nor Gaelic over English, nor rural over urban (quite the contrary). Produced on an epic scale with unambiguous ideological content, these historical pageants sought to be as inclusive as possible. Despite being commodified, they attracted a large number of participants and huge audiences. More people saw the military tattoo or the parades than attended all Abbey performances of O'Casey's plays in the 1920s. Some, like the commentators in *Honesty* in 1929, regarded them as self-serving efforts to unify or at least to pacify the people of Dublin after the end of a bitter civil war. Informed by a spirit of boosterism that often accompanies pageants, the Dublin Civic Weeks offered an anodyne and in some ways ahistorical version of Irish history. In *Modern Ireland, 1600–1972*, R. F. Foster observed that in the newly created Free State, "it was important to stress the supposed message of Irish history—which involved a necessary degree of deliberate amnesia. . . . [T]he real nature of pre-1916 Irish society had to be glossed over."[105] Much else in both the distant and the recent past was glossed over or gussied up in these pageants, but such selectivity is an intrinsic quality of historical pageantry, of all public history.

The concept of public entertainment is inherently vexed.[106] Like any period, the early years of the Free State did not have a monolithic public or a single standard for entertainment. O'Casey's plays, like Synge's, demonstrated how hotly contested ideas of entertainment or of a national theatre were in early-twentieth-century Ireland. Although the civic weeks did not survive the economic and political upheavals of the 1920s, they, and their tattoos in particular, provided the models for civic celebration and public history that would be revisited and revised over the coming decades.

Critical perspectives on pageantry in the post–World War I era are sharply divided. Patrick Wright memorably referred to the modern heritage industry in Britain as "amnesia . . . in historical fancy dress."[107] On the other hand, Fischer-Lichte sums up the aspirations of the *Thingspiel*, populist pageants from the early 1930s in Germany, as "unfold[ing] the potential to evoke quasi-religious feelings in spectators and to unite actors and spectators into a community."[108] To describe the Dublin Civic Weeks in such a way indicates that the European context for its pageantry may be as important as its more obvious Irish one. Driven by overt political motives and ideological intentions, the historical and mythological pageantry of the civic weeks effectively blended indigenous, demotic celebrations and theatrical traditions. Presentational rather than representational, these pageants prefigured the extremely popular military tattoos and stage shows of the 1930s and 1940s as well as the Tóstals and recuperative pageantry of present-day companies such as Macnas.

Plate 1. Jack Morrow's illustration of the program cover for *The Pageant of Castleknock*. Signed "Jack Morrow '08" in the lower left and "Seaghan Mac Murchada" in the lower right. Personal copy.

Plate 2. Seamus MacCall's costume design in pen and ink with watercolor
for the Irish in the tenth, eleventh, and twelfth centuries in the 1927 Dublin
Civic Week. Courtesy of the Seamus MacCall Collection.

IRISH! 16th Century Design No. 5.

string bound.

If spear is carried it should be accompanied by round metal shield about 2' 6" diam.

= rib of helmet

Helmet.

cloth or leather cap.

under helmet.

This short weapon hangs in scabbard from the shoulder, slung diagonally across the chest.

Fringe ornamented

2' 6"

Large sword in scabbard to be carried in hand.

Patterned cloth without embroidery

leather scabbard with leather metal mount-ings and finishing with fringe.

shoes of yellow leather

detail of shirt sleeve opening.

IRISH COSTUME 16th Century.
Cap can be of cloth or leather. Shirt generally saffron, — can also be
unbleached white. Coat of cloth, embroidered or striped. Legs can
be as shown, or with "hose," or quite bare. Coat is high waisted and
ties at front. Shirt reaches nearly to ankles but is tied round waist and
gathered up above knees.

Plate 3. Seamus MacCall's costume design for the Irish in the sixteenth century, 1927 Dublin Civic Week. Courtesy of the Seamus MacCall Collection.

Plate 4. Maurice MacGonigal's cover design for the *Dublin Civic Week, 1929: Official Handbook*. Courtesy of Ciarán MacGonigal for the estate of Maurice MacGonigal, RHA (1900–1979).

Plate 5. Micheál macLíammóir's watercolor costume design for Dervogilla in *The Ford of the Hurdles*. © Estate of Edwards-macLíammóir.
Courtesy of the Edwards-macLíammóir estate and the Dublin Gate
Theatre Archives in the Charles Deering McCormick Library of Special Collections at Northwestern University.

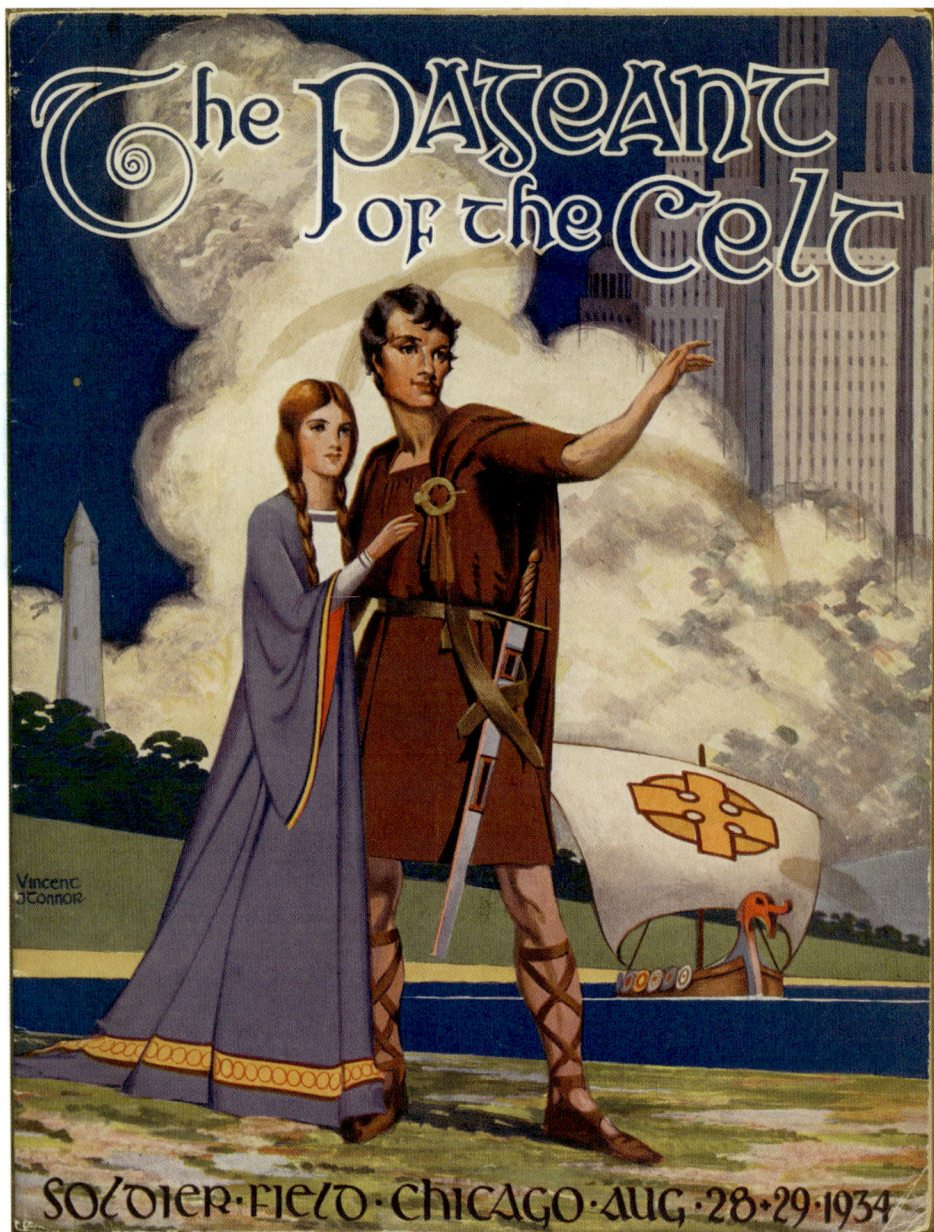

Plate 6. Program cover *The Pageant of the Celt*.

Plate 7. *The Roll of the Drum*, souvenir program, 1940. Courtesy of the National Library of Ireland.

Plate 8. *Táin*, Expo Festival, Seville, Spain, 1992. Courtesy of Macnas and the Macnas Archive, James Hardiman Library, National University of Ireland Galway.

3

North and South of the Border

The largest and most memorable public spectacle in twentieth-century Ireland was the Eucharistic Congress held in Dublin in 1932. In good weather over five days, June 22–26, 1932, "the congress demonstrated that the Irish Free State was, to all intents and purposes, a Catholic state. There was a definite air of Catholic triumphalism about the congress."[1] Dominated by the rites and rituals of the Catholic Church, the Eucharistic Congress itself did not partake of historical pageantry. Students at Sion Hill Convent school at Blackrock performed a modest but highly inventive historical pageant, *Eire: Handmaid of the Eucharist*, portraying Ireland's relationship with Catholicism, cleverly told through the span of a single day: from before dawn (druids), to daybreak (St. Patrick), and noon (saints and scholars), through the darkest hour (penal laws), to another dawn (Catholic Emancipation), and finally "the radiant morn" of the 1932 Eucharistic Congress.[2] Held in part to honor the fifteen hundredth anniversary of St. Patrick's return to Ireland, the Eucharistic Congress celebrated what Catholics saw as their Patrician Church. Even the collusion of the Free State government and the Catholic Church, however, did not preclude the Church of Ireland from asserting its claim to be a Patrician Church in Ireland. While the Eucharistic Congress anticipates the "special relationship" between Ireland and the Catholic Church in the 1937 Irish constitution, at least four large-scale religious historical pageants explored Protestant heritage in Ireland in the 1930s: Richard Rowley's *The Pageant of St. Patrick*, Ethel G. Davidson's *The Pageant of St. Patrick*, Magdalen King-Hall's *The Pageant of Greyabbey*, and M. Beatrice Lavery's *Presbyterianism through the Ages*.

The Church of Ireland celebrated St. Patrick even if its pageants could not compete with the bombast and scale of the Eucharistic Congress. In 1932, in addition to a four-day conference in Dublin in October, the Church of Ireland organized two elaborate pageants to honor St. Patrick as its patron saint. The first, staged in Northern Ireland in June, was Rowley's *The Pageant of St. Patrick*; the second, by Davidson, was performed at the Mansion House in Dublin in October. Scripts for both were published as the pageants' programs. Like the Eucharistic Congress and the historical pageants earlier in the century, these Patrician pageants hoped to inspire modern audiences by recalling a distant past. Rather than looking to mythological heroes, however, these pageants located the defining moment in Ireland's past as the island's conversion to Christianity. A prefatory note to Rowley's pageant reminded audiences, "Countless missionaries from Ireland spread through Europe the Gospel that Patrick brought to the Irish. Can we not dare to hope that his spiritual children may again revive the splendour of the past?"[3] The golden age Rowley recalled was not the time of Fionn or Cúchulainn, but the age of Patrick.

The first iteration of *The Pageant of St. Patrick*, a massive open-air production held in Northern Ireland shortly before the Eucharistic Congress in Dublin, was produced by the Church of Ireland and scripted by Rowley (pseudonym of Richard Valentine Williams, b. 1877), remembered for his poetry, his play *Apollo in Mourne* (1926), and his publishing enterprises.[4] His script, published by United Diocese of Down and Connor and Dromore, was illustrated by the costume designs of Mabel Annesley, best known for her wood engravings and watercolors, and William Conor, the Belfast artist born in 1881 who served as president of the Royal Ulster Academy between 1957 and 1964. Both Rowley and Conor are often identified with their depiction of the Ulster working classes, but in 1932 they collaborated to present this Church of Ireland pageant.[5] To defray expenses for *The Pageant of St. Patrick*, special collections were taken at Church of Ireland services around St. Patrick's Day in 1932.[6] A small core of actors with speaking roles was supplemented by a large choir, youth groups, the Belfast

Folk-Dancing Society, and members of the Prince of Wales's North Staffordshire Regiment.

Like Parker's pageants early in the century, Rowley's *The Pageant of St. Patrick* claimed site specificity, particularly through Patrick's attachment to Saul, where he landed in returning to Ireland from Europe and very near where he is buried in Downpatrick. The foreword by the Archdeacon of Dromore spells out these geographical associations: "Close to this place he [Patrick] first proclaimed the name of Christ and won his earliest converts in the household of Dichu, the local chieftain. There was his first church placed, named ever since Saul, from the barn (Sabhall) that Dichu gave to him to worship in" (11). Like Rowley's poetry, his pageant celebrates Ulster as a "beautiful and peaceful country" (24). "This place is very dear to me," says Patrick, with its "peaceful waters, the green pastures, the full leaved trees" (37). On his deathbed, Patrick singles out Saul: "I have had here foretastes of Paradise, and of all the scenes of my earthly exile, I have loved Saul best" (38). This Edenic depiction of Ulster and the site specificity of the pageant underscored Patrick's association with Northern Ireland and his status as the Church of Ireland's patron saint. The first performance of Rowley's *The Pageant of St. Patrick* on the shores of Strangford Lough at Castleward was an aquatic spectacular: Patrick returned to Ireland with his monks in "a graceful craft manned by hooded seamen [that] sailed majestically up the lough."[7] A second performance held at Belfast Castle on June 18, 1932, had to forego Viscount Bangor's ship bringing Patrick back to Ireland, but attracted even larger crowds.

In seven scenes Rowley's pageant covers the span of Patrick's life from his boyhood abduction by pirates (not Irish ones, but "The Scots! The Scots!" [17]), his escape from slavery in Slemish, his return to Ireland as a Christian missionary, his conversion of Dichu, his confrontation with druids at Tara, his meeting with King Laoghaire, and his death in Saul. Although the young Patrick's language is graphically violent ("My father is noble. . . . My father will have your heads. You will be crucified" [17]), the mature Patrick is serene, pacific, and modest. "I am the weakest and the poorest of men" (29), he says, "the most unlettered of them all" (37). Indeed, Patrick was played by two actors: as a headstrong young man by J. C. Cullen and as the venerable missionary by Rev. Cuthbert Peacocke, son of the then and himself later bishop of Derry.

As the pageant nears its end, Rowley shifts into an allegorical mode associated with Renaissance masques to show how Patrick united all of Ireland. In a scene set in Armagh, Coarb (the medieval Irish term for heir or successor) avers that Patrick chose the place for his cathedral, "the Mother-Church," because it was on that spot that he nursed a wounded deer back to health: "He gathered all the Churches, all the souls of Ireland in his arms, and the place where the deer lay will be a sacred place until the end of time; and his Church will be the Mother-Church of all the Churches of Ireland. *From the crowd, four masked female figures emerge, each emblematic of one of the four provinces*" (33–34). The four women, representing Ulster, Munster, Leinster, and Connaught, rhapsodize about Patrick and "tell of all his wanderings, all his perils, all his mighty acts amongst them" (34). Patrick's unification of Ireland seems to be less a political aspiration than an assertion of the common ground shared by the Church of Ireland and the Catholic Church. Although there is an element of chauvinism in that the warm and welcoming people of County Down warn Patrick that he will face grave danger in venturing south, the play's politics are more reconciliatory and nostalgic than sectarian or triumphalist. In the final scene, Patrick returns to Saul, where he "shall embark on the last voyage of all" (36). As in other treatments of the legend, Patrick does not convert Laoghaire, but wins his respect: "I am too old for such a change," says Rowley's Laoghaire, "but you may go in and out among my people with none to gainsay you" (32).

One photograph of the performance at Castleward in County Down shows a dozen of Dichu's men-at-arms perched menacingly in the battlements watching Patrick's arrival at Saul; another shows King Laoghaire's six queens and several of his soldiers on horseback. A striking panoramic photograph of Patrick surrounded by his followers meeting Dichu and his soldiers documents scores of participants plus a large choir seated at a distance. The *Belfast Telegraph* enthusiastically reported the event as "Ulster's first outdoors pageant, in modern days at all events, marking a new epoch in dramatic art in this Province." Its reportage reads very much like the coverage of a society gala. The pirates on horseback were "from the Prince of Wales' North Staffordshire Regiment at Ballykinlar, by kind permission of Major-General Gridwood and Lieut.-Colonel Mackenzie Kennedy"; playing Laoghaire's queen, Maud Kennedy "wore Lady Kennedy's [her mother's] beautiful amethyst jewels, bracelets, necklet, two brooches, and a star in her crown."[8] The Belfast *Irish Press* offered a quite different view of the pageant under the front-page headline "The Pageant in Co. Down: Non-Catholic Idea of Days of St. Patrick: Unconscious Comedy." The account was unmerciful about the acting, content, and quality of the performance: "We found a Patrick of little personality, and the Patrician ideal was further obscured by Rev. C. Peacocke's monotonous interpretation. . . . The long waits between scenes are not on the lines of the best pageantry." The review went on to criticize the staging and Annesley's and Conor's costumes as well, "but the most amazing thing about the Pageant was the silence concerning the part played by women in the days of Patrick."[9] Although Rowley imagined a united Ireland, his pageant only antagonized the Catholic press.

Another *Pageant of St. Patrick*, one written by Davidson and directed by Lennox Robinson, was staged in conjunction with the Church of Ireland conference held in Dublin on October 11–14, 1932, which published a 275-page book of proceedings. Performed indoors at Dublin's Mansion House on a more modest scale, Davidson's pageant was fully scripted and cast dozens of participants, with at least three different actors playing St. Patrick at various stages of his life. In twelve scenes the pageant moved between Dumbarton in Scotland, the Cistercian abbey in Lerins and later Auxerre in France, as well as more familiar locales in Ireland: Downpatrick, Armagh, Crochan, Saul, Tara, and Slane. Davidson's script relied even more heavily than most pageants on choral interludes, recitations, and tableaux. Like Rowley's pageant and the Patrician pageants to come in the midfifties, the recitation of *The Breastplate of St. Patrick* was a focal point.

Other historical pageants celebrating foundational religious events in Northern Ireland emulated the example of the Church of Ireland's 1932 Patrician pageants. M. Beatrice Lavery designed *Presbyterianism through the Ages: Historical Pageant* (1935) for performance by youth groups, each of which took responsibility for one of the seventeen scenes. The first scene, set in 1,250 BC (featuring the burning bush, which became the church's emblem), and the second, showing how "Ireland gave Christianity to Scotland through St. Columba" in 563, are prelude to eleven scenes set in the late sixteenth and seventeenth centuries that depict the great men of Presbyterianism—John Knox, Andrew Melville, Andrew Hislop (who was only sixteen when martyred). Although principally set in Scotland and Iona, *Presbyterianism through the Ages* features scenes of the closing of the gates of Derry and of the Siege of Derry (1689), both of which, as Ian McBride demonstrates, were focal points in Ulster Protestant history.[10] The finale of Lavery's pageant, "In Their Footsteps," invited participants to sign a covenant renewing their commitment to their faith.[11] The incorporation of fixtures of displays of Protestant identity in Northern Ireland, especially the signing of a covenant, may, in retrospect, seem to politicize the pageant and to make it a sectarian spectacle, but the covenant signing may gesture more toward a public performative act, not unlike the contemporary practice of signing a book of condolence, that could involve the entire audience. Lavery's pageant was tailor-made for youth conferences because individual groups could each take responsibility for the performance of one scene and form an audience for the entire production. *Presbyterianism through the Ages* was revived in December 1935 in Coleraine and periodically over at least the next thirteen years, including in October 1947 at Belfast's Assembly Hall and at the Metropolitan Hall in Dublin in October 1948.[12]

Far more spectacular than Lavery's youth pageant was Magdalen King-Hall's *The Pageant of Greyabbey: The Story of Sir John de Courcy and Affreca His Wife and How They Brought the Cistercians to the Barony of Ards* (1935), previewed by the *Irish Times* as "the 12th century romance of the Conquest of Ulster by the Norman Knight, John de Courcy."[13] Another pageant to claim site specificity, it was performed six times, for matinees and evening performances, on June 12, 13, and 15, 1935, on the Abbey grounds, Greyabbey, County Down, as a charity event to benefit the Queen's Institute of District Nursing, Northern Ireland. The program, which contains a complete script, was illustrated by costume sketches by Richard Douglas Perceval[14] of Norman knights, upright, manly, armored, and armed. The only visual representation of the natives, an "Irish Native of the Twelfth Century," shows a wizened, osteoporotic white-bearded man leaning on his cane.

The contrast between the Normans and the Irish begins at the opening banquet: "*Several important chieftains are present. They look barbaric but dignified in their native dress, and are attended by wild looking retainers*" (25).[15] Those Irish chieftains silently witness the pageant's central conflict between William de Burgo (d. 1206, remembered in *The Annals of the Four Masters* as one who "plundered Connacht, as well churches as territories; but God and the saints took vengeance on him for that; for he died of a singular disease, too shameful to be described") and John de Courcy (d. 1219). The Norman knights argue over how best to subdue and to pacify the native population. In the first scene, de Courcy accuses de Burgo of taking bribes from the Irish chieftains and thereby wasting the talents of "some of the best fighting men in Christendom here under his standard in this country, which has been occupied but never subdued" (27). With that allegation King Henry II makes a gift of Ulster to de Courcy: "The people there are as fierce and untamable as you yourself. Ulster is yours! I give it to you freely—if you can subdue it, that is to say!" (29). De Courcy's conquest of Ulster amounts to little more than the surrender of the native Irish: "The Chief of the Sept (*mournfully, but with dignity*)—We have no choice, stranger knight. Look at your men and then at us. Your men are clad in strong mail, we in these garments of peace. Your men are fully armed. We, in our haste, have had to snatch up sticks and stones as weapons. . . . It seems that even God is on your side, and that our own saints prophesy against us" (39). The Chief hopes that the people of "Ulidia" will offer resistance, but de Courcy orders the Irish to be taken away: "De Courcy—Take these natives to the city. They belong to me now. *The Irish, guarded by the soldiers, pass out in a long file. The men bear themselves with dignity; the women weep, but some of the younger ones cast covertly admiring glances at John de Courcy as they pass him. He waits until they have all gone by, then glances up at the heraldic device on his standard, throws back his head with a sudden laugh and, followed by his bodyguard, gallops away"* (39). The Irish language is referred to as "their outlandish tongue" (23) spoken by the barbarians in "this savage country" (29).

The pageant celebrates the hegemonic colonialism of a community that for centuries has ruled precisely by setting itself apart from the "natives." The "admiring glances" that native girls cast at de Courcy caution against intermarriage between the Normans and natives. As in her novels, King-Hall celebrates the civilizing Normans in time-worn tropes: de Courcy, for instance, enters riding a white charger and wins Affreca's hand when, disguised as "the stranger knight," he defeats all comers in a jousting tournament. Like the press accounts, the program is at pains to emphasize the ancestral connection between the performers and these twelfth-century characters. Closer, in fact, to aristocratic masque than to populist pageant, *The Pageant of Greyabbey* was a unionist spectacle "in which many people prominent in Northern society took part. . . . Miss Montgomery of Greyabbey, was the organiser of the pageant. . . . Lady Dervogilla, daughter of 'The O'Mahoney,' and here again we have an interesting case of the part being played by a namesake, Mrs. Rennie O'Mahoney."[16] John de Courcy (played by Captain Perceval Maxwell) and Affreca (Elizabeth Blakiston-Houston) were directed by A. S. G. Loxton, who played Jove in Rowley's *Apollo in Mourne*.[17]

All pageants are self-congratulatory, but King-Hall's *The Pageant of Greyabbey* stoked and was stoked by a triumphalism that is more often associated with the pageantry of July 12 and the commemorative Battle of Scarva. As chilling as treatment of native Irish in *The Pageant of Greyabbey* is, such attitudes, as Gillian McIntosh observes, were shared by several Ulster academic historians in the 1920s and 1930s who similarly saw the Irish as incapable of ruling themselves.[18] In 1926, for instance, Walter Alison Phillips in *Revolution in Ireland, 1906–1923*, wrote that there were "weighty authorities to support the opinion that the Celtic race is, by virtue of its inherent qualities, incapable of developing unaided a high type of civilization."[19] As McIntosh demonstrates, extensive pageantry in Northern Ireland in the mid-twentieth century was intimately connected to the British monarchy—royal visits, funerals, coronations, and the like. The vogue for religiously oriented pageants in Northern Ireland between 1932 and 1936 responds partly to the Eucharistic Congress yet is also an expression of what Ian McBride calls "a constant process of commemoration, rediscovery and popularization [in Ulster] since 1689."[20]

THE MILITARY TATTOO (1935)

Between 1935 and 1947, and especially during the Emergency (World War II), the record of historical pageantry in the Free State is virtually synonymous with the history of military spectacles. Drawing on the success of the 1927 and 1929 Military Tattoos, the Defence Forces undertook the majority and the most spectacular of Ireland's historical pageants in the 1930s and '40s. Supplemented by technical civilian expertise (in searchlights and costume design, for example), the Defence Forces created the Military Tattoos of 1935 and 1945 and the many Step Together pageants staged in provincial towns during the Emergency. The Defence Forces also sponsored three military stage shows at the Theatre Royal that relied substantially on Louis Elliman's production expertise and commercial theatre professionals—popular actors such as Noel Purcell, successful writers such as Dick Forbes, musicians, chorus girls. Over the decade between 1935 to 1945, these military theatricals incorporated historical pageantry to enhance the image and reputation of the Defence Forces, to advance a consistent message about Irish neutrality that reinforced government policies, and to construct, sometimes in highly inventive ways, a vivid, proud heritage for the Irish people.

The Irish Defence Forces had a large cadre of disciplined personnel as well as a well-trained cohort of musicians available for ceremonial occasions. In March 1923 two Germans, Fritz Brase and Frederick Christian Sauerzweig, appointed to the ranks of colonel and captain, respectively, reported to the Curragh to inaugurate the Army School of Music. Only months after the departure of British troops from the Irish Free State, importing officers from Germany was one way to break away from British military and musical traditions. The debut of the army band "was so unqualified a success that it laid the foundation of the reputation which the No. 1 Band has never ceased to enjoy."[21] Less than five years later, three separate army bands performed at the 1927 *Grand Military Tattoo*. The popularity of the army bands continued to grow after successful appearances at the 1928 and 1932 Tailteann Games and at the 1932 Eucharistic Congress. By the time of the 1935 Military Tattoo, there were four army bands, plus five pipe bands as well as various brass and percussion ensembles. Over the next decade, the Defence Forces provided integral, indispensable musical accompaniment to the Step Together pageants, the military's Theatre Royal stage shows, and the 1945 Military Tattoo.

Even more significant than a sophisticated musical infrastructure was the enthusiasm of Major-General Hugo Hyacinth McNeill, "high priest of the cult of military professionalism,"[22] whose appetite for historical pageantry was voracious. Nephew to Eoin MacNeill, Hugo McNeill attended St. Enda's, where he saw pageants garner support and goodwill in the community. In 1924 he was involved in thwarting the would-be Irish Army mutiny that resulted in the resignation of two government ministers and one hundred officers.[23] Later in that decade, he spent several months at the Command and General Staff College in Fort Leavenworth, Kansas, and, after returning to Ireland, achieved the rank of major-general while still in his twenties. In the 1930s and 1940s, McNeill shaped the public perception of the Defence Forces through military tattoos, massive stage shows, films, and radio broadcasts that all garnered extensive positive coverage in the press. During the Emergency, for example, he "employed a full-time cameraman, Jack Millar, to document the activities of the army: 'Most of this was put together by Gen. MacNeill himself, who had a great talent for that sort of work—wonderful fellow—anything to do with the theatre or films or entertainment, MacNeill was an enthusiast, and wouldn't allow anything to stop it.'"[24] In his forays into pageants

McNeill was not alone. His brother Olaf organized several of the Step Together pageants. In the 1950s Hugo McNeill became the first director of the Tóstal, the tourist initiative responsible for the extravagant national pageants in the midfifties. No less important were McNeill's many collaborations with the military historian G. A. Hayes-McCoy, including the first of the Tóstal's lavish pageants of identity, *The Pageant of St. Patrick* (1954). Hayes-McCoy was involved in the creation of several other historical pageants in the forties and fifties, sometimes drafting the scripts and other times acting as a historical consultant. Nicholas Canny writes that Hayes-McCoy "attributed his abiding interest in military affairs to the tattoos of the Connaught Rangers which, as a boy, he saw enacted opposite his parental home on Eyre Square" in Galway.[25]

Even after Fianna Fáil rose to power and de Valera became taoiseach in 1932, the image of the Free State Army remained troubled. A month before the 1935 Military Tattoo, the *Irish Times* editorialized: "The Free State Army has made considerable progress since 1929: it was a fine force then, but it is considerably smarter, more efficient and better disciplined to-day. There still lingers in a few quarters the belief that it consists of an almost unkempt body of men, badly officered, and barely able to keep in step on the march."[26] Indeed, as Labhras Joye writes, "Overall the army was in a poor state by March 1932 when Fianna Fáil took over government. After playing a key role in the Civil War it had been largely neglected, continuously under strength and barely trained."[27] As in the 1920s, a military tattoo afforded the opportunity to project a positive, progressive image of a modern, well-disciplined force in 1935. British tattoos had continued to attract large audiences, and not only in Britain: tattoos from Aldershot and Tidworth were broadcast over radio in Ireland. And again, as in the 1920s, the tattoo would visualize Irish history through processions, reenactments, and historical pageants. For the 1935 Military Tattoo, McNeill promised "one of the most spectacular and impressive displays of military and historical pageantry ever seen in Ireland."[28] And he delivered.

In late 1934 Minister for Defence Frank Aiken arranged for the Defence Forces to stage a military tattoo at the RDS facilities at no charge with the provision that "members of the [Royal Dublin] Society to be admitted free to the Tattoo and the Members' Stands to be reserved for their exclusive use."[29] Over the next ten months, publicity for the tattoo took pains to emphasize that no public moneys funded the tattoo: "It will cost the taxpayer nothing," wrote the *Irish Times*. "It has been financed entirely by the personal contributions of Army officers, and all the profits will go to Army charities."[30] Costing the taxpayer nothing, of course, assumed that the tattoo would not reimburse the Free State for the time and services of the officers and enlisted men. Despite the fact that the state appropriated no dedicated funds for the tattoo, considerable resources—time, matériel, personnel, and other assets—were marshaled to support the event. The *Irish Times* reported that by September 1935, "approximately one-third of the regular Army and the officers have been transformed into a huge theatrical cast."[31] Even beyond the training, transport, housing, feeding, and outfitting of thousands of military personnel, the tattoo incurred additional extraordinary costs. The *Irish Times* noted, "The pipers' band [was] splendid in their new saffron cloaks and kilts and their green tunics."[32] A chariot was designed and constructed for Cúchulainn. A script was developed. Hundreds of performers in the Sokol (calisthenic) drills had battery-powered lamps installed in their caps. The Corps of Engineers constructed a half-scale replica of the GPO. Extravagant fireworks ended each evening's performance.[33]

The army turned to professionals for several aspects of the production, most notably for the costumes designed by Micheál macLíammóir, fresh from his engagements in the United States, most recently Chicago's *The Pageant of the Celt* (Plate 6). For an Irish American audience, nine scenes spun the fabric of Irish (and Celtic) history from the fourth to the twentieth centuries. Irish and Scottish dancers, an orchestra, and a one-thousand-voice massed choir performed to great acclaim. The pageant depicted Cúchulainn, St. Patrick, "Celtic Light in Europe's Night" (featuring, inter alia, Sts. Colmcille, Columbanus, and Brendan), Brian Boru, the Norman invasion, "The Celtic Alliance" between Ireland and Scotland, the Wild Geese in Europe, "The Rise of Republicanism" (James Napper Tandy and Wolfe Tone, et al.),

"Up from the Ashes," and finally "Easter Week, 1916."[34] The *Chicago Herald* reported that John V. Ryan composed the "richly poetic version of Ireland's history," but a note on the clipping in the Dublin Gate Theatre Archive written in Hilton Edwards's hand disputes this claim: "Narration was written by Micheal from a scenario by Ryan."[35] Further complicating the authorship question and indeed the impossibility of knowing exactly what was staged are the many discrepancies between the scenes described in Matthias J. Harford's "Legend" (or libretto) in the program and the surviving macLíammóir script for "The Narrative of *The Pageant of the Celt*." The macLíammóir script, for instance, treats the Norman invasion by reworking the three episodes of *The Ford of the Hurdles* that deal with Diarmuid MacMurrough.

Whether the reported attendance figure of twenty-five thousand for the first performance included thousands of performers is unclear, but Soldier Field (still home to the Chicago Bears) could accommodate nearly three times that number. The weather was unfavorable and attendance disappointing, especially if anyone ever expected capacity crowds. MacLíammóir's recollection of the event in *All for Hecuba* is hilarious, insightful, and scathing: "The darkest side of Irish America with its subtle air of conquest, its mania for power and largess, its furs and jewels and smuggled liquor, its dim airtight background of shamrock, harp, and round tower, its wistful patronage to both countries, seemed incarnate in these two [unnamed] men who arrived to ask me to write and Hilton to help produce *The Pageant of the Celt*." He recalls the pageant's rehearsals as "the marshalling of the entire slum-population of the city [who were paid for their participation] into various groups of warriors, bards, and druids" and its performance with his "black velvet voice [winding] through the convolutions of my script, while in dumb show St. Patrick plucked huge shamrocks from the grass of Illinois, the Danes were driven out by pious Brian, Sarsfield thundered his silent way through Limerick, and the men of Easter week passed to their execution followed by Scottish pipers, Welsh bards, and the usual druids and dancers from Brittany and Penzance."[36]

Fresh from salvaging what he could of *The Pageant of the Celt* in Chicago, macLíammóir designed exquisite costumes for historical personages, including Cúchulainn, Brian Boru's officers, Diarmaid MacMurrough, Owen Roe O'Neill (cover image), Red Hugh O'Donnell, and dozens of others for the 1935 tattoo. Miss Rogers, wardrobe mistress at the Gaiety Theatre, executed macLíammóir's designs. More recent army uniforms from the Irish Volunteers (1916–21), the Irish Citizen Army, the Fianna, Cumann na mBan, and the Free State Army were authentic or exact replicas. Mr. J. Golden, the Dublin artist, collaborated in the production of the enormous GPO set piece, specifically in reproducing the three statues atop the pediment. MacLíammóir was not the only participant whose experience in the Dublin Civic Weeks and Tailteann Games informed the 1935 tattoo: Herbert Bailey, MacCall's collaborator in 1927, was responsible for the technical production; Elizabeth Young, seen in 1924 as Queen Tailte at the Theatre Royal, incarnated Eire, not as the Shan Van Vocht, but as a beautiful woman. Members of the Portobello dramatic society served as extras, the ordinary citizens, in the reenactment of Easter 1916.

Prelude to the September tattoo was the Easter commemoration staged at the actual GPO on O'Connell Street. On April 21, 1935, a large military parade marched to the GPO, where government dignitaries witnessed the unveiling of Oliver Sheppard's statue *The Death of Cuchulainn* to mark the nineteenth anniversary of the Rising. James Moran sees the 1935 Easter Sunday parade and ceremony as Fianna Fáil's appropriation of the 1916 Rising. He describes "a horde of ten thousand," "snaking" through the streets of Dublin before de Valera "unveiled the Cuchulainn statue to the noise of drum beats and bugle blasts" inside the GPO.[37] In the day nothing about the popular response to the April 1935 festivities deterred the organizers of the September tattoo, the first "stand-alone" tattoo in the Free State. On the contrary, the tattoo was strategically and energetically developed as a military campaign that built on the commemoration at Easter.

Extensive promotional publicity for the tattoo, in news stories as opposed to paid advertisements, appeared regularly from July on. More than a month before the first performance, this tattoo claimed historical authenticity: "Considerable attention has been devoted to this pageant to ensure historical accuracy in regard to costumes, arms, equipment and banners, and general settings."[38] The program was arranged to be suitable to children and teenagers as well as adults, although admission prices were not inexpensive: 3/6 and 2/6 for reserved seats; 2/ for unreserved seats, and 1/ for standing room. The extensive circulation of attractive visual images, both photographs of rehearsals and macLíammóir's exotic costume designs, as well as nearly identical wording in articles in the *Irish Times*, the *Irish Independent*, and the *Irish Press* indicate how well planned and effective the publicity campaign was. Display ads enticed audiences to "see the armies of the past come to life again. See the army of the present carry on the great tradition."[39] Unsurprisingly, the *Irish Press* was the most enthusiastic of Dublin's daily papers. On September 13, 1935, the *Irish Press* previewed scenes of "Brian blessing his army on the eve of Clontarf; the Chieftains of the North leading their men into battle against the Elizabethan invaders; the Volunteers of '82 raising the standard of independence; Emmet leading a forlorn hope; and so on up to the 'Easter Dawn' of 1916 and the unfurling of the Tricolour in the G.P.O."[40] The next day the *Irish Press* ran a publicity photo of "Irish Officers of All the Ages" featuring twenty-three pageant participants in distinctive historic uniforms and costumes. On September 16, 1935, the *Irish Press* offered further details: "In the item, 'the Easter Dawn,' an endeavour would be made to reproduce the occupation of the General Post Office on Easter Monday, the opening of the enemy attack, its gradual development until it reached its climax when the building burst into flames."[41] After the premiere, additional items in the daily press reported the impressive attendance figures and, in 1936, the transfer of the tattoo to Cork, where again it exceeded expectations.[42]

Military tattoos, like most historical pageants, are populist spectacles, overtly propagandistic, typically festive, rarely nuanced. In the Free State, military tattoos not only aimed to enhance the reputation of the contemporary Defence Forces and to demonstrate the imperative need for an army but also to infuse an educative and affective understanding of a noble Irish history. All four of the Irish military tattoos (1927, 1929, 1935, and 1945) used the March of the Nation to construct a heritage of Irish fighting men that was as noble as it was

16. An *Irish Press* clipping of the GPO replica constructed for the 1935 Military Tattoo. Courtesy of the Dublin Gate Theatre Archives in Charles Deering McCormick Library of Special Collections at Northwestern University.

venerable. After the first tattoo in 1927, the tattoos referred back to earlier iterations, recycled popular elements, yet spoke to their particular moment in time.

On September 17, 1935, the army premiered its third military tattoo at Dublin's RDS to benefit military charities. The tattoo was a two-and-a-half-hour extravaganza held for five evening performances, supplemented by a full dress rehearsal for children on September 16, 1935, and began at 8:00 p.m. The tattoo's more than twenty-five hundred performers were drawn largely from the ranks of the Free State army. Nine army bands, including pipers arrayed in new uniforms of green and saffron kilts, performed patriotic songs. Once darkness fell, a new variant on the "torchlight tattoo" used modern technologies, as performers wore caps with battery-powered lights in one of four colors. Audiences saw "the modern Army at work in the display of infantry drill, which concludes with a double square of men, in total darkness, firing a *feu de joie*."[43] Four powerful searchlights illuminated performers as the historical procession entered the darkened stadium. Nighttime performance facilitated *son et lumière* effects: plunging a massive arena into darkness, training powerful searchlights on participants, and detonating pyrotechnics.

The fullest surviving record of the production is the silent Pathé newsreel of daytime rehearsals for the five-performance revival at the Show Grounds in Cork in 1936. Three hundred bare-chested recruits wearing immaculate white trousers perform mass gymnastics in a show of physical fitness, military discipline, and hygienic deportment. Intricate chalk marks guide the elaborate field configurations. The newsreel's intertitles note, "In the Grand Finale Eire summons the Armies of all Ages to her banner"; Eire (Elizabeth Young), seen with long dark braids, waves her scepter to beckon the March of the Nation.

The two historical events selected for reenactment were the "Ride to Ballyneety," when in 1690 "Galloping Hogan" led Jacobite troops under Patrick Sarsfield to destroy the Williamite siege train, and Easter 1916. Nightly for the run of the tattoo and to the great delight of the audience, the siege train sent to force the capitulation of Limerick, "the greatest assembly of heavy artillery ever seen in Ireland up to that period," was itself destroyed. Tipped off with the password by a Williamite camp follower, Sarsfield swept down on the train the night before it would have reached Limerick:

> [Colonel Patrick] Sarsfield slipped through the besiegers' lines one dark night at the head of a selected Cavalry force and made for Keeper Mountain, over-looking the probable last bivouac of the siege train before it joined William's main forces. . . . The huge train went into its last bivouac under the eyes of hidden troops, who as soon as darkness fell, came stealing down from their eyrie. Bluffing their way past the outposts with the discovered pass word [sic] they were riding right into the sleeping camp before the alarm was given. The Dutch gunners and their escort had not a chance to save themselves. . . . The great guns were rammed with powder, their muzzles buried in the earth, the stores and ammunition were piled on top of them, a powder trail laid, the Williamite great train went thundering in ruin to the skies. Successfully evading the force sent to cut him off, Sarsfield and his Dragoons got back within their own lines to safety, bringing with them several hundred captured horses, welcome remounts for the sadly thinned Irish Cavalry Regiments.[44]

Such a reading of the Irish past allowed for an equestrian and pyro-technical spectacle that Michael Bay might envy. Nightly for the run of the tattoo and to the great delight of the audience, Sarsfield and his commandos captured the siege train, turned its artillery to the ground, detonated the explosives, and destroyed the train with spectacular effects. Historically, William defeated Sarsfield at the Battle of Aughrim the next year, but the dramatization of the siege train at Ballyneety destroyed by a crafty Irish force defending the people of Limerick against powerful invaders conveyed no sense of Sarsfield's eventual defeat. Audiences loved it.

Recourse to seventeenth-century history was and would remain de rigueur in twentieth-century Irish military tattoos.[45] In 1927 Sergeant Custume was seen to defend the bridge at Athlone in 1691; in 1929 the army depicted the Siege at Clonmel in 1649–50; in 1945 the tattoo represented Owen Roe O'Neill's return from exile and his transformation of despondent Irish troops into the well-disciplined fighting force that defeated Robert Monroe's forces at the Battle of Benburb in June 1646. The 1935 staging of "Easter Dawn" was unique in representing an event not only within the past century, but also within memory; in every other instance of historical reenactment, the four Irish military tattoos staged after Independence looked exclusively to the seventeenth century for historical episodes to reenact. In each of those instances, the Irish military was seen not only as victors, but as protectors and defenders of the native population against brutal imperial forces.

The representation, commemoration, and celebration of the events of Easter 1916 had and would vex Ireland for decades, especially in light of O'Casey's *The Plough and the Stars*. On April 8, 2012, for instance, the Easter Rising Commemorative Ceremony was held outside Dublin's GPO. Not carried live by the national television stations, but only streamed on the RTÉ (Radió Teilifís Éireann) website, the brief ceremony was a solemn affair: the president arrived, the taoiseach arrived; the minister of justice arrived; troops were inspected; a band played; a wreath was laid; a prayer asked for, among other things, relief from austerity; Captain Shane Keogh read the Proclamation;

planes flew overhead; people went home. The 2012 commemorative ceremony was utterly unlike the September 1935 tattoo.

With the twentieth anniversary of the Easter Rising only eight months away, the September 1935 tattoo staged its spectacular reenactment. The representation of 1916, referred to in the press as "Easter Dawn," centered on a half-size replica of the GPO and took as its inspiration, if not its source, the final act of macLíammóir's *The Ford of the Hurdles*, "Easter: The City at Dawn." The accounts of the 1935 "Easter Dawn" in the *Irish Independent* and the *Irish Press* offer details, unlikely to be coincidental, that affirm a direct connection with macLíammóir's "Easter: The City at Dawn":

> The scene opens outside the G.P.O.; a few people pass up and down, and the newsboys shout the *Irish Independent* and the "Freeman's Journal." The Volunteers arrive, and there is the reading of the historic Proclamation from the steps by Padraig Pearse. The bombardment is faithfully portrayed, the shrapnel bursts around the doomed building, fires break out everywhere, and then from the darkness comes the rattle of the firing squads as the heroic defenders are executed for their part in the battle for Irish freedom. The last scene in the pageant, "Easter Dawn," is the Tricolour rising majestically over the ruins of the G.P.O.[46]

The reenactment moved from a busy Dublin cityscape to the appearance of the Volunteers, the Proclamation of the Irish Republic, the occupation of the GPO, and the unfurling of the Irish tricolor. The GPO, now the rebel stronghold, was bombarded and set on fire by the British. The tricolor fell, as did silence broken only by "the rifles of the firing squads and the lonely notes of the 'Last Post.' . . . Then 'Reveille' rang out defiantly and the red glow over the [burning] building was transformed into the Rising Sun of Resurgence. The Tricolour floated once again more proudly over the Post Office and Dublin."[47] "Easter Dawn" moved from armed insurrection through defeat, including the execution of the Rising leaders, to eventual freedom and independence.

The name "Easter Dawn," the newspaper boys hawking the names of their papers as Dublin citizens begin the day, the reading of the Proclamation, the fatal gunshots that execute the rebel leaders (not seen, but heard ringing out of the silence) all link the 1935 representation of the Rising directly to macLíammóir's "Easter: The City at Dawn," last seen in Dublin some sixteen months earlier in April 1933 and thirteen months earlier in *The Pageant of the Celt* in Chicago. The twelve-hundred-word typescript for this episode, "Narrative Pageant of the Celts [*sic*]. Easter 1916," in the Dublin Gate Theatre Archive, offers a nearly identical account.[48] MacLíammóir writes that the Irish "with their capacity for living for the moment—have forgotten war and political strife and are here in the streets of their chief city, jostling each other on the pavement, telling good stories and hearing them, roaring with laughter in a way that would be regarded as bedlam in the street of many a more studiously merry-making capital" (1). Amazed and confused by the reading of an abbreviated Proclamation of the Irish Republic, some of the Dubliners see the insurgents as mad; others see the rebels as "inspired" (1). "The British troops, the Khaki troops of England" respond under the take-no-prisoners order "Don't spare Dublin" (2). After a battle sequence, Pearse and then Connolly surrender in their memorable phrases. Stage directions indicate "*Death sentences are read. Pause. Music. Narrator resumes*" with a fifty-word encomium of each of the seven Proclamation signatories in macLíammóir's voice: "Pearse . . . going to his death like a lover to his bride"; "And last, poor Connolly, like a wounded lion, lying so helpless on his stretcher, burning with fires that even the laws of the Stranger cannot quench the love of the poor and outcast, hatred of injustice and tyranny—borne by his faithful friends to a felon's death. (*A single volley follows each leader's exit.*)" (2). This dolorous moment, however, is immediately followed by jubilation:

(*Cue for exit of Britain.*)
But now, now the strangers move, and slowly they will go for this great and memorable week of Easter, though it be blackened by fire and flames, and torn by shells, though it is dark with blood and

bitter with the storm—will bear the "Golden fruits of sacrifice" and in the light that rises from the east, there on the scorched and smouldering ruins of the stones, the flag of Ireland surges, furls and unfurls like a song:

(*Cue for trumpet call and Flag Up.*)
—in addition, all the tears and all the curses, all the blood and death, are lighting steadfast torches throughout the land. Now, let us all rise together and give thanks and, in the dawn of freedom, sing the songs of Ireland, and the children of the Celt. (3)

The Rising here is directly tied to Irish Independence. MacLíammóir created the costumes for the 1935 tattoo; his authorship of and involvement in creating its 1916 reenactment remain all but conclusive.

Once more the March of the Nation, here called "a great cavalcade of Irish military history," depicted the modern army as the direct inheritors of glorious military traditions that reached back to Fionn mac Cumhaill. The order of procession was again chronological: the Red Branch knights of Ulster, the Fianna Éireann, soldiers of Clontarf, armies of the Anglo-Norman wars, Art MacMurrough and his Leinster clansmen, the northern princes and their bonnaughts and gallowglasses, Owen Roe O'Neill and the soldiers of the Confederacy, Sarsfield and his dragoons, the secret armies of later days, the pike men of '98, the Fenians, and the Irish Republican Army (IRA) of 1916–21. Finally, the troops of the modern Army—Regular, Reserve, and Volunteer; horse, foot, and artillery—along with Elizabeth Young incarnating Eire were brought together in "Rally Round the Nation." Arrayed on the field were twenty-five hundred performers, many in historical costumes, sixty on horseback, others in chariots, in a spectacular tableau of the Irish past and present. The premiere of the tattoo on September 17, 1935, also honored veterans of the Easter Rising, including eleven members of the original Cumann na mBan for whom replica uniforms were fitted.

The response to the 1935 Military Tattoo was everything Hugo McNeill might have hoped. Press reports were very positive, the crowds massive. Even the *Irish Times* acknowledged that the spectacle of the Easter Rising "seemed very real again last night, even to the red glow creeping up into the sky as the building was fired."[49] The *Irish Independent* gushed: "Here and there the searchlights, while flooding the newcomers as they entered the arena, gave us fleeting, phantom glimpses of the armies that had passed, glinting on spears and battleaxes as well as on the bayonets of the later years . . . the most impressive spectacle that these grounds have ever witnessed."[50] On September 21 the *Irish Independent* speculated, "It is possible it will be found that there were more people in Ballsbridge [at the RDS] last night than at any single day before."[51] Lord Mayor Byrne "received many letters requesting him to make representations to the Ministry of Defence urging the continuance of the Tattoo for at least another week." The *Irish Press* reported that the tattoo did more than entertain: "Whatever the 1935 Tattoo achieved or did not achieve, [McNeill] said, it certainly tended to bring the Army and the people closer together."[52] Whatever aesthetic judgment might be passed, the tattoo accomplished its primary purpose: to improve the image of the Defence Forces.

At first glance there may be chilling echoes of the annual Nuremberg Nazi conventions, especially the 1934 rally, the subject of Leni Riefenstahl's celebrated documentary, *Triumph of the Will* (*Triumph des Willens*), in the 1935 Military Tattoo. After its premiere on March 28, 1935, *Triumph of the Will* won a gold medal at the 1935 Venice Biennale and the Grand Prix at the 1937 World Exhibition in Paris. By deleting the last seven words, Ken Kelman's account of the film might accurately describe the 1935 Military Tattoo: "There are scenes where the earth is lost in darkness, and people and objects move in indeterminate space. Thousands of torches become flickering stars, and fireworks shot high complete the confusion of heaven and earth, confirming and celebrating the union of the lower world with that from which the Führer descended."[53] Of course, Riefenstahl's film did not change the way that many people felt about massive military displays in Ireland in the thirties because it was so widely banned. Despite its importance in film history and its inspiration of a conspicuous homage in Disney's *The Lion King* (when Scar reviews his troops), *Triumph of the Will* remains banned in Germany. It was, however, shown in Dublin in the year of its release. On October 27, 1935, with the permission of the Department of Justice, *Triumph of the Will* was screened at the Olympia Theatre. The letter from Seán Murphy to Dr. J. Schlemann, chargé d'affaires of the German Legation dated October 15, 1935, indicated that "the Department of Justice are prepared to provide police protection," but stipulated that "it would be inadvisable to invite members of the Irish public to assist at this performance. It is felt that if the invitations to the showing of the film are confined to the German Colony here, no objection can be made."[54] Of course, the "German Colony" in Ireland included at least two people, Fritz Brase and Frederick Christian Sauerzweig, who were directly involved in the army bands that performed at the 1935 Military Tattoo.

There were, of course, obvious differences between Hitler's mass rallies and the 1935 Military Tattoo: whereas the former glorifies a single individual, the Irish tattoo celebrated a nation's heritage, or at least an army's; the former sought to prepare a nation for war, while the latter ameliorated the army's unsteady reputation. *Triumph of the Will* displays an entirely modern force armed to the teeth with the latest in military technology, while the tattoo in Dublin was deeply rooted in the past, its soldiers outnumbered and outgunned in the historical episodes. Most important, the solemn atmosphere at Nuremberg was anything but in Dublin. A vastly more intricate and immediate debt of the Irish tattoos was to the British military tattoos that in the 1930s had become perennial fixtures in Aldershot and Tidworth.

THE EMERGENCY I: MILITARY STAGE SHOWS AT THE THEATRE ROYAL

On September 2, 1939, Ireland's declaration of the Emergency affirmed its neutrality in World War II. Neutrality, however, did not mean a diminished Defence Force. On June 8, 1940, Major-General Hugo McNeill outlined an aggressive recruitment drive to increase the ranks in the Defence Forces, particularly the Local Defence Force (LDF). Over the next five years, the recruitment campaign used stage shows in Dublin, specially produced films, radio broadcasts, newspaper articles, and regional recruitment weeks that all deployed the same motto: "Step Together." The phrase derives from a Young Irelander marching song by Michael Joseph Barry: "Step together—be your tramp / Quick and light—no plodding stamp."

In now-familiar terms, the short recruitment film *Step Together* describes the Irish Volunteer as the "proud bearer of tradition." Produced by the Defence Forces' Spearhead film unit under McNeill, this *Step Together* film records the training life of the volunteer with an emphasis on cleanliness, "healthy vigorous manhood," and modernity. Appearance is key: the recruit becomes part of a "well-turned out unit, smart and erect." Highlighting modern technologies including grenade launchers, antiaircraft guns, antitank rifles, and the "mobile striking forces," or motorcycles, the film exhorts viewers to "join up and step together."[55] In print, the same message appears in the Defence Forces' *Irish Army Pictorial: A Pictorial Record Which Brings to You in Life-Like Pictures and Vivid Articles the Story of Ireland's New Army*, published in 1943.

Ten weeks after McNeill first announced the recruitment campaign, as part of National Defence Week, August 25–31, 1940, *The Roll of the Drum* opened at the nation's largest theatre: the four-thousand-seat Theatre Royal in Dublin. Not only did the stage show appear in the nation's largest theatre, but it also ran for three "continuous performances" daily between 2:00 p.m. and 11:00 p.m. *The Roll of the Drum* was the first of three highly successful military shows, ones whose popularity rivaled the 1935 tattoo, produced at the Theatre Royal during the Emergency. Under Louis Elliman, who preferred the moniker T. R. Royle, the Theatre Royal was a mecca for popular entertainment during the Emergency. Elliman's ability to attract Dublin audiences was prodigious; he produced what may be the most successful stage show in Irish theatre history before *Riverdance*: the *Mother Goose* pantomime (1944), "seen by 258,000 people—one out of every three Dubliners—during its six-week run."[56]

Written by J. B. O'Sullivan, *The Roll of the Drum*, "Ireland's first military stage show," opened on August 25, 1940. The cover of the souvenir program features a chorus girl, a Hussarette, sporting a sexy military uniform in the blue and gold of the Royal Hussars (Plate 7) designed by Micheál macLíammóir, whose historical costumes were here recycled from the 1935 Military Tattoo. MacLíammóir's meticulous costume designs, reproduced as decorative miniatures, illustrated the program as well as appearing onstage. The program for *The Roll of the Drum* includes a remarkable prefatory essay, "The Call to Duty," that propagandizes the ideology of Irish neutrality: "For seven hundred years we had been forced to make history with sword and musket and rifle" to establish Ireland as "a veritable oasis of peace in Europe," an oasis now threatened by the "maelstrom" of war: "To-day in all Western Europe one Nation alone keeps the Flag of Peace flying — this Ireland of ours." Ireland is not configured as a nation that cannot choose between England and Germany; its neutrality emanates from its commitment to peace. The essay negotiates a delicate balance celebrating both a venerable military tradition and a nation dedicated to peace. Moreover, the program's essay pursues an aggressively nonsectarian, inclusive direction: "All creeds and classes have rightly united in raising their voices in tribute to the Soldiers of Ireland."[57]

The *Irish Times* elided the potential, some might say self-evident, contradiction between the army defending the nation and staging a theatre gala: "As far as the emergency permits, quite a large number of members of the Defence Forces will take part in this remarkable production, and their training is being brought to a high state of efficiency by constant rehearsals."[58] As for the tattoos, the deployment of military personnel as performers was justified to the public and to politicians as inculcating the discipline intrinsic to military preparedness. The stage show borrowed more than uniforms and costumes from the military tattoos: mass Sokol calisthenics, the performances by the army bands, the now-routine March of the Nation, and the invitation for the audience to join in singing the national anthem at the end were effectively recycled from the tattoos. *The Roll of the Drum* began with instrumental selections performed by the No. 1 Army Band and regimental songs sung by the Hy-Breasil Choir (composed of IRA veterans and led by Tommy Bevan as Count Thomond) in what was described as "a typical camp fire scene." Historical pageantry figures not only in the March of the Nation, but also in an episode entitled "Battle Eve of the Brigade," a "historical song-scena [sic] . . . based on Thomas Davis' stirring ballad written in tribute to the Irish Brigade in the French Army" (13). The program recalled that more than twenty thousand soldiers and officers who fought against William of Orange "sailed with Patrick Sarsfield to France. . . . What Irishman or woman to-day would not fervently echo the words of their first chief, gallant Patrick Sarsfield, dying on the stricken field of Landen in Flanders: 'Oh, that this was for Ireland!'" (15). "Battle Eve of the Brigade" reminded the audience that the pain of exile was far worse than the privations of wartime austerity or the inconvenience of the ban on foreign travel. Over the next four years, "Battle Eve of the Brigade" was the standard dramatic vignette performed in the Step Together pageants.

The "Army of To-day" performed Sokol exercise and a modern rifle drill followed by comic skits and chorus girls, transformed into the Royal Hussarettes. As the program notes, "We Irish never lost our morale or sense of humour no matter how grave the crisis confronting us. Even in the days gone by when we had to fight to the death for our liberties, the 'lilt of Irish laughter' was heard at least as often as the fierce skirl of the war pipes playing our men into action."[59] In the grand finale was a procession of the "Soldiers of Ireland: A Cavalcade of History" featuring the historical military men in the period costumes "loaned by Army Tattoo, General Committee," seen in the 1935 Military Tattoo.

The *Irish Times* called it a "brilliant production . . . [o]ne of the best presentations ever given by an Irish theatre"; the *Irish Press* noted that the Theatre Royal was "packed . . . to its utmost capacity" for a show "truly well done."[60] At the time, the combination of George Shiels's *The Rugged Path*, then entering a record-breaking and unprecedented seventh week at the Abbey, the O'Dea-O'Donovan Gaiety revels, and Frank O'Donovan's *The Show Goes On* prompted the *Sunday Independent* article "Theatres Make History in Dublin" for the record number of people attending Dublin theatres.[61] Were there any doubts about the appeal of scaling down the military tattoo and employing chorus

17. "Battle Eve of the Brigade." Step Together Scrapbook. Courtesy of the Military Archives of Ireland, Dublin.

girls and popular comedians in comic skits alongside the members of the Defence Forces, they were completely dispelled by the extension of *The Roll of the Drum* for first a second and then a third week's run. By the time it closed at the Theatre Royal and headed off to its runs in Cork and then Limerick, *The Roll of the Drum* had attracted audiences of more than 140,000 in Dublin, surpassing even the crowds of the wildly successful 1935 tattoo.

At Easter 1941, for the twenty-fifth anniversary of the Rising, Lorcan Bourke presented *The March of Freedom* twice daily at the Olympia Theatre in Dublin. The *Irish Times* reported, "Mr. Lorcan Burke assembled fifty artistes to carry out the historical scenes, the review was specially written by Peadar Kearney and Seamus de Burca."[62] Lorcan Bourke, his brother Seumas de Burca, and their uncle Peadar Kearney produced several patriotic pageants to mark the anniversaries of the Easter Rising. In 1937, with "the assistance of the Free State Army authorities," Kearney's *The March of Freedom* dramatized episodes from Irish history, including "the signing of the Treaty of Limerick, the death of Father Murphy at Oulard Hill [1798], the famine of 1847, and the surrender of the General Post Office in 1916."[63] Just before Easter in 1937, the Queen's presented "The Battle of Clontarf" on a program with the film *Texas Rangers*; on Easter Radio Athlone broadcast Niall C. Harrington's "Resurgence: Cavalcade of Easter Week" as a "radio pageant." The Easter 1941 show, billed as a "Cavalcade of Irish History," covered the period between 1690 and 1941 and was presented with the cooperation with the 26th Battalion. The presentation featured a performance by the army pipe band, which appeared in the massive parade on Easter and, like the tattoos and *The Roll of the Drum*, dramatized episodes from Irish history. At the Theatre Royal, *The Roll of the Drum* was followed by *Tramp, Tramp, Tramp*, "a stirring tribute to the Army in Eire," that opened in September 1942. Featuring, among others, Noel Purcell, *Tramp, Tramp, Tramp* was a musical comedy revue that shared the bill with the military film comedy *Hay Foot*, starring Noah Beery Jr., and was a far less elaborate production than *The Roll of the Drum*.

The next spring Louis Elliman of the Theatre Royal and Lorcan Bourke collaborated in presenting *Signal Fires*. Beiner notes that bonfires became a "popular act of commemoration [of 1798], reminiscent of the signal fires that had been lit on hills in Wexford to mark the outbreak of the Rebellion (26 May 1798)."[64] Opening at the Theatre Royal on Easter Sunday, April 25, 1943, *Signal Fires*, like *Tramp, Tramp, Tramp*, was a much shorter pageant performed with a Hollywood film and without chorus girls. The *Irish Times* described *Signal Fires* as "a pageant of Irish history in the making. . . . In graphic and dramatic fashion there is strung together a series of incidents in the various revolutionary movements from '98 to the present day."[65] Adapted from a script by actor Liam Redmond with additional dialogue by Dublin's resident script doctor, Dick Forbes, and historical costumes by Lorcan Bourke, *Signal Fires* was more like a commercial stage revue than a military tattoo. Performed by a core of versatile, professional actors, including Eddie Byrne, Gertrude Quinn, Michael Clarke (who played Pearse), and W. O'Gorman, supplemented by various military personnel and the No. 1 Army Band, the show relied more on dialogue than spectacle and ranged from 1867 through an "American Wake," the Easter Rising, the Frongoch Camp, and the Irish War of Independence to the present. At the outset, time is dissolved as "the camp fires recall the Signal Fires of long ago" as an Old Fenian and young soldier of 1943 discuss the Irish Army of today. The deliberate anachronism that brings soldiers from the mid-1800s and 1940s together creates a sense of a continuous past. Blending lighthearted treatment of fraught historical moments with a dreamy nostalgia, *Signal Fires* reaches for more human, more intimate bonds with the past through the camaraderie among soldiers. The first scene, "The Forge," sees soldiers preparing for the 1867 Rising: "Song and merriment cloaked the real purpose of the meetings of this secret army, but when their call to arms—the Signal Fires on the hills—came, we find a more resolute and grim body of men about to embark on another nightly escapade in the nations [*sic*] march of freedom." Another scene of "song and dance" blends with the sorrow of emigration in depicting an "American Wake." The first act ends with two scenes at the GPO where "we see the gallant little band of soldiers battling against overwhelming odds and fighting the catastrophic fire which is shown in all its terrifying splendour." The episode in Frongoch, for instance, dwells not on the defeat and imprisonment of the eighteen hundred Irish interned in the Welsh camp, but on their lively 1916 Christmas celebrations, complete with singing, dancing, and boxing. The "Last Ambush" touches on 1921 and the Irish War of Independence just before the finale: "Proudly we present them—the men of 1916 and after, standing on guard again, all differences forgotten. Side by side with the youth of the present generation, they are seen in this huge Finale Scene."[66] Not only does *Signal Fires* seek greater intimacy with the past, but it also acknowledges and aspires to overcome the bitter divisions from the Civil War. In 1916 the Frongoch Camp housed the insurgents, only later divided into the pro- and anti-Treaty factions, and in what "became a veritable political university and military academy."[67] Instead of a March of the Nation

18. *Signal Fires* program cover. Joseph Holloway Ephemera Collection. Courtesy of the National Library of Ireland.

reaching back to mythic and prehistoric times, *Signal Fires* focuses on a more recent, contentious past, one that earlier generations scrupulously avoided in the tattoos of 1927, 1929, and 1935. The time frame of the Irish historical pageants has become a moving wall pressing toward the present: whereas the 1927 tattoo was to reach back to an ancient past but proscribed everything after 1800, *Signal Fires* began in 1867 and moved right up to the present.

THE EMERGENCY II: STEP TOGETHER

The Step Together pageants drew heavily on the success of the Theatre Royal spectaculars but were modest affairs held in provincial venues, often as part of a military program that ran several days, as did National Defence Week in 1940. Step Together Weeks were held in July 1942 in Athlone, in September 1942 in Rathfarnham, in Bray and later Cavan in 1943, in Dun Laoghaire in July 1944. Perhaps typical was a Step Together Week held in 1942 when a "Step Together Revue" was performed three times in Mullingar on March 22, 23, and 24 and broadcast on radio as well. In conjunction with the GAA, the Defence Forces arranged for a variety of inexpensive entertainments: a hurling match between the army and LDF, a church parade, table quiz, tug-of-war, field and track events, and band performances. Performed at the County Hall in the evenings, the "Step Together Revue" featured vocal performances by Chrissie Manning and Philip Dore and a cast of forty in the performance of "Eve of the Battle," a version of the dramatic episode that appeared in *The Roll of the Drum.* Any profits from the events went to the Army and LDF Comforts Fund, "to provide the immediate necessities for the Defence Forces to make their lot a happier one."

The first historic episode, "Eve of the Battle," finds Irish exiles who joined the French army after the Treaty of Limerick singing of their longing for their native land and their joy at the prospect of avenging their defeat by Williamites. The program offered this summary:

Their singing inspires a Soldier of 1912. The commentary following the scene follows the Spirit of Freedom through the ages up to

19. Program cover from the 1942 Mullingar Step Together Week. Courtesy of the Military Archives of Ireland, Dublin.

1916, when the men of Easter week made their gesture and stamped upon their particular generation the clamorous demand for Ireland's release from bondage. The theme is carried into the war-worn days of 1921. The final commentary and Finale takes us to the Ireland of to-day through the early anxious years of our freedom up to the present tense moment of 1942 when Ireland, free and at peace, calls on her sons to guard that peace and that freedom, to "Step Together" in the grand Cause of her Protection.[68]

Surviving photographs in scrapbooks show the performers, accompanied by a small orchestra, against two drop cloths, a generic rural scene representing continental exile and another depicting the GPO.

A planning memorandum from Olaf McNeill set out very specific objectives for the Mullingar Step Together Week:

20. Rehearsal for the finale of a Step Together pageant. Step Together Scrapbook. Courtesy of the Military Archives of Ireland, Dublin.

[The] purpose is to (a) stimulate recruiting for Army and L.D.F. in the Area, (b) to make all classes, male and female realise that they have a duty to the State, and the fact that they cannot assist by being a member of the Defence Forces, does not exonerate them from performing that duty, as the various organisations such as the L.S.F. [Local Security Force], A.R.P. [Air Raid Precautions], Red Cross, and St. John Ambulance, and Army and L.D.F. Comforts Fund affords an opportunity for *everybody* to *do something* to help the defence of this country.[69]

The Step Together pageants targeted sectors of the population that were unlikely to have seen (and perhaps even to sympathize with) the tattoos and military stage shows. Not only were they often staged away from Dublin, but they also sought women volunteers as well as men.

THE MILITARY TATTOO (1945)

With the defeat of Germany and the end of World War II nearing, planning for another military spectacular was well under way. In his foreword to *The Illustrated Book of the Military Tattoo and Exhibition 1945*, the minister for defence, Oscar Traynor, writes, "I requested the Council of the Army Benevolent Fund to take upon themselves the responsibility of raising not less than £10,000 this year to meet the increased calls likely to be made on the resources of the Fund during the period following the demobilisation of the Defence Forces."[70] Indeed, in April 1945 that exact amount of the fund-raising goal was well publicized, as everything about the tattoo would be.[71] John P. Duggan indicates that the 1945 Military Tattoo celebrated the end of the Emergency,[72] but 1945 was also the centenary of the death of Thomas Davis, an occasion marked by public exhibitions, lectures, and meetings. The announcer's script for the tattoo and an article in Irish in the program of the 1945 tattoo also commemorated Davis. As frivolous as some components of the 1945 tattoo were, these commemorative acknowledgments struck somber patriotic notes that would reverberate through the 1966 commemorations of the Easter Rising.

The venues for the Military Exhibition and Tattoo as well as a gala Tattoo Ball were announced on February 12, 1945.[73] As in 1935, the Royal Dublin Society placed its grounds and premises in Ballsbridge at the disposal of the minister for defence without charge for the tattoo. The records of the finance subcommittee of the 1945 tattoo indicate that seed money, totaling £250, was collected from each of the four regional commands, plus £10 "from the Canteen Account (from a balance available from the last Tattoo)."[74] The financial arrangements were spelled out in detail and, in the case of transport at least, nearly "on the same terms as those given to the 1935 Tattoo Committee, viz., actual cost of petrol and oil, plus 1/2d per mile for depreciation of tyres, plus 10% Departmental charges."[75] When the Department of Finance charged the Department of Defence £114.1.10 for motorcycle replacement as a result of the "unusually heavy" use, which in 1945 included ramp jumping, stunt riding, and balancing a pyramid of nine men on a single moving motorcycle, the army argued that performing under these extreme conditions was just the sort of training they wanted the motorcyclists to have. The Department of Finance didn't buy it; in 1947 they were still arguing over the bill, but eventually the army reimbursed the Department of Finance.

By April 1945 the publicity committee was drip-feeding the press enticing details of events at the RDS. In addition to the tattoo, patrons could tour an elaborate military exposition at the RDS during the day. "Visitors will be encouraged to handle weapons, climb in and out of modern craft and armoured fighting vehicles." Children would be allowed to play in tank-like Bren gun carriers. By May 3, 1945, five days before VE day, illustrations based on "original drawings in small water colours . . . by Dr. Hayes McCoy who is responsible for their accuracy"[76] were passed on to Captain S. McNeill to reproduce as twenty-seven life-size illustrations of Irish military figures with historically accurate uniforms, weapons, and accoutrements, including Cúchulainn and the Red Branch knights (dated at the "Beginning of the Christian Era"); Fionn Mac Cumhaill (AD 200); Niall of the Nine Hostages; Brian Boru; Diarmuid MacMurrough; Art MacMurrough Kavanagh; Garrett More, the Earl of Kildare; Hugh O'Neill and Red

Hugh O'Donnell; Owen Roe O'Neill; Patrick Sarsfield; Irish Volunteers; United Irishmen; Young Irelanders; and Fenian Brotherhood (1867).[77] More recent uniforms were carefully researched, sourced as original or created as replicas, for display on mannequins at the RDS exhibition.

As festive and celebratory as the tattoos were, in 1945 there was a concerted effort to educate the Irish people about the Battle of Benburb, at which on June 5, 1646, Owen Roe O'Neill defeated Robert Monroe. On May 18, 1945, Commandant Niall Harrington forwarded copies of the "the Historical Pageant Script prepared by Major [Olaf] McNeill," brother of Major-General Hugo McNeill, for careful review by the historical subcommittee, chaired by Colonel A. T. Lawlor. Harrington, who was attached to the Military Archives in the mid-1930s and a frequent creator of radio programs on military subjects, broadcast *The Story of Benburb: A Documentary* on Radio Éireann in August 1945. Whereas earlier pageants asserted historical accuracy, the 1945 tattoo undertook vastly more sophisticated research that drew on scholars and military historians. In June 1945, for instance, Hayes-McCoy wrote Hugo McNeill an eight-page letter explaining the military salutes used through the centuries. In early June a team of four researchers, including Hayes-McCoy, visited the site of the Battle of Benburb and consulted with Mr. Patterson of the Armagh Museum. Workshops in the Clancy Barracks manufactured costumes, breastplates, helmets as well as muskets and ten thousand cartridges—their designs all vetted by Hayes-McCoy at the National Archives. By July 1945 the military tattoo pageant committee arranged for hundreds of eight- and twelve-foot pikes, scores of swords, numerous muskets, and sixty horses. Major Justin MacCarthy was cast to play Owen Roe O'Neill and Commandant J. Stack, of the Irish Jumping Team, to play General Monroe.

A month before the Tattoo Ball in 1945, the *Irish Times* reported a black market in tickets, which were sold out "many weeks ago." Journalists were invited to visit the barracks, view the preparations, and even participate in the commando training regime. Frank Jeffares reported that the "soldiers of the Benburb age also wore full armour—a suit of it faces you in Dr. Hayes McCoy's office. Army engineers and scrap metal are to-day coming together to produce 220 such suits. The Cromwellian-type helmet, technically a lobster-tailed burgonet, gives full head protection."[78] The next week "An Irishman's Diary" explained the source of the armor: "For some time armourers in a Dublin barracks have been breaking up the remnants of German planes that crash-landed upon the unyielding soil of the twenty-six counties during the late war."[79] Some of the tattoo's helmets were recast from tin ammunition boxes. Enticing photo opportunities of rehearsals paid off with regularity. Further details kept the coming tattoo in the public eye: the 16-mm army films made during the Emergency would be screened in a small cinema, there would be an arts and crafts exhibition, champion Irish horses like Ireland's Own were seconded to perform. Newspapers were not the only outlets cultivated for free publicity. Radio Éireann broadcast regular performances by various army bands and presentations by Hugo McNeill and other officers. In addition to the production of hundreds of historical costumes and weapons and the training and rehearsal of thousands of participants, organizers prepared inexpensive programs as well as a seventy-two-page souvenir program, whose cover pictured members of the contemporary Defence Forces in the shadow of Owen Roe O'Neill on his white charger. The illustrated program, which was made available while the tattoo was still running, included photographs of the 1935 tattoo and of rehearsals for the 1945 event as well as articles on military affairs. The Irish Travel Association ran an article in *Irish Travel*. Hoping to lure tattoo patrons, hotels, restaurants, and pubs mentioned the tattoo in their ads. Other companies took out ads in newspapers in support of the tattoo. Three stage shows in Dublin theatres capitalized on the tattoo's popularity: *Tattoo Topics* at the Olympia, *Irish Cavalcade* at the Queen's, and *Royal Brocade*, "where the dancers . . . give a revudeville [*sic*] version of the Sokol drill."[80]

National historical pageants such as the 1945 tattoo can be anodyne in seeking the widest approval, but "The Army of the People," an essay by J. B. O'Sullivan (author of *The Roll of the Drum*) is a notable exception in raising the question of the Defence Forces' role in the

21. *The Illustrated Book of the Military Tattoo and Exhibition* (1945). Papers of G. A. Hayes-McCoy, James Hardiman Library. Courtesy of the National University of Ireland Galway.

early years of the Free State: "That first Regular Army of ours [was] only the military machine of a political party, and for many a long year after the civil war the Defence Force of the Irish Free State continued to be, in the minds of half our population, the army of a political party"; only the third military tattoo in 1935 "following as it did a change in Government . . . proved that the armed forces of the State were above politics."[81] Here the attitude toward the recent past underwent revision, while the understanding of the mythic past had changed utterly: the 1945 tattoo souvenir record included a photo captioned "The Cuchullain of To-Day was Applauded on his Remote Control Motor Cycle" with the mythic Ulster warrior sporting helmet, goggles, and a mustache and brandishing an enormous spanner in a chariot drawn by two remote-controlled motorcycles rigged together.

The 1945 tattoo employed a now-proven formula. The massed army bands, "over 300 performers, the largest assembly of musicians ever to perform in Ireland under the baton of one conductor,"[82] played stirring melodies. Cavalry units displayed motorcycle trick riding and jumping; precision Sokol calisthenics were performed by 600 men, "not professional soldiers," but members of the Dublin Battalions of the Local Defence Force, "ordinary citizens in civilian occupations," who, the program twice mentioned, trained "in their spare time" (38, 41). Demonstrations of battle training and ceremonial infantry drill brought thousands of soldiers onto the field. The historical pageant and reenactment of the Battle of Benburb came next, followed by "illuminated figure marching," and the Grand Finale—the March of the Armies. The final "reveal" was the massed forces: "When the Flag has been lowered the arena is lit up and the public sees for the first time the entire cast of the Tattoo—numbering some 3,000 performers" (43). Despite the fact that Benburb is in Country Tyrone, the choice of the Battle of Benburb as the focus for the historical pageant seemed apposite: the tercentenary of the battle was approaching, and Owen Roe O'Neill was a well-known military hero celebrated in song and ballad. But the *Irish Press* summed up the most obvious attraction: "We have all too often staged historical pageants of battles which we lost. The point about Benburb is that, for a change, we won it."[83]

A single announcer narrated the Benburb pageant. The first scene opens in the Irish camp with "no proper order . . . [in a] general atmosphere of 'desolation and despair'" (39), the later phrase attributed to J. F. Taylor's 1896 study, *Owen Roe O'Neill.* O'Neill "and his trained staff at once set to work to transform the raw Irish levies into a disciplined trained army . . . [using] the newest weapons of the time . . . the fearsome 18 foot pike of the unbeaten Spanish Infantry . . . [and] the musket. Above all O'Neill instills into his men the spirit and supreme value of discipline" (39). With his Spanish allies, O'Neill leads the Irish force against General Robert Monroe, the "sturdy veteran of the 30 years war, greatest general of the invading forces [who is determined to] break into Leinster and bring the war to a conclusion and the Confederacy to disruption and collapse." After O'Neill's training, "the Irish army, trained, equipped, confident—stand ready. And at their head, mounted on his white horse in his gorgeous uniform of Spain rides Owen Roe O'Neill, surrounded by his Staff, bearing his army colours of Green with a Gold Harp, and carrying into battle too, not for the first nor the last time his personal standard the Red Hand of Ulster."[84] The Irish forces, marshaling 180 Irish pikemen, 100 Irish musketeers, 31 McDonald Highlanders, 31 Creaghts, 30 cavalry, and 3 officers (whose plumes and sashes were provided by Mssrs. Bourke), were ready to defeat Monroe's army. Whereas *The Roll of the Drum* affirmed Ireland's commitment to peace, the 1945 tattoo celebrated a rare but brilliant military victory.

The finale offered another March of the Nation. The Announcer's script for the "Grand Finale":

> The Finale opens with the "March of the Armies"—a Pageant of Two Thousand Years of Irish Military Tradition. In the first group we have the Fighting Forces of the Ancient Gael . . . An Craobh Ruadh, the Red Branch Knights of Ulster, led by the Great Cuchulainn himself in his War Chariot . . . Next the Fianna Eireann of the Second Century, Ireland's first Regular Army, with their renowned high-Fheinnidhe, Fionn Mac Cumhail at their head . . . Then the

Army of Clontarf under their famous warrior—King Brian Boru. . . .
In the second group march the Armies of the Conquest. They are
headed by Art MacMurrough Kavanagh and his Leinster Clansmen. . . . Next we see the Standards of the Ulster Princes, O'Neill
of Tyrone and O'Donnell of Tirconnail. . . . And now come the
soldiers of Benburb, worthy representatives of the War of the Confederacy. . . . The Boyne and Aughrim, Athlone and Limerick are
recalled by the Jacobite Army represented by a troop of Sarsfield's
famous Dragoons, led by the great Cavalry leader and his dauntless
henceman [sic], "Galloping Hogan" the Rapporee [sic]. . . . Now we
come to the Era of the Secret Armies. . . . First we have the United
Irishmen of 1798. . . . Next the Irish Republican Brotherhood-the
Fenians of 1867. . . . Then the most potent and successful of all
the Irish Republican Army. . . . See them march past wearing the
uniforms they wore twenty-five years ago; the Irish Volunteers, the
Citizen Army, the boys of Na Fianna Eireann and the girl soldiers
of Cumann na mBan. . . . This cavalcade of the past is brought to
a close with the entry of the inheritors of this Twenty Centuries of
proud Tradition-the Defence Forces of To-Day.[85]

Earlier in the century, the March of the Nation dwelt on mythic heroes and waves of Viking, Danish, and Norman invaders and culminated before the end of the eighteenth century. By 1945 the tattoo
eagerly celebrated republican ancestors of the late eighteenth, nineteenth, and early twentieth centuries as the conduit to the ancient
past. Like the Gaelic League Language Procession in 1907, the 1945
March of the Nation constructed the Irish past with no distinction
between the mythic and the historic. All the better to construct the
recent past in mythic dimensions.

Surviving footage of the 1945 Military Exhibition and Tattoo in
the Military Archives shows President Seán T. O'Ceallaigh's visit to
the RDS, where the life-size renderings of historical uniforms are displayed on the walls. Huge crowds view the antiaircraft guns, arma-
ment exhibits, and a massive scale model of the Battle of Benburb.
Very young boys swarm over military vehicles and weapons. The film

22. Cartoon from *Dublin Opinion*, September 1945. Courtesy of Katy O'Kennedy for the estate of Niel O'Kennedy (1923–2010).

coverage of the tattoo itself records a daytime rehearsal without an audience present and captures little of the drama on show, but documents thousands of participants in colorful uniforms.[86]

The 1945 tattoo, coming after years of economic privation, isolationism, and war and less than a month after atomic bombs were dropped on Hiroshima and Nagasaki, was even more popular than previous tattoos. Treating the tattoo as an occasion of state, the president arrived in evening dress in an open carriage. "First came the massed bands, 360 strong, marching ten deep, a solid block of instrumentalists, dressed in the saffron kilt, in the ordinary green Army uniform, and in the ceremonial blue uniform," then battle training, and "a lecture from the announcer on modern assault tactics. . . . And the strong point a most realistic house, was most realistically blown sky-high."[87] Without a trace of irony, the humor magazine *Dublin Opinion* wrote: "The show of shows at the moment in Dublin is the *Military Tattoo*. The Army has staged a brilliant varied and exciting show. Prodigious pains and prodigious rehearsing must have gone to its making. It is spectacular, ingenious and thrilling, and it bears the hallmarks of hard work and imagination."[88] Like its predecessors, the tattoo was secular, especially in comparison with an openly confessional event like the Eucharistic Congress. Its religious dimension was confined to O'Neill's rising in his stirrups to exhort his Irish troops: "Now you have arms in your hands as good as they have! So, let manhood be seen by the push of the pike. Your word is Sancta Maria, and so, in the name of the Father, Son and Holy Ghost, advance and give not fire till you are within pike-length."[89]

The run of the tattoo was not without incident. On September 5 the *Irish Times* reported that Jimmy Corbett, one of the motorcycle stuntmen who "finishes a bottle of stout while standing erect on the saddle of his machine[,] was thrown to the ground by the crash, but he held on to the glass containing the stout, which he succeeded in finishing before he lost consciousness" and was transported to St. Briein's military hospital; three days later the *Times Pictorial* ran a photo of Trooper Corbett standing on his motorcycle. De Valera got into hot water over his attendance at the Tattoo Ball and was threatened with expulsion from the Gaelic League, but in late October the league lifted its long-standing ban on attending foreign dances so that it would not have to expel the taoiseach. On June 2 members of the United Pacifist Council of Ireland wrote to the *Irish Times* complaining about the militarism on display at the tattoo; the group sold, apparently with some success, copies of *Peace News* to people queuing for admission. Even the lengthy lines themselves were the subject of extensive press coverage. The total attendance at the Military Exhibition and Tattoo, 418,718 (218,778 at the exhibition and 199,940 at the tattoo), represents a significant portion of the population of Greater Dublin (not just the city), which in 1946 was 827,725.

The strength of popular support for the tattoo helped the minister of defence, Oscar Traynor, respond to questions in the Dáil Debates seven months after the 1945 tattoo:

In the exhibitions the public were given an intelligent insight into the weapons, machinery and instruments which must be known, mastered and handled by a modern Army and, in the tattoos, they were given an idea of the training and tactics employed and of the use in warfare of the various weapons. The hundreds of thousands of people who attended the exhibitions and tattoos had an opportunity of judging for themselves the pitch of efficiency which the Defence Forces attained during the Emergency and I feel there can have been nobody who did not bring away with him a feeling of appreciation and pride.[90]

Although the tattoo raised considerable revenue and attracted vast crowds, it was the last time the army took responsibility for a national pageant.

After the end of World War II, Carrickfergus hosted at least three pageants billed as *The Landing of William*. Press accounts report a modest affair in 1946, a lavish spectacle in 1947, and a "happy medium" struck in 1948.[91] That year King William, played all three years by Br. Hugh McAteer (the title "Brother" indicative of his status in the Black Preceptory), arrived in a "flower-bedecked barge" in the Carrickfergus harbor where a twenty-one-gun salute, the mayor, town clerk, and other officials welcomed him.[92] Although the pageant was a single formalized symbolic episode with few, perhaps only one, historical character, the *Belfast Telegraph* compared it with its better-known counterpart, the Sham Fight of the Battle of Scarva. Celebrated annually on July 13 (unless that date falls on a Sunday, in which case it takes place on July 14), the Battle of Scarva is one of few loyalist public spectacles that can be described as a historical pageant. Closely allied to the Sham Fight are the elaborate banners that depict historical scenes from 1688–91 whose "emphasis is on [King] William, the man, and his relationship with Ulster, rather than on the battle fought. . . . [The banners] do not recount history so much as illustrate the relationship of King Billy to the Ulster Protestant people."[93] Belinda Loftus documents the preeminence of King William III in loyalist banners and parades in *Mirrors: William III and Mother Ireland*, which includes photographs of the Battle of Scarva and the personation of William

III in a 1975 parade in Holywood, County Down.[94] More prominent, of course, is the well-documented unionist parading tradition.[95]

The annual Battle of Scarva begins as musical contingents, more often silver flutes and as opposed to the "blood and thunder" marching bands associated with July 12, progress down a narrow lane to Scarva House, where a handful of men perform a symbolic reenactment recalling "four Williamite Irish battles: the battles of Derry, Enniskillen, Aughrim and the Boyne."[96] In 1937 *The Bell* published "The Battle of Scarva," H. L. Morrow's account of his visit to the pageant. One man on horseback, King William, Morrow wrote, "wore a cocked hat, a blue tunic with gold lace and a broad orange sash. . . . He carried a sword in one hand and an orange-coloured flag in the other . . . followed by ten or fifteen men in some sort of rough-and-ready fancy-dress clothes, and carrying rook-rifles on their shoulders." His opponent, King James, met with hearty booing from a crowd that numbered in the thousands, "mostly women and children in their white summer clothes, sprawling on the ground, with parcels of cut-cake and sandwiches," and was in an identical cocked hat, but with "a green flag and a tunic that had at one time or another unmistakably belonged to a 'B' Special. . . . In just under fourteen minutes from the start, the famous Sham-Fight—Derry, Aughrim, Enniskillen and the Boyne—was fought and finished."[97] Morrow's account accords with Ruth Dudley Edwards's description of the pageant as performed sixty years later: "King William and his main henchman, General Schomberg on the one hand, and King James and General Patrick Sarsfield on the other, appear on horseback to thunderous applause followed by motley footsoldiers more or less dressed for the part. After riding around for a while, the kings and generals, still on horseback, fight each other with swords, while their followers use swords, pistols with blanks or just generally tussle."[98] When the green flag of King James is finally shot to ribbons, the episode has reached its end. In 2000 Bryan wrote that at Scarva, "the whole event has a relaxed but 'respectable' atmosphere." Videos posted on YouTube confirm Bryan's estimate that more recently, "the whole performance lasts no more than about 5 minutes."[99] The event may have remained largely stable over the

past century. In *Thompson in Tir-na-n-Og* (1912), Gerard MacNamara
has his title character, a Scarva native, Andy Thompson, describe the
Sham Fight: "We have one [battle] every 13th of July. Ach, it's a great
sight. They come from all arts and parts to see the show. Excursion
trains from Derry and Belfast. The papers used to make fun of us. Ach,
but times is changed, for now the *News Letter* calls it a 'pageant.'"[100]

In the South the pageants staged after the 1945 Military Tattoo
and before the Tóstal were much more modest affairs. In July 1947
the *Nenagh Guardian* reported a "Colourful Procession at the Dun
Drom Feis" that included "a portrayal of the soldiers of Ireland adown
the ages."[101] Captain John Dowling of the Defence Forces successfully organized the Tara Memorial Ceremonies and Pageant, held in
Navan on October 2 and 3, 1948, to commemorate the 150th anniversary of the 1798 rising and the Owen Roe O'Neill Tercentenary in
1949. Both of these pageants marshaled supernumeraries from local
GAA clubs, dramatic societies, and the Fórsa Cosanta Áitiúil (FCA,
the army reserve). Guy Beiner observes "a significant change" in the
commemorative practices surrounding the 150th anniversary of the
1798 rising: "With government officials endorsing commemoration
of Ninety-Eight . . . mainstream commemoration lost its oppositional
edge." Whereas many sesquicentenary events centered on statues or
monuments connected to the 1789 rising, the celebrations in Castlebar on August 1, 1948, also included a reenactment of the Battle of
Castlebar and "military pageant."[102] On October 10, 1948, a pageant
in Buncrana commemorated the Battle of Lough Swilly. The biggest sesquicentenary events were in Dublin, where the Gaelic League
organized a series of lectures, meetings, and civic events. The Dublin
historical parade represented Dublin in 1798 (including Wolfe Tone,
Lord Edward Fitzgerald, and Mollie Weston), Dublin and the IRA
in 1916–21 (including the Dublin Brigade, the Irish Volunteers, the
Irish Citizen Army, the Fianna Éireann, and the Cumann na mBan),
and "Dublin of Yesterday and To-Day." The week concluded with the
1798 Commemorative Concert at the Olympia Theatre, where Maire
nic Shiubhlaigh made one of her last stage appearances, here in Lady
Gregory's *Gaol Gate*.

Other small-scale pageants continued to appear. In 1950 a scaled-back tattoo with motorcycle riders, massed calisthenics and gymnastics, a demonstration of army training exercises, a *feu de joie*, and fireworks honored the tercentenary of the Siege of Clonmel. As in the 1929 *Grand Military Tattoo*, a "Historical Item" presented a reenactment of the Siege of Clonmel, "an effort . . . to reproduce, within the limits of available space, a few of the historical highlights of the famous siege . . . [and] a complete Pageant of Irish Military Forces from the dawn of the Christian era down to our own times."[103] A Clonmel paper published a *Siege of Clonmel Commemoration: Tercentenary Souvenir Record*. Similarly, the *Leader* (Limerick) published the *Tercentenary of the Siege of Limerick Souvenir Book* in 1951.

The army, specifically "the men of the Eastern Command of the Defence Forces,"[104] also facilitated the 1947 staging of a pageant, *The Common People (An Gnath Phobal)*, on the grounds of Trinity College Dublin. On the occasion of the 50th Oireachtas of the Gaelic League, *The Common People* was held in conjunction with the Pan-Celtic Congress, whose delegates came from Brittany, Wales, Cornwall, Isle of Man, Scotland, India, England, and Africa and that first formally met at the National Eisteddfod in Birkenhead in 1917. With a cast of two thousand sporting five thousand costume items, *The Common People* was performed in Trinity College Park. Translated into Irish by Aindrias O Muimhneachain and directed by John Stephenson, the pageant was written by Hayes-McCoy. Some photographic images of *The Common People*, along with a program containing a scene-by-scene summary, survive in the Hayes-McCoy Papers. Lieutenant Tomas O Faolain, who wrote for the *Dublin Evening Press* as Terry O'Sullivan, worked for the Irish Tourist Association, and was the father of writer and journalist Nuala O'Faolain, is credited as the "chief announcer."

Located well within recorded history rather than evoking a mythic past, *The Common People* begins with a prologue depicting the "Golden Age of Civilisation in Ireland, when Brian Boru, having vanquished the Scandinavian invaders and firmly established native rule, reconvened the Fair of Tailteann, the Oireachtas of 1007." Dalcassian warriors on horseback stand guard over the fair; Boru himself arrives on a white charger. As *The Common People* moves through "the collapse of the Confederacy and the coming of Cromwell in the period 1649 to 1652," with the defeat of "the last remnants of the old Gaelic order . . . it remains for the 'Gnath Phobal' to preserve both their civilization and culture." In covering the next three centuries, the pageant touches on the Repeal movement, the Famine, the Young Irelanders, the 1916 Rising, and the guerrilla warfare of 1921, but also represents the New Ireland with personnel from Aer Lingus and CIÉ (Córas Iompair Éireann, the public transport body): "Symbols of the new Ireland are everywhere, interwoven in the traditions and spirit of the past."[105] The *Irish Press* praised the inclusion of "pilots, air hostesses, bricklayers, carpenters and uniformed C.I.E. men. The evolution of the citizen is complete."[106]

The pageant was among the first to acknowledge phases of Irish history as troubling as the Famine. *The Common People* shows no shortage of great men—Brian Boru, Daniel O'Connell, et al.-but it also looks beyond them to more ordinary citizens, even if the common people depicted were all employees of state or semistate agencies. Like so many earlier pageants, a chronological format elides centuries, but in comparison with earlier pageant narratives, *The Common People* is more forthcoming about not only the recent past, but also the sorrows of Irish history.

These anniversaries and tercentenaries anticipate the increasingly commemorative focus of historical pageantry in the second half of the twentieth century. The Defence Forces would support other pageants in conjunction with the Gaelic League and local organizations, but the entertainment mission of the army, like the army itself, contracted after 1945. Historical pageantry, however, followed Hugo McNeill to the Tóstal.

4

The Tóstals

In the summer of 1951, the Festival of Britain, marketed as "the auto-biography of a nation," celebrated the one hundredth anniversary of the Great Exhibition; by early the next year, news of a "proposed Festival of Dublin in 1953" appeared in the Irish dailies.[1] What became the Tóstal was only one element in a paradigmatic shift in Ireland's tourism policy and cultural agenda in the early 1950s. Recognizing the importance of international tourism as an industry, the Inter-Party coalition that came to power in early 1948 under John Costello looked to theatre, the Abbey in particular, to attract foreign visitors to Ireland. In 1949 the Cultural Relations Committee of Ireland, operating in the Department for External Affairs, produced a series of short, informative paperback books, Saol agus Cultúr in Éirinn (Life and Culture in Ireland), designed "to give a broad, vivid, and informed survey of Irish life and culture."[2] The next year Seán Mac-Bride founded the Irish News Service. In 1951 the Republic of Ireland established the Arts Council (An Chomhairle Ealaíon), the first National Fleadh for traditional music was held in Mullingar, Liam Miller founded the Dolmen Press; Comhaltas Ceoltóirí Éireann was established to promote Irish music, song, dance, and language. Even after the 1951 election returned de Valera and Fianna Fáil to power, organizational infrastructures to support the arts continued to appear: Bord Fáilte, charged with developing tourist accommodations, ameni-ties, and facilities, was created on July 3, 1952; Gael-Linn debuted that same year. Cork held its first International Choral and Folk Dance Festival in 1953. These agencies and events all sought to project a positive, progressive image of Ireland, particularly in the arts, and to attract foreign visitors. Most important, they all mark a departure from the isolationism that prevailed in Ireland before and during the Emergency and that characterized de Valera's tenure as taoiseach in the 1930s and '40s. As a tourist initiative, the Tóstal took responsibility for national historical pageants in the midfifties.

Having accepted loans from the Marshall Fund that would be repaid in US dollars, Seán Lemass, appointed minister for industry and commerce when Fianna Fáil returned to power in 1951, saw the possibility that tourism might become "a cornerstone of the national economy."[3] Transatlantic air travel was now a reality, but Ireland faced two serious impediments to foreign, especially North American, tourism: the paucity of attractive accommodations and amenities, especially outside of Dublin, and the brevity of the tourist season. As Irene Furlong observes, Lemass framed government policy on international tourism, which demanded improvements in transport, dining, and cultural facilities as well as the expansion of suitable accommodations, not only as addressing the expectations of foreign visitors, but as raising the standard of living for ordinary Irish people.[4] Terence Brown's observation of the period suggests a larger context for Lemass's policies and for the genesis of the Tóstal: "The 1950s were troubled by crises in the balance of payments, in 1951 and 1955, owing to fluctuations in the conditions of external trade which, together with the continuing exodus of emigration, were widely felt to reflect an Irish stagnation that was increasingly unacceptable."[5] Although state funds were not specifically appropriated to the first Tóstal, statutory bodies like the CIÉ and the Irish Tourist Board, civil servants in government departments as various as Posts and Telegraphs and Defence all made indispensable contributions. Now retired, Major-General Hugo McNeill, having won praise for the 1945 tattoo, oversaw the first Tóstals. Especially in its early years, the Tóstal, billed as "Ireland at Home," was conceived as nationwide and decentralized; local councils throughout the country were encouraged to plan festive events.

One of the many Irish cultural enterprises that had its origins in the 1950s, the Tóstal sought to extend the tourist season since, as the *Irish Times* noted in 1958, "the primary function of An Tóstal has been, and is, to attract visitors to Ireland."[6] The first Tóstal, held for three weeks between the fifth and the twenty-sixth of April 1953, featured spectacles with a strong patriotic flavor, a model sustained in 1954, when the Tóstal again coincided with Easter. As such the first two Tóstals imbricated the religious observance of Easter, the commemoration of the Easter Rising, the coming of spring, and the cultural agenda of the state. J. P. O'Brien, chairman of Fogra Fáilte, the agency charged with publicizing the work of the Irish Tourist Board and the Irish Tourist Association,[7] hoped that "An Tóstal will establish itself not merely as a major target for tourist traffic, but as a rallying point for Ireland's exiled children from all parts of the earth."[8] Luring the descendants of the diaspora back to Ireland had been an ambition since the Irish Race Congress in 1922, if not before. In the Tóstal's second year, for instance, President O'Kelly described it as "a period of national reunion and celebration. Once again Ireland was at home to her many exiles and friends."[9]

The growing isolationism after the 1932 Eucharistic Congress, the implementation of Fianna Fáil's economic protectionist policies, and severe restrictions on foreign travel during the Emergency brought about an inward turn toward domestic audiences in the pageantry of the 1940s. Fogra Fáilte's prospectus for the first Tóstal highlighted "pageants and parades" among its attractions: "Foreigners for a long time have labored under the illusion that Ireland is a sad, mournful country, inhabited by a sad, mournful people. This impression is false and has no true application to the real Ireland, either to the Ireland of the past or to the Ireland of the present."[10] Despite Eric Bentley's observation that a visitor to the Abbey Theatre in 1952 "feels himself the victim of a hoax, a gigantic hoax that has been written into the history books and engraved on the general mind,"[11] Tóstal planners recognized the potential of Irish theatre to attract international tourists, although the Dublin Theatre Festival did not emerge until 1958. In the early 1950s, however, with Dublin's most famous theatre gutted by fire in 1952 and the Abbey in temporary residence at the Queen's, the Tóstal looked to historical and mythological pageantry as theatrical attractions. The labor-intensive technology of these pageants drew thousands of nonprofessionals into performances of Ireland's heritage and attracted hundreds of thousands of spectators.

From the outset some saw the Tóstal as an opportunity to tap national resources. On April 4, 1952, the Arts Council submitted to the minister for industry and commerce wildly ambitious plans for the development of the cultural infrastructure: "one Theatre to be built within two years i.e. the Abbey" (not realized until 1966) and "a proper concert hall . . . in Iveagh Gardens" (not realized until 1981) as well as an open-air folklore museum, an extension of the National Museum, and a series of historic monuments, initially in timber to be replaced by marble or stone, in St. Stephen's Green.[12] In the face of such massive, expensive proposals, all centered in Dublin, the first Tóstal encouraged local councils to plan events best suited to existing resources. One problem was that some local councils were not accustomed to such advanced planning, so national promotional materials did not include all local events. In Dundalk, for instance, the 1953 historical pageant was not presented until more than two weeks after the official Tóstal program ended. Principally a pageant of local history, the Dundalk pageant anticipated Mac Anna's pageant in the 1966 commemoration. During the first Tóstal, Dublin's Gaelic League sponsored a single performance of a historical pageant covering "the period from the Battle of Clontarf in 1014 to Easter Week, 1916," in the Phoenix Park on April 19, 1953;[13] another two historical pageants were performed in Waterford.[14]

Back on January 19, 1953, a group of seasoned professionals, including Louis Elliman and Lieutenant Colonel T. Gunn, met with G. A. Hayes-McCoy, then still at the National Museum of Ireland, to plan a stage presentation for the first Tóstal. *Trumpet Call* was a music-hall show in twelve scenes sponsored by the Department of Defence that featured Theatre Royal regulars who had appeared in the Defence Forces stage shows during the Emergency: Jack Cruise, Noel Purcell, chorus girls (now "the Royalettes"), and Eddie Byrne. About a third of *Trumpet Call*'s scenes were patriotic ballads (performed by the massed army bands and singers), musical interludes, or physical stunt work; another third were comic skits by members of the Theatre Royal professional acting ensemble. The remaining third were historical vignettes scripted by Hayes-McCoy, although the program credits him only as a historical adviser. Influenced less by Brechtian theory than by the need to relate one thousand years of Irish history using only fifteen professional singers and actors, Hayes-McCoy's presentational histories relied on narration supplemented by relatively short set speeches by historical characters. The seventh scene, "One Thousand Years a' Growin'," was a pastiche of the Irish struggle to wrest independence from the British. Speaking in the timeless voice of authority, the Spirit of the Liffey (Eddie Byrne) narrated the historical scenes, much as did the narrator in *Signal Fires*. In four brief dramatic vignettes, featuring Silken Thomas (1534), "Red Hugh's Escape" (1592), "After the Boyne" (1688), and John Mitchel (1848), *Trumpet Call* celebrates the resolute Irish against the fickle British, sometimes with humor. Defeated at the Battle of the Boyne, King James is an object of ridicule given only a single line: an agitated James rushes onstage to report, "It came to a fight at the Boyne, but it grieves me to say that your countrymen have run away," to which Lady Tyrconnell replies, "Well, Sire, I see that your Majesty has won the race" (5/3).[15] Through the ages, Irishmen endure the perfidy of Albion. They suffer and sometimes die for the sake of Ireland in anticipation of the freedom the present-day audience enjoys. As in *The Common People*, Hayes-McCoy offered an inclusive understanding of the Irish: in a scene of feasting and conviviality, the lord mayor of Dublin welcomes "Danes, merchants, sea-adventurers, . . . Norman knights, . . . city guildmen, soldiers, merchants' wives" (5/1).

The last lines spoken by the timeless Spirit of the Liffey appeal to the audience's patriotism:

> And on one Easter Monday thirty-seven years ago Dublin kept that promise. . . . Thus was Mitchel's pledge redeemed. I am the Voice of the Spirit of the Liffey. I am the spirit of Dublin—Dublin of the Dane and Norman and Irishman—and I can foretell for Dublin's future nothing but what you can make of Dublin's past. A thousand years lies behind you. That is *your* pledge. Will you honour it? When

the call goes up in the name of Ireland will you—remembering the dead—will you too cry "Promise for me! Promise for me!" (5–6)

Like so many pageants, *Trumpet Call* ended with communal singing—in this instance of "A Nation Once Again."

Trumpet Call was much closer to the military shows at the Theatre Royal in the 1940s than to Hayes-McCoy's more pacific Gaelic League pageant, *The Common People*. Like the Emergency stage shows, it was more a recruiting vehicle for the Defence Forces than an attraction for Tóstal tourists. A lighthearted vaudeville show that incorporated historical vignettes filled with nationalist pieties, *Trumpet Call* received scant press coverage. The *Irish Independent*, for instance, wrote, "Something of the tragedy of Ireland's history and the glory of her recent past is conveyed by tableaux, pageantry, mime and music. At times, mime and tableau tend to be over-weighted with symbolism; but in general it is history without tears."[16] History without tears was what historical pageantry did best.

The first Tóstal was hardly without problems, first among them the ludicrously undersized "Bowl of Light," what "Myles na Gopaleen called . . . The Tomb of the Unknown Gurrier,"[17] that attracted derision and hooliganism. The British tabloids had a field day. London's *Daily Mirror* ran an unflattering photograph of Hugo McNeill with a malicious caption and gleefully mocked all of the Tóstal's shortcomings.[18] In Ireland there was criticism as well: the Royal Hibernian Academy unanimously passed a resolution calling for the removal of the unimpressive Bowl of Light. Worse, as Furlong notes, the overall figures for foreign tourism dropped in 1953.[19] J. P. O'Brien, chairman of Fogra Fáilte, however, argued that "in spite of the hooligans, heartachers and humbugs" and even if the Bowl of Light was a "tawdry contraption," the Tóstal was still a worthy undertaking. He urged people to start working "now for a more magnificent Tóstal in 1954."[20]

After the first Tóstal, pageants must have seemed an especially attractive option. A national pageant could be administered and overseen by Hugo McNeill himself. *Trumpet Call*, like the 1935 and 1945 Military Tattoos, had proved profitable, not least because military personnel were seconded as supernumeraries. Because admission was charged, rowdyism could more easily be controlled. Costs could be effectively managed. Moreover, even if potential visitors from overseas did not know what a Tóstal was, they knew what a pageant was. And Hugo McNeill knew someone who could write one.

THE PAGEANT OF ST. PATRICK (1954)

In its second year, 1954, the Tóstal began on April 17 and 18, Holy Saturday and Easter Sunday. By again involving local authorities as widely as possible, organizers hoped that events throughout the country would attract visitors to and beyond Dublin. The National Spring Clean Campaign, which morphed into the Tidy Towns initiative in 1958, promoted civic pride and practical improvements in towns throughout the country. The *Irish Times* editorialized that the Tóstal aimed "to enhance our people's pride in their own country—particularly, in its appearance."[21] Regional pageants, a popular component in the provincial programs in 1953, were held in Athenry, Bray, Wicklow ("Wicklow through the Ages"),[22] and Arklow, Aughrim, Belmont, Dundalk, Galway, Kilkenny, Kilcullen, Kildare, and Waterford in 1954. Donegal and Killarney held "rallies of the clans" for the Donegal and O'Donoghue clans, respectively. Two episodes of the Killarney rally of the O'Donoghue clan, "The Return from Limerick" and "The Chieftains of Lough Lein," figure in Colm O Laoghaire's newsreel *Ireland in Spring*, made for the Irish Edition of Universal News. Narration of the newsreel describes the men on horseback in a "victorious return to Glenflesk from the Siege of Limerick." Another episode from the Killarney pageant, according to the newsreel narration, revived "an ancient ceremony" in which "the present head of the clans is to receive the homage of his chiefs," demonstrated by "breaking their wands or staffs before him."[23] Dundalk again staged its own historical pageant, a "War of Independence Pageant."[24] The most elaborate pageant staged by a local authority in 1954 was Waterford's tribute to native son Thomas Francis Meagher. In twenty-two scenes, a cast of seventy outlined Meagher's career in both Ireland and the United

States. To advance overseas tourism, a color guard from the Fighting 69th, the 165th Infantry Regiment of the New York Irish, was invited to participate.[25]

In Dublin the opening parade for the second Tóstal included three central elements: a parade of the Defence Forces, the march of the thirty-two counties, and the festival of flowers featuring "30 floats representing Irish industrial firms."[26] Newsreel narration produced by Universal News–Irish Edition describes the opening parade as a "young nation marching towards its day of golden fulfillment."[27] Organized by the Dublin City Committee of the Gaelic League, the march of the thirty-two counties, grouped as the four provinces, personated figures associated with each county. "Leading each provincial contingent was a mythical princess in a horse-drawn chariot, preceded by a standard-bearer, and escorted by warriors dressed in traditional costumes."[28] Newsreel footage shows a modest procession with fewer than twenty people dressed in period costumes representing each province's contingent. Although diasporic observers might have been hard-pressed to identify them all, the Irishmen and -women personated on Dublin's streets that day offered an unfettered inclusivity ranging across the millennia and over both fact and fiction: Louth sent Cúchulainn along with Father Lorcan Murray; Antrim was represented by Muircheartach of the Leather Cloaks, Henry Joy McCracken, Roger Casement, and Eoin MacNeill; in Sligo's contingent Diarmuid O Duibhne ("hero of the romantic Fianna saga of Diarmuid and Grainne") marched next to Constance, Countess Markievicz, and the trad fiddler Michael Coleman. Representing all thirty-two counties (and all four provinces) in the parade was less political in 1954 than it would become in later decades;[29] before 1969 several Irish historical pageants, notably ones by Bryan MacMahon, represented all thirty-two counties.

In July 1953, shortly after the first Tóstal, a committee for a 1954 national pageant was already constituted and planning the centerpiece of the 1954 Tóstal: a national pageant, *The Pageant of St. Patrick*. It would be performed in three episodes over two days, April 12 and 13, Holy Saturday and Easter Sunday, at three locations described in the *Irish Press* as "the first bridgeheads of the Catholic faith [in Ireland]":[30]

Drogheda, Slane, and Tara. Hugo McNeill brought to the Patrician pageant not only immense organizational skills, but also assumptions that he could access the same resources under the same terms that created the military spectacles in the 1940s. He soon found himself ensnared in contending power structures. The Tara Central Committee wanted Bord Fáilte to indemnify local authorities and the committee members personally against any and all possible losses. The parish priest chairing the Tara Central Committee, Father G. Cooney, hoped that the pageant "can in time develop into an Irish Oberammergau of world-wide fame." Drogheda wanted its share of the pageant to represent its local history. Some delegates saw the pageant as a cash cow, a chance "of getting some money out of the Government."[31] The Department of Defence initially waffled at McNeill's requests for army musicians and the gratis cooperation of FCA units in the Boyne area for the 1954 pageant. McNeill, however, kept the focus on a single Patrician theme; the army units eventually (and indispensably) did cooperate.

It was not inevitable that Hayes-McCoy would write the national Patrician pageant for the 1954 Tóstal. Father Cooney suggested Micheál macLíammóir, the only person in Ireland whose record for creating historical pageantry surpassed Hayes-McCoy's, but Hayes-McCoy's academic credentials and extensive experience in working with McNeill prevailed. Throughout his careers, first at the National Museum and then University College Galway, Hayes-McCoy demonstrated an abiding commitment to popularizing Irish history. Not only did he create pageants, but he also wrote children's radio programs and historical series for newspapers; he participated in the Thomas Davis lectures broadcast on Radio Éireann and the Teilifís Éireann documentary series on Irish battles. In the 1945 Military Tattoo, he demonstrated his ability to collaborate with the Defence Forces. A talented draftsman with an acute visual sense, Hayes-McCoy created exquisite maps and illustrations for his own articles and books as well as for the journal he founded with Hugo McNeill, the *Irish Sword*. Although not a playwright, he had crafted dramatic episodes that not only educated but also entertained audiences that would number in the thousands, even the tens of thousands. And unlike macLíammóir, he was a trained historian, an Irish one at that, who could ensure the accuracy of the pageant's presentation of historical events.

At a meeting of the Tara Central Council on October 20, 1953, Hayes-McCoy struck a solemn tone that helped to quell the bickering among rival constituents. The minutes of the meeting record Hayes-McCoy's explanation that "the proposed Patrician Pageant must be founded on an entirely different and even more noble basis [than earlier tattoos, commemorations, and pageants]. The events which it was proposed to commemorate in this Pageant, in effect, signified the actual birth of the Irish Nation as we know it to-day."[32] The year 1954 marked a decisive departure from the narrative of earlier historical pageants, indeed, from a wide array of Cúchulainnoid works that located the origin of the modern Irish nation in ancient mythology. Earlier generations used historical pageantry to forge an originary bond between an emergent or nascent independent Ireland and its mythological or military ancestors. Whereas before Independence, Castleknock, St. Enda's, and the North Monastery attempted to depict, with varying degrees of success, links between Irish myth and Christian virtue, a Patrician pageant located the defining moment of the modern state, now the Republic of Ireland, in the island's conversion to Christianity. And whereas almost all of the national pageants of the 1920s, 1930s, and 1940s were scrupulously secular, the Patrician pageants, first in the 1930s and then in the 1950s, were anything but.

The early stages of planning for *The Pageant of St. Patrick* consistently referred back to earlier pageants and centenaries. One of McNeill's first moves in planning the 1954 pageant was the secondment of Captain John Dowling as pageant coordinator, a post Dowling took up on December 7, 1953. Dowling had successfully organized the Tara Memorial Ceremonies and Pageant in 1948 and the Owen Roe O'Neill Tercentenary in 1949. Again, as in 1948 and 1949, local GAA clubs, dramatic societies, and the FCA would be marshaled as supernumeraries. Similarly, planners hoped that "the bulk of costumes might be made up in local Convents, as was the practice in the 1948 '98 Ceremonies."[33]

Both handwritten drafts and the complete typescript of *The Pageant of St. Patrick* survive in Hayes-McCoy's papers. The scripts for the three episodes run between fourteen and twenty-six double-spaced sheets of A4, although stage directions take up the majority of the text. The Announcer, who narrates the highly choreographed movement of thousands of performers, has as many lines of dialogue as all the other characters combined. The newsreel coverage of the 1954 pageant provides about eight minutes of black-and-white footage drawn from all three episodes (at all three venues) with detailed voice-over commentary of the pageant's action by the newsreel narrator.[34] Amateur color footage of the first episode at Drogheda, held at the Irish Film Institute, documents a colorful spectacle held on a sunny day.

The 1954 *The Pageant of St. Patrick*, an open-air extravaganza of costume and song in three site-specific acts, featured Anew McMaster in the title role. As advertised in the *Dublin Evening Mail*, the pageant featured a "Cast of 1,700 . . . Massed Choir of 400 voices . . . Greatest Pageant ever produced in Ireland . . . Four episodes extending over two days." St. Patrick arrived at Drogheda on Holy Saturday; the lighting of the Paschal Fire and the conflict with the druids at Slane took place that night; on Easter Sunday evening St. Patrick confronted the high king of Ireland, as well as the druids and the Brehons at the Royal Court of Tara, and "confound[ed] Paganism, symbolised by his destruction of Crom Cruach and his 'sub Gods twelve.'"[35] All three episodes broadcast the Announcer's narration of the pageant's action over loudspeakers. Whereas the first episode was played on the banks of the Boyne in front of bleachers erected for spectators, the second and third episodes employed platform stages. Hayes-McCoy's script for the Slane episode calls for a "small, flat stone altar . . . wired for a microphone" (Slane 1),[36] with a temporary structure for the choir. The second and third episodes were performed at night; the script indicates that the action at Slane should begin as late as possible "to secure adequate darkness" for the spectacular bonfire and pyrotechnics.

At Drogheda the Announcer describes Patrick's return to Ireland as the fulcrum of Irish history and the Irish people as including the diaspora:

an tóstal

THE PAGEANT OF
SAINT PATRICK

APRIL 17th–18th

★

Cast of 1,700—Massed Choir of 400 voices — Greatest Pageant ever produced in Ireland — Four episodes extending over two days.

HOLY SATURDAY, APRIL 17th

DROGHEDA : 2.30 — 4.30 p.m.
● The Landing of St. Patrick on the Banks of the Boyne ● Reception by Chiefs and People.

SLANE : 8.0 — 10.0 p.m.
● The lighting of the Paschal Fire in defiance of Paganism ● The arrest of St. Patrick.

EASTER SUNDAY, APRIL 18th

AN UAIMH (Navan) : Gaelic Festival 2.0 — 5.0 p.m.
● Traditional Sports (2.0 p.m.). ● Tableau Vivant (3.0 p.m.).
● Hurling Match (3.30 p.m.) — **Cork** (All-Ireland Champions) and **Wexford** (Oireachtas Champions).

HILL OF TARA : 8.0 — 10.0 p.m.
Patrick, Champion of Christianity, confronts the High King of Ireland, the Druids and the Brehons at the Royal Court of Tara and confounds Paganism, symbolised by his destruction of Crom Cruach and his "sub Gods twelve."

This Pageant will be re-enacted on the actual sites where these epoch-making events took place over 1,500 years ago.

● PRICES OF ADMISSION

HOLY SATURDAY : APRIL 17th
Drogheda : Grand Stand 6/-
Slane : Reserved Enclosure 2/-

EASTER SUNDAY : APRIL 18th
An Uaimh (Navan): Reserved Enclosure 1/- (Stand tickets available on ground).
Hill of Tara: Grand Stand 7/-. Reserved Enclosure 2/-.

● TRANSPORT

C.I.E. and G.N.R. are providing special train and bus services for the Pageant of St. Patrick on April 17th and 18th. Details of these services will be found in the Companies' advertisements in the public press or on application to:—C.I.E. Road Passenger Office, 59 Upr. O'Connell Street, Dublin, or G.N.R. District Traffic Manager, Amien Street, Dublin.

● ADVANCE BOOKING

Messrs. Clery & Co., O'Connell Street.

Messrs. Brown Thomas Ltd., Grafton Street.

Messrs. Elvery's, O'Connell Street.

For details of travel and other arrangements from centres other than Dublin apply to:—Tostal House, 7/8, Mount St. Crescent, **Dublin;** Phone 61991. Pageant Headquarters, Beechmount House, **Navan;** Phone Navan 103. I.T.A. Bureau, 17, Queen's Arcade, **Belfast;** Phone 28338; or any C.I.E., G.N.R. or U.T.A. Office.

23. Advertisement for *The Pageant of St. Patrick* in the *Dublin Evening Mail*, April 3, 1954.

Out of the past of our race comes, shining and splendid, the story of
Patrick. . . . He and those with him brought hither the Message of
Life. Soon the Message shaped our Irish world into the great bright-
ness of intention and of art that is our noblest heritage of an heroic
past. It sustained us in evil times. . . . Think then, my friends, as we
see Patrick, that with us, watching too, are all that mighty host, his
Irish children, our Irish forefathers-all that vast multitude, departed
hence, far scattered, many stories, the Irish race of fifteen hundred
years. (Drogheda 2)

As saffron-clad oarsmen appeared to row the boat (the craft was actually powered by motor)[37] bringing St. Patrick back to Ireland, the narration echoes Yeats's "Easter 1916": "a new age is about to dawn, and
all—all—must be changed. From this moment their world slips back-
ward in their lives, for life awaits them" (Drogheda 4d). Unarmed,
Patrick alights with white-surpliced men and boys. No sooner does
Patrick overcome the initial resistance of the native lord and his warriors who respect Patrick's serenity in the face of menace, but the high
king's troops surround Patrick and his followers. Suddenly, the sail
of his boat is brilliantly illuminated; Hayes-McCoy's stage directions
specify, "Every effort should be made to have this lighting up of the
boat as surprising and spectacular as possible." Bells rings, white birds
fly overhead, and *"as Patrick's arm comes slowly round, all those under it,
from left to right, fall flat on the ground"* (Drogheda 6). The Christians
kneel in prayer and the native lord in submission, but the high king's
troops lie supine, immobilized, overwhelmed. The newsreel footage
shows how all are quite subdued by Patrick's rapport with supernatural powers and provides this narration: "But a strange thing happens.
Before the calm gaze of the tall stately stranger the soldiers of the
high king falter and cower on the ground, powerless to move. Not
before St. Patrick raises the local chieftain from the ground can the
bewildered army find the strength to rise to its feet again."[38] Patrick
prophesies the future greatness of the Irish: "And if I may speak to you
of the future, the far distant future of this land of Ireland, I would say
to you: Rejoice, people of Ireland, this race of yours will yet be famous

among men, even to the ends of the earth" (Drogheda 6–7). The scene ends with a choir of children welcoming Patrick to Ireland as young girls dance around a doll atop a tall pole, reminiscent of the spring fertility dances around a priapic maypole.

The episode on Saturday night at Slane opens with King Laoghaire (Godfrey Quigley), his family, his priests, and the massed supernumeraries celebrating the pagan gods Lug and Crom Cruach with a feast, music, and dancing. The Announcer's prologue warns: "Here—here at Slane—Patrick will meet this awful power of evil" (Slane 2). Followed by his disciples and new converts, forty men and women ("simple folk, the dwellers in this place"), Patrick stands behind the altar as verse speakers recite Mangan's "St. Patrick's Hymn before Tara." Under paganism the Irish are reduced to spiritually famished zombies: twenty-four *"young men and women clad in dark garments and each holding a staff in one hand and having the other stretched forward in supplication towards the Christians . . . mournfully and repeatedly call 'Patrick, Patrick'"* (Slane 4) and approach the saint, hungry for salvation. As the choir sings the "Hymn of St. Patrick," Patrick touches their staffs so that *"the light at the top is switched on, and it shows up—a bright cylinder—as a lighted candle."* Their dark cloaks are reversed, showing bright linings. As Patrick lights the Paschal Fire with his torch, the Announcer explains it as "a symbol of the fire of faith that, once lighted in their [the Irish people's] hearts, may nevermore until the end of days be quenched" (Slane 4). A martial drumming "like distant thunder is heard outside the arena, towards Tara," heralding the high king's troops: *"as many armed figures as possible."* Patrick continues to pray serenely through thunderclaps and a "blood curdling yell from the surrounding darkness" (Slane 7), through a second and then a third yell. Laoghaire's troops advance uttering a *"rough chant"* and move, *"snake-like,"* in what the newsreel narration describes as a ritual counterclockwise movement of hundreds of men in tight columns weaving an intricate pattern at a slow run. The newsreel captures an imposing, highly choreographed spectacle of menace. One of the two chief priests, Lochru, surrounded by a phalanx of ten bodyguards, accuses Patrick: "Throughout all this land it is well known—it is a long established rule—that, until the King's fire burns, none other may be lit that may be seen from royal Tara. . . . [Is] this open challenge of the king?" (Slane 6). Again, *a simple, barbaric music with again the drum beating*" heralds the arrival of yet another thousand to fifteen hundred of the high king's forces that accompany Laoghaire, his queen (Pauline Flanagan), and their two daughters in his chariot. When Erc, the first in Laoghaire's camp to embrace Christianity, runs toward the Christians, who welcome him as a convert, Lochru becomes enraged. Lochru begins a slow ritual dance of "*barbaric movement,*" enters a trancelike state, and uses his rod to trace figures, which "*causes the firework with which it is charged to ignite*" (Slane 12). Chaos ensues, but when Patrick advances carrying his large cross, Laoghaire's troops collapse, prostrate on the earth, again subdued by an unseen power. As one of Laoghaire's daughters kneels before him, Patrick tells the high king: "These men were sent to kill me and to kill my followers. We are the servants of God and God protected us. His power—no devil's power, and no power of mine—upset them. But they are not dead, or even harmed" (Slane 13a). With a "*sudden explosion . . . Lucetmael appears between Patrick and Laoghaire. His robes must be luminous.*" Literal fireworks explode when Lucetmael, denouncing his lighting the Paschal Fire as blasphemy, conjures against Patrick. The ending of the Slane episode is a cliffhanger: "still haughty" Laoghaire is "irresolute" (Slane 14), impressed with Patrick, but unwilling to dismiss his priests Lucetmael and Lochru. Because they now serve Patrick's "God of Love," Laoghaire's queen and daughters intercede for Patrick and ask that no one be executed and that they accompany Patrick to Tara.

The stage set constructed at Tara was designed for the decisive triumph of Christianity over paganism. At the rear of a large platform stage where Laoghaire holds a banquet to honor his pagan gods stand "*13 erections, one larger than the others to represent the false gods, Crom Cruach and his satellites*" (Tara 1). The narrator describes Tara as "the centre of that world, the place of highest majesty in Ireland. And in those long ages when other minds than ours imposed their will on Ireland it was to this place our people hearkened [*sic*] back, so that the dim memory of native power, here displayed, worked in us like a fever of unrest until we should redeem our birthright. Of all our Irish ground, this is the spot most sacred" (Tara 3). Erc and the queen and her daughters argue that Patrick and his followers did not know that lighting their Paschal Fire violated the law. The crowd howls for Erc's death until a princess (Mary Rose McMaster) steps forward to defend Erc and Patrick and to denounce Lucetmael. The great doors slowly open, and Patrick, *"dressed regally in his most elaborate vestments,"* slowly advances, causing panic and *"extreme fear"* (Tara 9) in all except his followers who kneel before him. Laoghaire offers Patrick protection and seems, at least momentarily, to side with his wife and daughter against his pagan priests. Lucetmael extends a poisoned cup of welcome to Patrick; before drinking from it, Patrick blesses the cup, which causes it to explode. Erc then attacks Lucetmael, and Laoghaire enjoins them all to "stop this unseemly brawling" (Tara 15); instead, Lucetmael and Erc will meet in single combat. Despite Lucetmael's underhanded tactics, Erc soon has Lucetmael at his mercy, but the crowd surges forward to rescue Lucetmael and attack Erc. The princess comes to Erc's rescue, and both of them kneel before Patrick. Laoghaire now asks Patrick to explain his religion, but before he can, Lucetmael returns filled, as the Announcer explains, with the powers of his gods: "Now Lucetmael mingles with his gods, and, casting all on the issue, seeks to loose the fury from below on Patrick's head. He stands in his most sacred place, among the graven images of the gods of Tara, whom he worships, and whom all these people have worshipped. And, as the ultimate throw in his satanic game, he conjures up the very persons of the gods—He calls them, and they come!" (Tara 20). With spectacular lighting effects behind the ridge where the thirteen idols perch, sinister figures emerge from each of the idols to perform a *"weird and sinuous"* (Tara 21) dance as Lucetmael works himself into a pagan frenzy. Patrick finally steps forward to denounce "these foul motions from the world beneath! These are not gods, but devils!" and smites the idols: *"For each [idol struck by Patrick] there is the same disintegration, the same whistling and rocket burst, and the same cry from the onlookers"* (Tara 22–23). With Lucetmael, Crum Cruach, and his twelve subgods now destroyed, Laoghaire, although he does not embrace Christianity, tells

Patrick to "go in peace, and preach in peace with my protection" (Tara 24). Patrick and his followers exit, and as they do more fireworks are set off behind the stage and a *"large and brilliant Cross"* (Tara 25) now takes the place of the pagan idols. The pageant ends with the choir leading the audience in singing the national anthem.

Although serene, Patrick channels supernatural forces to subdue the high king's soldiers at Drogheda and again in Slane, to defeat Lochru and Lucetmael, and to destroy the pagan idols. There are plenty of demonstrations of the power of paganism, but it is no match for Christianity. Throughout the pageant Christianity is portrayed as an inclusive, democratic religion of love, whereas the pagan beliefs are a set of barbaric, totalitarian controls over the people. The pageant also echoes features of Irish myth, particularly the disabling spell cast on the Ulster warriors in the Cúchulainn tales. Despite the fact that Robert Briscoe, a Jew, would soon be elected lord mayor of Dublin, *The Pageant of St. Patrick* asserted the centrality of Christianity to the nation and positioned Patrick as the forefather and savior of the Irish. In his opening address at the performance of the first episode in Drogheda, Taoiseach Eamon de Valera proclaimed that "the coming of St. Patrick to Ireland and the ancient seat of government at Tara was the most important event in the history of the country."[39]

As unsophisticated, essentialist, and hokey as this performance may seem to us, in 1954 *The Pageant of St. Patrick* was extremely popular with the Irish press and audiences. Episodic as it was, the pageant attracted huge crowds: more than ten thousand paid admission for each episode. The *Irish Independent* praised *The Pageant of St. Patrick* as "unforgettable in its brilliance and its manifest success."[40] The *Irish Times* described the pageant as "the most ambitious open-air pageant ever staged in either this or the neighbouring island and the first attempt in any European country, other than Greece, to represent historic happenings on the actual scenes where they had originally taken place" and wrote that the pageant "justified the money and care that were lavished on it."[41] A photograph of the episode staged at Drogheda captures a sense of the pageant's epic scale: hundreds of "pagan warriors" outfitted with ten-foot pikes, large shields, broadswords, headdresses, and period costumes standing on the shore of the Boyne River in front of St. Patrick's boat. On closer inspection many of these pagan warriors seem delighted with their performative postures. As is clear from photographs and newsreel footage, many of the pageant participants were children or adolescents. One measure of how readily the audience and participants embraced their own performativity was that, when Anew McMaster stepped off his boat as St. Patrick, unscripted onlookers rushed forward to kiss the hem of his robe. As well as affirming the affective potential of pageantry on this scale, *The Pageant of St. Patrick* raised questions about the ability or willingness of audience members and participants to distinguish between staged spectacle and reality. In 1968, in a series of reminiscences in the *Irish Times*, McMaster recalled that after the Drogheda episode concluded, "it was almost impossible to get through the crowds as the people recognised me, they even climbed onto the top of the car, and stood on the running-board, and mothers held up their children to be blessed. I kissed but did not bless them, for episode one was over, and I was Anew McMaster again and no longer our Patron Saint."[42]

In the history of twentieth-century pageants, the 1954 pageant is the first to locate the defining moment in the nation's history as its conversion to Christianity (and, many might have said, Catholicism). Whereas early pageants had depicted several Christian saints and the 1932 Protestant pageants for the fifteen hundredth anniversary foregrounded the return of St. Patrick to Ireland, Hayes-McCoy's pageant and macLíammóir's 1955 revision stake the claim for Ireland's identity as a Christian and Catholic country. Such an assertion is either conspicuously absent or only dimly foretold in earlier pageants performed in the century's first decade. By claiming that the pageant represented the nation's most sacred moment at its most sacred site, the jubilant, even raucous, atmosphere of the military tattoos yielded to the somber moment of transition from the pagan to the Christian. The *Sunday Independent* reported "a reverent audience" for what many saw as an occasion of faith.[43] No military heroes would parade. No Celtic princesses would primp and preen. No Cúchulainn would stand in a motorcycle chariot.

24. Pagan warriors in the first episode of Hayes-McCoy's *The Pageant of St. Patrick* (1954) as seen in the *Irish Times*, April 19, 1954. The boat in which Patrick arrived at Drogheda appears in the upper right. © and used by kind permission of the *Irish Times*.

Quite unlike the military tattoos, the Tóstal pageants were held not as fund-raising charity events, but as part of a tourist initiative, an investment of state funds that might not break even, let alone yield profits in the short term. Indeed, the 1954 pageant received a grant of £3,500 from Bord Fáilte.[44] From a financial perspective, the 1954 pageant was hugely profitable. Attendance and revenue from ticket sales exceeded budget estimates by more than a factor of three. The crowd of 15,000 at Drogheda was better than the 11,500 anticipated. With the added attraction of pyrotechnics, the big successes were the evening performances at Slane and Tara, where audiences of 3,100 and 9,000 were expected but 13,000 and 35,000 paid admission. Favorable weather as well as fireworks surely helped to create such vast audiences. In comparison with the estimates from January 1954, which projected income from the three sites and "general" income at £3,157,[45] the actual income of £10,260 reported in the *Times Pictorial* exceeded expectations by 325 percent.

Although popular with audiences and with the press, the 1954 Tóstal pageant attracted some criticism, much of it focused not on the identification of the foundational moment of the Irish nation as its conversion to Christianity, but on financial issues. After the second Tóstal in 1954, vocal opponents surfaced. In Meath Captain P. Giles told the Meath County Council that the Tóstal was "the biggest racket ever in this country. . . . They would be much better concerned in catering for the people of this country in a decent Irish way instead of their being forced to 'trek outside' in order to earn a living. They were inviting to this country every type of 'spiv' who had money to splash around."[46] Other problems with historical pageants emerged: the Waterford Council faced the worst of them as the Meagher pageant left debts of £1,314, but a national historical pageant seemed established as a popular and profitable Tóstal fixture.

THE PAGEANT OF ST. PATRICK (1955)

After the second Tóstal, the festival's date was moved from Easter to mid-May, partly because English visitors might well be put off by Easter 1916 commemorations, but mainly because, although organizers were lucky in 1954, the weather around Easter was rarely conducive to open-air performances. The Tóstal was intended as an annual event; in its early years there was a willingness to experiment in what did work (a national pageant) and did not (a Bowl of Light). In its third year Tóstal activities crystallized around the successes of 1953 and 1954. The popularity of the Cork international music and choral festival emboldened organizers to plan an international film festival in Cork. So impressed were the organizers with the Patrician pageant that they decided to consolidate *The Pageant of St. Patrick* for six performances at Croke Park, the Dublin home of the GAA, in 1955. Transport and accommodation problems could be more easily overcome in Dublin. The local committee that needled McNeill with petty demands in 1954 would be eliminated. With the Abbey players performing at a theatre festival in Paris, the Queen's Theatre dark, the Gate shut down for repairs, and the Gaiety closing for renovations midway through the

1955 Tóstal, a pageant at Croke Park offered at least some dramatic performances in a city renowned for theatre.

MacLíammóir and Edwards were natural choices to recast the Patrician pageant as a more coherent theatre event for performance in a single venue. Their Dublin Gate Theatre Company's "bent was toward the drama as theatre rather than as literature,"[47] and their aesthetically conscious, often avant-garde, visual style in costumes, set design, and décor served the demands of pageantry. Of course, macLíammóir and Edwards had practical and varied experience in pageantry, both in Ireland and abroad. In 1953–54, moreover, the Arts Council had bailed out their Gate Theatre Company with a £3,000 grant stipulating that "plays by Irish dramatists should, as far as reasonably possible, be performed by your company."[48] Now "rumours of untold wealth . . . placed at the disposal of An Tóstal" for pageant production reached their ears.[49] Why Edwards and macLíammóir sought the commission is obvious: they were in debt up to their eyeballs and without a theatre base, their company reduced to two or three yearly productions at the Gaiety Theatre.

Edwards's and macLíammóir's plans for the 1955 St. Patrick pageant were especially ambitious. Their experience with Orson Welles in Dublin, in Illinois, and only three years earlier in filming Welles's version of *Othello* brought home the importance of star power. On December 31, 1954, the chairman of An Bord Fáilte wrote to Liam Cosgrave, the minister for external affairs, to inquire about recruiting Hollywood stars who would lure international tourists to the pageant: "It is felt that the association of such well-known celebrities would contribute in very large measure to achieving the desired success for the Pageant." In February 1955 the Irish Embassy in Washington, DC, extended invitations to two Irish-born Hollywood stars, Barry Fitzgerald and Maureen O'Sullivan, to perform in 1955 *The Pageant of St. Patrick*. Although both expressed a willingness to do so, neither could make the necessary commitment to rehearsals and performances in Dublin.[50]

The previous year's site-specific treatment of St. Patrick provided a structural outline, and, drawing on his experience in creating *The*

Ford of the Hurdles, macLíammóir undertook the creation of a second *Pageant of St. Patrick* for six performances at Croke Park. Ecclesiastical as well as academic authorities vetted macLíammóir's script. Interestingly, the priestly authorities were not in Drumcondra with Archbishop John Charles McQuaid but with the Jesuits in Rathfarnham, whence the analysis of Father L[eonard] Sheil, SJ: *"The Pageant of St. Patrick* is magnificent. I consulted four of my colleagues who are all agreed on this."[51] Hayes-McCoy's response to macLíammóir's draft raised questions about the use of the word "druid" ("'druid' is historically out of context and since 'priest' is a perfectly good word for what is wanted 'priest' is the better word to use")[52] and challenged the inclusion of special terms for the Irish at the Last Judgment: "Is it not open to the objection of being a shade 'too Irish'? After all, why should we—except as a joke—advertise ourselves as meriting preferential treatment just because we're Irish?"[53] The preferential treatment was, indeed, altered in subsequent scripts, but the druids remained. A small core of professional actors was again supplemented by thousands of supernumeraries, more than eight hundred of whom came from the sodalities and confraternities at Our Lady of Good Counsel in Drimnagh. The premiere of the pageant took place at Croke Park on Sunday, May 8, 1955, a mere two and a half hours after Kerry defeated Cavan in the All-Ireland Senior Football Championship.

The spectacle was nothing less than what might be expected from Edwards and macLíammóir on a substantial budget. The first scene of Patrick's captivity at Sliabh Mis opened with a procession that included fourteen male slaves bound to a chariot, slave drivers with lashes, nine women slaves, two boy slaves, and three girl slaves as well as "12 mountebanks (Male)—2 of whom are dwarves . . . [performing] a fantastic jigging dance."[54] Opting for even more sensational and sensationalized effects, the 1955 pageant incorporated strong elements of sadism and the grotesque only suggested by the war dance of Laoghaire's troops and the frenzied trance of Lucetmael in the 1954 pageant. Luan's daughter is abducted and presumably raped, since "when she comes back no man will look for her in marriage . . . [but] the gods will not punish [her abductors because] they have sacrificed ten goats at the feast of Lu."[55] Whereas a children's dance welcomed St. Patrick in 1954, in the 1955 pageant dancers who appeared by permission of the Irish Ballet Society performed four ballets: a Dance of the Sun, the Dance for Dana, the Rites of the Snow, and the Ballet of the Clowns.[56] To perform the pagan rites that celebrate the festival of spring by honoring the Feast of Beal, a *"monstrous hunchback [dances] grotesquely . . . [to] shrill discordant music."* The hunchback and mountebanks are forced to dance, the Announcer explains, until they collapse:

> then they must dance again—
> Till they foam at the mouth—the sacred foam—
> For that is the madness of the gods! (5)

Further evidence of the barbaric, depraved religion of the pagans is seen by bloodstained cages that housed the bird and goat sacrifices, for "the Gods must be fed. . . . The gods are greedy." After the frenetic spectacle of pagan depravity, the second episode shows a contemplative Patrick in a cloister in Rome who, in a dream, hears the "Guth na Gael / Voice of Ireland," calling him back to Ireland.

25. *The Pageant of St. Patrick* (1955) as seen in the *Irish Times*, May 16, 1955. © and used by kind permission of the *Irish Times*.

MacLíammóir's script is more poetic as well as more hyperbolic than Hayes-McCoy's. Although both celebrate the Irish landscape, macLíammóir's Patrick offers this lush description of an idyllic land:

> There are mountains in that country lonely and pure under cloudy crowns. The hawks fly above their heads. The salmon leap in the rivers and the young deer walk over the hills. In the Springtime the children play with bare feet on the tender grass under blossoming hawthorn boughs. In the winter they tell of strange wonders by the fires of turf. The sheep graze in the meadows in the long summer days, and the woods in the autumn are full of nuts and berries. There, as night falls the waters are brimmed with stars, the cattle in the glens are at peace, the moorhen sleeps among the rushes. (8)

Structurally, the 1955 pageant alternates between pagan depravity and Christianity serenity. In the third episode, Patrick witnesses a salacious rite in which "half-naked" Dancers of the Sun *dance in revolving circles . . . whirl to and fro, their heads thrown backwards and downwards and backwards again in ecstasy*" (10). Laoghaire's druids denounce Patrick and his monks as thieves and robbers, but one local man, Dichu, offers his barn, where Patrick says the first Mass in Ireland.

Patrick's lighting of the Paschal Fire again upstages King Laoghaire's fire at Tara and precipitates the confrontation between Laoghaire and his druids and Patrick. After the conversions of Erc, the queen, and Dufach (Laoghaire's poet), Luchru denounces Patrick as a blasphemer. When Laoghaire demands a demonstration of the power of the Christian God, Patrick offers "a vision of God's mission on earth": "As the music of the [monks'] chant rises on the air the dark-cloaked crowds of people turn into white-robed singers: their spears become lighted candles, and they add their voices to the Hymn of Easter. This causes Luchru to writhe in pain and then vanish" (21), his death keened in Irish the priestesses of the Sun. With his high priest dead, Laoghaire expresses his admiration for Patrick in vintage macLíammóir dialogue: "There is some curious beauty in your treason. And your courage is fabulous" (19).

The second act begins at Tara, where Laoghaire's chieftains ridicule Patrick's strange religion that worships three gods in one. Now on the run, Patrick comforts his monks by reciting "St. Patrick's Breastplate" in Irish as, hidden by a herd of deer, they elude their pursuers. In the climactic confrontation between paganism and Christianity, "The Cross in Tara, 433 A.D.," the evil Luchamaol has taken Luchru's place. At Laoghaire's feast the dancers perform "The Dance of the Sacrifice of the Unveiled Virgin of the Spring to Dana, Goddess of the Earth." The final episode, a coda of sorts, takes place after the comprehensive triumph of Patrick at "Cruach [sic] Padraic" (34) in AD 440.

Throughout their pageants macLíammóir and Edwards deploy a hybrid patriotic and religious typology that recalls Pearse's fusion of the Christian and Celtic. The mob cries out for Erc, who has converted to Patrick's Christianity, just as an earlier mob cried out for Barabbas. In a stunning and deliberate anachronism, the evil heathen priest Lucetmael calls for "death to the scheming cropheads." The tonsured monks who travel with Patrick, rather than the anti-wig-wearing French revolutionaries of the 1780s, are the models for "Croppies" of 1798 and, by extension, the true prototypes of Irish patriotism.

Both Tóstal Patrician pageants portrayed a Christianity quite unlike the brand of Catholicism alternatively described as Jansenist or Maynooth. As if in anticipation of Vatican II, Patrick's faith is joyful, life-affirming, cerebral, and inclusive, quite unlike the experience of Irish Catholicism in the fifties described by John Banville, among others.[57] Although his enemies denounce his religion as a cult of suffering, Patrick condemns the cruelty, elitism, and blood sacrifice of the worshippers of Angus, Dana, and Lu. In proclaiming "the blessing of God is waiting in His hand to sanctify us all" (33), Patrick brings warmth and light to melt the snow conjured by Luchamaol. The snow, by the way, cleverly recycled a similar effect from the 1954 pageant: scores of women unfurled voluminous white capes to represent the snow and gathered them up to enact Patrick's power to melt the snow.

The *Irish Times* applauded the pageant for "moments of excellence and of extraordinarily effective theatre . . . one of the most effective and spectacular *coups de theatre* ever seen in this country—the destruction of the old gods—and the excellent 'Snow Dance,'" but criticized the final episode at Croagh Patrick as anticlimactic and "overwordy."[58] The *Irish Independent* wrote that the production "at times . . . transcends the theatre and becomes almost a religious experience."[59] At its premiere the pageant was performed before an audience of 30,000 and reached even larger national audiences via Radio Éireann in a broadcast that was favorably reviewed.[60] Initially, the 1955 pageant took three hours and twenty minutes to perform, but by Saturday, May 14, "the pageant was shortened by the deletion of the Croagh Patrick episode, and by cutting the interval to five minutes, performance concluded by 11 p.m. so that the spectators were able to get transport home."[61] Poor weather and the pageant's running time drew audiences of fewer than 10,000 for much of the run, but on Thursday, May 26, Children's Night, played for "children from orphanages and other institutions throughout the city"[62] and with reduced admission prices for children and adults, the crowd was 75,000. Estimates placed the total attendance at the 1955 *The Pageant of St. Patrick* between 115,000[63] and 160,000.[64] If 100,000 could be counted in the premiere and Children's Night, that result left paltry audiences in a huge arena for four other performances. After the 1954 pageant, expectations were for even larger crowds in a venue that could have accommodated more than 450,000 in six performances. Micheál macLíammóir recalled the production with little fondness as "an open-air pageant play about St. Patrick written by myself with Anew McMaster as the Saint surrounded by hordes of monks, druids, clowns, dancers, worshippers of the sun, and royal personages at Tara, their teeth, during most of the performances, chattering like castanets in a smart north-east gale."[65]

THE PAGEANT OF CUCHULAINN (1956)

In late 1955 Bord Fáilte Éireann decided that the pageant for the fourth Tóstal would draw on the legend of Cúchulainn. To vet two scripts for the Cúchulainn pageant, organizers of the 1956 Tóstal turned to the single person in Ireland with the greatest experience in staging and directing Irish historical pageants: Hilton Edwards. Edwards reported on the relative merits of two scripts: one by Denis Johnston and one other, quite possibly by Phillip Rooney, author of the historical novel (1946) and film screenplay (1947) *Captain Boycott*, then head of script writing at RTÉ, where Johnston had a regular radio spot as a theatre critic while in Dublin.[66] Edwards's report set out what he saw as the obvious principles for pageants, ones that served as his criteria in judging the entries:

> I cannot state too strongly my belief that a rule of the theatre applies with even greater force to a Pageant production, and this is that if the audience is to be entertained they must understand what is happening, that one can only make them understand by making one statement at a time, whether by word of mouth or by action (preferably these should coincide to make the point doubly clear), and that no actor or actors can express to a large audience completely surrounding them anything but the simplest of statements.[67]

After Johnston's script was selected for production, Bord Fáilte Éireann consulted Hayes-McCoy on the historical merits of the script[68] and commissioned Edwards to provide the "synoptic layouts" for the staging at Croke Park, although Brendan Smith is credited with "production" and Michael O'Herlihy with "direction and design."

The Pageant of Cuchulainn was composed relatively quickly, probably in late 1955, while Johnston was in Ireland on a Guggenheim fellowship to research his projects on Jonathan Swift. Johnston (b. 1901) probably did not remember the frenzy of pageantry when he was a youngster living in Dublin during the first heyday of historical pageants, but he had vivid recollections of the pageants of the Dublin Civic Weeks of 1927 and 1929 and the 1932 Tailteann Games, to which in 1931 he submitted *The Moon in the Yellow River* in the playwriting competition. Johnston would also have been aware of Yeats's Cúchulainn plays. Writing as E. W. Tocher, he endorsed pageantry in "A National Morality Play" in the very first issue of the Gate Theatre magazine *Motley* in 1932.[69] Nine years later *The Bell*, for which

Johnston would become drama critic, published Johnston's letter to the editor, nearly identical to the 1932 *Motley* article, advocating, "Once a year on a public holiday—Easter Monday—a kind of National Morality Play should be performed in O'Connell Street, re-enacting in conventionalised form the events of Easter Week 1916. . . . The play should include the Fairyhouse crowds—the little band of marching men—the seizure of the Post Office—the Proclamation read at the foot of the Pillar—the charge of the Lancers—the closing in—the siege—the surrender—the Volunteers march out to prison and to death—fifteen men march ahead—the people follow."[70] What Johnston describes draws on elements of macLíammóir's "Easter 1916: The City at Dawn," originally performed as the final scene in *The Ford of the Hurdles*, first staged in 1929 not long after the premiere of *The Old Lady Says "No!"* In 1932 and again in 1941, Johnston envisioned a reenactment of the Easter Rising staged as a public performance: O'Connell Street "would provide one of the finest open-air, Street Theatres in the world"; the year 1916 would "provide a heroic theme as rich in dramatic values as anybody could wish." Twice he had proposed an annual site-specific pageant, one that would grow in ritual, for which "as few people as possible should pay or be paid." In 1956, in advance of the Tóstal, he returned to this idea: "I think that the Rising could be commemorated much more effectively by a sort of pageant in which the actual happenings of Easter Monday, 1916, could be re-enacted round the G.P.O."[71] This was, in fact, perfectly consonant with Johnston's views on theatre. "Theatre," he wrote in 1933, "is at its best when it is most theatrical."[72] Like Fischer-Lichte's call for the retheatricalization of theatre, Johnston rejected realism as inherently untheatrical.

Johnston's *The Pageant of Cuchulainn*, under the revised title *The Tain: A Pageant*, appeared in 1977 in the second volume of *The Dramatic Works of Denis Johnston*.[73] Johnston's biographers relegate the work to the dustbin of pageantry: Harold Ferrar and Gene A. Barrett completely ignore it; Bernard Adams offers a paltry eleven words. In the pageant's program, Johnston's "A Note on the Theme" describes Celtic mythology both as an "essentially Irish contribution to the heritage of mankind" and as "surprisingly human and up-to-date." His essay high-lights the links between the Cúchulainn tale and Greek myth:

> In the final part, one should note how the fundamentally pre-Chris-tian elements of the story come into their own—the cult of animal totems, and the working of the *Geasa* or prohibitions that corre-spond (to some extent) with the immutable decrees of the Fates in the Greek myths. For example, Cuchulainn is a hound and is bound by his personal *geas* never to eat "himself," or to refuse the offer of hospitality. We will see in this final section, how this dilemma brings him to his death, so strikingly depicted by the statue in the vestibule of the General Post Office in Dublin.[74]

Indeed, images of Oliver Sheppard's GPO sculpture appeared in the pageant's publicity and on the program cover of *The Pageant of Cuchulainn*.

Johnston's pageant ran for six consecutive nights, May 16–21, 1956. Like earlier pageants and military tattoos, *The Pageant of Cuchulainn* commenced at twilight in order to avail of pyrotechnics and cel-ebratory fireworks. All the dialogue was prerecorded and broadcast over loudspeakers. Johnston maps the geography of Ireland onto the pitch at Croke Park: at the south end is Rathcrogan, the seat of the Connaught tribes in County Roscommon; at the north end Ulster, Cúchulainn's home. The River Dee lies at midfield, where most of the combat takes place and where Ferdiad and Cúchulainn meet to share food and wine the night before their final battle. Like so many pageants performed in the open air, *The Pageant of Cuchulainn* mined the inventory of audio effects: chanting, thunder, the Brown Bull's tre-mendous roar, music, song. The cast of twelve hundred includes eight major roles (Cúchulainn, Shanahan, Medb, Ferdiad, Bricriu, the Mor-rigan, Láeg, and Finnabair), twenty-five other speaking roles, another twenty-five nonspeaking parts (including Calatin's three misshapen sons and three misshapen daughters), eighty dancers—who perform as the Red Bull of Connaught, other beasts, crows, puffballs, and sprites—as well as hundreds of supernumeraries.

26. Denis Johnston's *The Pageant of Cuchulainn*, 1956. Courtesy of the Board of Trinity College Dublin.

Johnston foregrounds Cúchulainn's bravery and self-sacrifice, but, like Yeats, he also deals with Cúchulainn's grief, despair, and death. *The Pageant of Cuchulainn* places particular emphasis on malignant supernatural interventions: *geasa*, prophesies, curses. Indeed, the Morrigan (Iris Lawler), a bird-witch, is Cúchulainn's nemesis. The first act stresses the hero's youth: Medb mocks Cúchulainn as "Boy" (374), and Lech asks, "Do you suppose that I, a man of fifty battles / Would condescend to fight a beardless boy?" (379). But unlike Pearse's *The Boyhood Deeds of Cúchulainn*, Johnston's pageant cast a thirty-year-old Ray McAnally in the title role.[75]

The pillow talk of Ailill and Medb establishes their competitive rivalry (with displays of pots and pans, jugs, plates, pitchers, rings and jewelry, clothing, livestock), which stands in stark contrast to the friendship vows of Cúchulainn and Ferdiad. The foster brothers "swear to be friends . . . now and forever . . . to the Death" (356), but the cynical, demonic bird-woman Morrigan advises them to "swear by the summer, lads, for friendship / is as fleeting as the sun and cannot bear / the cold" (356). Dara, the owner of the Brown Bull, who speaks with a broad Northern Irish accent, initially agrees to lend Medb the "baste" without charge, but when he hears rumors that he did so only because he feared her, Dara rescinds his offer. The Brown Bull is deliberately made to appear ridiculous: Johnston's stage directions, for instance, specify: *"The Brown Bull of Cooley is an enormous garlanded, brazen property, drawn on a truck. It is constructed so that at the required moment its great mouth opens and it belches smoke, and its eyes light up"* (344). Fabricated in papier-mâché with a touch of Godzilla about him,[76] the bull was fifteen feet high and thirty feet long.[77] Like Medb's and Ailill's displays of material possessions, the Brown Bull is outsize, overblown, devoid of any spiritual dimension.

A succession of warriors, warlords, and tribes first present themselves to Medb, each performing a war dance (that is, the war dance of the men of Leinster, then of Munster, then of Connaught), which probably bore some resemblance to the Maori Haka dance and recalls the bellicose choreography of Laoghaire's troops in the Patrician pageants. Throughout each of Cúchulainn's battles with the provinces, Medb's forces edge toward the mechanical Brown Bull, getting a little closer to it each time. This movement divides the spectator's attention between the center-stage single combats of Cúchulainn in which he kills scores of warriors and Medb's minions cowardly scurrying to highjack the bull while Cúchulainn fights for his life. Meanwhile, at the south end, in Rathcrogan, Finnabair entertains and seduces Ferdiad, delaying his climactic battle with Cúchulainn.

After Ferdiad is killed by the deadly Gae Bolg in the final combat, Cúchulainn carries the body of his foster brother to the Ulster side of the river and cradles him while the forces of Connaught finally carry off the snorting Brown Bull to Rathcrogan. No sooner has the Brown Bull been won than it is lost: *"Then DARA's voice is heard, calling the Bull, and for the first time its roar is heard. It opens its mouth, and smoke pours from its throat and nostrils. Its eyes blaze with light, and with a shriek of terror, everybody runs away . . . the Red Bull being the last in the rout. In the gathering darkness DARA and the attendants run the Brown Bull as rapidly as possible back to the North and out by the North-west entrance"* (390). In the final section, "The End of Cuchulainn," the descendants of the slain warriors return to a despondent Cúchulainn. First to appear are the children of Calatin: his daughter Beve leads *"six misshapen ones— three males and three females . . . [who] dance and weave spells around a cauldron"* (391) into which one of them throws a dead dog. Then to "strange tremulous music" appear "dancers dressed as Wraiths, Puff-balls, Thistles and Leaves" (392), bizarre revenants of Cúchulainn's victims or perhaps projections of his sorrow over Ferdiad's death.

Johnston's pageant pits the youthful idealism of Cúchulainn and Ferdiad against the cynicism and materialism of the powerful: the Morrigan, Bricriu, Ailill, and Medb. His pageant was in some ways a gore-fest worthy of a Quentin Tarantino. Quite early in the pageant, while the debilitating curse of Macha is still on the Ulster warriors, Conchobar decapitates Sualtam and places the severed head on the Pillar of Emain, where it remains for the duration of the pageant. Corpses are strewn over midfield. When Cúchulainn obeys his *geas* to accept the hospitality of the misshapen daughters of Calatin by eating the food that they offer him, the Morrigan appears to say:

> Dog, Hound of Cullin, Dog!
> You have eaten yourself.
> Haha! Haha!
> Where are your sinews now? (394)

Ensnared by his two *geasa*, to accept the hospitality offered by women and never to eat dog's flesh, Cúchulainn is doomed. At the end of the pageant, when the god Lug appears to claim his son, the Hound of Ulster, Cúchulainn's severed head and one hand are placed in a casket on a pyre and consumed by flames.

27. The Brown Bull in Johnston's *The Pageant of Cuchulainn*, 1956. Courtesy of the Board of Trinity College Dublin.

Johnston's pageant incorporates the Irish language, mainly in Cúchulainn's frenzied battle trance (*risteárd*) and Shanahan's choric songs. Johnston freely and syncretically interpolates elements from Arthurian legend, Shakespearean drama, and classical tragedy in his retelling the Irish epic. Ferdiad, for instance, vows "upon my honour as a Knight" (384). Underpinning the pageant is Johnston's trademark irreverence and iconoclastic humor that informed *The Old Lady Says "No!"*:

MAC ROTH: Son of Factna, I am Mac Roth.
DARA (*dryly*): A name I never heard tell of hereabouts.
MAC ROTH (*proudly*): I am the Chief Herald of Connacht . . .
DARA: Think of that now. (365)

Just as Cúchulainn's dual *geasa* doom him, Johnston's pageant under-scores the dilemma of Cúchulainn by pitting the militaristic values of bravery and strength against his vow of friendship to his foster brother, Ferdiad. The wholesale slaughter of scores of warriors that litter the pitch to serve the vanity of a materialistic ruler suggests the banality and futility of war, especially one waged over something as ridiculous as this snorting, fire-belching bull.

The sense of Irish identity suggested by Johnston's pageant was vastly more complex and potentially more problematic than that pro-posed by the two recent versions of *The Pageant of St. Patrick*. John-ston's pageant foregrounds the internecine struggles that pit Irishman against Irishman and brother against brother. Unlike the Cúchulainn pageants earlier in the century, *The Pageant of Cuchulainn* subverts the understanding of Cúchulainn as purely heroic, challenges republican pieties, and anticipates the treatment of the myth by Macnas's *Táin* thirty-six years later. Johnston's sense of an unheroic Irish past figures prominently in many of his plays, beginning with his very first play (*The Old Lady Says "No!"*) and featuring in his works in the later 1950s and 1960s.

The reception of *The Pageant of Cuchulainn* was mixed. The front-page account in the *Irish Times* on May 17, 1956, praised the pageant as written "on a heroic scale, full of moments of great theatre and sparkling with witty dialogue. Last night's performance proves that pageants are in a department in which Tóstal goes from strength to strength and learns from each year's experience." Ken Gray, the drama critic of the *Irish Times* who found macLíammóir's Patrician pageant "a little disappointing,"[78] praised Johnston's work, but was especially negative about pageants: "Does anybody really believe that an historical pageant, even a good one, is likely to bring American and British tourists hotfoot to Ireland?"[79] Although fourteen thousand people attended the gala's final performance, earlier shows were only sparsely attended, and the overall attendance, estimated at fifty thou-sand,[80] was disappointing, less than half of the number that attended either of the previous two pageants. The *Connaught Sentinel*'s coverage of Johnston's pageant appeared under the headline "'Satchmo' Beats

Cuchullain in Popularity Test in Dublin," to report that while Louis Armstrong packed the National Stadium on the South Circular Road, the attendance at *The Pageant of Cuchulainn* was lackluster: "This magnificent spectacle, recalling our storied past, must have caused a loss of 15,000 pounds."[81] In the run-up to the opening of the 1956 Tóstal, the daily press ran far fewer articles and photographs to publicize the festival in general and the pageant in particular than in earlier years. Although Tóstal promoters put many eggs in Dublin's basket, the combination of poor weather and Johnston's sophisticated treatment of Irish mythology lacked the appeal of the Patrician pageants. After May 21 the press, especially the *Irish Times*, was highly critical not only about Johnston's pageant, but about the very idea of a substantial investment in a pageant of any description. With attendance at less than half, if not a third, of the previous year, in 1956 the state's investment in the Tóstal (£39,500) was less than half what it had been in 1954 (£81,500), and it would continue to diminish over the next two years. After 1957 the Tóstal abandoned its national pageants.

The importance of the Tóstal pageants to Ireland's cultural and theatre history lies not only in the sheer number of people who participated and attended, but also in their construction of a post-Emergency Irish identity. Even before the Tóstal, the merit of spectacular pageants was questioned. In February 1956, Aladair MacCaba wrote that "tourists want something more than a few pageants held in often chilly and inclement weather, to anchor their interest in a country."[82] More than a month before it was seen, Johnston's pageant suffered in comparison to the first Cork international film festival: "And are we Dubliners green with envy at the thought of the films that will be seen [in Cork], not to mention the film stars lounging along the banks of the Lee while we're 'making do' with Queen Maeve, Cuchulainn and company, up in Croke Park."[83] After the performances, "An Irishman's Diary" wondered, "How do the citizens of the languorous [*sic*] town by the lazy Lee contrive, on a slender enough budget, to organise for themselves a ballet festival, a film festival, an international choral festival, and the Vienna Philharmonic, while Dublin limps along on one pageant and a few odds and ends?"[84] At the end of the year, the *Irish Times* recalled that "the highlight of the Tóstal in Dublin was the pageant of Cúchulainn in Croke. . . . Much more successful, however, was Cork's first film festival."[85] Johnston's was the last of the Tóstal national pageants. The cost, logistics, and risks of these bombastic productions led organizers to consider other ways in which the Tóstal might incorporate theatre, with the result that they created the Dublin International Theatre Festival, one of the few components of the Tóstals that, despite intense controversy, survives from the 1950s into the twenty-first century.

In its early years the Tóstal looked to historical pageantry to attract tourists and to create a version of the Irish past that could involve thousands of citizens in performative supporting roles. In 1954 and 1955, Patrician pageants plainly celebrated an independent nation whose defining moment was its conversion to Christianity; in 1956 *The Pageant of Cuchulainn* located ancient Irish legend in the much wider context of Indo-European myth and literature. The early Tóstals were not arts festivals, but, in A. J. Leventhal's words, "a rather inchoate jumble of national aesthetic jollifications illumined by fireworks."[86] By the summer of 1956, the Tóstal pageants had run their course. As an occasion of faith and blessed by good weather, Hayes-McCoy's 1954 pageant exceeded expectations, while others did not. For three years the Tóstal facilitated national pageants of Irish identity, but they were too costly, too logistically complex, and, perhaps most important, too vulnerable to Irish weather. Public enthusiasm for pageantry on this scale began to fade after 1956 and waned quickly, perhaps as quickly as it had in 1914. But with state funding, it returned in time for the fiftieth anniversary of the Easter Rising.

5

1966 and the Recuperative Pageantry of Macnas

When on December 31, 1961, television broadcasting began in the Republic, the nature of public entertainment in Ireland shifted yet again. Along with the other social and cultural upheavals that characterized the post-Emergency era, television transformed the way in which people perceived their heritage, demonstrated civic engagement, and, perhaps most important, viewed authority. In the sixties and seventies, historical pageants evolved as civic spectacles and moved decisively into a commemorative mode. As Mary Daly writes:

> After 1966 the anniversaries of major historical events attracted at best low-key commemorations, (as in the case of the 50th anniversary of the founding of Dáil Éireann in 1969), and sometimes almost nothing at all. The only memorable celebrations were those organised at a local level, such as the 1988 celebration of Dublin's millennium, Cork's 800th anniversary in 1985, the 300th anniversary of the Treaty of Limerick in 1691. The 75th anniversary of the 1916 rising was marked, or not marked, largely by embarrassment.[1]

With pageantry tied more often than ever to anniversaries and centenaries, its festive and celebratory dimensions yielded to ones of solemnity and reverence. With the conspicuous exception of the fiftieth anniversary of the Easter Rising, pageants were shorter, less lavish, more localized affairs.[2] In comparison with the Tóstal pageants, their politics, at least before the terror of the Troubles began in the late 1960s, would be more overtly republican and their tenor somber.

The increasing use of professional theatre practitioners and actors in the 1950s had made pageantry an expensive undertaking. At the same time, the engagement of visual artists and craftspeople waned. The promotional materials, programs, and ephemera from the pageants of the 1950s (including the Tóstal pageants) and beyond lack the elegance and vernacular energy seen in the 1920s. After 1966 and before its revivification by Macnas in the 1990s, historical pageantry languished.

The title of the official publication documenting the Rising's fiftieth anniversary, *Cuimhneachán, 1916–1966: Commemoration*, plainly signaled the shift from festivity to solemnity. In his foreword Taoiseach Seán Lemass wrote that the state intended "to mark the 50th Anniversary of the Easter Rising of 1916 to honour those who took part in it and to emphasise its importance as a decisive event in our history."[3] Over fourteen days, beginning on Good Friday, April 8, 1966, with a ceremony at Banna Strand in Kerry honoring the men, Roger Casement, Robert Monteith, and D. J. Bailey, associated with the gunrunning on the German ship the *U19*[4] and ending with a special Mass at Arbour Hill on April 24, 1966, the state programmed a series of commemorative exercises. UCD awarded honorary academic degrees to surviving relatives of six of the Proclamation's signatories; statues were unveiled, exhibitions opened, wreaths laid. All of these exercises might be described as performances; one, Tomás Mac Anna's *Aiseirí: Gloir-reim na Cásca* (Resurrection: The Easter Pageant), was expressly crafted as a pageant. Another historical pageant, MacMahon's *Seachtar Fear, Seacht Lá* (Seven Men, Seven Days), commissioned by the GAA, was performed three weeks before the official government commemorations began.

TOMÁS MAC ANNA AND BRYAN MACMAHON

In the mid-1950s, while the Tóstal pageants were staged as national spectacles, Tomás Mac Anna and Bryan MacMahon were creating regional historical pageants performed by (and for) a specific constituency. Neither of their pageants commemorating the Easter Rising,

Mac Anna's *Aiseirí* and MacMahon's *Seachtar Fear, Seacht Lá*, was cut
from whole cloth. Both, as Roche observes of *Aiseirí*, are pastiches that
rely upon well-known ballads, poetry, music, and iconic images to tap
affective responses in their audiences. Both 1966 pageants reflected
their authors' earlier experience in local pageants. Indeed, the dramaturgy, rhetoric, imagery, structure, and performance strategies in the
pageants of the Easter Rising's fiftieth anniversary owe much to the
pageants created by Mac Anna and MacMahon before 1966.

Tomás Mac Anna spent his lifetime (1926–2011) in the Irish theatre. Mac Anna's portfolio ranged across the theatrical spectrum.
Deeply engaged in producing representations of the Irish past, his
theatrical career began, he recalls, with a play about local history
that "was accepted and produced by Radio Éireann."[5] Mac Anna was
only twenty-one when he started directing Irish-language plays at the
Abbey. He had long experience in directing and creating the annual
Christmas pantomimes, including the 1952 Irish-language *Setanta
agus an chu* (written with Tarlach i hUid) and the 1979 *Táin bo cu* (written with Eoghan O Tuairisc). In 1965 his direction of a celebrated
production of Brecht's *Galileo* at the Abbey "earned [Mac Anna] a
reputation for his Brechtian stagecraft."[6] Like Johnston, Mac Anna
bridled against the constraints of realism. In an interview with Christopher Murray, Mac Anna said that in his Gaelic productions as in his
direction of *Galileo*, "I always tried to get away from the rather solid
traditional, ever-expected, fourth-wall naturalistic idea."[7] In addition
to his experience with populist productions such as Christmas pantomimes, he directed more than 150 plays and wrote a dozen of his own,
including the provocative *A State of Chassis* (1970). His work in theatre
administration was also extensive: in 1967 he became artistic adviser
to the Abbey and served the Abbey as artistic director between 1973
and 1978 and again in 1985.

In 1966 Mac Anna had already been involved in the creation of
pageants for more than a decade, often in connection with the historical pageants staged in Dundalk. On May 13, 14, and 15, 1955, for
instance, Dundalk staged Mac Anna's *Historical Pageant of a Northern
Town*, advertised as "Spectacular Drama! Scenes depicting the life and

times of: St. Brigid, Blessed Oliver Plunkett, and Maeve, Cuchullain, Ferdia, and modern times. Nightly at 9:30. Floodlights. Cast of 100."[8] The press previewed, "It will tell of the Brown Bull of Cooley, the crowning of Edward Bruce, the arrest of Blessed Oliver Plunkett and many other stirring chapters in the history of the Gap of the North."[9] The selective, episodic glimpses at the past targeted not the entire nation, let alone foreign tourists, but a specific community that would perform and attend these pageants.

Mac Anna's *Aiseirí* had about sixty principal players supplemented by "a cast of 800 drawn mainly from the Defence Forces."[10] In constructing his script, Mac Anna collaborated with the Department of Defence, which produced the pageant. Several of the pageant's episodes were battle reenactments, most of which involved a large number of the participants in period costumes or in authentic or replica uniforms. Mac Anna's proposal for the pageant's finale echoes the Military Tattoos in 1935 and 1945: "In final tableau, then, we see the Volunteers of 1918–21, the Irish Army and the Republicans—here there would be a moment of tribute to the Civil War dead—the Army of the Emergency, and finally today's Army."[11] The emphasis on military encounters, the "Call to Arms," and the procession of various Irish armies over the ages recall the formulas of the earlier military tattoos.

A ninety-minute pageant, *Aiseirí* ran for five nights at Croke Park beginning on April 12, 1966. Huge photographic portraits of the sixteen republicans executed in 1916, running along the length of the stadium, flanked the raised platform stage and its dais. Speaking parts were again limited, "interpreted through three symbolic figures of 'Ireland,' 'The Poet' and 'The Soldier.'"[12] Mac Anna, like MacMahon, brought to the 1966 anniversary a long-standing advocacy of the Irish language. He, too, created a bilingual script, although, as Anthony Roche observes, English predominates and Irish appears "as a kind of seasoning along the lines of *ag labhairt cupla focail* ['speaking a few words']."[13] Micheál macLíammóir brought his vast experience with pageantry and his "black velvet voice" to perform the principal narration, which was prerecorded.

Mac Anna constructed an arc of Irish republicanism that swept over nearly two hundred years. The official publication of the Department of External Affairs describes *Aiseirí* as locating the Rising in an international context by tracing "the idea of the Republic from its beginnings in the United States and the French Revolution, through the Easter Rising to the first Dail in 1919." The pageant begins with the landing of the French in aid of the United Irishmen and their catastrophic defeat at the Battle of Ballinamuck. From the 1798 insurrection, *Aiseirí* moved to "Emmet's rising" in 1803, through the Famine, to the Young Irelanders and the Fenian Rising of 1867. The pageant paid tribute not only to the sixteen executed patriots but to several nationalist organizations: the GAA, the Gaelic League, Fianna Éireann, the Irish Citizen Army, the Irish Volunteers, and Cumann na mBan.[14] Mac Anna enlarged his pageant's appeal not only by recognizing the contributions of these groups, but also by honoring the Rising's survivors as well as its martyrs.

The most spectacular and best received of the historical scenes staged in *Aiseirí* was a reenactment of the baton charge during the 1913–14 Dublin Lockout. In the *Irish Times*, Eileen O'Brien described it as "the most zestful thing of the evening and the cheers of the audience for the Citizen Army and the Starry Plough which echoed across the whole North Side of Dublin could not leave anyone who heard them entirely unmoved."[15] The choice to stage this episode, which occurred more than two years before 1916 and to link it directly to the Easter Rising, paid special tribute to James Connolly and the Irish Citizen Army (and in doing so shifted the emphasis away from Pearse). Roisín Higgins observes, "James Connolly emerged as the most clearly realised figure of the jubilee. His life and political writings resonated in the difficult economic circumstances and strike action of the mid-1960s."[16] Cathal Brennan notes that this was consonant with other events in the official commemoration: "The prominent role of Connolly during the commemorations led many to take an interest in his writings. Lectures and publications on the role of Connolly's socialism and the Irish Citizen Army appeared."[17] Although Pearse's image was struck on the commemorative ten-shilling silver coin in 1966, in *Aiseirí* as elsewhere, Connolly was no less central a figure than Pearse.

Press accounts suggested that *Aiseirí* incorporated modern technology less than successfully: "To enjoy the pageant one must be able to enter into the spirit of the thing, to booh General Lake, to weep for Robert Emmet, to cheer unrestrainedly for the French at the Races of Castlebar. The strip neon explaining what was going on was an unnecessary touch of vulgarity."[18] *Aiseirí* was performed in "polar conditions" with poor attendance. Mac Anna had hoped for a box office of 30,000 or more (an average of about 6,000 in an arena that later that year accommodated 84,516), but audiences for *Aiseirí* were disappointing, perhaps because Irish audiences could watch Hugh Leonard's eight-part televised documentary-reenactment, *Insurrection*, from the comfort of their homes.[19]

Both Mac Anna and MacMahon took the image of resurrection as central to their 1966 pageants. The program cover of *Seachtar Fear, Seacht Lá* shows a phoenix rising from the ashes of the burning GPO; the subtitle of Mac Anna's pageant, *Gloir-reim na Cásca* [The Pageant at Easter], links it directly with Christ's resurrection. Whereas the sunburst (or sunrise) was an iconic visual trope much earlier in the century, the linkage of Easter and resurrection was hardly secular, although accessible to Protestants as well as Catholics. In both instances, images of rebirth locate the Easter Rising as key to the emergence of the independent Irish nation.

MacMahon's pageant production before 1966 was not unlike Mac Anna's: extensive engagement with amateurs, most often young people from the GAA in MacMahon's case, to stage a straightforward message of patriotism. For decades MacMahon was deeply involved with amateur theatre in Ireland as playwright, adjudicator, and enthusiast. He wrote at least seven pageants of Irish history, some spanning millennia, some focused on a few decades; some were allegorical, others commemoratively biographical. After nearly thirty years' experience with pageantry, he reached conclusions about the dramaturgy of pageantry that echo the convictions of Hilton Edwards: a pageant that "can stand on its own," MacMahon wrote, "is characterized by a strong simple story line—a steel wire as it were, upon which the beads of episode are strung. If the wire breaks the beads are scattered."[20]

In the mid-1950s MacMahon wrote two short historical pageants, *The Pageant of the Four Green Fields* and *The Pageant of the Flag*, expressly for performance at GAA events. In a letter to the editor of the *Sunday Press* in 1962, MacMahon explained that he designed his short scripts to accommodate the demands and to serve the needs of particular places and particular times: "These pageants have been produced, on ceremonial occasions, in field and on stage, in various parts of Ireland, U.S. and Britain. With my permission and approval, various producers have adapted, expanded or contracted the scripts to meet the needs of the time and locality."[21] Both *The Pageant of the Four Green Fields* and *The Pageant of the Flag* were periodically revived for performance in connection with GAA events, and some variations appear in press reports of different performances as well as in MacMahon's papers.

The Pageant of the Four Green Fields, first performed at halftime in the Meath-Kerry Gaelic football championship on September 26, 1954, found a very large audience: 75,276 spectators at Croke Park on the day of the dedication of the then-new Hogan stand, the large cantilevered grandstand closest to Jones Road on the west side of the stadium. Surviving film shows the pageant performed at the game's interval by young boys and girls wearing not fake beards and elaborate costumes, but simple modern clothing.[22] MacMahon's *The Pageant of the Flag* first appeared, along with *The Pageant of the Four Green Fields* (accompanied by army bands, Irish dancers, and choirs), under the evocative title *The West's Awake* for the opening of the Countess Markievicz Park in Sligo on July 21, 1957.

Two or three announcers, variously called heralds or criers, narrate the symbolic movement and configuration of groups on the pitch in *The Pageant of the Four Green Fields*. The physical action in both pageants is processional and employs a variable number of supernumeraries to represent Ireland's four provinces. As the synoptic tributes of the four provinces' histories were broadcast over loudspeaker, each accompanied by a familiar tune, *The Pageant of the Four Green Fields* "depicted Mother Ireland calling her sons from the Four Provinces. Thirty-two

230 • ALL DRESSED UP

boys with flags of the counties of Ireland came to the center of the field from the four corners."[23] By using abstractions, including the personification of Eire as a woman, here played by Joan Beardshaw,[24] rather than historical figures, MacMahon's pageant obviated the need for elaborate costumes and realized maximum participation and flexibility in the few minutes available for performances at halftime. Like Pearse's pageants and others performed at Castleknock and the North Monastery in Cork before the Rising, MacMahon's early pageants were written to be performed by young people: GAA members, typically both girls and boys. Mainly, these supernumeraries were playing themselves, the direct inheritors of Irish republican tradition.

boys with flags of the counties of Ireland came to the center of the field from the four corners."[23] By using abstractions, including the personification of Eire as a woman, here played by Joan Beardshaw,[24] rather than historical figures, MacMahon's pageant obviated the need for elaborate costumes and realized maximum participation and flexibility in the few minutes available for performances at halftime. Like Pearse's pageants and others performed at Castleknock and the North Monastery in Cork before the Rising, MacMahon's early pageants were written to be performed by young people: GAA members, typically both girls and boys. Mainly, these supernumeraries were playing themselves, the direct inheritors of Irish republican tradition.

The Pageant of the Four Green Fields may now seem anodyne, but by choreographing all of the thirty-two counties coming together as one Ireland, its message was charged in 1954, and within fifteen years it would be inflammatory. Only the previous month, in June 1954, the IRA successfully raided the Gough barracks in Armagh in its effort to rearm. In May 1955 two Sinn Féin (abstentionist) candidates were elected to Parliament in Northern Ireland. Of this "Northern success," writes J. Bowyer Bell, "some felt it was a straight sectarian protest vote. Others felt it was a patriotic gesture. Still others saw it as moral authority for the use of physical force."[25] By the end of 1956, the IRA Border Campaign, "Operation Harvest," was under way and would last more than six years. Eleven people, including six Royal Ulster Constabulatory members, died in guerrilla actions focused on the border between the Republic of Ireland and Northern Ireland. Given that youngsters and young adults performed *The Pageant of the Four Green Fields*, its republican message, like the one that Pearse's pageants inculcated in his pupils, was highly charged.

The Pageant of the Flag, subtitled *The March of a Nation, 1798–1920* for its performance in Sligo in 1957, fully inverted the selectivity of the historical pageantry in the 1920s. Now, like *Aiseirí*, rather than excluding the nineteenth and twentieth centuries, as had the military tattoos in the 1920s, it was the mythological and medieval past that yielded to the exclusive emphasis on a discernibly republican version of Irish history between the 1798 Rising and Independence in 1922. *The*

Pageant of the Flag memorializes nationalists from the United Irishmen, through the Fenians, to the republicans of the Easter Rising,
and it pays special tribute to Terence MacSwiney, Thomas Ashe, and
Kevin Barry, all of whom died (and died young, at forty-one, thirty-
two, and eighteen, respectively) between 1917 and 1920 at the hands
of the British or in British custody. Even though some individuals are
singled out, MacMahon's early pageants represented these republicans
as involved in populist movements whose sacrifices produced modern
Irish freedom.

A musical overture, "Let Erin Remember," an announcement in
Irish, and a ceremonial prelude begin *The Pageant of the Flag*. Its central action is the entry of a band, a drum roll, a bugle salute, and the
introduction of the flag. For the 1957 performance in Sligo, a female
and two male criers narrated the main action that shows the United
Irishmen, the 1867 Fenians, John Devoy and O'Donovan Rossa (both
among the "Cuba Five," the leaders of the Irish Republican Brotherhood who died in exile in America), the "Stalwarts of Easter Week,
Men of the Columns' ranks," all of whom fought, suffered, and died
so, in the pageant's final words, that, "in God's air, above us, free /
This, our Flag, might fly."[26]

Pearsean declamation and sentiment infuse *The Pageant of the Four
Green Fields* and *The Pageant of the Flag*. The rhetoric and imagery of
MacMahon's early pageants replicate Pearse's, sometimes quoting him
directly. In *The Pageant of the Flag*, a "strange dark voice" channeling
Pearse from "the dead generations" says that foes "cannot undo the
miracles of God who ripens in the breasts of young men the seeds
sown by the young men of a former generation. And the seeds sown
by the young of '65 and '67 are coming to their miraculous ripening
to-day. Life springs from death and from the graves of patriot men
and women spring living nations" (3–4). Echoing Pearse, MacMahon
conflates Christian and republican sacrifice. Similarly, in *The Pageant
of the Four Green Fields*, the Herald summons his sons to his side from
each of Ireland's provinces. Calling out to Antrim, Tirconaill (Donegal), Monaghan, Down, Derry, Cavan, Armagh, Fermanagh, Tyrone,
most of which constitute Northern Ireland, the Herald says:

Province dearest to my heart,
Province first in my thoughts, dominant in my dreams.
Province that is flesh of my flesh, bone of my bone, blood of my
    blood. one ireland—ireland one. I call on Cuighe Uladh . . .
    restore my language!
Go, my sons.[27]

The pageant ends by inviting audience performativity in the communal singing of "A Nation Once Again." Irish historian Gearóid Ó Tuathaigh recalls seeing a pageant in the 1950s that may well have been MacMahon's *The Pageant of the Four Green Fields*: the Republic of Ireland was configured on the pitch and in the finale; the Ulster counties joined the other provinces to show a united Ireland composed of all thirty-two counties.[28] Within little more than a decade, such sentiments would be seen as not only provocative, but possibly inflammatory.

The imagery, structure, and rhetoric of *The Pageant of the Four Green Fields* and *The Pageant of the Flag* resurface in *Seachtar Fear, Seacht Lá*. Again, the GAA commissioned MacMahon in 1966 to create a pageant celebrating the "National Holiday,"[29] March 17. Again, MacMahon wrote for performance by young GAA members, consistently referred to as boys and girls. Again, MacMahon was not paid for his script. Again, an indispensable feature of the production is music, which in March 1966 in Dublin was provided by the Artane Boys' Band, the Black Raven Pipe Band, the Emerald Girls' Pipe Band, and Comhaltas Ceoltóirí Éireann. Music was no less an essential component of MacMahon's historical pageants than of his successful 1960 Abbey play, *The Song of the Anvil*, for which Seán Ó Riada composed an original score. MacMahon's papers include an outline of his memory of the music and poetry used in the first production of *Seachtar Fear, Seacht Lá*, possibly for an unrealized revival. The music ranged from the Clancy Brothers to "Step Together," from traditional tunes to "A Nation Once Again"; extracts of poetry, sometimes only a line or two, came from Joseph Mary Plunkett's "The Stars Sang in God's Garden" and "I See His Blood upon the Rose," Francis Ledwidge's "I

Heard the Poor Old Woman Say," James Stephens's "Spring 1916," and dozens of other Irish writers.[30]

The debate between a Young Man and Young Woman who lament the irrelevance of events that took place "so long and long ago—ere we were born" frames *Seachtar Fear, Seacht Lá*. The timeless "Narrator Over-and-Above" (Martin Dempsey) answers them:

NARRATOR (*with mounting momentum*):
    I am Narrator Over-and-Above
    I know the many Masks of Nationhood
    I saw Cúchulainn struggle ere he died
    I saw the Northmen come and go
    The Normans come and hold
    I stood beside Cave Hill above Belfast
    When first the principles of separation were laid down
    I was a shaft of sunlight in the cell of Tone
    I saw the Fenians stumble in the snow
    And I was a bystander in O'Connell Street
    When, fifty years ago to-day,
    Seven men in seven days

(*The bells . . . fade down*)[31]

In its omniscience and transcendence of time, the narrative stance recalls the Spirit of the Liffey in Hayes-McCoy's *Trumpet Call*, which in turn evokes the time-transcending trope in *Signal Fires*. Although the Narrator is "Over-and-Above," the pageant itself is specifically set in the present day, "Eastertide, 1966." During the students' discussion of the meaning of Easter 1916, all seven signatories of the Proclamation appear on the pitch accompanied by "two hundred members of the Dublin G.A.A. Clubs and one hundred girls from the Camogie Association [who] represent the following groups: the Fenians, the Workers, the Monks, the Heralds, the Volunteers, the Young Men and Young Women."[32]

Seachtar Fear, Seacht Lá was performed in March 1966, outside of
the official government commemorative ceremonies in April, at Croke
Park, where "each night, for a week, three powerful Searchlights with
filters of green, white and orange" could be seen.[33] The production
was also televised.[34] Two weeks later, on Sunday, April 3, 1966, seven
thousand nationalists saw *Seachtar Fear, Seacht Lá* performed in Casement Park in Belfast by three hundred of the Dublin cast who traveled to the North, where they were joined by members of the Antrim,
Armagh, Derry, and Down GAA clubs. A young man who attended
the Belfast performance recalled "'a carnival atmosphere with can-
dyfloss and toffee apples,' and maintained that the nationalist community turned out in such large numbers merely because the floodlit
event provided a welcome relief from the dull aimlessness with which
Ulster Sundays were usually spent."[35] Press coverage of *Seachtar Fear,
Seacht Lá* in Dublin was largely positive. The *Irish Times* reported that
the pageant "pulled at the heartstrings, not through sentimentality,
but because it succeeded in crowding into two memorable hours the
smile and tear of our history, with their inevitable lacings of despair
and hope."[36]

Seachtar Fear, Seacht Lá targeted younger audiences who could have
no memory of 1916 and aspired to provoke an affective response in the
young. Higgins argues that in the 1966 pageants, "The young represented a destabilising presence who threatened the redemptive acts
that were now the preserve of old veterans and the dead."[37] Like Mac-
Mahon's earlier pageants, *Seachtar Fear, Seacht Lá* was performed by
and, to some extent, for adolescents and young adults and invited them
to emulate in life the politics they performed in the pageant as surely
as did the pageants at Castleknock, St. Enda's, and the North Monastery. Noteworthy is the prominence of young women. In the pageants
associated with elite boys' schools, with the Defence Forces, and even
in the Patrician pageants, women are marginalized. Although the 1935
tattoo recognized women of Cumann na mBan, only Johnston's *The
Pageant of Cuchulainn* and the pageants by MacMahon approach gender parity. No less important is that *Seachtar Fear, Seacht Lá* presented
Pearse not only as the descendant of the long tradition reaching back

through the centuries but as the progenitor to whom young people should look. Despite Pearse's use of physical force, the Narrator urges the audience to embrace "the principles for which these Seven Men lay down their lives," "not in the rancorous idiom that is rifle-fire,"[38] but in the peaceful pursuit of their ideals.

One of the challenges of any commemoration of the Easter Rising is the representation of a failed physical-force revolt that resulted in death and destruction and was seen even by some of its central participants as doomed.[39] Over the next few years and especially after the beginning of the Troubles, the legacy of Irish republicanism was vastly and perhaps irrevocably complicated by the violence and rhetoric of the Troubles. Cultural commentators were increasingly critical over the next decades about the 1966 commemorative events, especially about the military parade and Hugh Leonard's televised quasi reenactment, *Insurrection*. As Declan Kiberd notes, although a clear majority of Irish people in 1991 took "celebratory pride in the Rising," only "a brief, sheepish ceremony" marked the seventy-fifth anniversary; even then the taoiseach was asked why any such event was held. Kiberd sees the 1966 ceremonies as "a last, over-the-top purgation of a debt to the past, which most of the celebrants secretly suspected would go unpaid."[40] In the 1970s and 1980s, the 1966 commemorations would be decried as triumphalist and causally linked with republican violence, specifically with contemporary IRA terrorism, by what Kiberd calls "anti-nationalist revisionism" (8): "In Ireland, those who would erase or diminish the memory of 1916 are actuated by one simple conviction," argues Kiberd, "glorification of the Easter rebels leads young people to join the IRA" (11).

After the 1966 commemorative exercises, the national appetite for large-scale pageantry was again sated, if not glutted; the Rising pageants were the last pageants staged for the entire nation. In 1967 MacMahon wrote a pageant to commemorate the death of Thomas Ashe that was produced on the local GAA pitch in Dingle, its "principal parts in the pageant . . . played by Elizabeth Devane and Celsus Sheehy (relatives of Ashe), Padraigh O Mathuna and P. O Lionsigh,"[41] before an audience that included President de Valera and General Richard Mulcahy, bitter opponents in the 1920s. MacMahon here moved away from the largely processional mode that dominated his earlier pageants; he described *The Pageant of Thomas Ashe* as allegorical and as having site specificity: "His story will be interpreted on a stage symbolic of a small quay in West Kerry against the background of the sea and the things of the sea—the medium which dominated the youth of Tomás [Ashe]. Actors and actresses, choirs, verse-speakers and dancers will play their parts. An important part of the pageant which has been written entirely in Irish will be interpreted by the Black Raven Pipers Band [from Lusk], which Tomás himself founded."[42] In fine June weather, *The Pageant of Thomas Ashe* along with another short pageant by MacMahon, *Mise Eire*, were well attended by both pro- and anti-Treatyites.[43] MacMahon's tribute to Ashe was a striking instance of a commemoration that succeeded in bringing former opponents together.

MacMahon created a more ambitious two-and-a-half-hour historical pageant based on a thousand years of Limerick history, *Remember Limerick* (the city's motto), performed March 14–20, 1976, at the Savoy Theatre as part of its fourth civic week. The pageant's program is unambiguous in its mission: "To-day's pageant honours four generations of militant patriots from whose efforts to secure the freedom of Ireland from foreign domination our nation must continue to draw inspiration."[44] Directed by Martin Dempsey (MacMahon's frequent collaborator) and narrated by Des Ronan, the pageant attracted positive response in the local and national press: "It was superb drama from a group of amateurs numbering about 80 and including housewives, office clerks, bus drivers and dustmen."[45]

Three years later, to mark the centenary of Pearse's birth, Martin Dempsey (as Mairtin O Diomasaigh) again worked with MacMahon, not as a narrator, but now as the producer of *A Pageant of Pearse*. In 1979, after ten years of traumatic violence on the island of Ireland, the legacy of Pearse had shifted, even from what it had been in 1966. Now Pearse was routinely linked with and evoked by the Provisional IRA. The immediate context for *A Pageant of Pearse* was that only nine weeks earlier, on August 27, 1979, eighteen soldiers died in an explosion in Warrenpoint and, on the same day, Lord Mountbatten and three others were killed when terrorists blew up his boat near Sligo. A month earlier the Provisional IRA rejected the pope's call for peace in Ireland.

With a cast of one hundred, *A Pageant of Pearse* appeared for both matinees and evening performances over five days (plus a preview), November 6–10, 1979, at Dublin's National Stadium, where a two-tiered stage offered sixteen thousand square feet of stage space. Minister for Education John Wilson "said that children's attendance at and participation in the pageant will be regarded as time spent in school."[46] The pageant costs ran near fifty thousand pounds, with an unspecified amount of subvention coming from the government. A press release from Coiste Chomoradh an Phiarsaigh (Committee to Commemorate Pearse) described it as "A Fair Effort to present all the facts" and quoted MacMahon as intending to present Pearse "as a human being caught in the toils of superhuman events . . . as a character displaying human flaws and fears as well as heroism." The press release highlighted the professionalism of the production: a full (prerecorded) orchestral score, a cast of twenty-six professional actors including Patrick Dawson as Pearse and Barry Cassin as Yeats, and MacMahon's "hope to excite the audience theatrically through the visual, the spoken word, poetry, song, dance and instrumental music and to build up a spectacle in which Pearse the man can be seen in a warm light."[47] MacMahon took a year to write the bilingual script, not least because Ruth Dudley Edwards's 1977 *Patrick Pearse: The Triumph of Failure* cast a very cold eye on their subject. Moreover, the popular imagination now saw Pearse as the patron of physical-force violence that beset Northern Ireland and had recently moved south.

As he had in *Seachtar Fear, Seacht Lá*, MacMahon frames the pageant as a debate between two students, Brid and Eoin, outside the GPO. Four old women (Ogbhean) invoke the memory of Pearse as "poet . . . teacher . . . barrister . . . playwright . . . sculptor . . . leader of men," but the mob denounces him as "fanatic . . . dreamer . . . Mock Messiah! Exploiter of the young . . . Pederast. Eleutheromaniac! . . . Mystic! Introvert! . . . Egoist! Blasphemer! And scorner of Women! Him with his dropped eyelid and his Lisp! Martyr Supreme!

Dangerous Nationalist! Slyboots!"[48] In the course of the three-hour spectacle, "the broad spectrum of legend and history from Naoise to 1916 got an airing in the National Stadium," wrote the *Irish Times*. The ghosts of Wolfe Tone, Robert Emmet, John Mitchel, Fintan Lalor, Thomas Davis, and scores of other characters, including Margaret Pearse, Grace Gifford, and the editors of the *Irish Times* and the *Irish Independent*, appeared onstage as so many ghosts of Christmases past. After three hours of portraying Pearse as a man of great action, "suddenly—and without reason—the voice of a pacifist MacMahon calling, through his young Trinity student, for no more blood but for unity through love."[49] As in the admonition against violence in *Seachtar Fear, Seacht Lá*, *A Pageant of Pearse* tried to disassociate Pearse from physical force and to position him "in a warm light."

Even where the pageant might have expected to attract positive reviews, the press coverage was harsh. The *Irish Press*, for instance, wrote that "Pearse's life is presented in a sprawling ream of history that lacks dramatic sense or scope. . . . The device used to establish continuity: two U.C.D. students outside the G.P.O. debating on Pearse's life within the hearing of a tipsy street singer, cannot balance the uneven tone of the piece; indeed at times the trio are in danger of being trampled on by the endless procession of political and literary figures." *A Pageant of Pearse* was one of the only pageants reviewed by a theatre critic; it took as bad a drubbing as a theatre production ever took. The actors, prerecorded music, and three-hour length were all lambasted, as were the "irrelevantly multi-coloured lighting effects. . . . Hundreds of ill-fitting costumes paraded before and around Gerry O'Sullivan's ugly mural of a set."[50] Attendance was as poor as the reviews. For some performances the performers might have outnumbered the audience members.

In 1979 another of MacMahon's pageants, the most widely seen of his historical pageants, perhaps of all Irish historical pageants, was entering its thirteenth year: the Knappogue Castle *Pageant of Ireland*. When transatlantic service between Ireland and the United States began in 1945, Shannon was the sole destination and departure city. Brendan O'Regan's 1947 duty-free shopping scheme was one inventive response to the many foreign tourists passing through Shannon Airport; medieval banquets at nearby castles were another. By the 1960s tens, perhaps hundreds, of thousands of North America tourists found themselves booking hotels near Shannon Airport the night before their return flights. The most durable of MacMahon's pageants, perhaps of any Irish pageant, can be traced back to the early 1960s when the Shannon Free Airport Development Company "introduced the idea of such banquets to this country."[51] The medieval banquets offered an evening's entertainment that provided something "more Irish" than drinking in the hotel with other tourists awaiting their morning flights. Bunratty Castle, purchased by Lord Gort in 1954, began its medieval banquets in 1963; Dunguaire Castle in Kinvara followed suit in 1966. In 1967 Knappogue Castle offered not only a banquet but also MacMahon's *Pageant of Ireland*, which was still running in the 1980s.

As an entertainment devised for North American tourists, Mac-Mahon's Knappogue pageant was among the most highly scripted of pageants. With a running time under an hour, thirty-seven minutes in one iteration, it offered "glimpses and impressions of Ireland spanning a period of over 2,000 years."[52] A young man and young woman, Finn and Grania, beget the Seneschal ("From her the lovely / And from him the feared / The primal poet sprung").[53] MacMahon considered the Seneschal, the storyteller, "the bearer of the story line—the wire on which the beads were threaded."[54] Those beads were many. MacMahon's *Pageant of Ireland* began in the fourth century BC with the Celts and Fionn mac Cumhaill, moved to St. Patrick's conversion of Ireland in 432, after which

> . . . the cream of Europe's youth
> Flocked to our schools, were housed and taught
> And from this island
> Went forth a band of wandering Irish monks
> To spread the peace of Christ. (4)

This golden age of peace and learning prevailed until the Danes defeated Brian Boru,

> . . . and thus it was that in the very soil
> Immediately outside these walls of Knappogue
> There rose a valorous Confederation of the Clans
> Known by the name . . . Dalcassians. (5)

"The long night of slavery" was the legacy of Dervogilla and Diarmuid: "A sorry pair! Seven and a half centuries of bondage / These two brought upon our land" (6). Despite the draconian English laws that set down the penalty of death for any Norman taking an Irish name, playing an Irish game, or speaking the Irish language, the Normans "felt the pull of Ireland's ways" (6). Cromwell's time in Ireland was represented, as at the 1935 tattoo, by Galloping Hogan leading Patrick Sarsfield out of Limerick to blow up the siege train at Ballyneety. Robert Emmet, "that rebel debonnaire [*sic*]" (9), ended his speech from the dock with the phrase "let me [*sic*] epitaph be written" (10). In the nineteenth century, "two dark strangers stalked the land / Their names were Famine and the brother Death" (10). As an epilogue the *Pageant of Ireland* looked to a "schoolmaster called Pearse" (12) and the Easter Rising of 1916 in anticipation of the freedom of the modern Irish state.

MacMahon's *Pageant of Ireland* is keenly aware of its largely American audience and gestures toward internationalism. Particular tribute, for instance, is paid to the origins of the Fenian brotherhood: "After the American Civil War many officers and men of Irish birth or descent assembled in U.S. and Canada and decided to free Ireland from British Rule. Thus was founded the Fenian Brotherhood."[55] At another moment a "snatch of 'La Marseillaise'" is heard. The pageants at Knappogue did for Irish history what the Reduced Shakespeare Company did for the world's greatest dramatist: rendered them accessible, entertaining, uncomplicated, and, perhaps most important, painlessly brief. Nonetheless, its enduring popularity suggests it was, for many, better than the hotel bar.

There were other pageants in the 1970s and 1980s. In October 1984 the GAA celebrated its centenary with a play-pageant, *Purple and Gold, 1884–1984*, written by Nicholas Furlong and directed by Tomás Mac Anna. In 1989, for the seventieth anniversary of the meeting of the first Dáil at the Mansion House, Mac Anna created yet another pageant, one of those that Daly describes as "low-key." On May 5, 1990, the Derry City Council sponsored "possibly the largest outdoor pageant ever staged by a local authority in Ireland" to commemorate the tercentenary of the Siege of Derry.[56] Drawing on wide cross-body support, Mitchel McLaughlin, later general secretary of Sinn Féin, said that "the pageant was seen as 'marketing a normalising image of Derry.'"[57] Indeed, the pageant, written and directed by Andy Hinds, appeared on a bill with Shaun Davey's specially commissioned "Relief of Derry Symphony" and performances by several pipe bands.[58] Wary of ostentatious bombast, triumphalism, and whatever might be construed as offensive, official representations of the past were now very cautious in their representation of the past and sometimes underwhelming in their brevity and formality.

In 1993 Knappogue Castle replaced its pageant of Irish history with a similar show focused on women in Irish history. These entertainments were highly commodified presentations for the sometimes-inebriated tourist's gaze. Their performers were professionals, their audience alien, their message more anodyne than ever. In 1991 Seamus Deane lamented that "in so far as it can, Ireland now treats the past as a kind of supermarket for tourists, a place well-provided with 'interpretative centres' that will allow Newgrange and Joyce, the flora and fauna of the Burren, the execution cells at Kilmainham, the Derrynaflan hoard and the Blarney stone to be viewed as the exotic debris thrown up by the convulsions of a history from which we have now escaped into a genial depthlessness."[59] Cut off from its community and from its populist base, pageantry was literally deracinated. Only by returning to its roots did historical pageantry live another day.

THE RECUPERATIVE PAGEANTRY OF MACNAS

At the end of the twentieth century, Ireland experienced a festivalization that provided destinations and programming for Irish as well as foreign tourists. Furlong notes, "Many of the particular festivals which sprang from the Tóstal have survived for almost 50 years, including the Dublin theatre festival, the Cork film festival, the Waterford light opera festival and the Cork choral festival, and none of these (and the multitude of other festivals which now attract thousands every year to these shores) could exist with the continued support of tourist bodies."[60] In 1959 Bord Fáilte published a brochure, *Ireland of the Festivals*, to suggest tourist destinations, especially ones outside Dublin. Today, in addition to the annual gatherings spawned by and surviving the Tóstal, festivals around the country center on everything from food to film, from lace to literature, from yachts to Yeats. Festivals like the Galway Arts Festival, founded in 1978, brought international performers to Irish audiences. Exposure to these international companies and their often radically nonrealistic theatricality provided the spark for several new Irish companies, including Operating Theatre in 1980, Macnas in 1986, Barabbas Theatre Company in 1994.[61] Irish theatre practitioners, Mikel Murfi among them, might train outside Ireland, as Murfi did at École Jacques Lecoq in Paris. Rather than pursuing a career in Britain or the United States, they returned to work in Ireland. This internationalism was one of the germs for the globalization that Patrick Lonergan describes as shaping the vibrant Irish theatre of and beyond the Celtic Tiger. Indeed, Lonergan observes the "reduction of the importance of spoken language in favour of visual spectacle" and the experience of theatre practitioners outside Ireland to ask, "What does 'nation' or 'region' mean in a globalizing world?"[62] The 1995 Arts Council reported, "The Galway Arts Festival about 10 years ago were involved in bringing very radical European productions to Ireland. Macnas was born from such a European experience. The mask making, circus influence and style of performance all came from direct foreign influence."[63] But there was another, perhaps underreported, critical spark: state funding in the arts sector. Through the Arts Council, FÁS (the Irish Training and Employment Authority) schemes, and other agencies, the state was investing in these performance companies and arts enterprises. Macnas, for instance, not only received Arts Council funding, but also benefited from employing people through an FÁS wage-subsidy program whereby the unemployed or underemployed received professional training.

At the same time, the Abbey explored new dramturgical frontiers. Bernadette Sweeney documents the emergence of one of the most startling of these interventions: the landmark collaboration among director Patrick Mason, playwright Tom Mac Intyre, and actor Tom Hickey to adapt Patrick Kavanagh's 1942 poem *The Great Hunger* for theatrical performance.[64] The production was a striking appropriation of a well-known if not well-loved literary text, liberated from any debt to the literal or literary. In his essay on the production, Vincent Hurley locates the Mason–Mac Intyre–Hickey production in the tradition of practitioners and theorists who advocated "reawakening the primitive power of theatre by freeing it from the constraints of formal texts and appealing directly to the unconscious mind through gesture, movement and spectacle."[65] Nor was *The Great Hunger* an isolated instance of nonrealistic dramaturgy from the Abbey in the 1980s. Mason's brilliant premieres of Mac Intrye's other plays, of Frank McGuinness's plays, especially *Observe the Sons of Ulster Marching toward the Somme* (1985), and of Tom Murphy's *The Gigli Concert* (1983), Stewart Parker's *Pentecost* (1987), and Friel's *Dancing at Lughnasa* (1990) redefined what the world understands to be an Abbey play.

In the 1980s a host of Irish theatre practitioners and scholars demonstrated that text and performance were often not discrete entities. Anna McMullan chronicled a robust theatre scene in Ireland fueled by "the emergence of theatre practices which foreground performance: the visual, kinesic and the corporeal as major means of expression and signification."[66] Christie Fox and Sweeney argue that recent Irish theatre adopted and popularized new approaches to physicality and the human body. As Fox observes, that this sea change occurred when it did was not coincidental: "The fluidity of borders between text and performance comes at a time when other borders, markers, and definitions are called into question or are undermined by social relations."[67] Macnas was neither the first nor the only Irish company to take up the challenge of reimagining the possibilities for the performance of Irish historical and mythological characters in the late twentieth century. *Stage* magazine praised the "ritualistic pageantry" of James W. Flannery's 1989 staging of five of Yeats's plays as *Cúchulainn Cycle* with Ciaran Hinds and Olwen Fouéré and a score by "Billy" Whelan. Theatre Omnibus staged Michael Harding's *The Waking of Brian Boru* in Ennis in 1990. In 1995 Big Telly Company produced Zoe Seaton's *Cúchulainn* in Coleraine.

One representative instance of Macnas's treatment of the Irish past and its inventive, eclectic dramaturgy, the *Táin*, suggests the trajectory of historical pageantry in Ireland as the twentieth century drew to a close. As remote as this production was from Pearse's *The Boyhood Deeds of Cúchulainn*, the resurgence of Irish mythology in Irish theatre at the end of the twentieth century recalls its popularity at the century's beginning. Like the pageants in the century's first decade, the Macnas *Táin* drew heavily on community support; enlisted the participation of large numbers of amateurs, including children and adolescents; and attracted huge audiences. What set Macnas apart from other contemporary companies pursuing performance-based work were its systematic excavation of indigenous performance traditions, its involvement of the community, and its interrogation of whose Ireland it was.

Inspiration for Macnas came from the appearance of two European companies, both founded in 1971, with ties to the Galway Arts Festival: Els Comediants, the Catalan theatre company, and Footsbarn, originally based in the barn of the Foot family in Cornwall. In the early 1980s the Galway Arts Festivals featured performances by these troupes, both of which, like Macnas, draw on highly theatrical traditions that emphasized music, elaborate costuming and masks, clowning, dance, and acrobatics and, especially for Els Comediants, minimized the centrality of a text-based script and the exalted status of the playwright. These companies typically performed outside purpose-built theatres: in the open air, in tents, or in appropriated, especially disused, spaces. One of the hallmarks of Macnas has been the reclamation of public and unlikely private spaces for the performance of community-specific and community-participatory spectacles. Its mission statement was on one occasion formulated thusly: "We hope to create opportunities for celebration and ritual through creating spectacles with the community."[68] Macnas took theatre out of theatres by bringing it directly to the larger community, enlisting large numbers of volunteers, developing performances that were not based on a playwright's text, and amusing all they encountered with aggressively anti-elitist entertainments.

Macnas established its early reputation in Ireland and throughout Europe on the basis of parades and festivals that Fox and others have chronicled. The annual Galway Arts Festival parade, for which they are probably best known and which, until 2013, was a highlight of the Galway Arts Festival, recruited hundreds of volunteers to produce a cleverly themed spectacle grounded in the particularities of Galway life. Macnas's productions routinely comment politically and socially—sometimes overtly, as in an installation on a Galway roundabout of a giant cigarette stubbed out on Quit Smoking Day, but more often obliquely. In 2004, for instance, the parade wryly commented on global warming with an elaborate tropical float accompanied by the booming sounds of Martha Reeves and the Vandellas performing "Heat Wave." In 2007, after Galway residents had endured a four-month ban on drinking tap water (a ban that continued until September 17, 2007), the Macnas parade featured a huge green cryptosporidium caged in what resembled a circus wagon. When the cryptosporidium escaped and menaced spectators, nurses attended the stricken Galwegians. The final float in the parade was encumbered by hundreds of empty plastic water bottles, dragged along as if it were a rigidly geometric mobile sculpture by Carl Andre. With the parades, spectacles, and plays, Macnas, perhaps no less successfully than the Galway Arts Festival, has become, in geographer Bernadette Quinn's assessment, "deeply embedded . . . in the artistic life of the city."[69]

The word "Macnas" is now often translated from the Irish as "joyful abandonment," but in earlier days it was defined by the less concise but more descriptive phrase "the act of playing or disporting oneself, romping and horseplay." Fox notes the Irish word means "'playfulness, act of playing, frolicking,' but which also has a secondary meaning of 'wantonness,' referring to the 'lusts of the flesh.'"[70] In pursuing its ludic agenda, the pageantry of Macnas recovers important features from paratheatrical traditions: garish makeup and costumes, elaborate floats, grotesque puppets, stilt walkers, gargantuan forms—an eighty-foot-high (or -long) Gulliver, a giant whale, oversize heads (seen, for instance, in their creations for the 1993 U2 Zooropa tour)— as well as a whole range of spectacular effects to assail and to delight the senses.

Macnas also asserted a distinctive Irish heritage of festive social traditions that had been repressed by church or state. Founder Páraic Breathnach sees the festive dimension of Macnas as intimately related not only to both what the company took from Els Comediants and the venerable traditions of carnival described by Mikhail Bakhtin but also to the long-repressed forms and spirit of an expressly Irish festivity: "My parades were deliberately commenting on the society we live in. . . . The idea of carnival is that you have license—license to give out to people, license to dance, license to take off your clothes. Those elements had been severely repressed in Ireland from the 1840s by the Catholic church—dancing, crossroads dancing, fair days, all those things had been severely proscribed by the Catholic Church so it was very repressive. Ireland was very repressive in the fucking eighties so there was a distinct anti-clerical element in all the work I did at that time."[71]

As decisive as the exposure to El Comediants and Footsbarn was, Macnas was not merely interested in imitating or importing foreign models. Especially in its first decade, Macnas methodically mined Irish myth and culture to exploit existing but now-submerged Irish traditions of public spectacle and performance. One of its first projects in 1986 was a series of school visits by Wrenboys that featured actors and musicians dressed in the distinctive straw ruffs and capes and the conical straw headgear that masks the face.[72] For New Year's Eve in 1986, Macnas devised a journey through the city center for children who encountered a Watchman, "Dark Drummers," a Gateman, and finally a Priestess of Light. The next year Macnas devised *The Big Game*, celebrating the Galway three-in-a-row team that won the senior football championship in 1964, 1965, and 1966 with nineteen oversize replica heads, in "a 10-minute mock football game between Macnas performers taking the place of Galway and Mayo footballers. Those 10 minutes of football were featured highlights from the 1960s re-enacted live before an audience of 35,000 people; one of the largest if not *the* largest, audiences ever to watch a theatre event in Ireland."[73] The performance, televised during the halftime of the Connaught finals, brought Macnas national recognition. As one early participant writes, it was "a way of bringing art to the masses at a Gaelic football match."[74] In 1991 *Tir Faoi Thoinn* (The Land beneath the Waves) featured Breathnach as that "master of tricks and illusions, Manannán mac Lir . . . a spiritual being associated with rebirth and procreation" and recruited women, men, and children, all to perform as seductive mermaids.[75] In these early projects, Irish legend, of ancient or recent vintage, was the point of departure: the Fir Bolgs, Gráinne Mhaol, and the Galway champion senior football teams from 1964, 1965, and 1966 provided themes for Macnas spectacles. Similarly, in 1994 the Macnas parade portrayed the Tribes of Galway. These performances sought to recuperate specifically Irish folk traditions and legend, even if they, like those legendary Galway football squads from the 1960s, were within living memory. Like the historical pageants in 1907–14, Macnas looked back to native stories, but unlike their predecessors, Macnas reclaimed festivals and carnivals of ancient Ireland that were subject to the repression of neither the English nor the Catholic Church. Unlike St. Enda's and Castleknock at the beginning of the century, pagan Ireland appealed to Macnas not because of its unredeemed prefiguration of Christian virtue, but precisely because it was pagan. Indeed, many of the early Macnas performances imagined a pre-Christian world of carnival as defining the Irish past. The revival of this pagan Ireland was a radical departure from the religious and historical pieties of the pageantry of a much earlier Revival.

Based in one of the regions of Ireland most committed to the Irish language and with Irish speakers among its founders, Macnas negotiated challenges of bilingualism principally by using "a minimum of words, focusing their activity on mime, music, and movement."[76] By incorporating Irish as the language heard daily on the streets of Galway and placing it in a festive context expressing joyful abandon, Macnas treated Irish not as a lifeless school subject but as an organic component of Galway life. The use of the Irish language was entirely consonant with the determination of Macnas to appropriate familiar spaces. Fox rightly notes that performance-based companies such as Macnas responded to Peter Brook's seminal interrogation of the very nature and location of theatre. Macnas sought out and reclaimed disused buildings in Galway: Fisheries Field, McDonagh's Flood Street warehouse, and the building that once housed the University College Galway wind tunnel. The Macnas parades, like most public parades, went right through the heart of this city, another means of taking theatre to the people. The parades were accessible, inviting, free, and extremely popular. They were also irreverent, outlandish, and politically oriented. By sacralizing the secular, Macnas transformed ordinary spaces and offered the community the opportunity to celebrate itself. Macnas's focused regionalism, its determination to be local—employing local volunteers, local heroes, local legends—not only attracted community support to create ever more epic productions but also gave Macnas performances authenticity. Paradoxically perhaps, the intensity of community support, pride, and participation also facilitated Macnas's international reputation.

The year 1992 was an extremely productive and busy one for Macnas and for the arts in Galway more widely. In January 1992 Macnas extended the run of *Circus Story*. Over the next three months, they revived *Tir Faoi Thoinn* for production in Holland and did their part for the St. Patrick's Day parade. In May and June they rehearsed and took the *Táin*, along with *Gulliver*, to Expo 92 in Seville. In addition to the Irish premiere of the *Táin* during the Galway Arts Festival in July, they presented a street spectacle, *Capall*; both toured Ireland in August and September. In October the *Táin* won Best Irish Production in the Dublin Theatre Festival, and, in November, it appeared at the Glasgow Festival, the Belfast Festival, and the Patrick Kavanagh Festival in Carrickmacross. By December they had another children's show, *The E P Moran Christmas Circus Show*, running in Galway and appeared with the Saw Doctors at the Point in Dublin on New Year's Eve.

For the 1992 Expo in Spain, Macnas departed from its more expansive parades and spectacles to bring the company's performance skills to bear on a more narrative theatre performance: the Macnas *Táin*. This was neither Macnas's first stage play nor its first performance in a conventional theatre space; indoor performances of *Alice* (in Wonderland), *Treasure Island*, and *Circus Story* preceded the *Táin*, and Macnas eventually realized a trilogy of mythologically based works. The strength and cohesion of these non-text-based narratives grew out of and incorporated techniques and stagecraft developed in their performance-based spectacles.

The poster for the *Táin* conveys only a modest sense of the company's use of huge flags, elaborate costumes, exotic helmets and other headgear, pikes, and similar props to fill the often-large playing spaces and to convey the epic quality of the action. In part to break away from the perception that their productions were mere entertainments and ones suited to, if not directed toward, children, the 1992 production of the *Táin* was performed in a less participatory and more formal relationship between actors and audience. *Táin* offered a carefully structured narrative whose mise en scène brought talents acquired on the streets to more conventional theatrical spaces. The non-text-based narratives found strength and were meticulously rehearsed, blocked, and performed to a full musical score. Breathnach recalls that Thomas Kinsella's 1969 translation of *The Táin* provided an inspiration for the production and that a philologist with Irish researched original manuscript sources for Macnas as well. The surviving records of the Macnas *Táin* include a complete videotape of one of its performances, press clippings and promotional materials, and a four-page typescript, "Draft Scenario," labeled by hand as "1st draft."[77]

The stage for the *Táin* was a raked circular platform with three large standing stones (Plate 8). Performed with "dialogue" in neither Irish nor English, the Macnas *Táin* uses mime, a heavily percussive score by John Dunne, and athletic choreography to convey its narrative. Structured on an arc that begins in a carefree, even comic mode and ends in the tragic, their *Táin* opens with the young Cúchulainn and his foster brother, Ferdiad, playfully batting around a hurley ball (or sliotar). A grand marriage procession interrupts their games as chariots bearing Medb and Ailill circle the main playing area.

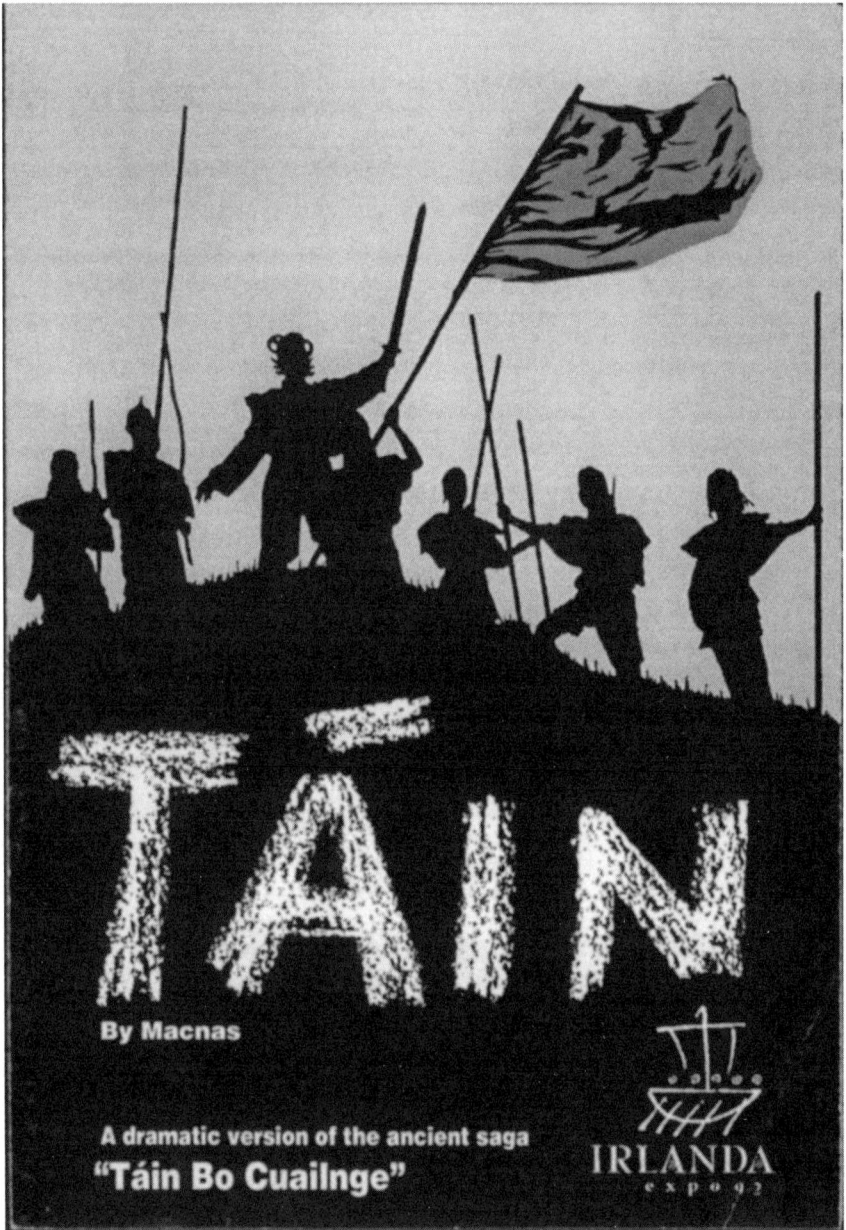

28. Program cover for the Macnas *Táin*, 1992. Courtesy of Macnas and the Macnas Archive, James Hardiman Library, National University of Ireland Galway.

Powdered and pampered by their attendants, the bride and groom glory in the physical delights of their honeymoon night in acrobatic performances beneath their bridal sheets, a green quilt representing "the fields of Ireland."[78] Using broad physical humor and slapstick, their relationship quickly devolves into an aggressive and ludicrous display of material possessions: crowns and headdresses, ornate pillows, treasure boxes stuffed with jewels. When Medb shows off her golden bull and Ailill counters with his immense white bull, the mood changes from silly to sober as Medb's jealousy turns from childish to sinister. When Conchobar's even more immense Brown Bull passes by, Medb and Ailill, a couple perfectly matched in their need to possess what they do not have, collapse in a tantrum of jealousy. Consumed by envy, Medb makes up to Ailill and implores him to join forces with her; together they dispatch two emissaries to Conchobar to acquire the bull. The emissaries come across Cúchulainn, again intently honing his hurling skills. They steal his hurley ball and taunt him in a game of keep-away that soon turns violent: they knock him to the ground and sadistically shove the sliotar in his mouth. Just as one of Medb's men is about to send the sliotar flying by slamming the back of Cúchulainn's head with the caman, Conchobar arrives in his chariot. Conchobar's men behead one of the emissaries and dispatch the other back to Connaught with the severed head of his comrade.

Outraged, first by the failure of the emissary's mission and then by the display of the severed head, Ailill and Medb summon their armies, the Connaughtmen, to war against Ulster. Otherworldly female figures, wielding black nets and crimson cloths that foretell a fate of defeat and death, hardly deter Medb and Ailill, who press on with their army to Ulster where they encounter Conchobar. Medb tries to bargain with Conchobar, offering first her golden bull, then her daughter, and finally herself. With Connaught stage right and Ulster stage left, the battle is set. After initial single combats, a wailing woman afflicts the Ulstermen with the pain of childbirth; the men crumple in agony as their bellies grow huge. Cúchulainn, the sole Ulsterman unaffected by the curse, defeats Medb's warriors one after another in brutal single combats. By impugning his manhood, Medb finally goads the last

Connaughtman, Ferdiad, to fight Cúchulainn. Ferdiad and Cúchulainn greet as the long-lost brothers they are before beginning in a series of exhausting single combats—first with short spears, then long spears, and finally with swords. Cúchulainn's *risteárd*, his warp spasm, a phrase borrowed from Kinsella's translation of *The Táin*, transports him to a superhuman and inhuman killing mode. By now the production's tenor has moved to the realms of tragedy. Pitting friend against friend, brother against brother, the combat of Ferdiad and Cúchulainn will, the audience knows, be as horrific as it is pointless. The scenario concludes: "The scene is now one of utter senseless desolation and destruction. A large black raven enters from the audience and flies over the stage. It perches on top of the standing stone with its black multi layered tail covering the whole stage. All is black."[79]

In its interpretation of the *Táin*, Macnas foreground the deadly internecine combat between Ferdiad and Cúchulainn, which in 1992, with the Good Friday Agreement six years off and nowhere in sight, plainly evoked an ongoing struggle of Irish people killing other Irish people. That the conflict originates in Medb's jealousy and initially targets her own husband's worldly possessions underscores the puerile nature of the encounter. The Macnas *Táin*, like Johnston's *The Pageant of Cuchulainn* thirty-six years earlier, transformed the narrative from an epic celebration of military prowess (if indeed it ever was only that) to a twentieth-century exploration of the pointlessness and horror of violence. In this retelling Ferdiad and Cúchulainn are pawns manipulated to fight each other with tragic consequences. The implications for their deadly combat, its senselessness and futility, had obvious analogues in the sectarian struggle in Northern Ireland.

The Macnas *Táin*, like most of their stage plays, was performed by the company members that gave Macnas its core stability in the late eighties and early nineties. Using doubling, tripling, and quadrupling, a cast of about a dozen, accompanied by five musicians, performed twenty-seven roles. The authorship of the work is attributed to Páraic Breathnach, who describes a highly collaborative process in working with a researcher, the director (Rod Goodall), the composer (John Dunne), and the company. The program from October 1992 credited its creation to "Paraic Breathnach, Tom Conroy, John Dunne, Rod Goodall, Peter Sammon, and Owen MacCarthaigh."[80] The reliance on ancient myth, the absence of a fixed dialogue, and the collaboration of the company combine to expose how problematic the notion of authorship is in performance-based work like the *Táin*. But for all of the collaboration and improvisation that brought the Macnas *Táin* to fruition, the performances were precisely blocked to a full musical score. They had to be because their performance of the *Táin* relied heavily on highly physical choreography, especially the fights between Ulstermen and Connaughtmen, which included stunt work such as the realistically mimed beheading of one of Medb's emissaries. The original score by John Dunne, using five musicians playing keyboards, guitar, bass guitar, bodhrán, and other percussion instruments, perfectly suited the action onstage: a somber percussive dirge as the dead are carried from the field of battle and wailing guitar riffs during the battles between Cúchulainn and Ferdiad.

The performances at the Seville Expo 92 garnered a nomination for a UNESCO award and attracted avid coverage in the Irish press. Lorcan Roche's response to the *Táin* in the *Irish Press* described Macnas as "one of the country's most innovative theatre companies" and the *Táin* as "a celebration of that Celtic identity and pride."[81] After seeing the *Táin* performed at the Galway Arts Festival, Paddy Wordworth wrote that "on the considerable strengths of this production Macnas must now be recognised as a vital force in Irish theatre, without any qualifications whatsoever."[82] The political dimension of the Macnas interpretation of the Irish national epic was even more keenly observed in reviews from Scotland and Northern Ireland. The Glasgow *Herald*, for instance, described it as "an outsize drama of feudal quarrels and internecine violence in which (giving it a relevance that can hardly escape anyone) warrior brother slays warrior brother and the monarchs of Connacht and Ulster look on in horror at the bloodshed they have caused."[83]

Press coverage of the success of the *Táin* at Expo 1992 paved the way for extensive touring both in Ireland and in the United Kingdom. Over the remainder of 1992, Macnas toured, performing the

29. *Táin*, Expo Festival, Seville, Spain, 1992. Courtesy of Macnas and the Macnas Archive, James Hardiman Library, National University of Ireland Galway.

Táin more than eighty times in a wide variety of venues, both indoor and open-air, including the Sligo Sports Centre, Fellows Square at Trinity College, McDonagh's Flood Street warehouse in Galway, Festival Hall at Queen's in Belfast, and the National Stadium in Dublin. Breathnach estimates an average audience size of about seven hundred or, conservatively, a total audience of more than fifty thousand, a larger audience than could be accommodated at a sold-out fifteen-week run on the Abbey Theatre's main stage. At the end of the year, the Macnas *Táin* won Performance of the Year at the Telecom Éireann Entertainment awards.

Macnas's treatment of historical pageantry burst the constraints that had emerged in the straitened commemorative pageantry of the fifties, sixties, and seventies. The Macnas *Táin*'s notion of what Ireland was or is was light-years removed from 1954's and 1955's *The Pageant of St. Patrick* and similarly subverts the nationalism in the 1966 commemorative pageants. This Ireland was lusty, pagan, and vibrant. It was as if de Valera had never existed. Just as the counterhegemonic pageants in the early twentieth century contested what was Irish, so Macnas's recuperative pageantry asserted an Irish heritage of robust, unashamed sensuality in communal celebration. The *Táin* was the first in what is sometimes referred to as Macnas's Celtic Trilogy, theatre spectacles grounded in Irish mythology, including *Buile Suibhne* (*Mad Sweeney*, 1994) and *Balor* (1996). For several years after the *Táin*, Macnas regularly produced plays, the most remarkable of which was 1998's stage adaptation of Patrick McCabe's *The Dead School*, which, though a qualified success, contains some of the most amazing stagecraft to grace an Irish stage in the late twentieth century.

The Macnas *Táin* also informed *The Story of the Bull*, the production from the Fabulous Beast Dance Company for the 2005 Dublin Theatre Festival. The production evokes Karl Marx's famous line that history repeats itself, first as tragedy and then, the second time, as farce. Set in a contemporary, avaricious Celtic Tiger Ireland, Michael Keegan-Dolan's script uses Thomas Kinsella's translation of *The Táin* as a point of departure to transform Medb and Ailill into Maeve and Alan Fogarty, high-powered, grasping wheeler-dealers who are fixated upon the bull of title, which belongs to the rural Cullen family. Maeve not only covets the Cullen bull, but keeps a stable of virile young male step dancers, all parodies of Michael Flatley, to perform in her wildly successful stage show, *Celtic Bitch*. This Maeve runs through champion step dancers the way her namesake ran through warriors. Exhausted by their grueling performances (both on the boards and in her bed), they are regularly replaced by even younger, more studly men. The highlight of *The Story of the Bull* was the swan song of one of these dancers in the remarkably self-deprecating dance of an aging arthritic performed and choreographed by one of the original stars of *Riverdance*, Colin Dunne.

Breathnach recalls the 1992 *Táin* as wedding form and content: "A new style of theatre we had created: a non-verbal visual theatre based on Irish mythology and stories from Irish myth. And, indeed, it presaged the whole Celtic revival of *Riverdance* and others. We were way ahead of the game in that respect, in reviving Celtic mythology and the stories of Celticism."[84] A happy paradox of the work of companies like Macnas is that access and exposure to dramaturgies, training, and theatrecraft from outside Ireland did not result in turning away from Irish traditions, themes, and performance strategies, but intensified their recuperation of what was specifically national and regional.

Today Macnas is best known for its annual street parade in Galway and its presentations at the St. Patrick's Day parade in Dublin (and often elsewhere as well). Since the mid- to late 1990s, the Galway Arts Festival, as Bernadette Quinn observes, shifted its attention away from the Galway community and to the attraction of national international tourism: "The historical privileging of Galway residents and the place of Galway was now altered."[85] The Macnas entry in the 2012 St. Patrick's Day parade in Dublin, for instance, featured a sixteen-foot humanoid rhinoceros that moved along the parade routes in Dublin as well as Moscow seated in an enormous wheelchair. The rhinoceros may have gestured toward Eugene Ionesco's absurdist classic or to Beckett (who initially proposed having Nell and Nagg in *Endgame* confined to wheelchairs rather than trash cans), but Macnas's focus on Irish performance traditions was distinctive of its early years.

Whereas spectacles like Macnas's draw on the carnivalesque possibilities of pageantry, commemorative ceremonies have grown increasingly formal, solemn, and restrained. That Macnas so successfully demonstrated the possibilities for pageantry begot a range of similar enterprises, notably Bui Bolg, the Wexford street theatre company founded in 1994. Over the years Macnas collaborated with hundreds of theatre practitioners, including Mikel Murfi, Vincent Woods, Pat McCabe, and Mick Lally. No less important is that a six-year-old who can remember a New Year's Eve walkabout through Galway city is now a thirtysomething whose commodious understanding of theatre was shaped by Macnas.

Conclusion

Ireland still does not have a festive national holiday that celebrates the state, as does the Fourth of July in the United States or Bastille Day in France. Before Independence, Lady's Day, August 15 (the Feast of the Assumption, still a Catholic holy day), was often marked by nationalist gatherings, including Daniel O'Connell's monster meeting at Tara in 1843. Kenmare and other localities still hold a fair or festival around Lady's Day. Whereas St. Patrick's Day was once a solemn occasion, a holy day of obligation when pubs closed, it now is a wholly secular, gala attraction associated with almost-obligatory festivity and drink, lots and lots of drink. Today its celebration accomplishes what eluded organizers of the civic weeks and Tóstals: the extension of the tourist season beyond the summer months. At the same time that St. Patrick's Day grew increasingly secular, the ceremonies to mark the anniversary of the Easter Rising have, over the past half century, become more troubled, often subdued, and much contested. Now no one thinks of celebrating the Easter Rising as they did in 1935 by setting fire to a replica of the GPO and cheering when the Irish tricolor ascends, but only of commemorating a problematic but pivotal event in the history of the state.

Throughout the twentieth century, historical pageantry relied heavily on pastiche, incorporating often-familiar ballads, poems, speeches, tableaux, songs, stories, and iconic images. Pageants seized upon a fragmentary understanding of the past that was already shared by the audience and built upon it by crafting narratives that spoke to specific moments. Historical pageants played to, developed, and, most important, gratified the audience's horizon of expectations. The audience sought by historical pageants was rarely the intelligentsia or the cognoscenti, but the ordinary citizens, especially impressionable, young ones. So suited to particular moments were these populist spectacles that they invariably had a short shelf life. Pageantry spun its confections like candy floss and usually lasted no longer.

Over the century features distinct to Irish pageantry surfaced and accreted importance, the most enduring of which, the March of the Nation, morphed from its appearances in the Gaelic League Language Week Processions into a chronological presentation of the Irish past, especially its warriors. Like any theatrical idiom, pageantry in twentieth-century Ireland referred to its predecessors. The military productions that dominated Irish pageantry after 1932, for instance, directly referred to earlier tattoos, which in turn drew on nineteenth-century British tattoos. Not only were the costumes used in the 1935 tattoo recycled for some of the stage shows during the Emergency, but so were structural features: gymnastic displays, the March of the Nation, reenactments of seventeenth-century military encounters. Before midcentury the vigor, courage, cunning, and strength of military men were central to historical pageantry. After the Emergency there was a greater candor in looking at the more traumatic history of the nineteenth and early twentieth centuries, even at the Famine.

A survey of Irish historical pageantry reveals confluences of many tributaries. For art and design historians, the engagement of artists and craftspeople in historical pageantry as well as pageantry's vibrant expressions of vernacular forms, particularly in the first several of the twentieth century's decades, remain avenues of further inquiry. Historians may discover the flash points in the debates and controversies underlying these pageants, especially ones sponsored, funded, or otherwise supported by the state. For folklorists and anthropologists, the religious orientation of the Patrician pageants and other hagiographic representations of Irish saints may disclose further links to pilgrimages, patterns, and other occasions of faith. Even in musicology, a field sadly neglected here, a rich vein of vernacular music, some of it originally composed for these pageants, was intrinsic to the pageants and a mainstay of their affective powers.

Other continuities may invite theatre historians to read these pageants in dialogue with the mainstream of Irish drama. The careers of Fred Morrow, Bryan MacMahon, Denis Johnston, and especially of Hilton Edwards and Micheál macLíammóir might profitably be assessed in light of their engagement with historical pageants. Morrow, macLíammóir, and Hayes-McCoy in particular brought to pageant making potent combinations of visual and verbal skills. The use of the theatrical idiom of pageantry, especially in the first half of the twentieth century, can be also seen as challenging the Abbey's presentation of the nation's past. Although pageants rarely competed with mainstream theatres for the same audience, on at least one occasion, the 1909 *The Return of Lug Lamfada*, a historical pageant provided a nationalist alternative to a specific Abbey production, Shaw's dreadful, much-ballyhooed *Blanco Posnet*. Here and throughout the century, pageantry offered the opportunity to perform an affiliation. Participation in spectacles like the military tattoos or the Patrician pageants could be a memorable experience even for the humblest spear carrier, probably especially for the humblest spear carrier. Pageants, after all, sought affective responses in their audiences and performers. Especially significant were the many times children and adolescents were drawn into the act of personation. Throughout the twentieth century, historical pageants very rarely developed nuanced characters as did mainstream theatre. Instead, they deployed extravagant effects to play into the political convictions and the affective responses to which their audiences were predisposed. Because pageantry taps emotional chords that offer a populist idiom in which to stage the history of the nation, its relationship with the moment of its performance is worthy of exploration. The challenge of locating these pageants in their historical context, an undertaking this study only touches on, is especially intriguing. In the face of the violence of the Border Campaign, for instance, the meaning of MacMahon's *The Pageant of the Four Green Fields* was newly charged with political significance. No less inviting are the many faces of Dervogilla imagined by Gregory as a grieving dowager, by Yeats as a penitent girl, but by macLíammóir as a gorgeous woman in a loveless marriage.

Historical pageants reflect their time, much as history plays do. The recourse to mythological figures drawn from the mists of the Celtic Twilight in historical pageants is unsurprising in a decade that was "Cúchulainn-mad." Like the vogue for Irish mythological tales, the pageants crafted and performed between 1908 and 1914 located the Irish heritage reenacted by schoolboys and Gaelic Leaguers in a remote golden age. Through the very act of personation, participants, especially the supernumeraries who were often children, adolescents, and young adults, affirmed and expressed aspirations that pageant makers hoped they would carry through their lives. Just as historians scrambled to publish narratives of the Irish pre-Union past after Independence, the pageants of the Civic Weeks of 1927 and 1929 paraded a range of military heroes, sometimes including the rebels of the Easter Rising. By 1966 Pearse and the other signatories of the Proclamation were no longer seen as the descendants of a tradition, but the progenitors of one. The more recent reluctance to celebrate the Rising owes much to the very facts that not only was the Rising unsuccessful, but it was predicated on physical-force violence. The failure of MacMahon's *A Pageant of Pearse* may be read as indicating that Ruth Dudley Edwards's biography was profoundly influential or that, in one of the worst years of the Troubles, Pearse's legacy was directly tied to the physical-force violence that beset the island, or that the idiom of pageantry had lost its appeal.

The enduring power of myth lies in its ability to speak to generation after generation—rarely with the same voice, sometimes in mutually exclusive meanings. The relationship between twentieth-century historical pageantry to the mainstream of theatre in Ireland is highly problematic. Early in the twentieth century, pageantry closely paralleled theatrical explorations of Irish myth in scores of playwrights, ranging from Yeats to Alice Milligan, AE to James Cousins. Later in the century, the enticing comparison with pageantry lies principally in the Irish history play. Like the Irish history play, historical pageantry addresses an appetite to understand or to create the Irish past. In 1983 Lynda Henderson lamented that the "concern for history is a perverse desire to remain fallen, to make no attempt to rise, to spend your life contemplating your navel. . . . Too many contemporary Irish plays bleat plaintively of old wounds."[1] In 1991 Gerald Fitzgibbon described the interest of playwrights such as Friel, Murphy, Leonard, and McGuinness in Irish history as nothing less than an obsession.[2] Claire Gleitman observed in 2004 that "Ireland's blood-stained history provides dramatic material aplenty, and it is a rare Irish author who opts to disregard it altogether."[3] Bernhard Klein explored what he saw as the "radical historical 'methodology'" adopted by Friel, Stewart Parker, and Frank McGuinness.[4] Other critics suggest that the engagement of drama with history fuels an energetic atmosphere for the arts. Tom Maguire, for instance, located the plays of Marie Jones, Parker, Tom Paulin, Gary Mitchell, and Martin Lynch in a vibrant theatrical scene in Northern Ireland driven by the need to come to terms with Irish history, both contemporary and remote. The arts' interest in Irish history is hardly limited to playwrights. Two productions of the Coisceim dance theatre company, *Reel Luck* (1995) and *Touch Me* (2012), both might be described as state-of-the-nation works that explore Irish history. Coisceim's most recent production is simply called *Pageant* (2013).

In his prescient 1988 essay on the Irish history play, Christopher Murray writes, "In Ireland history tends always towards myth, for what shapes political attitudes are the versions and images of the past standing as symbols rather than as factual records of experience."[5] Historical pageantry sought to actualize, to renovate, and usually to invest with heroic meaning those "versions and images of the past." Playwrights often do something quite different. Deploying a radically unrealistic dramaturgy, Thomas Kilroy's *Talbot's Box* (1973) undoes the popular understanding of ascetic piety of Dublin's worker-saint Matt Talbot. McGuinness freely speaks of his plays *Mutabilitie* (1997), which portrays the encounter between a shipwrecked gay, Catholic Shakespeare and Edmund Spenser in Ireland, and *Speaking Like Magpies* (2005), which reimagines the Gunpowder Plot, as travesties of history: "At the heart of the play [*Speaking Like Magpies*]," says McGuinness, "there's a Jacobean masque and that's where the details of the Gunpowder Plot come through. *Mutabilitie* was spoken of as a 'travesty of English and Irish history'—so it's another travesty."[6] In his epic enterprise to chronicle generations of his family, Sebastian Barry "determined to rescue figures adrift in history's flood, and salvage a sense of belonging . . . redeeming the forgotten, marginalized and awkward minor actors of Irish history."[7] Whereas pageants gratified the audience's knowledge, contemporary Irish history plays thrive on destabilizing the audience's expectations.

In *Making History* (1989), Brian Friel deconstructed the pieties of Irish nationalists as well as those of Irish historians. A meditation on Irish historiography, *Making History* found Archbishop Peter Lombard asking, "Are truth and falsity the proper criteria? I don't know. Maybe when the time comes my first responsibility will be to tell the best possible narrative. Isn't that what history is, a kind of story-telling? . . . maybe imagination will be as important as information."[8] For Tony Corbett, Lombard is "the essence of the historical vindicator [who] writes history as an idealized *exemplum* for the present."[9] Lombard's historiographical sense in not simply a comment on the contemporary upheavals of Irish revisionism. Characteristic of modern Irish pageantry is the attitude toward *The Ford of the Hurdles* expressed by Hilton Edwards in 1929: "The play as a whole is presented in a free and imaginative fashion." Friel's Lombard more directly echoes Thomas Davis. As Mary Helen Thuente observes of the liberties with history taken by nineteenth-century nationalists: "Thomas Davis expressed the creed of many nationalists when he declared that the 'exact dates, subtle plots, minute connections and motives' found in the most superior prose history did not serve what he identified as 'the highest ends of history.'"[10] Stephen Dedalus famously hoped to awake from "the nightmare of history." Historical pageantry offered a dreamy alternative to that nightmare.

Appendix

Notes

Glossary

Bibliography

Index

English Translation of Pearse's
Macghníomhartha Chúchulainn

Seán Ó Briain

Seán Ó Briain holds a master's in Old and Middle Irish and a bachelor's in Modern Irish and English from University College Galway. He has been a translator and editor on the staff of the Translation Section of Dáil Éireann (the Irish Parliament), providing Irish-language translations of the acts of Parliament, and previously an assistant editor in *An Gúm*, the Irish Language Publications Branch of the Department of Education in Dublin with responsibility for dictionaries and textbooks.

He was previously a tutor in Irish and Old Irish at University College Galway and since 2009 has been an occasional lecturer in translation studies in the Department of Irish at University College Dublin.

THE BOYHOOD DEEDS OF CÚCHULAINN[1]
MARTIAL CAREER

CAST

Choir, a grouping of bards and monks
Conchúr Mac Neasa, King of Ulster
Warriors of the Branch-Red:[2]
Fearghas Mac Róigh
Conall Cearnach
Laoire Buach,

The Branch-Red:
Cafach the Druid
Follún Mac Conchúir, Leader of the Band of Youths
Lads of the Band of Youths:
Eon
Ainle
Ardán
Iollann Fionn
Buinne Rua
Aodh Caomh
Seatanta Mac Sualtaimh (Seatanta son of Sualtamh), Cúchulainn
Cualann Ceard (Cualann the Artisan), A noble artisan of the Ulstermen.
Iúr Mac Riangabhra, Conchúr's Charioteer
Fear Faire, Sentinel
Soldiers, attendants, artisans, musicians, performers, female attendants, etc.

PLACE

Eamhain Macha

TIME

The First Century

I
Incipit: The Martial Career

Music playing. The Choir enters and moves about the field performing the following verses:

THE CHOIR. (*Air: Slowly and thoughtfully. Arranged by Tomás Mac Domhnaill*)
　　A story for you, Nobles of the Gael,
　　Heroic knowledgeable band,
　　A story unsurpassed
　　In the ancient annals of Ireland.

　　One day when the son of Neasa arose
　　Strong king of the youths of Ulster,

He sat on the height of the Eamhain
Together with his warriors and valiant men.

While the youthful warriors played there,
On the field of the royal household,
There came among them a fair youth,
Who was greatest in power and valour.

He challenged them to three contests
proceeding to slay and defeat them
Until they joined with him in battle
and had him as their leader.

The high king asked the strong vigorous and victorious youth
who he was;
I am son of your brother,[3]
I am Seatanta son of Sualtamh.

The First Part

*Eamhain Macha. Conchúr's fort in the centre of the field. The lawn of Eamhain
fronting on to it. A small wood to the left. Conchúr and Fearghas enter the lawn,
surrounded by warriors. They sit in the doorway of the fort playing chess.[4] The
young troop of Eamhain arrive, running, with Follún Mac Conchúir in their
midst, hurleys in hand, standing centrefield. Follún speaks:*

FOLLÚN. I challenge you, Eon!

EON. I'll take you on!

FOLLÚN. I'll have Naoise! (*Naoise sides with Follún, behind him*).

EON. I'll have Ainle! (*Ainle sides with Eon, behind him*).

FOLLÚN. Ardán!

EON. Iollann Fionn!

FOLLÚN. Buinne Rua!

EON. Aodh Caomh!

*And so on to the end. Each youth taking his place behind his captain when he
is called. And then each team proceeding to their own goal, with their captain.
The captains then placing the youths in their playing position after that, i.e. each*

captain advancing out from his own goal in front of his team; raising his hurley, with two standing. Follún throws in the ball; and they start the game.

The game continues for some time. Seatanta enters, approaching them from the wood, wearing a red tunic and a bright puckered shirt next to his skin with a fine purple mantle; hurley in hand. Standing now and then to observe the youths. Upon arriving at the edge of the wood, he stands in the shade of a tree watching carefully. Things continue so for a while. A youth strikes the ball towards Seatanta. Seatanta saves it with his foot. Follún speaking in a loud voice:

FOLLÚN. You have the ball, boy! Hurl it over here to us!

SEATANTA. Look out, young Ulster lads!

He strikes the ball while saying this: he continues to strike it from one end of the plain to the other in spite of the youths, until he strikes it over the edge of the goal line on the far side. Follún speaks:

FOLLÚN. Right well, boys, respond together to this fair youth!

THE YOUTH BAND. We shall respond!

Follún and Eoghan drop the ball at the mouth of Seatanta's goal; the other youths defending the other goal; Seatanta strikes the ball from one end of the plain to the other again and over the edge of the goal line on the far side in spite of them. Follún speaks:

FOLLÚN. We're disgraced having this small youth getting the better of us on the plain of Eamhain. Give him his answer this time boys!

THE YOUTH BAND. We'll do that!

Seatanta takes them on a third time with the same result. The youths get angry. Follún speaks.

FOLLÚN. Right, boys, let's take him on together and make him pay for breaking our taboos, since it is taboo to permit a young boy to come into our game without first seeking our permission. Take him on!

THE YOUTH BAND. We'll do that!

They take him on with ferocious vengeance, beating him with their hurleys. Seatanta defends himself with his own hurley, knocking them over on all sides. The king hears the commotion; he stands and approaches them surrounded by warriors. Conchúr takes hold of Seatanta's hand and speaks with a regal voice:

CONCHÚR. Stop this commotion, boys; and you stop too, little fellow, from attacking the youth band. It's obvious that you're not playing fair with them.

SEATANTA. I didn't get a fair welcome from them, my king, having come from far distant lands to befriend them.

CONCHÚR. Weren't you aware of the taboos of the band of youths? Every young lad who comes to them must come under their patronage.

SEATANTA. I wasn't aware of that. If I had, I would have done so.

CONCHÚR. Right, boys, take it upon yourselves now to let this child go.

THE YOUTHFUL BAND. We'll do that.

SEATANTA. I don't accept that, my king! By the gods that I worship, if they do not come under my patronage, I will not stay my hand against them.

THE YOUTH BAND. We accept your patronage!

They bend the knee and bow their heads in his presence. Conchúr speaks.

CONCHÚR. Tell me now, young lad, where did you come from, which path did you take or what's your name and surname?

SEATANTA. I came over Sliabh Fuaid, from the plain of Muirheivna and Seatanta son of Sualtamh is my name, and my mother is Deachtaire, who is your own sister, o king of Ulster.[5]

CONCHÚR. You are very welcome, young boy. Happy the one who is your mother! I am glad to see your beauteous head and your strong hand, so quick to wound!

He clasps the youth and kisses him and presses him to his chest. Fearghas speaks:

FEARGHAS. Welcome, young lad!

Fearghas grasps the youth, lifts him into his two hands and places him on his shoulder. The bands of youths and warriors speak out in praise with one voice:

THE YOUTHS AND THE WARRIORS. You're very welcome! You're very welcome!

They enter the fort, surrounding Conchúr and Fearghas, Seatanta being on Fearghas's shoulder.

II
Incipit: The Second Part

Music is played. The Choir enters and moves about the field, singing the following verses:

A story for you, nobles of the Gael,
Heroic, knowledgeable band,
A story unsurpassed
In the ancient annals of Ireland.

One day when the son of Neasa,
The strong king of the youths of Ulster,
Went drinking and feasting
at the request of the chief artificer, Culann.

The military son of Sualtamh
was left at the royal household,
Until he went after them
In heroic victory.

Prosperous Culann
had a brave hungry ravenous hound,
Who attacked the youth savagely,
Until it was defeated in the combat.

The youth said, 'O Culann,
'I will henceforth be your hound'
'Following that deed,' Cafach said,
'O fair youth, Cuchulainn is your name.

The Second Part

Cúchulainn's forge. A very large fire therein. Young craftsmen hammering on anvils in front of the doorway. They commence reciting the following verses:
(Air: Quick and with feeling. Arranged by Tomás Mac Domhnaill)

THE CRAFTSMEN.
Ding, dong, dideró,
Let us strike, o youths,
Ding, dong, dideró,
On the anvils.

Ding, dong, dideró,
Let us strike bravely,

Ding, dong, dideró,
with heavy sledge hammers.

ONE CRAFTSMAN.
Strike that, o young smith,
Low and light,
Let us all strike it together,
All together.

THREE OF THEM REPLY.
Let us strike it again,
And strike it together,
And let us strike it all around,
With ease and agility.

ALL THE CRAFTSMEN.
Ding, dong, dideró, etc.

THE FIRST CRAFTSMAN.
Strike it, form it,
Craftsmen of the Forge,
A golden widefurrowed sword,
for Conchúr, for the high king.

ALL THE CRAFTSMEN.
Ding don dideró, etc.
Culann speaks.

CULANN. Conchúr Mac Neasa and the Branch-Red are coming to us to celebrate tonight. Cease the beating, as I hear the sound of the young and the clash of the weapons and the royal household approaching.

The craftsmen cease work and enter the forge. Conall, Fearghas, Laoire, Cafach and the Branch-Red are already coming on location. Culann and the craftsmen welcome them. They sit down in the forge and drink heartily. Culann speaks after they sit down.

CULANN. Is there anyone else of your company due to come tonight, o king of Ulster?

CONCHÚR. No. Of whom do you speak?

CULANN. A brave hound of hungry teeth that I have and it is his duty to mind the house every night, and woe betide anyone who would try to enter the house in spite of him, since he would maul them though and through.

CONCHÚR. Seal the doorway and let out the hound.

Culann closes the doorway as he lets out the hound. The king's musicians play music and perform. Meanwhile, Seatanta enters and heads for the forge: since it was understood that he was left at home and that he came in the wake of Conchúr and the Branch-Red, shortening the way for himself with his hurley and ball. He arrives at the door of the forge (it's understood that this door is at the back; the listeners hear a fearsome and abhorrent racket).

Conchúr arises and speaks:

CONCHÚR. A pity it is, o youths, that we came here tonight to feast!

THE ULSTERMEN. Why so, o king?

CONCHÚR. The little lad I left behind, my sister's son, felled by the hound!

The Ulstermen stand up, seize their weapons and go out, led by Fearghas. They re-enter with Seatanta on Fergus's shoulder. Culann stands in the doorway looking in front of him. Conchúr speaks:

CONCHÚR. Welcome, little lad!

Culann arrives and stands in front of Conchúr and Seatanta. He speaks:

CULANN. Welcome for the sake of your father and mother, but you are not welcome in your own right.

CONCHÚR. What have you against the boy?

CULANN. I'm very sorry I made this feast for you, Conchúr, since my value is worthless henceforth, and my life is worthless. Good indeed was the fellow you took from me, little lad. He was one who guarded my clothes, my cattle and my territory!

SEATANTA. Don't be angry with me, o Master Culann, since I will undertake that true commitment.

CONCHÚR. What commitment will you make about it, son?

SEATANTA. If there be a pup of that hound's progeny in Ireland, I will train it until it will be as useful as its father. And I will be a hound to protect his cattle and territory for Culann for that period of time.

CONCHÚR. You have promised well, young son.

CAFACH. I would not do better myself; and your name shall be Cú Chulainn, the Hound of Culann, as a result.

CÚ CHULAINN. Not at all. I prefer my own name, Seatanta son of Sualtamh.

CAFACH. Don't say that, sonny, since the men of Ireland and Scotland will hear that name, and the mouths of the men of Ireland and Scotland will be full of that name.

SEATANTA. If what you say is true, Cafach, I will take that name.

THE ULSTERMEN. Cúchulainn! Cúchulainn!

Conchúr and the Ulstermen sit down once again to the drinking feast. Cúchulainn sits on the threshold of the doorway, as a protective hound. The musicians take up playing again. They continue so for a while. Having finished their feasting, Conchúr and the Ulstermen arise, bid farewell to Culann and go their way, but Cúchulainn remains sitting on the threshold defending the forge.

III
Incipit: The Third Part

Music is played. The Choir enters and moves about the field reciting the following verses:

A story for you, nobles of the Gael,
O heroic, knowledgeable band,
A story unsurpassed
In the ancient annals of Ireland.

One day when the son of Neasa arose,
The strong King of the youths of Ulster,
There came to him the youth,
The brave heroic hound of Culann.

He asked for weapons and equipment,
Gave his blessing to the youths,
Set forth in his chariot,
to do battle and contest.

He refrained not from frenzied deeds,
Until he reached the edge of the province,

Until he killed the three sons of Neachtan,
Although the churls were manly.

A story for you, nobles of the Gael,
O heroic, knowledgeable band,
A story not found
In the ancient annals of Ireland.

The Third Part

The field of Emain. Cafach enters the field with Cúchulainn and Follún and the band of youths surrounding him. Follún speaks:

FOLLÚN. Tell us, o master Cafach, what is the sign put on this day over the days of the year? Is it a good sign or a bad sign?

CAFACH. Yes indeed, son, the youth who will receive weapons today, he shall be illustrious and renowned, but his life will be short and impermanent.

FOLLÚN. How so, Cafach?

CAFACH. He shall do deeds which shall be reckoned among the most valorous deeds of the world, but he shall have a short life.

Cafach and the band of youths leave the scene. Cúchulainn waits and sits on his own. Conchúr and the Ulstermen arrive on the field with their hounds and [other] dogs, together with their huntsmen and attendants. Cúchulainn arises and bows in the presence of Conchúr, speaking as follows:

CÚCHULAINN. Every good wish to you, king of the Ulstermen!

CONCHÚR. That is the speech of one who is seeking something. What do you want, little son?

CÚCHULAINN. To bear arms.

CONCHÚR. Who inspired you thus, little son?

CÚCHULAINN. Cafach the Druid.

CONCHÚR. In that case, you won't be refused. Give weapons to this fair youth!

One of the heroes gives a sword and a spear to the youth. Cúchulainn tests the weapons and breaks them in so doing. He speaks:

CÚCHULAINN. These weapons are no good, my king.

CONCHÚR. Give him other weapons.

He is given other weapons and he breaks them in the same way. Cúchulainn speaks:

CÚCHULAINN. These weapons are no good, my king.

CONCHÚR. Give him other weapons.

He is given other weapons and breaks them in exactly the same way. Cúchulainn speaks.

CÚCHULAINN. These weapons are no good. Give me weapons that are my match.

CONCHÚR. I will give you my own weapons, little Hound.

He is given the king's weapons. Cúchulainn bends and tests them but does not break them.

    Cúchulainn speaks:

CÚCHULAINN. These weapons are good weapons: These weapons are my match. Happy the king who is the match of these weapons and equipment. Happy the land whence he came!

Cafach enters and speaks:

CAFACH. Did he take weapons?

CONCHÚR. Yes.

CAFACH. I am not happy that your sister's son has done that.

CONCHÚR. Why so? Are you not the one who encouraged him to do so?

CAFACH. It was definitely not I.

CONCHÚR. What's this, enchanted sprite? Have you lied to me?

CÚCHULAINN. Do not be angry with me, master Conchúr. He is indeed the one who incited me in this matter since, on Follún asking him what sign was on the day, he said—the young son who takes weapons today he shall do deeds which shall be reckoned among the most valorous deeds of the world, but he shall have a short life.

CAFACH. That indeed is true. Young hound, you shall be illustrious and noble but your life will be short.

CÚCHULAINN. It means little to me were I to live but one day and one night but that tidings of me and my deeds would endure after me.

CONCHÚR. Good, my little son. Get into your chariot.

CÚCHULAINN. Bring me my own chariot, Conchúr, since no other chariot is good enough for me.

CONCHÚR. Where is Iúr mac Riangabhra?

IÚR. Right here, my king.

CONCHÚR. Get here with my own two horses and set up my chariot.

Iúr exits and re-enters having captured the horses and set up the chariot. Conchúr speaks:

CONCHÚR. Get up into the chariot, son.

Cúchulainn gets up into the chariot. The chariot does a round of the field. Conchúr and the Ulstermen set off hunting and killing game. Cafach heads off into the fort. The band of youths enter the field, go to one side of the fort, and play games. The chariot returns and stands in front of the doorway of the fort. Iúr speaks:

IÚR. Well done, sonny. Le me unyoke the horses from the chariot.

CÚCHULAINN. It's too early to unyoke them just yet. Drive on ahead of me so that the band of youths can salute me on my taking weapons.

They drive on to where the band of youths is located.

FOLLÚN SPEAKS. Did you take weapons today, Cúchulainn.

CÚCHULAINN. I did indeed.

THE BAND OF YOUTHS. Victory to you in battle and slaughter, Hound of the Forge!

IÚR. Well done, little Hound. Let me unyoke the horses now.

CÚCHULAINN. It's too early to unyoke them just yet. Where does this road lead?

IÚR. To the Ford of the Sentry in The Mountain of Fuad [Sliabh Fuaid] on Ulster's frontier.

CUCHULAINN. Drive on ahead of us to that Ford, since, by the gods worshipped by my people, I shall not return to Eamhain Macha until I see that ford and redden my weapons with the enemies of the Ulstermen.

They proceed onwards, with the band of the youths celebrating. The band of youths resume their games, i.e., the game of the hole, the game of the wheel and the other games of the band of youths. This continues for a while. Conchúr and the Ulstermen return from their game killing. Boars, deer, hinds, hares, birds, etc. are being carried by the attendants.

They enter the fort. The band of youths follow them. Conchúr and Fearghas emerge, surrounded by warriors, and sit in the doorway of the fort, playing chess.[6] A sentinel stands on the roadway on watch. Conchúr speaks after a period of silence:

CONCHÚR. Do you see anything?

SENTINEL. I don't see anything, my king.

CONCHÚR SPEAKS AGAIN.

CONCHÚR. Do you see anything?

SENTINEL. I don't, but I hear the sound of a chariot approaching.

They remain silent for another while. Conchúr speaks a third time.

CONCHÚR. Do you see anything?

SENTINEL. I see a single charioteer approaching, and he comes in a frightening manner. A fine firmly boarded chariot beneath him. Two beautiful swift highly adorned horses under that chariot. The horses travel at great speed. The chariot is full of swords and spears and warrior shields.

CONCHÚR. Describe the charioteer.

SENTINEL. A small sad black-haired boy, the fairest of the sons of Ireland.

CONCHÚR. I know that charioteer. It is the little lad who took weapons today, having returned from the province's frontier. I believe he has reddened his weapons and, nobles of Ulster, unless he is overcome, he will bring death to all in the fort tonight.

FEARGHAS. What shall we do, my king?

CONCHÚR. Let the womenfolk of Eamhain face him on the plain to welcome him.

Some of the warriors enter the fort. The womenfolk of Eamhain emerge and proceed to welcome Cúchulainn. Cafach, the band of youths, the warriors, the musicians, the attendants, etc. come onto the field. Cúchulainn arrives with the chariot at great speed. The womenfolk welcome him. Cúchulainn dismounts from the chariot and enters the presence of the king, having the swords and spears and shields of his enemies in his hands. Some of the attendants remove other swords, spears and shields from the chariot, laying them in front of the king. Cúchulainn speaks in a loud crystal clear voice.

CÚCHULAINN. I have brought you swords and spears and shields of the enemy, Conchúr.

CONCHÚR. Your coming is welcome, o Hound of the Ulstermen!

FEARGHAS. Your coming is welcome, o Hound of the Forge!

CAFACH. Your coming is welcome, Cúchulainn!

The Ulstermen, with one voice. Your coming is welcome, Cúchulainn!

Cúchulainn mounts the chariot again. All of the Ulstermen, including the warriors, youths, druids, musicians, craftsmen, womenfolk, attendants, etc., etc. go around the field three times and proceed afterwards into the fort. Cúchulainn at the rear, surrounded by the Branch Red.

Source Text

Pearse, Patrick. *Macghníomhartha Chúchulainn.* In *Na scríbhinni liteartha le Pádraig Mac Piarais: Scríbhinni i nGaeilge,* edited by Séamas Ó Buachalla, 142–55. Dublin: Mercier, 1979.

Notes

ARCHIVAL SOURCES

BMacM	Bryan MacMahon Papers, privately held
DGTA/NU	Dublin Gate Theatre Archive, Charles Deering McCormick Library of Special Collections at Northwestern Univ., Evanston, IL
HMcC/NUIG	G. A. Hayes-McCoy Papers, National Univ. of Ireland Galway
IFI	Irish Film Institute, Dublin
IWM	Imperial War Museum, London
MAI	Military Archives of Ireland, Dublin
MA/NUIG	Macnas Archive, National Univ. of Ireland Galway
NAI	National Archives of Ireland, Dublin
NLI	National Library of Ireland, Dublin
RCBL	Reorganized Church Body Library, Dublin
SC/QUB	Special Collections, Queen's Univ. Belfast
SRL/KU	Spencer Research Library, Univ. of Kansas, Lawrence
SmacC	Seamus MacCall Papers, privately held
TCD	Trinity College Dublin

INTRODUCTION

1. Diane Taylor, *The Archive and the Repertoire: Performing Cultural Memory in the Americas*, 24.

2. The dramatist St. John Ervine recalls that in his youth, Belfast Protestants associated the theatre with damnation: "The pleasure I drew from my visits to the play in my aunt's company . . . was marred by the panic into which she occasionally fell when she thought of what would be the state of her immortal soul if God should call her home while she was in the theatre. . . . I mention this matter because the belief that the pit of the theatre was only another name for the pit of hell was prevalent at that time [1880s], and has not yet [1930s] died out." Ervine attributes this belief

279

to "the conviction that the mummer violates the commandment that we shall not make unto ourselves graven images." St. John Ervine, *The Theatre in My Time*, 15–16.

3. Pierre Nora, "Preface to the English-Language Edition," in *Realms of Memory: Rethinking the French Past*, xvii.

4. See Marvin A. Carlson, *Places of Performance: The Semiotics of Theatre Architecture*.

5. See Joan FitzPatrick Dean, *Riot and Great Anger: Stage Censorship in Twentieth-Century Ireland*, 166–77.

6. W. B. Yeats, "The Reform of the Theatre," 9.

7. On audience deportment in Irish theatre, see Adrian Frazier, *Behind the Scenes: Yeats, Horniman, and the Struggle for the Abbey Theatre*, esp. chap. 3, "Author and Audience," 64–107; and Cheryl Herr, *For the Land They Loved: Irish Political Melodrama, 1890–1925*.

8. Press clippings, bk. 6, DGTA/NU.

9. The play's title is often translated as *The Boy Deeds of Cúchulainn*, but "Boyhood" is used by many, including Maire Heaney in *Over Nine Waves*.

10. Rev. Myles V. Ronan, "Religious Life in Old Dublin," 53.

11. See Alan J. Fletcher, *Drama, Performance and Polity in Pre-Cromwellian Ireland*, 90–113. See also Alan J. Fletcher, *Drama and the Performing Arts in Pre-Cromwellian Ireland*.

12. Joseph C. Walker, "An Historical Essay on the Irish Stage."

13. Gary Owens, "Nationalism without Words: Symbolism and Ritual Behaviour in the Real 'Monster Meetings' of 1843–45," 247.

14. Ian McBride, *The Siege of Derry in Ulster Protestant Mythology*, 67.

15. Stephen Howe, *Ireland and Empire: Colonial Legacies in Irish History and Culture*, 95.

16. Sean Farrell, *Rituals and Riots: Sectarian Violence and Political Culture in Ulster, 1784–1886*, 156.

17. See Janette Condon, "The Patriotic Children's Treat: Irish Nationalism and Children's Culture at the Twilight of Empire."

18. Erika Fischer-Lichte, *Theatre, Sacrifice, Ritual: Exploring Forms of Political Theatre*, 33.

19. Brenna Katz Clarke, *The Emergence of the Irish Peasant Play at the Abbey Theatre*, 51.

20. Dawson Byrne, *The Story of Ireland's National Theatre: The Abbey Theatre, Dublin*, 57.

21. See Herr, *For the Land They Loved*.

22. Fischer-Lichte, *Theatre, Sacrifice, Ritual*, 3.

23. Erika Fischer-Lichte and Jo Riley, *The Show and the Gaze of Theatre: A European Perspective*, 72 and passim.

24. Matthew Jefferies, *Imperial Culture in Germany, 1871–1918*, 188.

25. John Hutchinson, *The Dynamics of Cultural Nationalism: The Gaelic Revival and the Creation of the Irish Nation State*, 179.

26. Francis Joseph Bigger, "'Hugh Roe O'Donnell': An Irish Historical Masque," 172.

27. Standish O'Grady, *Hugh Roe O'Donnell: A Sixteenth Century Irish Historical Play*, 32.

28. Joseph McBrinn, "The 1904 Feis na nGleann: Craftwork, Folk Life and National Identity." See also Joseph McBrinn, "The Princess Taise Banner at the 1904 Feis na nGleann."

29. Alan Gailey, *Irish Folk Drama*, 31.

30. A typical evening was the Brian Boru Centenary in the Round Room at the Mansion House on August 23, 1915, when the Father Mathew Orchestra and Celtic Glee Singers performed, Maire nic Shiubhlaigh recited, Gerard Crofts and others sang, and St. Enda's students presented tableaux vivants. Program, *Brian Boru Centenary*, Joseph Holloway Ephemera Collection, NLI.

31. Robert Withington, "Louis Napoleon Parker," 513.

32. Percy MacKaye, *The New Citizenship: A Civic Ritual Devised for Places of Public Meeting in America*, 5. Subsequent references given in the text.

33. See chapter 1. The Aberdeens recall this production in their memoir, *"We Twa": Reminiscences of Lord and Lady Aberdeen*. The *Irish Independent* reported two performances of what it identified as O'Grady's *The Coming of Finn* in August 1906.

34. See Nicola Gordon Bowe and Elizabeth Cumming, *The Arts and Crafts Movements in Dublin and Edinburgh, 1885–1925*, 163–68.

35. Diarmuid Ó Giolláin, "The Pattern," 201.

36. *Belfast Newsletter*, July 12, 1888.

37. *Belfast Newsletter*, Aug. 20, 1896.

38. "Fashion and Varieties," *Freeman's Journal*, Jan. 15, 1891.

39. Maria Tymoczko, "Tableaux Vivants in Ireland at the Turn of the Century," 93.

40. Elizabeth, Countess of Fingall, *Seventy Years Young*, 235.

41. Herr, *For the Land They Loved*, 46–48.

42. "Belfast Gaelic League," *Belfast Newsletter*, May 9, 1898.

43. Catherine Morris, *Alice Milligan and the Irish Cultural Revival*, 273.

44. Christopher Morash, *A History of Irish Theatre, 1601–2000*, 121.

45. Louis Napoleon Parker, "Historical Pageants," 145.

46. Louis Napoleon Parker, *Several of My Lives*, 284.

47. See Victor Turner, *The Anthropology of Performance*.

48. Withington, "Louis Napoleon Parker," 512.

49. Meghan Lau, "Performing History: The War-Time Pageants of Louis Napoleon Parker," 265.

50. Kathleen M. O'Brennan, "The Drama as a Nationalising Force," *Sinn Féin*, Nov. 10, 1906, 3. Two weeks later another article under the same title, this one by T. B. Cronin, appeared in *Sinn Féin*.

51. See David Bergeron, *English Civic Pageantry, 1558–1642*; and Tracey Hill, *Pageants and Power: A Cultural History of the Early Modern Lord Mayor's Show, 1585–1639*.

52. Eric Hobsbawm, introduction to *The Invention of Tradition*, edited by Eric Hobsbawm and T. O. Ranger, i.

53. Anthony Roche, "Stage Representations of the Rising," 309.

54. Victor Turner and Edith L. B. Turner, *Image and Pilgrimage in Christian Culture: Anthropological Perspectives*. Turner uses "pilgrimage" in place of "pageant."

55. Marie Coleman, *The Irish Sweep: A History of the Irish Hospitals Sweepstake, 1930–87*, 25.

56. "Drama of Iona," *Irish Times*, May 28, 1928.

57. "Cashel Tostal Council: Historical Processional Pageant," 1953, TSCH/3/S15297, NAI. Numerous other city and county historical pageants and parades were staged in the early years of the Tóstal, 1953–55.

58. See Robert Hogan, Richard Burnham, and Daniel P. Poteet, eds., *The Rise of the Realists, 1910–1915*.

1. DRAMA-MAD, CÚCHULAINN-MAD, PAGEANT-MAD

1. Roy Foster, "Remembering 1798," 77.

2. *Fáinne an Lae*, July 2, 1898, translated by and quoted in Philip O'Leary, *The Prose Literature of the Gaelic Revival, 1881–1921: Ideology and Innovation*, 164. See also Lawrence W. McBride, "Young Readers and the Learning and Teaching of Irish History."

3. See L. McBride, "Young Readers."

4. See, for instance, Christopher Innes, *Avant Garde Theatre, 1892–1992*.

5. Frazier, *Behind the Scenes*, 100–107.

6. Karen Vandevelde, *The Alternative Dramatic Revival in Ireland, 1897–1913*, 94.

7. Mary Colum, *Life and the Dream*, 95.

8. Brian Siggins, *The Great White Fair: The Herbert Park Exhibition of 1907*, 10.

9. See Fintan Cullen, *Ireland on Show: Art, Union, and Nationhood*; and "Centenary of the Irish International Exhibition."

10. "Ireland in 1907: An Editorial Appreciation," *World's Work* 9, no. 54 (1907): 563.

11. Bram Stoker, "The Great White Fair in Dublin," *World's Work* 9, no. 54 (1907): 571–72.

12. "Ireland in 1907," *World's Work* 9, no. 54 (1907): 565.

13. Maureen Keane, *Ishbel: Lady Aberdeen in Ireland*, 101.

14. Éamon Ceannt, "The Oireachtas Incident," *Leader*, Aug. 24, 1907.

15. "A National Exhibition," *Leader*, June 3, 1911.

16. Hutchinson, *Dynamics of Cultural Nationalism*, 179.

17. P. J. Mathews, *Revival: The Abbey Theatre, Sinn Féin, the Gaelic League and the Co-operative Movement*, 24. For a comprehensive view of Gaelic League membership, see Timothy G. McMahon, *Grand Opportunity: The Gaelic Revival and Irish Society, 1893–1910*.

18. *Sinn Féin*, May 18, 1907.

19. Colum, *Life and the Dream*, 154.

20. "Irish Language Procession," *Sinn Féin*, May 25, 1907.

21. McMahon, *Grand Opportunity*, 198.

22. James Stephens, "Builders," *Sinn Féin*, May 11, 1907.

23. *Irish Times*, June 10, 1907.

24. *Sinn Féin*, June 8, 1907.

25. Timothy G. McMahon, "The Gaelic Summer Colleges," 123.

26. *Irish Times*, June 10, 1907.

27. The *Irish Independent* reported that Moonan was "the author of a book describing the tableau, which had a large sale yesterday" (June 10, 1907). Moonan wrote *A Short History of Ireland* with Mary Hayden, which became a standard history textbook in the early years of the Free State. See McMahon, "The Gaelic Summer Colleges," 137–39.

28. Máire Ní Mhaonaigh observes in her entry in the *Dictionary of Irish Biography* that the "metamorphosis and in particular the liberty taken with facts in the formation of Brian's legend create difficulties when trying to access the historical ruler."

29. "Irish Language Procession," *Irish Times*, June 1, 1907.

30. *Irish Times*, June 10, 1907.

31. *Sinn Féin*, June 15, 1907. In the same issue of *Sinn Féin*, the Abbey production of *The Playboy of the Western World* touring England was said to be "received with groans by the Irish who witnessed the production, and prolonged applause by the English. The world knows now what kind of savages those patient English have to deal with in this country."

32. Jeanne Sheehy, *The Rediscovery of Ireland's Past: The Celtic Revival, 1830–1930*, 148.

33. The phrase comes from Charles Stewart Parnell: "No man has the right to fix the boundary to the march of a Nation."

34. Nellie O Cleirgh and Cecilia Saunders Gallagher, "A Political Prisoner in Kilmainham Jail: The Diary of Cecilia Saunders Gallagher," 14.

35. *Irish Times*, May 2, 1907.

36. *Irish Times*, June 22, 1907.

37. *Irish Times*, June 8, 1907. The Aberdeens paid a vice-regal visit to the pageant on June 28, 1907.

38. *A Twelfth Century Pageant Play: Portraying Scenes of Irish History*. No author is identified in the publication, but the *Irish Times* attributed the play to Percival Aungier. Subsequent references given in the text.

39. Sir Richard Wallace donated Maclise's painting to the National Gallery of Ireland in 1879. See Síghle Bhreathnach-Lynch, *Ireland's Art, Ireland's History: Representing Ireland, 1845 to Present*, 255.

40. Diarmuid Ferriter in the *Dictionary of Irish Biography* records that Lord Iveagh's philanthropy was especially generous in 1907 and 1908: "In 1907 the opening of the Iveagh markets, situated in the Francis St. and Patrick St. areas of Dublin city, were made possible with his financial backing. Generous contributions were also made to TCD [Trinity College Dublin] (of which he was elected chancellor in 1908), and he donated land in Iveagh Gardens to UCD."

41. Shortly after *A Twelfth Century Pageant Play*, the *Irish Times* (July 8, 1907) reported that Viscount and Viscountess Iveagh would entertain Prince and Princess Christian at Elvedon for the Bury St. Edmunds Pageant.

42. "Dramatic Pageant in Lord Iveagh's Grounds," *Irish Times*, May 23, 1907.

43. *Irish Times*, June 26, 1907.

44. *College Chronicle* 33 (1908): 17–18.

45. "The Castleknock Pageant," *Freeman's Journal*, June 1, 1909.

46. The president of Castleknock in 1908 was a Vincentian priest, not to be confused with the first Irish cardinal, also named Paul Cullen (1803–78).

47. James H. Murphy, *Nos Autem: Castleknock College and Its Contribution*, 104.

48. "For some years Historical Pageants were done in England, and with great success. The York Pageant was one of the most famous. It was produced in the old surroundings of the events. Father Bodkin went to see it, and was greatly struck by the idea. Father Paul Cullen, the President, made up his mind to initiate the idea for Castleknock." *St. Vincent's College, Castleknock: Centenary Record, 1835–1935*, 240.

49. http://www.castleknockcollege.ie/About-the-School/history-castleknock-college.html.

50. *College Chronicle* 23 (June 1908), 17. See also William John Fitzpatrick, *Irish Wits and Worthies, Including Dr. Lanigan, His Life and Times, with Glimpses of Stirring Scenes since 1770*, 278. Coohal is believed to be buried "beneath the vast tumulus, Knock-maroon Hill."

51. *The Battle of Castleknock*, *College Chronicle* 29 (special pageant number, June 1914). Subsequent references given in the text.

52. Thomas Moore used the term both in his history of Ireland and in "Dear Harp of My Country." Today, it is familiar in video gaming.

53. The caoine was written by Tadgh Ó Donnchadha (Torna) who was later professor of Irish at University College Cork (1916–44).

54. Cecil Lavery served as attorney general in Costello's coalition government and later as Supreme Court judge.

55. *College Chronicle* 29 (special pageant number, June 1914): 8.

56. Born in Dublin in 1873, Father John P. Campbell, CM, was one of the founders of the Old Dublin Society. He is not to be confused with Joseph Campbell's younger brother, also named John P. Campbell, known primarily as a visual artist and associated with the 1913 *An Dhord Fhiann: An Irish Historic Pageant*, performed at the 69th Regiment Armory in New York City. Very confusingly, in 1909 the *College Chronicle* reproduced three signed illustrations by the artist along with the pageants by the priest.

57. In June 1908 the Morrow brothers held an exhibition of their works at their recently opened Dublin branch of their shop at 15 D'Olier Street. The firm was short-lived, not least because when the Theatre of Ireland closed its books, the Morrow brothers were still owed money. "The Theatre of Ireland," O'H B3664, SRL/KU.

58. J. W. Good, "The Ulster Literary Theatre," *Uladh*, Feb. 1905, 8.

59. Seosamh de Paor, "The Ulster Literary Theatre," *Uladh*, Sept. 1905, 7.

60. Sam Hanna Bell, *The Theatre in Ulster: A Survey of the Dramatic Movement in Ulster from 1902 until the Present Day*, 16.

61. Another image of Jack Morrow's work, of a copper "Shield of Heroes," from this period appears in McBrinn, "1904 Feis na nGleann," 29.

62. Hibernicus, "The Castleknock Pageant," *Leader*, June 13, 1908.

63. "St. Vincent's College Castleknock," *Freeman's Journal*, June 1, 1908.

64. *An Claidheamh Soluis*, June 27, 1908.

65. *Freeman's Journal*, June 30, 1908.

66. Through 1910 the Theatre of Ireland featured mythologically based plays every year, bringing AE's *Deirdre* to the rented Abbey stage in 1907; Edward Martyn's *Maeve* to the Abbey in 1908; another version of this 1908 pageant, *The Fate of the Children of Tuireann*, to the Oireachtas and then to Kilkenny in 1909; and an Irish version of *Deirdre* to the Rotunda and to the Oireachtas in 1910. "The Theatre of Ireland," O'H B3663, SRL/KU.

67. "Go mairidh ár nGaedhilg slán" (The Rallying Song of the Gaelic League) was composed as a poem by Dermot Foley (Diarmuid Ó Foghludha) and set to music by Annie W. Patterson in 1905. It became a popular anthem at Gaelic League events. See McMahon, *Grand Opportunity*, 157–58.

68. L. P. B., "Open Air Drama," *Leader*, Mar. 27, 1909.

69. Cuan Dor, "Irish Drama in the Open Air," *Leader*, Apr. 3, 1909.

70. Patrick Maume, *Daniel Patrick Moran*, 4.

71. "The Procession—Afterthoughts," *Leader*, June 29, 1907.

72. Cuan Dor, "Irish Drama in the Open Air," *Leader*, Apr. 3, 1909.

73. James Cousins and Margaret Cousins, *We Two Together*, 179–80.

74. See Keane, *Ishbel*.

75. *Irish Times*, May 6, 1911.

76. *Irish Times*, June 5, 1913.

77. Mike Cronin and Daryl Adair, *The Wearing of the Green: A History of St. Patrick's Day*, 129; Mike Cronin, "'Funereal Black Trucks Advertising Guinness': The St Patrick's Day Industrial Pageant."

78. Aberdeen and Temair and Aberdeen and Temair, *"We Twa,"* 182–83.

79. *Irish Independent*, Mar. 16, 1909.

80. *Irish Industries Pageant: Illustrated Souvenir of the Irish Industries Pageant, Held in Dublin, St. Patrick's Eve, 1909*, 10.

81. Griffith explained to his readers what the symbol meant in the context of his ideology and in relation to his newspaper on Oct. 16, 1909: "That is our registered Irish Trade Mark number. *Sinn Féin* is the only journal in Ireland entitled to use the Irish Trade Mark. The reason why is that 'Sinn Féin' is the only daily journal in Ireland printed on Irish paper. 'Sinn Féin' is printed with Irish ink. All the materials procurable in Ireland that go to make up a newspaper are used in 'Sinn Féin.' All other daily journals in Ireland import their paper from England, America, France, or Holland. . . . [For the trademark] a sign peculiar to Ireland was agreed upon, namely a scroll device representing the legendary Collar of Malachi, surrounded by the words, Déanta i nÉirinn [*sic*] (Made in Ireland). The use of this sign was permitted to manufacturers who could show that their goods were made in the country, and every infringement was prosecuted under the British Trades Mark Law, the Irish people being for once able to use British law to their own advantage."

82. Aberdeen and Temair and Aberdeen and Temair, *"We Twa,"* 183. Patrick Maume notes that in 1889, O'Grady also published *Red Hugh's Captivity*, later revised as *The Flight of the Eagle*. See Maume, "Standish James O'Grady: Between Imperial Romance and Irish Revival," 24.

83. "Journalists Come from All Parts to Irish Conference," *Irish Independent*, Sept. 1, 1906.

84. "Pageant at Dublin Castle," *Irish Times*, Mar. 16, 1909.

85. Nicola Gordon Bowe, "A Contextual Introduction to Romantic Nationalism and Vernacular Expression in the Irish Arts and Crafts Movement, c. 1886–1925," 189, 192.

86. *Irish Times*, May 29, 1911.

87. Desmond Ryan, *The Man Called Pearse*, 65.

88. "'Irish' Literary Theatre,' *An Claidheamh Soluis*, May 20, 1899; "All Ireland," *United Irishman*, May 6, 1899; "All Ireland," *United Irishman*, May 13, 1899.

89. Louis N. LeRoux states that Pearse also attended the Eisteddfod in Cardiff in 1909. See *Patrick H. Pearse*, adapted from the French of Louis N. LeRoux and revised by the author, translated by Desmond Ryan, 20.

90. Ibid., 20. The Welsh National Eisteddfod often included pageants. In 1909, for instance, a pageant ended as "the whole five thousand actors, at one swift movement, fell into groups making a Map of Wales, with 'Dame Wales in the midst.'" *Freeman's Journal*, July 28, 1909. Such a configuration of a nation appears in Bryan MacMahon's *The Pageant of the Four Green Fields*.

91. The uncial inscription originally executed by the Morrow brothers has since been replicated for the Office of Public Works' renovation of the Hermitage as the Pearse Museum. See Elaine Sisson, *Pearse's Patriots: St Enda's and the Cult of Boyhood*, 210.

92. *Diaries of Joseph Holloway*, MS 1806, NLI.

93. Finola O'Kane, "Nurturing a Revolution: Patrick Pearse's School Garden at St Enda's," review of *The Twentieth-Century Landscape*, 78.

94. Cathaoir O'Braonain, "Poets of the Insurrection II: Patrick H. Pearse," 346.

95. Padraic Pearse, *The Story of a Success*, 17.

96. O'Leary, *Prose Literature of the Gaelic Revival*, 249–58.

97. See Edward A. Hagan, *High Nonsensical Words: A Study of the Works of Standish James O'Grady*, 137: "*The Coming of Fionn* masque was written years since in Kilkenny for Lady Desart, and was acted in her grounds at Aut-Evin on the banks of the Nore," with lights hanging from tree branches, "acting was by night," supervised by Captain Otway Cuffe. *Hugh Roe O'Donnell* was "to be performed in woods of Sheestown, in the County of Kilkenny, 15 Aug. 1902." Standish O'Grady, *Hugh Roe O'Donnell: A Sixteenth Century Irish Historical Play*, 1. O'Grady's play ends with the recitation of a genealogy tracing Hugh Roe O'Donnell's direct lineage back through, inter alia, Niall of the nine hostages; Milesius, king of Spain; Magog; Noah; to Adam, "the son of God" (32).

98. *Diaries of Joseph Holloway*, MS 1806, NLI.

99. Ibid.

100. Ibid.

101. Standish O'Grady, *The Masque of Fionn*, 26–27. *The Coming of Fionn* is the first part of *The Masque of Finn*, which was published in a compendium volume, *Finn and His Companions*, with separate pagination.

102. *Diaries of Joseph Holloway*, MS 1806, NLI.

103. "St. Enda's School, Rathmines," *Irish Independent*, Mar. 22, 1909.

104. "The Return of the Fianna," *An Claidheamh Soluis*, Mar. 27, 1909.

105. W. P. Ryan, *Irish Nation*, Mar. 27, 1909.

106. Pearse, *The Story of a Success*, 17–19.

107. Ibid., 40.

108. Ibid., 19–20.

109. Sisson, *Pearse's Patriots*, 91.

110. All quotations from *The Boyhood Deeds* refer to the translation published as the appendix.

111. Philip O'Leary, "'The Dead Generations': Irish History in the Gaelic Revival," 93–96.

112. See Sisson, *Pearse's Patriots*; and John Springhall, *Youth, Empire, and Society: British Youth Movements, 1883–1940*.

113. Stephen MacKenna, "Pageants," *Freeman's Journal*, June 23, 1909.

114. Ibid.

115. Brendan Walsh, *Boy Republic: Patrick Pearse and the Weapon of Education*, 155.

116. "Dr. Douglas Hyde at the Frankfort Feis," *Irish Times*, June 6, 1910.

117. Milo Mac Garry recalls a famous episode when the performers returned to Dublin drew a receptive crowd of onlookers as "battleaxes, tall gilded spears which glinted like polished bronze in the lamp-lit streets." "Memories of Sgoil Eanna," *Capuchin Annual* (1930): 38.

118. See Sisson, *Pearse's Patriots*, 8; and Milo Mac Garry, "Memories of Sgoil Eanna," 37.

119. *Diaries of Joseph Holloway*, MS 1806, NLI.

120. Sean Mac Giolla An Atha, *An Claidheamh Soluis*, Mar. 27, 1909.

121. *Irish Times*, June 17, 1912.

122. *Irish Times*, Apr. 15, 1913.

123. *An Macaomh* 1, no. 2 (1913).

124. Jones Road was the site of Croke Park. The previous year, on June 29 and 30, 1912, the Gaelic League Carnival was held at Jones Road. On June 14, 1913, a fire broke out at Jones Road "where the St. Enda's *fete* is at present being held." See Patrick Pearse, Róisín Ní Ghairbhí, and Eugene McNulty, *Patrick Pearse: Collected Plays*, 48–52.

125. Sean O'Casey, "The Irish Fete in Jones's Road," in *The Letters of Sean O'Casey, 1910–1941*, 1:28.

126. Sean O'Casey, "No Flowers for Films," in *The Green Crow*, 174.

127. Brian Crowley, *Patrick Pearse: A Life in Pictures*, 101.

128. "St. Enda's College," *Irish Times*, June 15, 1914. See also Raymond J. Porter, *P. H. Pearse*. Porter asserts that because Pearse was in America, St. Enda's performed no pageants in 1914.

129. Joseph Holloway Ephemera, NLI.

130. *Irish Times*, June 23, 1909.

131. See Dean, *Riot and Great Anger*, 166–77.

132. "A National Pageant," *Sinn Féin*, Aug. 21, 1909.

133. *Sinn Féin*, Aug. 26, 1909.

134. Frazier, *Behind the Scenes*, 91.

135. Morris, *Alice Milligan*, 30.

136. Hyde's preface distinguishes the Children of Tuireann from the Children of Lir and the Children of Uisneach (the tale of Deirdre) because the former "belongs to purely mythological times, perhaps many hundreds of years before Christ. All the characters are mythological." Douglas Hyde, *Children of Tuireann*, 6.

137. Ibid., 5.

138. Ibid., 54–55.

139. Alice Milligan, "The Return of Lugh-Lamh-fada," in *Hero Lays*, 13.

140. *Diaries of Joseph Holloway*, MS 1806, NLI.

141. *Sinn Féin*, Sept. 4, 1909. Molloy's political cartoons would regularly illustrate *Sinn Féin* with allegorical representations of insurgent nationalism. On Molloy, see Brian Ó Conchubhair, *"An Gúm*, the Free State and the Politics of the Irish Language," 106–13.

142. The sunrise and the sword of light, already potent symbols of the nationalist cause, appeared on the mastheads of the Gaelic League newspapers, *Fáinne an Lae* (Dawn of Day) and *An Claidheamh Soluis* (The Sword of Light).

143. "A National Pageant," *Sinn Féin*, Aug. 25, 1909.

144. *Diaries of Joseph Holloway*, MS 1806, NLI.

145. Seán Farrell Moran, *Patrick Pearse and the Politics of Redemption: The Mind of the Easter Rising, 1916*, 92.

146. McMahon, *Grand Opportunity*, 199.

147. *College Chronicle*, 29 (1914): 15.

148. Song translated by George Sigerson from *Gaels and Gall*.

149. *Castleknock College: Boy Actors from St. Patrick's College at Castleknock*.

150. *Diaries of Joseph Holloway*, MS 1809, NLI.

151. "The Castleknock College," *Irish Independent*, May 25, 1910.

152. *Diaries of Joseph Holloway*, MS 1811, NLI.

153. *Irish Times*, July 27, 1911.

154. *Diaries of Joseph Holloway*, MS 1811, NLI.

155. "Attack on King," *Irish Times*, Aug. 7, 1911.

156. "Cuchulainn's Fort, Dundalk," *Irish Times*, Aug. 12, 1911.

157. "Cuchullain's Fort," *Northern Whig*, Aug. 16, 1911.

158. "The Late Francis Joseph Bigger," 105.

159. "Cuchullain's Fort," *Northern Whig*, Aug. 16, 1911.

160. R. J. Ray, "A Notable Pageant," *Journal of the Ivernian Society* 3–4 (1910–12): 27. Ray was a journalist and the author of *The White Feather* (1909), *The Casting Out of Martin Whelan* (1910), and *The Gombeen Man* (1913).

161. Barry M. Coldrey, *Faith and Fatherland: The Christian Brothers and the Development of Irish Nationalism, 1838–1921*, 205.

162. "Christian Brothers Centenary," *Cork Free Press*, Sept. 2, 1911.

163. Ray, "A Notable Pageant," 28.

164. *Leader*, Sept. 16, 1911.

165. "Christian Brothers Centenary," *Cork Free Press*, Sept. 11, 1911.

166. Ray, "A Notable Pageant," 37.

167. Ibid.

168. Ibid., 27.

169. Coldrey, *Faith and Fatherland*, 205.

170. *Leader*, Sept. 16, 1911.

171. Coldrey, *Faith and Fatherland*, 205.

172. "The Final Act of the Pageant," *Cork Free Press*, Sept. 7, 1911.

173. Ray, "A Notable Pageant," 36.

174. Mac Garry, "Memories of Sgoil Eanna," 37. See also Sisson, *Pearse's Patriots*, 7–8.

175. "Daffodil Fete," *Irish Times*, Apr. 25, 1914.

176. Francis Sheehy-Skeffington, *The Prodigal Daughter*, 17. On April 12, 2014, the play was revived in a rehearsed reading by Donal O'Kelly at the Sheehy Skeffington Summer School in Dublin.

177. A program for *The Pageant of Great Women* displayed at the Victoria and Albert Museum, 2012.

178. *Freeman's Journal*, Apr. 25, 1914.

179. Rosemary Cullen Owens, *Smashing Times: A History of the Irish Women's Suffrage Movement, 1889–1922*, 65.

180. "Suffragist Fete in Dublin," *Irish Citizen*, May 2, 1914.

181. Guy Beiner notes that after 1898, "the nationalist press lauded Maud Gonne as the Irish 'Joan of Arc'" (253).

182. Maurice Gorman, *Dublin from Old Photographs*, n.p.

183. "Irish Women's Franchise League," *Irish Citizen*, May 2, 1914.

184. Quoted in Paul Larmour, "John Campbell (1883–1962): An Artist of the Irish Revival," 67.

185. Deborah Sugg Ryan, "Performing Irish-American Heritage: The Irish Historic Pageant, New York, 1913."

186. *Souvenir Program of Finn Varra Maa*, 1917, BK11, SRL/KU. The title refers to Finnbheara, "the king of the fairies in Irish folklore." James MacKillop, *Myths and Legends of the Celts*, 331.

187. T. H. Nally, *"Finn Varra Maa" (The Irish Santa Claus): An Irish Fairy Pantomime in Four Acts*, 19. Dialogue (as opposed to stage directions or musical scores) dominates the text; the subtitle's use of "pantomime" identifies it as a Christmas family entertainment or "panto."

188. Ibid., 42.

189. J. A. P., "Finn Varra Maa Is Still Worth Seeing," *Irish Independent*, Dec. 24, 1932.

190. Axel Klein, "Legends in Irish Opera, 1900–1930," 49.

191. Fintan O'Toole, "The Irish for Ho, Ho, Ho," 91.

192. Bowe and Cumming, *Arts and Crafts Movements*, 167–68.

193. On the mission in Chota Nagpur, see Oonagh Walsh, *Anglican Women in Dublin: Philanthropy, Politics, and Education in the Early Twentieth Century*.

194. Eva Jellett, *A Pageant of Irish Saints*, program, 1924, MS 159, RCBL.

195. "Irish Pageant," 1921, British Pathé, 236.15, http://www.britishpathe.com/video/irish-pageant.

196. Eva Jellett, *A Pageant of Irish Saints*, press clipping, 1921, MS 159, RCBL.

197. John Millington Synge to Stephen MacKenna, in *The Collected Letters of John Millington Synge*.

2. FORGING THE PAST IN THE IRISH FREE STATE

1. "Varadkar Hopes 'Gathering' Will Generate €200 Million," *Irish Times*, Mar. 8, 2012.

2. J. J. Walsh's enthusiasm for the Aonach Tailteann endured even after his abrupt departure from government in 1928. In his "hearty Cead Mile Failte" to the program of the second Aonach Tailteann, Walsh, who signed his name in Irish, Seamus Breathnach, described the games as "this quadrennial call of motherland [for] all who love and wish to serve the old land." In his memoir, *Recollections of a Rebel*, Walsh, although embittered by his experiences in government, is especially proud of his contributions to the Aonach Tailteann.

3. León Ó Broin, *Revolutionary Underground: The Story of the Irish Republican Brotherhood, 1858–1924*, 88.

4. Seamus Deane, "Irish Poetry and Irish Nationalism," 11.

5. Andrew Kincaid, *Postcolonial Dublin: Imperial Legacies and the Built Environment*, 62.

6. John Turpin, "Visual Culture and Catholicism in the Irish Free State, 1922–1949," 55.

7. See Paige Reynolds, *Modernism, Drama, and the Audience for Irish Spectacle*; and Mike Cronin, "Projecting the Nation through Sport and Culture, Aonach Tailteann and the Irish Free State, 1924–32" and "The State on Display: The 1924 Tailteann Art Competition."

8. The 1924 subsidy of £600 to An Comhar Drámaíochta, the "in-house production company at the Abbey," predates the £850 subsidy to the Abbey Theatre in August 1925. See Robert Welch, *The Abbey Theatre, 1899–1999: Form and Pressure*, 86.

9. Anne Dolan, *Commemorating the Irish Civil War: History and Memory, 1923–2000*, 25.

10. *Proceedings of the Irish Race Congress*, i.

11. John Brannigan, *Race in Modern Irish Literature and Culture*, 36.

12. *Proceedings of the Irish Race Congress*, xiv.

13. Brannigan, *Race in Modern Irish Literature and Culture*, 42.

14. *Irish Times*, July 14, 1914.

15. T. H. Nally, *The Aonac Tailteann and the Tailtenn Games: Their Origin, History and Development*, 7.

16. M. J. MacAuliffe, *The History of the Aenach Tailteann and the Ancient Irish Laws*, xiv.

17. Cronin, "Projecting the Nation," 404.

18. The signature and date "W. Victor Brown/22" appear on the cover of *Tailteann Games: Irish Race Olympic*, but not on subsequent uses of the image. W. Victor Brown illustrated F. R. Higgins's poetry collection *Salt Air*.

19. Program for *The Story of the Games*, JHE/NLI.

20. Reynolds, *Modernism, Drama, and the Audience*, 169.

21. "Pageant of Queen Tailte," *Irish Times*, June 16, 1932. A. T. Lawlor and Elizabeth Young as well as Dr. John Larchet and Miss Rock were later involved in creating other Irish historical pageants.

22. Dominic Bryan, *Orange Parades: The Politics of Ritual, Tradition and Control*, 60.

23. After Laurence O'Neill's departure on February 23, 1924, Dublin did not have a lord mayor until Alfred ("Alfie") Byrne took office on October 14, 1930. Dublin Corporation was likewise suspended during this period. Because of the number of anti-Treaty figures in Dublin government, the municipal government was replaced in 1924 by a direct state administration under the supervision of the minister for local government with three Dublin city commissioners: Seamus O Murchadha, Patrick J. Hernon, William C. Dwyer.

24. Micheál macLíammóir, *All for Hecuba: An Irish Theatrical Autobiography*, 83.

25. See http://www.bridgesofdublin.ie/gallery/view/oconnell-bridge-irish-civic-week-1927.

26. *Dublin Civic Week, 1927: Historical Costume Ball*, 3.

27. See Marnie Hay, *Bulmer Hobson and the Nationalist Movement in Twentieth-Century Ireland*.

28. "Trinity College Park Sept. 19 & 23, Mansion House Sept. 20 & 24," private collection.

29. Brian P. Kennedy, "The Failure of the Cultural Republic: Ireland, 1922–1939," 17.

30. See Fionna Barber, *Art in Ireland since 1910*, 70–71.

31. Reynolds, *Modernism, Drama, and the Audience*, 157.

32. Seamus Murphy, "Foreword," in *Dublin Civic Week, 1927: Official Handbook*, 7.

33. "Municipal Government in Dublin," in *Dublin Civic Week, 1927: Official Handbook*, 10.

34. The *Irish Times*, on September 22, 1927, described the Pageant of Irish Industry: "Six tall young Civic Guards marched in front. . . . St. John ambulance pipe band, two civic Guard bands and the Artane school band. Fire Brigade . . . City Technical Institute . . . Post Office . . . gaily decorated vehicles." Colorful floats displaying improved, modern municipal services paid tribute to the efficiency and legitimacy of the appointed Dublin city commissioners.

35. *Dublin Civic Week 17th to 25th Sept. 1927: General Programme*, n.p.

36. *Irish Times*, Sept. 20, 1927.

37. "Historical Pageants," *Irish Independent*, Sept. 10, 1927.

38. Seamus MacCall, *Historical Pageant (Official Guide)*, 4. Subsequent references given in the text.

39. Geoffrey Coulter, "History Brought to Life," *Sunday Independent*, Oct. 2, 1927.

40. *Dublin Civic Week: Historical Pageant*, n.p. On September 23, 1779, John Paul Jones, commanding the USS *Bonhomme Richard*, captured the HMS *Serapis* in the North Sea off the Yorkshire coast. See James C. Bradford, "The Battle of Flamborough Head."

41. "Attractions of Civic Week," *Irish Times*, Sept. 20, 1927.

42. "Historical Pageant," *Irish Independent*, Sept. 20, 1927.

43. *Honesty*, Sept. 24, 1927.

44. *Irish Times*, Sept. 21, 1927.

45. Tableaux vivants are discussed in greater detail in the previous chapter.

46. "Dublin's Gala Week," *Irish Times*, Sept. 21, 1927.

47. "Historical Pageant," *Irish Independent*, Sept. 21, 1927.

48. "Historical Pageant: Tableaux at the Mansion House," *Irish Times*, Sept. 21, 1927.

49. Four hundred costumes in several accounts, but the *Sunday Independent* claimed there were "nearly 1,000 costumes." M. A. T., "Stage and Platform," *Sunday Independent*, Oct. 2, 1927.

50. Patricia Boylan writes that in the 1920s, Toto Cogley ran "a cabaret-cum-nightclub-cum-shebeen called The Studio Art Club, at 41 Harcourt Street. She was a key figure in a truly Bohemian circle in Dublin, the Club version of which was genteel by comparison." Patricia Boylan, *All Cultivated People: A History of the United Arts Club, Dublin*, 234. Nicholas Allen identifies Toto Cogley as Helen Carter and associates Seamus MacCall with the cabaret on Hardwicke Street. Nicholas Allen, *Modernism, Ireland and Civil War*, 56–57.

51. Coulter, "History Brought to Life."

52. Clipping, "How DeValera Defied the North," *Sunday Dispatch*, Apr. 3, 1932, SmacC.

53. Seamus MacCall, "Ancient Irish Nights' Entertainments," SmacC.

54. Alec Newman was editor of the *Irish Times* from 1954 to 1961.

55. Clipping, *Honesty*, SmacC.

56. "How Life in the Army Is Publicised," *Irish Times*, Feb. 4, 1947.

57. Like Shakespeare in his history plays, Boucicault manipulated and fabricated historical episodes freely. In *Robert Emmet*, for instance, Boucicault arranged for Anne Devlin, rather than dying in abject poverty and being buried in Glasnevin cemetery, to escape to America with Michael Dwyer. See Herr, *For the Land They Loved*.

58. "Dublin's Gala Week," *Irish Times*, Sept. 21, 1927.

59. "Dublin Civic Week," *Irish Builder*, Oct. 1, 1927, 722.

60. "Civic Week," *Irish Builder*, Oct. 1, 1927, 736.

61. *Honesty*, Sept. 17, 1927. Art O'Murnaghan designed the cover for the *Saorstát Eireann Handbook* in 1932 and, after 1929, served as the stage manager at the Gate Theatre. His illustration of borders for the *Dublin Civic Week, 1929: Official Handbook* appears in figures 13 and 14 (pp. 120–21).

62. Sean Stafford notes Wolfe Tone's appearance with Humanity Dick Martin in Kirwan's Lane Theatre in Galway in August 1783. See Sean Stafford, "Taibhdhearc Na Gaillimhe," 183.

63. "Garrison Theatricals," O'H Q37, SRL/KU.

64. "Royal Irish Military Tournament," *Irish Times*, May 9, 1894.

65. *Northern Ireland Military Torchlight Tattoo* (1927), IWM.

66. Both tattoos were staged at Lansdowne Road, where the day after Britain entered World War I more than 350 members of the rugby union volunteered in the 7th Royal Dublin Fusiliers.

67. Alternatively, the imitative quality of these spectacles is characteristic of a postcolonial state struggling to define itself.

68. Eunan O'Halpin, "Politics and the State, 1922–32," 103, quoting G-2 report no. 6000, n.d., with Sterling (Dublin), to Marriner, Department of State, Washington, May 11, 1928 (US National Archives, RG75/841d 20/1).

69. Eunan O'Halpin, "The Army in Independent Ireland."

70. See Maryann Gialanella Valiulis, *Almost a Rebellion: The Irish Army Mutiny of 1924*; and Ciara Meehan, *The Cosgrave Party: A History of Cumann Na NGaedheal, 1923–33*.

71. "Aldershot Tattoo," *Irish Times*, May 18, 1928.

72. "Civic Week—Military Tattoo Rehearsal: Historic Curragh Ceremony," *Irish Independent*, Sept. 3, 1929.

73. *Grand Military Tattoo and Fireworks Display: Lansdowne Road, Dublin, September 17th, 21st & 24th*, 15, 17. Subsequent references given in the text.

74. *Grand Military Tattoo and Fireworks Display: Lansdowne Road, Dublin September 5th, 7th, 9th, 11th, & 14th*, 11. Subsequent references given in the text.

75. Clonmel Tercentenary Committee, *Siege of Clonmel Commemoration: Tercentenary Souvenir Record.*

76. "Tattoo Triumph," *Irish Independent*, Sept. 6, 1929.

77. "A Magnificent Military Spectacle," *Irish Independent*, Sept. 19, 1929.

78. "Editorial," *An tOlgach*, October 1927, 2.

79. "Tattoo Triumph," *Irish Independent*, Sept. 6, 1929.

80. "Ireland's Wars," *Irish Times*, Sept. 9, 1929.

81. "Honours of Dublin's Week," *Irish Independent*, Sept. 17, 1929.

82. "Dublin Civic Week," *Star*, Aug. 24, 1929.

83. MacLíammóir translated and adapted his *Diarmuid agus Grainne* from the Irish for performance at the Peacock Theatre in November 1928.

84. *Irish Statesman*, Sept. 14, 1929. Although the Dublin Gate Theatre did not attract sufficient subscription shares, Lord Longford capitalized the macLíammóir-Edwards venture.

85. The script for *The Ford of the Hurdles* survives in several heavily notated typescripts in the Gate Theatre Archive. The seven episodes were: episode 1, "The Coming of the Fair Stranger ('A Warrior from the North of the East')"; episode 2, "The Rape of Dervogilla"; episode 3, "Diarmuid [Mac Murchadha] of the Gall: How Tiarnan O Ruairc Avenged Himself on Diarmuid Mac Murchadha"; episode 4, "The Judas of the Gael: How Diarmuid Mac Murchadha Betrayed the Irish to Henry II"; episode 5, "Roundheads and Gingerbread; Interlude: Gavotte and Minuet"; episode 6, "Green Jackets and Pikes: The Trial of Robert Emmet for High Treason"; and episode 7, "Easter: The City in the Dawn." *The Ford of the Hurdles*, Production 76, DGTA/NU.

86. MacLíammóir was especially proud of "Diarmuid's Lament," which was later recorded as a 78 rpm record; he includes his lyrics in the first volume of his autobiography, *All for Hecuba.*

87. "The Coming of the Fair Stranger," in *The Ford of the Hurdles*, 1/2, DGTA/NU. Several versions of the play in typescript appear in the Gate Theatre Archive. Cited here are episode/page numbers to reflect that the pages for each scene are numbered separately.

88. Dervogilla's costume is comparable to his design for another role played by Coralie Carmichael, Oscar Wilde's Salome.

89. D. L. Kelleher, *Ireland of the Welcomes*, 52–54.

90. James Joyce, *Ulysses*, 34–35, 324.

91. On verbatim theatre, see Mary Luckhurst, "Verbatim Theatre, Media Relations and Ethics."

92. See Marianne Elliott, *Robert Emmet: The Making of a Legend*. Elliott describes *The Ford of the Hurdles* as macLíammóir's "traditional Emmet pageant" (231) and documents numerous linkages of Emmet and the Easter Rising.

93. See James Moran, *Staging the Easter Rising: 1916 as Theatre.*

94. Quotations given in the text refer to the 1932 revision of the seventh scene, "Easter 1916." MacLíammóir's script often revises, and sometimes profoundly alters, Pearse's and Casement's original words. Casement, for instance, wrote, "The government of Ireland by England rests on restraint and not on law," but macLíammóir's script offers "rests on restraint not on love."

95. H. S., "Pearse Play and Pageant at the Gate," *An Phoblacht*, Apr. 2, 1932, Press Cuttings, Book 6, DGTA/NU.

96. The Gate produced Ernst Toller's 1927 play *Hoopla!* Toller wrote three pageants performed at social democratic festivals in the 1920s: *Pictures from the French Revolution* (1922), *War and Peace* (1923), and *Awakening* (1924; coauthored with Adolf Winds). See Fischer-Lichte, *Theatre, Sacrifice, and Ritual*, 133.

97. J. J. Lee, *Ireland, 1912–1985: Politics and Society*, 270.

98. Dorothy Macardle, "An Artist's Tribute to the Men of 1916," *Irish Press*, Apr. 26, 1933; and M. G. MacB., *An Phoblacht*, Apr. 27, 1933, Press Cuttings, Book 6, DGTA/NU. Gonne, who originated the title role of "Cathleen ni Houlihan" in 1902, claimed ownership of the play and authorized its performance by the Ulster Literary Theatre later that year.

99. "'The Ford of the Hurdles': Pageant Play at the Mansion House," *Irish Times*, Sept. 10, 1929.

100. "Triumph of the Carnival," *Irish Independent*, Sept. 14, 1929.

101. "Under Our Microscope," in *Honesty*, Sept. 14, 1929.

102. "Dublin's Civic Week as Seen from the West," in *Honesty*, Sept. 21, 1929.

103. "March of Dublin Unemployed," *Irish Times*, Sept. 12, 1929.

104. The *Sunday Independent* reported a loss of £1,719 and 19s. for the 1929 Civic Week. The deficit for *The Ford of the Hurdles*, which cost £1,010 but brought in a mere £310, accounted for just under half of the total loss. "Dublin's Civic Week," *Sunday Independent*, Jan. 19, 1930.

105. R. F. Foster, *Modern Ireland, 1600–1972*, 535.

106. See, for example, Michael Warner, *Publics and Counterpublics*.

107. Patrick Wright, *On Living in an Old Country: The National Past in Contemporary Britain*, 74.

108. Fischer-Lichte, *Theatre, Sacrifice, Ritual*, 150.

3. NORTH AND SOUTH OF THE BORDER

1. Rory O'Dwyer, "Eucharistic Congress," 46.

2. See *Eire: The Handmaid of the Eucharist*.

3. Richard Rowley, *The Pageant of St. Patrick*, 14. Subsequent references given in the text.

4. Joseph McBrinn, "The Crafts in Twentieth Century Ulster: From Partition to the Festival of Britain," 70.

5. See ibid., 60–61. McBrinn also records that a "memorial to the Pageant [of St. Patrick] was devised for St. Anne's Cathedral" in Belfast (61–62).

6. "Church of Ireland Notes," *Irish Times*, Mar. 9, 1931.

7. "Triumph of Pageant," *Belfast Telegraph*, June 11, 1932.

8. Ibid.

9. C. E., "The Pageant in Co. Down: Non-Catholic Idea of Days of St. Patrick: Unconscious Comedy," *Irish Press* (Belfast), June 13, 1932.

10. Ian McBride in *The Siege of Derry* observes, "After 1916, the Somme replaced the siege [of Derry] as the great symbol of Ulster's willingness to pay the ultimate price for king and country" (71).

11. See M. Beatrice Lavery, *Presbyterianism through the Ages*.

12. *Irish Times*, Oct. 26, 1948.

13. "Founding of Grey Abbey," *Irish Times*, June 10, 1935.

14. Perceval (1858–1944), who served as an engineer in the British army in India, sometimes signed his visual works "Ooloo." In 1999 the Down County Museum acquired eight watercolors by him.

15. Magdalen King-Hall, *Pageant of Greyabbey: Handbook*. Subsequent references given in the text.

16. "Greyabbey Pageant," newspaper clipping, tipped in program, SC/QUB.

17. *Irish Times*, June 22, 1935. In 1929 Magdalen King-Hall married Patrick Perceval Maxwell.

18. See Gillian McIntosh, *The Force of Culture: Unionist Identities in Contemporary Ireland*.

19. Walter Alison Phillips, *Revolution in Ireland, 1906–1923*, 4.

20. I. McBride, *Siege of Derry*, 80.

21. Major [Christian] Sauerzweig, "Army School of Music," 58, 59. Sauerzweig writes, "The British system was found unsuitable for our own military organisation, and from the musical point of view it also contained grave defects. British bands at that time used a pitch different form that of every other country" (57).

22. Eunan O'Halpin, *Defending Ireland: The Irish State and Its Enemies since 1922*, 101. O'Halpin observes that Hugo McNeill "remained throughout his career hopelessly insensitive to political affairs" (101).

23. Dermot Keogh and Andrew McCarthy, *Twentieth-Century Ireland: Revolution and State Building*, 22.

24. Clair Wills, *That Neutral Island: A Cultural History of Ireland during the Second World War*, 105.

25. Nicholas Canny, "Gerard A. Hayes-McCoy," in *Dictionary of Irish Biography*, http://dib.cambridge.org/quicksearch.do;jsessionid=2F24990E4C9809E2D6AA40 CC6315F5F7.

26. *Irish Times*, Aug. 14, 1935.

27. Labhras Joye, "The Reserve of the Irish Army under Fianna Fáil," 144.

28. *Irish Times*, Sept. 9, 1935.

29. "After the Horse Show," *Irish Times*, Nov. 2, 1934.

30. "The Military Tattoo," *Irish Times*, Sept. 9, 1935.

31. "The Tattoo: One-Third of Army Busy," *Irish Times*, Sept. 10, 1935.

32. J. A. P., "Impressive Opening of Military Tattoo," *Irish Times*, Sept. 18, 1935.

33. The extant files in the Military Archives on the 1935 tattoo center on the fact that the files are missing. Apparently, the 1935 files were accessed for planning the 1945 tattoo and were not located after that event.

34. Matthias J. Harford, "Legend," 22–32.

35. Press Clippings, DGTA/NU. The *Chicago Sunday Times* made that exact attribution: *The Pageant of the Celt* was macLíammóir's script from Ryan's scenario. Ryan was a Chicago attorney; founder of Irish Historical Productions, Inc.; and the son of Frank J. Ryan, who wrote the 1904 *Ireland's Crown of Thorns and Roses; or, The Best of Her History by the Best of Her Writers: A Series of Historical Narratives That Can Be Read as Entertainingly as a Novel* (Chicago: M. A. Donohue, 1904).

36. MacLíammóir, *All for Hecuba*, 200–202.

37. J. Moran, *Staging the Easter Rising*, 69, 71. The army may well have hoped for an even larger "horde." Joye documents chronic attendance problems for the newly formed Volunteers (the forerunner to the FCA) in the mid-1930s.

38. "The Military Tattoo: Pageant of Irish History," *Irish Times*, Aug. 14, 1935.

39. "Military Tattoo," *Irish Times*, Aug. 24, 1935.

40. "The Military Tattoo," *Irish Press*, Sept. 13, 1935.

41. "The Military Tattoo," *Irish Press*, Sept. 16, 1935.

42. An image of the program for the Cork tattoo is available at http://irishgarrisontowns.com/wp-content/uploads/2012/06/Front-Tattoo-Cksm.jpg.

43. "Success of the Tattoo," *Weekly Irish Times*, Sept. 21, 1935.

44. "Irish Military Tattoo, 1935," *Leitrim Observer*, Sept. 14, 1935.

45. In *A Shrinking Island: Modernism and National Culture in England*, Esty notes that "Parker made it a generic prescription that no scene represent an historical era closer to the present than the mid-seventeenth century" (59).

46. J. A. P., "Impressive Opening of Military Tattoo."

47. "Veterans of the 'Easter Dawn,'" *Irish Press*, Sept. 18, 1935.

48. "Narrative: Pageant of the Celts, Easter 1916," DGTA/NU. Subsequent references given in the text.

49. "History Lives Again," *Irish Times*, Sept. 18, 1935.

50. J. A. P., "Impressive Opening of Military Tattoo."

51. "Record Crowds at Tattoo," *Irish Independent*, Sept. 21, 1935.

52. "104,000 See the Tattoo," *Irish Press*, Sept. 23, 1935.

53. Ken Kelman, "Propaganda as Vision: *Triumph of the Will*," *Logos, http://www.logosjournal.com/kelman.pdf*.

54. Letter from Seán Murphy (for Eamon de Valera) to J. Schlemann (Dublin), DFA 14/125, NAI.

55. *Step Together* (promotional film), Video 140, MAI.

56. John Finegan, *Evening Herald*, quoted in Philip B. Ryan, *Noel Purcell: A Biography*, 47.

57. *The Roll of the Drums*, souvenir program, Theatre Royal, 1940, 7, 6. Robert Fisk observes that de Valera had championed Ireland's neutrality in the Dáil in 1927 and continued to do so. Fisk, *In Time of War: Ireland, Ulster, and the Price of Neutrality, 1939–45*, 33.

58. "Defence Week at Theatre Royal," *Irish Times*, Aug. 22, 1940.

59. *Roll of the Drums*, souvenir program, Theatre Royal, 1940, 7.

60. *Irish Times*, Aug. 26, 1940; "Theatre Royal, Dublin," *Irish Press*, Aug. 26, 1940.

61. "Theatres Make History in Dublin," *Sunday Independent*, Sept. 15, 1940.

62. "The Olympia," *Irish Times*, Apr. 15, 1941.

63. "An Historical Pageant," *Irish Times*, Mar. 30, 1937.

64. Guy Beiner, *Remembering the Year of the French: Irish Folk History and Social Memory*, 249.

65. "'Signal Fires' History in the Making," *Irish Times*, Apr. 26, 1943.

66. *Signal Fires: 26th Battalion, Easter Week, 1943*, Joseph Holloway Ephemera, NLI.

67. Sean O Mahony, *Frongoch: University of Revolution*, 58. See also W. J. Brennan-Whitmore, *With the Irish in Frongoch*. The Frongoch internment camp was, in fact, being closed down during December 1916.

68. Step Together Scrapbook, DC/236B, MAI.

69. "Details of Army and L. D. F. Step Together," Step Together Scrapbook, DC/236B, MAI.

70. Oscar Traynor, foreword to *The Illustrated Book of the Military Tattoo and Exhibition*, 9.

71. *Irish Times*, Apr. 7, 1945.

72. John P. Duggan, *A History of the Irish Army*, 341.

73. "Army Plans Tattoo on Large Scale," *Irish Independent*, Feb. 12, 1945.

74. DC/236B, MAI. In the event, in 1945 the army paid 3/4d. per mile for depreciation of tires.

75. Domhnail MacCionnaith, Chief of Staff, to Secretary, Mar. 19, 1945, DC/236B, MAI.

76. Hugo McNeill to A. T. Lawlor, May 3, 1945, DC/236B, MAI. Some of Hayes-McCoy's illustrations of the uniforms and weaponry of historical fighting men, such as an Irish musketeer at the Battle of Aughrim in 1691, can be seen in small black-and-white reproductions in *Irish Army Pictorial: A Pictorial Record Which Brings to You in Life-Like Pictures and Vivid Articles the Story of Ireland's New Army*.

77. Uniform Exhibit: Historical Section, DC/236B, MAI.

78. Frank Jeffares, "Preparing for the Battle of Benburb," *Irish Times*, July 21, 1945.

79. "An Irishman's Diary," *Irish Times*, July 30, 1945.

80. *Irish Times*, Sept. 10, 1945.

81. J. B. O'Sullivan, "The Army of the People," in *Tattoo: An Illustrated Souvenir Record of the Great Military Tattoo and Exhibition*, 18.

82. "The Military Tattoo," in *The Illustrated Book of the Military Tattoo and Exhibition*, 36. Subsequent references given in the text.

83. "Observer Says—," *Irish Press*, Apr. 6, 1945.

84. Announcer's Script, 1945 Military Tattoo, 4, DC/236B, MAI.

85. Ibid., 7–8.

86. "Military Tattoo Rehearsal," Pathé, 1936, AF1365, IFI.

87. "Military Tattoo at Dublin Thrills Thousands," *Irish Times*, Sept. 1, 1945.

88. "Plays and Films," *Dublin Opinion*, Sept. 1945.

89. Announcer's Script, 1945 Military Tattoo, 5, DC/236B, MAI.

90. Dáil Éireann, vol. 100, Mar. 27, 1946, Committee on Finance.

91. "Landing of King William: Carrick Pageant," *Belfast Telegraph*, June 12, 1948.

92. Characters in Benedict Kiely's short story "Mock Battle" attend the Battle of Scarva and recall events at one of the Carrickfergus *The Landing of William* pageants and at the Drogheda episode in the 1954 *The Pageant of St. Patrick*. See *A Letter to Peachtree, & Nine Other Stories*, 35–50.

93. Neil Jarman, *Material Conflicts: Parades and Visual Displays in Northern Ireland*, 171–89.

94. Belinda Loftus, *Mirrors: William III & Mother Ireland*, iv.

95. See Jarman, *Material Conflicts*; Bryan, *Orange Parades*; and Ruth Dudley Edwards, *The Faithful Tribe: An Intimate Portrait of the Loyal Institutions*.

96. Edwards, *Faithful Tribe*, 17.

97. H. L. Morrow, "The Battle of Scarva," *The Bell* 2, no. 4 (1937): 18–20.

98. Edwards, *Faithful Tribe*, 17.

99. Bryan, *Orange Parades*, 152, 153.

100. Gerard MacNamara, *Thompson in Tir-na-n-Og*, 323.

101. "Colourful Procession at the Dun Drom Feis," *Nenagh Guardian*, July 5, 1947.

102. Beiner, *Remembering the Year of the French*, 265, 268.

103. Clonmel Tercentenary Committee, *Siege of Clonmel Commemoration*, 88.

104. *Irish Independent*, July 29, 1947.

105. Ibid.

106. *Irish Press*, July 22, 1947.

4. THE TÓSTALS

1. "Festival of Dublin Needs Financial Guarantee," *Irish Press*, Mar. 5, 1952.

2. "Note," in *Theatre in Ireland*, by Micheál macLíammóir, 4.

3. Irene Furlong, *Irish Tourism, 1880–1980*, 167.

4. Furlong sees the suggestion that Juan Trippe, president of Pan American World Airways, made to Lemass for a "'Come Back to Erin' festival aimed at Irish-Americans" as formative in the planning for a national festival.

5. Terence Brown, *Ireland: A Social and Cultural History, 1922–2001*, 200.

6. "Final Curtain?," *Irish Times*, Feb. 16, 1958.

7. The Irish Tourist Association was founded in 1923, the Irish Tourist Board in 1939. The latter had specific responsibility for establishing and enforcing standards for tourist accommodations. In 1955 a single Bord Fáilte Éireann was created. See Eric Zuelow, *Making Ireland Irish: Tourism and National Identity since the Irish Civil War.*

8. J. P. O'Brien, *An Tóstal*, n.p.

9. "Opening of Second Annual Festival Is Marked by Big Parades," *Irish Times*, Apr. 19, 1954.

10. O'Brien, *An Tóstal*, n.p.

11. Eric Bentley, "Irish Theatre: *Splendeurs et Misères*," 217.

12. "An Chomhairle Ealaion: Memorandum in Connection with National Festival," Apr. 4, 1952, TAOIS/3/S15297, NAI.

13. "Gaelic League Pageant," *Irish Times*, Apr. 20, 1953.

14. Zuelow, *Making Ireland Irish*, 129.

15. Gerard Hayes-McCoy, "Trumpet Call," A35/113, HMcC/NUIG. Subsequent references given in the text refer to scene and page number in Hayes-McCoy's typescript. His scene 5 became *Trumpet Call*'s scene 7.

16. Clipping, *Irish Independent*, Apr. 6, 1953, A35/12, HMcC/NUIG.

17. Brian Fallon, *An Age of Innocence: Irish Culture, 1930–1960*, 259.

18. Clippings, TAOIS/3/S15297, NAI.

19. Furlong, *Irish Tourism, 1880–1980*, 173.

20. Clipping, *Irish Times*, Apr. 22, 1953, TAOIS/S 15297, NAI.

21. "Auspicious Opening," *Irish Times*, Apr. 19, 1954.

22. "Provincial Centres Make Ready for the Festival Opening," *Irish Independent*, Apr. 16, 1954.

23. See *Ireland in Spring*, dir. Colm O Laoghaire, 1957, AA433, IFI.

24. "Pageant Is High Light of Tóstal Programme," *Irish Independent*, Apr. 2, 1954.

25. *Irish Independent*, Mar. 13, 1954.

26. *Irish Times*, Apr. 16, 1954.

27. *An Tóstal*.

28. *Irish Times*, Apr. 19, 1954.

29. Even in the early stages of planning for the first Tóstal, the Irish Anti-Partition League in Belfast approached organizers about setting aside Easter Sunday, 1953, as a national day of protest against partition. Seán Lemass as minister for industry and commerce was directed to tell the Anti-Partition League that "while anti-partition propaganda will not form an official part of the arrangements, the League could avail of the excellent opportunity provided by An Tóstal to distribute anti-partition information to the many visitors who, it is hoped, will come to Ireland next year." "Extract from Cabinet Minutes," Oct. 17, 1952, TAOIS/3/S15297, NAI.

30. "Tóstal Pageant Will Be Record," *Irish Press*, Apr. 3, 1954.

31. "Tara Central Council: Pageant of St. Patrick," minutes of Feb. 2, 1954, 4, TAOIS/3/S15297, NAI.

32. "Pageant of St. Patrick," minutes of Oct. 20, 1953, meeting, 1, TAOIS/3/S15297, NAI.

33. "Pageant of St. Patrick," minutes of July 23, 1953, meeting, TAOIS/3/S15297, NAI.

34. *An Tostal*, Universal News–Irish Edition, 1955 [1954], AB276, IFI; *St. Patrick's Pageant-Drogheda*, John J. Jennings Collection, roll 87, AE086, IFI.

35. *Dublin Evening Mail*, Apr. 3, 1954. Navan, the fourth site, hosted a Gaelic festival on Easter Sunday.

36. Hayes-McCoy's papers include several drafts of the pageant. The one used here has separate pagination for each of the three episodes; subsequent references given in the text.

37. St. Patrick's boat, the *Girl Pat II*, was refitted as a white Viking long ship with a sail featuring the Paraclete and a decorative gunnel for equally decorative oars.

38. *An Tostal*, AB276, IFI.

39. "Biggest Open-Air Pageant," *Irish Times*, Apr. 19, 1954.

40. "Of Drama," *Irish Independent*, Apr. 18, 1954.

41. "Auspicious Opening," *Irish Times*, Apr. 19, 1954.

42. Anew McMaster, "Pageant at Slane," *Irish Times*, Oct. 4, 1968.

43. "1500 Years Rolled Back," *Sunday Independent*, Apr. 18, 1954.

44. Eoin Nesson, "Tóstal Pageant Cost a Gift," *Times Pictorial*, May 29, 1954.

45. "Report on *The Pageant of St. Patrick*," 1954, TAOIS/S15297, NAI.

46. "The Biggest Racket Ever," *Meath Chronicle*, May 15, 1954.

47. Robert Hogan, *After the Irish Renaissance: A Critical History of Irish Drama since "The Plough and the Stars,"* 116.

48. Quoted in Christopher Fitz-Simon, *The Boys: A Double Biography of Micheál Mac Líammóir and Hilton Edwards*, 182.

49. Hilton Edwards to W. T. Balfe [Tóstal Council], Apr. 29, 1954, DGTA/NU.

50. DFA/6/415/267, NAI.

51. L. Sheil, SJ, to macLíammóir, 1955, Correspondence, DGTA/NU.

52. Gerard Hayes-McCoy to Micheál macLíammóir, Apr. 19, 1955, DGTA/NU.

53. G. A. Hayes-McCoy, "Observations on the Script for the Pageant of Saint Patrick, 1955," Mar. 8, 1955, DGTA/NU.

54. Hilton Edwards, production memorandum, *The Pageant of St. Patrick*, 1, DGTA/NU.

55. Micheál macLíammóir, *The Pageant of St. Patrick*, 3, DGTA/NU. Subsequent references given in the text.

56. Clipping, "The Pageant of St. Patrick: Facts and Figures," DGTA/NU.

57. See John Banville, "Memory and Forgetting: The Ireland of de Valera and Seán Ó Faoláin": "The society in which I grew up, and out of which I was striving to grow, seemed to me monolithic, impregnable, eternal. The structures of it appeared not man-made but the result of natural and inevitable forces before which the individual must bend, or break" (25).

58. "Pageant Enthralled Its 30,000 Audience," *Irish Times*, May 9, 1955.

59. Quoted in display ad, *Irish Times*, May 18, 1955.

60. G. A. Olden, "Crozier and Caman," *Irish Times*, May 12, 1955.

61. Caption to photo, *Irish Times*, May 16, 1955.

62. "Croke Park Hosting," *Irish Independent*, May 27, 1955.

63. "Last Performance of Pageant of St. Patrick," *Irish Times*, May 30, 1955.

64. "Cast of 1,200 for Tóstal Pageant," *Irish Times*, Mar. 22, 1956.

65. MacLíammóir, *Theatre in Ireland*, 73.

66. Bernard Adams, *Dennis Johnston: A Life*, 311.

67. Hilton Edwards, "Report as Requested upon Two Projects for *The Pageant of Cuchulainn*," 1955, DGTA/NU.

68. Hayes-McCoy and Johnston exchanged very cordial letters about *The Pageant of Cuchulainn* in 1956. See A35/125(4), HMcC/NUIG.

69. The title of Johnston's essay gestures not to moral drama, but to the subgenre of medieval and early Tudor morality plays.

70. Denis Johnston, letter to the editor, 90.

71. Denis Johnston quoted in "An Irishman's Diary," *Irish Times*, Mar. 29, 1956.

72. E. W. T., "Towards a Dynamic Theatre," 3.

73. Denis Johnston, *The Tain: A Pageant*, in vol. 2 of *The Dramatic Works of Denis Johnston*. Subsequent references given in the text.

74. Denis Johnston, "A Note on the Theme."

75. The casting of professional actors in the major roles drew some derision as "the policy [was] that every leading Dublin theatre company should be represented among the cast of principals." "Cast of 1,200 for Tóstal Pageant," *Irish Times*, Mar. 22, 1956.

76. Ishirō Honda's film *Godzilla* appeared in 1954.

77. "A Thousand Work for Pageant's Success," *Irish Times*, May 9, 1956.

78. Ken Gray, "St. Patrick's Story," *Irish Times*, May 14, 1955.

79. Ken Gray, "Good as the Tóstal Pageant of Cuchulainn Was, We've Had It," *Irish Times Pictorial*, May 26, 1956.

80. "Close-Down of Tóstal in Dublin," *Irish Independent*, May 22, 1956.

81. "'Satchmo' Beats Cuchullain in Popularity Test in Dublin," *Connaught Sentinel*, May 29, 1956.

82. "But the 'Home Front' Tourism Has Been Neglected," *Irish Times [Pictorial]*, Feb. 4, 1956.

83. [J. C. Davis], "Cork Has Best Tóstal Idea," *Pictorial Postbag, Irish Times*, Apr. 7, 1956, 18.

84. "An Irishman's Diary," *Irish Times*, May 23, 1956.

85. "Scrapbook for 1956," *Irish Times*, Dec. 29, 1956.

86. A. J. Leventhal, "Dramatic Commentary," 52.

5. 1966 AND THE RECUPERATIVE PAGEANTRY OF MACNAS

1. Mary Daly, "History à la Carte? Historical Commemoration and Modern Ireland," 35.

2. See ibid., 35–36.

3. "Foreword by the Taoiseach," in *Cuimhneachán, 1916–1966: Commemoration*, 11.

4. Max Caulfield, *The Easter Rebellion*, 34–35.

5. Tomás Mac Anna, interview by Karen Carleton, 278.

6. Richard Pine, "Tomás Mac Anna" [obituary], *Guardian*, July 10, 2011, *http://www.guardian.co.uk/stage/2011/jul/10/Tomás-mac-anna-obituary*.

7. Tomás Mac Anna, interview by Christopher Murray, 132.

8. "Dundalk An Tostal," *Irish Independent*, May 10, 1955.

9. "Tostal Attractions," *Irish Independent*, Apr. 19, 1955.

10. *Cuimhneachán, 1916–1966*, 54.

11. Quoted in Roche, "Stage Representations of the Rising," 307. Roche notes that the tribute to the Civil War dead did not materialize. He remarks that a reference to the armies of the Emergency seems "incongruous," but the inclusion of more recent Irish forces is perfectly consonant with practice in the military tattoos.

12. *Cuimhneachán, 1916–1966*, 54. Accounts vary in setting the number of participants from the Defence Forces between six and eight hundred.

13. Roche, "Stage Representations of the Rising," 308.

14. *Cuimhneachán, 1916–1966*, 54.

15. Eileen O'Brien, "President Attends 1916 Pageant," *Irish Times*, Apr. 13, 1966.

16. Roisín Higgins, "Remembering and Forgetting Pearse," 135. Higgins quotes an account in the *Boston Globe* that reported, "The greatest cheers came, not for any of the marching men, but for the strikers of 1913, when they burst onto the field with their placards. And the loudest boos were not for the red-coats, with their muskets and their cannons, but the baton charge by the police that helped to break the strike!" (135).

17. Cathal Brennan, "A TV Pageant: The Golden Jubilee Commemorations of the 1916 Rising." A special issue of the *Irish Socialist* published for the fiftieth anniversary of the 1916 Easter Uprising is available online: http://comeheretome. com/2010/06/14/1916-1966-irish-socialist-commemorative-booklet.

18. O'Brien, "President Attends 1916 Pageant."

19. *Insurrection* was broadcast by RTÉ and is available online at http://www.rte. ie/archives/.

20. Bryan MacMahon, memo to Cian O'Carroll, May 31, 1983, 1, BMacM.

21. Bryan MacMahon to the *Sunday Press*, Mar. 30, 1962, BMacM.

22. "All Ireland Football Championship Final," 1954, AA225, IFI.

23. "Big Day for Meath in Dublin," *Irish Times*, Sept. 27, 1954.

24. "Pageant Novel Croke Park Attraction," *Irish Independent*, Sept. 27, 1954.

25. J. Bowyer Bell, *The Secret Army: The IRA, 1916–1979*, 269.

26. Bryan MacMahon, *The Pageant of the Flag* typescript, 7–8, BMacM. Subsequent references given in the text.

27. Bryan MacMahon, *The Pageant of the Four Green Fields*, typescript, 7–8, BMacM.

28. Gearóid Ó Tuathaigh, in conversation with the author, Apr. 27, 2010.

29. Bryan MacMahon, *Seachtar Fear, Seacht Lá*, typescript, 1a, BMacM.

30. Bryan MacMahon, "Music and Poetry in Script," typescript, BMacM.

31. Bryan MacMahon, *Seachtar Fear, Seacht Lá*, typescript, 6, BMacM.

32. *Seachtar Fear, Seacht Lá* program, 1966, n.p., BMacM.

33. Bryan MacMahon, *Seachtar Fear, Seacht Lá*, typescript, 1a, BMacM.

34. Brennan, "TV Pageant." Planned broadcast of *Seachtar Fear, Seacht Lá* on RTÉ came only after a dispute over fees for actors and technicians to stage an extra daytime performance. Dermot Doolan, secretary of Irish Actors' Equity, quoted: "Equity told Telefís Eireann that one night's television performance fee should be equal to the week's salary for the pageant. While actors subsidise theatre in Ireland, they are not prepared to subsidise Telefís Eireann." *Irish Times*, Mar. 12, 1966.

35. Michael Parker, "Reckonings: The Political Contexts for Northern Irish Literature, 1965–68," 137.

36. Michael Foy, "Dramatic Pageant His Big Cast," *Irish Times*, Mar. 18, 1966.

37. Roisín Higgins, "'I Am the Narrator Over-and-Above . . . the Caller Up of the Dead: Pageant and Drama in the 1966 Commemorations," 152.

38. Bryan MacMahon, *Seachtar Fear, Seacht Lá*, typescript, 8, BMacM.

39. On expectations of the Rising's participants, see Fearghal McGarry, *The Rising: Ireland—Easter 1916*, esp. chap. 4, "Walking on Air," 120–65, and his essay "1916 and Irish Republicanism: Between Myth and History."

40. Declan Kiberd, "The Elephant of Revolutionary Forgetfulness," 19. Subsequent references given in the text.

41. Clipping, "Dingle Tribute to Thomas Ashe," *Kerryman*, June 3, 1967, BMacM.

42. MacMahon quoted in "Dingle Tribute to Thomas Ashe," *Kerryman*, June 3, 1967, BMacM.

43. Ibid.

44. "To-day's Pageant," in *Luimneach Civic Week, '76* (Limerick: n.p., 1976), n.p., BMacM.

45. Clipping, "City Sees Itself in Pageant," *Irish Press*, Mar. 15, 1976, BMacM.

46. Caroline Walsh, "Pearse Pageant Has Cast of Thousands," *Irish Times*, Nov. 7, 1979.

47. Jim Kennedy, "Information" (press release), Coiste Chomoradh an Phiarsaigh (the Committee to Commemorate Pearse), 1, BMacM.

48. Bryan MacMahon, *A Pageant of Pearse* typescript, 6, BMacM.

49. Walsh, "Pearse Pageant."

50. Des Cassidy, "Drama Sketches Life of Soldier, Writer," *Irish Press*, Nov. 7, 1979.

51. "The Boom in Medieval Banquets," *Irish Independent*, July 28, 1975, BMacM.

52. *Pageant of Ireland* program, BMacM.

53. Bryan MacMahon, *Pageant of Ireland*, typescript, 6, BMacM. Subsequent references given in the text.

54. Memo to Cian O'Carroll, BMacM.

55. *Pageant of Ireland* program, BMacM.

56. Anne Crilly, "Relief All Round after Siege Pageant," *Fortnight*, June 1990.

57. Quoted in ibid., 28.

58. "Siege of Derry Pageant," *Theatre Ireland* 22 (1990): 3.

59. Seamus Deane, "Wherever Green Is Read," 98.

60. Irene Furlong, "Tourism and the Irish State in the 1950s," 181.

61. See Olwen Fouéré's account of the history of the company she cofounded with Roger Doyle, "Operating Theatre and *Angel/Babel*"; and Carmen Szabo, *The Story of Barabbas, the Company*. See also Raymond Keane, "I a Clown."

62. Patrick Lonergan, *Theatre and Globalization: Irish Drama in the Celtic Tiger Era*, 4–5.

63. Quoted in Christie Fox, *Breaking Forms: The Shift to Performance in Late Twentieth-Century Irish Drama*, 2.

64. See Bernadette Sweeney, *Performing the Body in Irish Theatre*. Sweeney notes that Mac Intyre received a grant from the Irish Arts Council that contributed to the creation of *Doobally/Black Way* in 1979, which was well received in Paris, but the second performance in the Edmund Burke Theatre at Trinity College "was interrupted as police removed irate members of the audience" (74).

65. Vincent Hurley, "*The Great Hunger*: A Reading," 80.

66. Anna McMullan, "Reclaiming Performance: The Contemporary Irish Independent Theatre Sector," 30.

67. Fox, *Breaking Forms*, 22.

68. Macnas application to Gulbenkian Foundation, MA/NUIG.

69. Bernadette Quinn, "Changing Festival Places: Insights from Galway," 238.

70. Fox, *Breaking Forms*, 63.

71. Páraic Breathnach, in discussion with the author, May 28, 2012.

72. See Gailey, *Irish Folk Drama*. In *The I.R.A. and Its Enemies: Violence and Community in Cork, 1916–1923*, Peter Hart examines similarities between the Wren boys and IRA activities (178–83).

73. Terry Dineen, *Macnas: Joyful Abandonment*, 37.

74. Riona Hughes, "The Flateley Family," in ibid., 27.

75. Dineen, *Macnas: Joyful Abandonment*, 70.

76. Program for *Táin*, n.p.

77. "*An Táin*: Draft Scenario," 1, MA/NUIG.

78. "*An Táin*: Draft Scenario," 1, MA/NUIG.

79. "*An Táin*: Draft Scenario," 3, MA/NUIG.

80. Program for *Táin*, n.p.

81. Lorcan Roche, "Giant Steps from the Street," *Irish Press*, Oct. 16, 1992.

82. Paddy Wordworth, "'The Tain' at Galway Arts Festival," *Irish Times*, July 23, 1992.

83. John Linklater, "Big Idea's from Erin's Pagan Past," *Herald*, Oct. 19, 1992.

84. Breathnach, in discussion with the author, May 28, 2012.

85. Bernadette Quinn, "Shaping Tourism Places: Agency and Interconnections in Festival Settings," 73, http://public.eblib.com/EBLPublic/PublicView.do?ptiID=204114.

CONCLUSION

1. Lynda Henderson, "A Fondness for Lament," 18. To support her argument, Henderson pointed to Friel's *Translations*, Kilroy's *Double Cross*, and McGuinness's *Carthaginians*.

2. Gerald Fitzgibbon, "Historical Obsession in Recent Irish Drama," 41.

3. Claire Gleitman, "Reconstructing History in the Irish History Play," 218.

4. Bernhard Klein, *On the Uses of History in Recent Irish Writing*, 84.

5. Christopher Murray, "The History Play Today," 273.

6. Frank McGuinness, interview by Dominic Cavendish, 118. See Joan FitzPatrick Dean, "Advice to the Players, and the Historians: Metatheatricality of McGuinness's *Mutabilitie*."

7. Roy Foster, "'Something of Us Will Remain': Sebastian Barry and Irish History," 196.

8. Brian Friel, *Making History*, 8.

9. Tony Corbett, *Brian Friel: Decoding the Language of the Tribe*, 13.

10. Hilton Edwards, "The Historical Pageant," in *Dublin Civic Week, 1929: Official Handbook*, 42; Mary Helen Thuente, "The Folklore of Irish Nationalism," 52.

APPENDIX: ENGLISH TRANSLATION OF PEARSE'S
MACGHNÍOMHARTHA CHÚCHULAINN BY SEÁN Ó BRIAIN

1. Translation and notes by Séan Ó Briain of "Macghníomhartha Chúchulainn" from Patrick Pearse, *Na scríbhinni liteartha le Pádraig Mac Piarais: scríbhinni i nGaeilge*, 142–55.

2. An Chraobh Rua. Traditionally this has been translated as "Red Branch," the "Red Branch" knights, and so on. The original form is "Craebruad" or "Craobhrua," a compound word, and the correct translation is really "Branch Red." It was the title of Conchúr's residence at Eamhain Macha.

3. Note that in the first song, final stanza, third line, Cúchulainn replies to Conchúr, "Is mé mac do dhearthar" (I am son of your brother). However, elsewhere in the text Cúchulainn says he is son of Conchúr's *sister*. See note 5.

4. "Ficheall": This is translated as "chess," although it is believed the board game in question was not the modern one as we know it. Literally it means "wood sense." In some translations it is left as "fidchell" or "ficheall."

5. Note that in the final stanza of the Choir's opening verses, Cúchulainn replies to Conchúr, saying, "I am the son of your brother."

6. See note 4.

Glossary

aeridhearcht. Open-air entertainment.

Ard Ri. High king.

An Chomhairle Ealaíon. Irish Arts Council.

Comhaltas Ceoltóirí Éireann. Society for Musicians of Ireland.

craobh. A branch of the Gaelic League.

Dáil Éireann. Irish parliament.

eric: Fine paid by a murderer to his victim's family.

feis (pl. **feiseanna**): Festival.

Garda Síochána. Irish police (lit., Guardians of the Peace).

geas (pl. **geasa**). Unique obligation or prohibition.

Oireachtas. Irish parliament; also Gaelic League national festival.

Inghinidhe na hÉireann. Daughters of Erin.

Saol agus Cultúr in Éirinn. Life and Culture in Ireland.

slainte. Irish for health.

Bibliography

NEWSPAPERS AND PERIODICALS

Belfast Newsletter
The Bell
Capuchin Annual
An Claidheamh Soluis
College Chronicle (Castleknock)
Connaught Sentinel
Cork Free Press
Dublin Evening Mail
Dublin Magazine
Dublin Opinion
Fortnight
Freeman's Journal
Guardian
Herald (Glasgow)
Honesty
Irish Builder
Irish Citizen
Irish Independent
Irish Nation
Irish News
Irish Press
Irish Press (Belfast)

Irish Times
Irish Worker
Leader
Leitrim Leader
An Macaomh
Manchester Guardian
Mayo News
Meath Chronicle
New Ireland Review
Northern Whig
An Phoblacht
Sinn Féin
Standard
Star
Theatre Arts
Theatre Ireland
Threshold
Times (London)
An tOlgach
Uladh
United Irishman
World's Work

ARCHIVAL FILMS

All Ireland Football Championship Final. 1954, AA225, IFI.
Castleknock College: Boy Actors from St. Patrick's College. 1931, AD231, IFI.

Ireland at Home. 1953, AB955, IFI.

Ireland in Spring. Dir. Colm O Laoghaire, 1957, AA433, IFI.

Irish Pageant. 1921, British Pathé, 236.15, http://www.britishpathe.com/video/irish-pageant.

Military Tattoo Rehearsal. 1936, AF13365, IFI.

Opening of "An Tostal." Universal Irish News, 1953, AA839, IFI.

St. Patrick's Pageant-Drogheda. John J. Jennings Collection, roll 87, AE086, IFI.

Step Together. Ca. 1940, Video 140, MAI.

An Tostal. Universal News–Irish Edition, 1955 [1954], AB276, IFI.

BOOKS AND ARTICLES

Aberdeen and Temair, John Campbell Gordon, and Ishbel Gordon Aberdeen and Temair. *"We Twa": Reminiscences of Lord and Lady Aberdeen.* London: W. Collins Sons, 1925.

Adams, Bernard. *Denis Johnston: A Life.* Dublin: Lilliput, 2002.

Allen, Nicholas. *Modernism, Ireland and Civil War.* Cambridge: Cambridge Univ. Press, 2009.

Banville, John. "Memory and Forgetting: The Ireland of de Valera and Seán Ó Faoláin." In *Ireland in the 1950s: The Lost Decade*, edited by Dermot Keogh, Finbarr O'Shea, and Carmel Quinlan, 21–30. Cork: Mercier, 2004.

Barber, Fionna. *Art in Ireland since 1910.* London: Reaktion, 2013.

Bartlett, Rebecca. "Theatre Omnibus." *Theatre Ireland*, no. 24 (Winter 1990–91): 22–23.

Beiner, Guy. *Remembering the Year of the French: Irish Folk History and Social Memory.* Madison: Univ. of Wisconsin Press, 2007.

Bell, J. Bowyer. *The Secret Army: The IRA, 1916–1979.* Dublin: Poolbeg, 1998.

Bell, Sam Hanna. *The Theatre in Ulster: A Survey of the Dramatic Movement in Ulster from 1902 until the Present Day.* Dublin: Gill and Macmillan, 1972.

Bentley, Eric. "Irish Theatre: *Splendeurs et Misères.*" *Poetry* 53 (Jan. 1952): 216–32.

Bergeron, David. *English Civic Pageantry, 1558–1642.* Columbia: Univ. of South Carolina Press, 1971.

Bhreathnach-Lynch, Síghle. *Ireland's Art, Ireland's History: Representing Ireland, 1845 to Present.* Omaha, NE: Creighton Univ. Press, 2007.

Bigger, Francis Joseph. "'Hugh Roe O'Donnell': An Irish Historical Masque." *Ulster Journal of Archaeology* 8, no. 4 (1902): 172.

Bort, Eberhard, ed. *Commemorating Ireland: History, Politics, Culture*. Dublin: Irish Academic Press, 2004.

Bowe, Nicola Gordon. "A Contextual Introduction to Romantic Nationalism and Vernacular Expression in the Irish Arts and Crafts Movement, c. 1886–1925." In *Art and the National Dream: The Search for Vernacular Expression in Turn-of-the-Century Design*, edited by Nicola Gordon Bowe, 181–200. Dublin: Irish Academic Press, 1993.

Bowe, Nicola Gordon, and Elizabeth Cumming. *The Arts and Crafts Movements in Dublin and Edinburgh, 1885–1925*. Dublin: Irish Academic Press, 1998.

Boylan, Patricia. *All Cultivated People: A History of the United Arts Club, Dublin*. Gerrards Cross: Smythe, 1988.

Bradford, James C. "The Battle of Flamborough Head." In *Great American Naval Battles*, edited by Jack Sweetman, 27–47. Annapolis, MD: Naval Institute Press, 1998.

Brannigan, John. *Race in Modern Irish Literature and Culture*. Edinburgh: Edinburgh Univ. Press, 2010.

Brennan, Cathal. "A TV Pageant: The Golden Jubilee Commemorations of the 1916 Rising." Irish History Online, http://www.theirishstory.com/2010/11/18/a-tv-pageant-%E2%80%93-the-golden-jubilee-commemorations-of-the-1916-rising/.

Brennan-Whitmore, W. J. *With the Irish in Frongoch*. Dublin: Talbot Press, 1917.

Brophy, Thomas J. "On Church Grounds: Political Funeral and the Contest to Lead Catholic Ireland." *Catholic Historical Review* 95, no. 3 (2009): 491–514.

Brown, Terence. *Ireland: A Social and Cultural History, 1922–2001*. London: Harper Perennial, 2004.

Bryan, Dominic. *Orange Parades: The Politics of Ritual, Tradition and Control*. London: Pluto, 2000.

Byrne, Dawson. *The Story of Ireland's National Theatre: The Abbey Theatre, Dublin*. Dublin: Talbot Press, 1929.

Carlson, Marvin A. *Places of Performance: The Semiotics of Theatre Architecture*. Ithaca, NY: Cornell Univ. Press, 1989.

Caulfield, Max. *The Easter Rebellion*. Dublin: Gill and Macmillan, 1995.

"Centenary of the Irish International Exhibition." Ballsbridge, Donnybrook and Sandymount Historical Society. http://bdshistory.org/images/final _exhibition_panels.pdf.

Clarke, Brenna Katz. *The Emergence of the Irish Peasant Play at the Abbey Theatre*. Ann Arbor, MI: UMI Research Press, 1982.

Cleary, Joe. *Outrageous Fortune: Capital and Culture in Modern Ireland*. Dublin: Field Day, 2007.

Clonmel Tercentenary Committee. *Siege of Clonmel Commemoration: Tercentenary Souvenir Record*. Clonmel: Nationalist Newspaper, 1950.

Coldrey, Barry M. *Faith and Fatherland: The Christian Brothers and the Development of Irish Nationalism, 1838–1921*. Dublin: Gill and Macmillan, 1988.

Coleman, Marie. *The Irish Sweep: A History of the Irish Hospitals Sweepstake, 1930–87*. Dublin: Univ. College Dublin Press, 2009.

Colum, Mary. *Life and the Dream*. London: Macmillan, 1947.

Condon, Janette. "The Patriotic Children's Treat: Irish Nationalism and Children's Culture at the Twilight of Empire." *Irish Studies Review* 8, no. 2 (2000): 167–78.

Connolly, Sean J., ed. *Kingdoms United? Great Britain and Ireland since 1500: Integration and Diversity*. Dublin: Four Courts, 1999.

Corbett, Tony. *Brian Friel: Decoding the Language of the Tribe*. Dublin: Liffey Press, 2002.

Cousins, James, and Margaret Cousins. *We Two Together*. Madras: Ganesh, 1950.

Cronin, Mike. "'Funereal Black Trucks Advertising Guinness': The St Patrick's Day Industrial Pageant." In *Ireland, Design and Visual Culture: Negotiating Modernity, 1922–1992*, edited by Linda King and Elaine Sisson, 151–63. Cork: Cork Univ. Press, 2011.

———. "Projecting the Nation through Sport and Culture: Ireland, Aonach Tailteann and the Irish Free State, 1924–32." *Journal of Contemporary History* 38, no. 3 (2003): 395–411.

———. "The State on Display: The 1924 Tailteann Art Competition." *New Hibernia Review* 9, no. 3 (2005): 50–71.

Cronin, Mike, and Daryl Adair. *The Wearing of the Green: A History of St. Patrick's Day*. London: Routledge, 2002.

Crowley, Brian. *Patrick Pearse: A Life in Pictures*. Cork: Mercier, 2013.

Cuimhneachán, 1916–1966: Commemoration. Dublin: Department of External Affairs, 1966.

Cullen, Fintan. *Ireland on Show: Art, Union, and Nationhood*. Farnham: Ashgate, 2012.

Czira, Sidney Gifford. *The Years Flew By: Recollections of Madame Sidney Gifford Czira*. Edited by Alan Hayes. Galway: Arlen House, 2000.

Daly, Mary. "History à la Carte? Historical Commemoration and Modern Ireland." In *Commemorating Ireland: History, Politics, Culture*, edited by Eberhard Bort, 34–55. Dublin: Irish Academic Press, 2004.

Daly, Mary E., and Margaret O'Callaghan, eds. *1916 in 1966: Commemorating the Easter Rising*. Dublin: Royal Irish Academy, 2007.

Dean, Joan FitzPatrick. "Advice to the Players, and the Historians: Metatheatricality of McGuinness's *Mutabilitie.*" *Irish University Review* 40, no. 1 (2010): 81–92.

———. *Riot and Great Anger: Stage Censorship in Twentieth-Century Ireland*. Madison: Univ. of Wisconsin Press, 2003.

Deane, Seamus. "Irish Poetry and Irish Nationalism." In *Two Decades of Irish Writing: A Critical Survey*, edited by Douglas Dunn, 4–22. Cheadle: Carcanet, 1975.

———. "Wherever Green Is Read." In *Revising the Rising*, edited by Máirín Ni Dhonnchadha and Theo Dorgan, 91–105. Derry: Field Day, 1991.

Dineen, Terry. *Macnas: Joyful Abandonment*. Dublin: Liffey, 2007.

Dolan, Anne. *Commemorating the Irish Civil War: History and Memory, 1923–2000*. Cambridge: Cambridge Univ. Press, 2003.

Dublin Civic Week: Historical Pageant. Dublin: n.p., 1927.

Dublin Civic Week, 17th to 25th Sept. 1927: General Programme. Dublin: n.p., 1927.

Dublin Civic Week, 1927: Historical Costume Ball. Dublin, n.p., 1927.

Dublin Civic Week, 1927: Official Handbook. Edited by Bulmer Hobson. Dublin: Civic Week, 1927.

Dublin Civic Week, 1929: Official Handbook. Edited by E. M. Stephens. Dublin: Civic Week, 1929.

Duggan, John P. *A History of the Irish Army*. Dublin: Gill and Macmillan, 1991.

Edwards, Ruth Dudley. *The Faithful Tribe: An Intimate Portrait of the Loyal Institutions*. London: HarperCollins, 1999.

———. *Patrick Pearse: The Triumph of Failure*. London: Gollancz, 1977.

Eire: The Handmaid of the Eucharist. Dublin: n.p., 1932.

Elliott, Marianne. *Robert Emmet: The Making of a Legend*. London: Profile Books, 2003.

Ervine, St. John. *The Theatre in My Time*. London: Rich and Cowan, 1933.

Esty, Joshua. *A Shrinking Island: Modernism and National Culture in England*. Princeton, NJ: Princeton Univ. Press, 2004.

Fallon, Brian. *An Age of Innocence: Irish Culture, 1930–1960*. New York: St. Martin's Press, 1998.

Farrell, Sean. *Rituals and Riots: Sectarian Violence and Political Culture in Ulster, 1784–1886*. Lexington: Univ. Press of Kentucky, 2000.

Fingall, Elizabeth, Countess of. *Seventy Years Young*. As told to Pamela Hinkson. New York: Dutton, 1939.

Fischer-Lichte, Erika. *Theatre, Sacrifice, Ritual: Exploring Forms of Political Theatre*. London: Routledge, 2005.

Fischer-Lichte, Erika, and Jo Riley. *The Show and the Gaze of Theatre: A European Perspective*. Iowa City: Univ. of Iowa Press, 1997.

Fisk, Robert. *In Time of War: Ireland, Ulster, and the Price of Neutrality, 1939–45*. Philadelphia: Univ. of Pennsylvania Press, 1983.

Fitzgibbon, Gerald. "Historical Obsession in Recent Irish Drama." In *The Crows behind the Plough: History and Violence in Anglo-Irish Poetry and Drama*, edited by Geert Lernout, 41–59. Amsterdam: Rodopi, 1991.

Fitzpatrick, William John. *Irish Wits and Worthies, Including Dr. Lanigan, His Life and Times, with Glimpses of Stirring Scenes since 1770*. Dublin: Duffy, 1873.

Fitz-Simon, Christopher. *The Boys: A Double Biography of Micheál Mac Liammóir and Hilton Edwards*. London: Nick Hern, 1994.

Fletcher, Alan J. *Drama, Performance and Polity in Pre-Cromwellian Ireland*. Toronto: Univ. of Toronto Press, 2000.

———. *Drama and the Performing Arts in Pre-Cromwellian Ireland*. Cambridge: D. S. Brewer, 2001.

Foster, R. F. *Modern Ireland, 1600–1972*. New York: Penguin Books, 1989.

———. "Remembering 1798." In *History and Memory in Modern Ireland*, edited by Ian McBride, 67–94. Cambridge: Cambridge Univ. Press, 2001.

———. "'Something of Us Will Remain': Sebastian Barry and Irish History." In *Out of History: Essays on the Writings of Sebastian Barry*, edited by Christina Hunt Mahony, 183–97. Washington, DC: Catholic Univ. of America Press, 2006.

Fouéré, Olwen. "Operating Theatre and *Angel/Babel*." In *The Dreaming Body: Contemporary Irish Theatre*, edited by Melissa Sihra and Paul Murphy, 115–24. Gerrards Cross: Colin Smythe, 2009.

Fox, Christie. *Breaking Forms: The Shift to Performance in Late Twentieth-Century Irish Drama*. Newcastle: Cambridge Scholars, 2008.

Fraser, T. G., ed. *The Irish Parading Tradition: Following the Drum*. New York: St. Martin's Press, 2000.

Frazier, Adrian. *Behind the Scenes: Yeats, Horniman, and the Struggle for the Abbey Theatre*. Berkeley: Univ. of California Press, 1990.

Frehan, Pádraic. *Education and Celtic Myth: National Self-Image and Schoolbooks in 20th Century Ireland*. Amsterdam: Rodopi, 2012.

Friel, Brian. *Making History*. London: Faber, 1989.

Furlong, Irene. *Irish Tourism, 1880–1980*. Dublin: Irish Academic Press, 2009.

———. "Tourism and the Irish State in the 1950s." In *The Lost Decade: Ireland in the 1950s*, edited by Dermot Keogh, Finbarr O'Shea, and Carmel Quinlan, 164–86. Cork: Mercier, 2004.

Gailey, Alan. *Irish Folk Drama*. Cork: Mercier, 1969.

Geary, Laurence M. *Rebellion and Remembrance in Modern Ireland*. Dublin: Four Courts, 2001.

Glassberg, David. *American Historical Pageantry: The Uses of Tradition in the Early Twentieth Century*. Chapel Hill: Univ. of North Carolina Press, 1990.

Gleitman, Claire. "Reconstructing History in the Irish History Play." In *The Cambridge Companion to Twentieth-Century Irish Drama*, edited by Shaun Richards, 218–30. Cambridge: Cambridge Univ. Press, 2004.

Gorman, Maurice. *Dublin from Old Photographs*. London: B. T. Batsford, 1972.

Graham, B. J., G. J. Ashworth, and J. E. Tunbridge. *A Geography of Heritage: Power, Culture, and Economy*. London: Arnold, 2000.

Grand Military Tattoo and Fireworks Display: Lansdowne Road, Dublin, September 5th, 7th, 9th, 11th & 14th. Dublin: Dublin Civic Week, 1929.

Grand Military Tattoo and Fireworks Display: Lansdowne Road, Dublin, September 17th, 21st & 24th. Dublin: Dublin Civic Week, 1927

Grene, Nicholas. *The Politics of Irish Drama: Plays in Context from Boucicault to Friel*. Cambridge: Cambridge Univ. Press, 1999.

Hagan, Edward A. *High Nonsensical Words: A Study of the Works of Standish James O'Grady*. Troy, NY: Whitston, 1986.

Harford, Mattias J. "Legend." In *The Pageant of the Celt*. Chicago: Irish Historical Productions, 1934.

Hart, Peter. *The I.R.A. and Its Enemies: Violence and Community in Cork, 1916–1923*. Oxford: Clarendon Press, 1998.

Hay, Marnie. *Bulmer Hobson and the Nationalist Movement in Twentieth-Century Ireland*. Manchester: Manchester Univ. Press, 2009.

———. "The Propaganda of Na Fianna Éireann." In *Young Irelands*, edited by Mary Shine Thompson, 47–56. Dublin: Four Courts, 2011.

Henderson, Lynda. "A Fondness for Lament." *Theatre Ireland* 17 (1988–89): 18–20.

Herr, Cheryl. *For the Land They Loved: Irish Political Melodrama, 1890–1925*. Syracuse, NY: Syracuse Univ. Press, 1991.

Higgins, Roisín. "'I Am the Narrator Over-and-Above . . . the Caller Up of the Dead: Pageant and Drama in the 1966 Commemorations." In *1916 in 1966: Commemorating the Easter Rising*, edited by Mary E. Daly and Margaret O'Callaghan, 148–72. Dublin: Royal Irish Academy, 2007.

———. "Remembering and Forgetting Pearse." In *The Life and After-Life of P. H. Pearse*, edited by Roisín Higgins and Regina Ui Chollatáin, 123–38. Dublin: Irish Academic Press, 2009.

———. *Transforming 1916: Meaning, Memory and the Fiftieth Anniversary of the Easter Rising*. Cork: Cork Univ. Press, 2012.

Hill, Tracey. *Pageants and Power: A Cultural History of the Early Modern Lord Mayor's Show, 1585–1639*. Manchester: Manchester Univ. Press, 2010.

Historical Processional Pageant [program]. Clonmel: Sporting Press, 1953.

Hobsbawm, Eric J., and T. O. Ranger, eds. *The Invention of Tradition*. Cambridge: Cambridge Univ. Press, 1983.

Hobson, Bulmer, ed. *Dublin Civic Week, 1927: Official Handbook*. Dublin: Civic Week, 1927.

———, ed. *Saorstát Eireann, Irish Free State: Official Handbook*. London: E. Benn, 1932.

Hogan, Robert. *After the Irish Renaissance: A Critical History of Irish Drama since "The Plough and the Stars."* Minneapolis: Univ. of Minnesota Press, 1967.

———. *The Experiments of Sean O'Casey*. New York: St. Martin's Press, 1960.

Hogan, Robert, and Richard Burnham, eds. *The Years of O'Casey, 1921–1926*. Newark: Univ. of Delaware Press, 1992.

Hogan, Robert, Richard Burnham, and Daniel P. Poteet, eds. *The Rise of the Realists, 1910–1915.* Vol. 4 of *The Modern Irish Drama: A Documentary History.* Dublin: Dolmen Press, 1979.

Howe, Stephen. *Ireland and Empire: Colonial Legacies in Irish History and Culture.* Oxford: Oxford Univ. Press, 2000.

Hurley, Vincent. "*The Great Hunger*: A Reading." In "*The Great Hunger*": *Poem into Play.* Mullingar: Lilliput, 1988.

Hutchinson, John. *The Dynamics of Cultural Nationalism: The Gaelic Revival and the Creation of the Irish Nation State.* Boston: Allen and Unwin, 1987.

Hyde, Douglas. *The Children of Tuireann.* Dublin: Talbot Press, 1941.

The Illustrated Book of the Military Tattoo and Exhibition. Dublin: Parkside, 1945.

Innes, Christopher. *Avant Garde Theatre, 1892–1992.* London: Routledge, 1993.

Irish Army Pictorial: A Pictorial Record Which Brings to You in Life-Like Pictures and Vivid Articles the Story of Ireland's New Army. Dublin: Cahill, 1943.

Irish Industries Pageant: Illustrated Souvenir of the Irish Industries Pageant, Held in Dublin, St. Patrick's Eve, 1909. Dublin: Maunsel, 1909.

Jackson, Daniel M. *Popular Opposition to Irish Home Rule in Edwardian Britain.* Liverpool: Liverpool Univ. Press, 2009.

Jarman, Neil. *Material Conflicts: Parades and Visual Displays in Northern Ireland.* Oxford: Berg, 1997.

Jefferies, Matthew. *Imperial Culture in Germany, 1871–1918.* Basingstoke: Palgrave Macmillan, 2003.

Johnston, Denis. *The Dramatic Works of Denis Johnston.* Vol. 2. Gerrards Cross: Colin Smythe, 1979.

———. Letter to the editor. *The Bell* 1, no. 6 (1941): 90.

——— [as E. W. Tocher]. "A National Morality Play." *Motley* 1, no. 1 (1932): 4–5.

———. "A Note on the Theme." Program for *The Pageant of Cúchulainn.* Dublin: Bord Fáilte Éireann, 1956.

——— [as E. W. T.]. "Towards a Dynamic Theatre." *Motley,* Apr.–May 1933, 3–4.

Joyce, James. *Ulysses.* New York: Random House, 1934.

Joyce, James, Kevin Barry, and Conor Deane. *Occasional, Critical, and Political Writing.* Oxford: Oxford Univ. Press, 2000.

Joye, Labhras. "The Reserve of the Irish Army under Fianna Fáil." In *Ireland in the 1930s: New Perspectives*, edited by Joost Augusteijn, 143–62. Dublin: Four Courts, 1999.

Keane, Maureen. *Ishbel: Lady Aberdeen in Ireland*. Newtownards: Colourpoint, 1999.

Keane, Raymond. "I a Clown." In *The Power of Laughter: Comedy and Contemporary Irish Theatre*, edited by Eric Weitz, 95–102. Dublin: Carysfort, 2004.

Kelleher, D. L. *Ireland of the Welcomes*. Dublin: Irish Tourist Association, 1929.

Kennedy, Brian P. "The Failure of the Cultural Republic: Ireland, 1922–1939." *Studies* 81, no. 321 (1992): 14–22.

Keogh, Dermot, and Andrew McCarthy. *Twentieth-Century Ireland: Revolution and State Building*. New Gill History of Ireland 6. Dublin: Gill and Macmillan, 2005.

Kiberd, Declan. "The Elephant of Revolutionary Forgetfulness." In *Revising the Rising*, edited by Máirín Ni Dhonnchadha and Theo Dorgan, 1–20. Derry: Field Day, 1991.

———. *Inventing Ireland*. Cambridge, MA: Harvard Univ. Press, 1996.

Kiely, Benedict. *A Letter to Peachtree, & Nine Other Stories*. London: Methuen, 1988.

Kincaid, Andrew. *Postcolonial Dublin: Imperial Legacies and the Built Environment*. Minneapolis: Univ. of Minnesota Press, 2006.

King-Hall, Magdalen. *Pageant of Greyabbey: Handbook*. Belfast: n.p., 1935.

Klein, Axel. "Legends in Irish Opera, 1900–1930." *Proceedings of the Harvard Celtic Colloquium* 24 (2004): 40–53.

Klein, Bernhard. *On the Uses of History in Recent Irish Writing*. Manchester: Manchester Univ. Press, 2007.

Larmour, Paul. "John Campbell (1883–1962): An Artist of the Irish Revival." *Irish Arts Review* 14 (1998): 62–73.

"The Late Francis Joseph Bigger." *Journal of the County Louth Archaeological Society* 6, no. 2 (1926): 103–5.

Lau, Meghan. "Performing History: The War-Time Pageants of Louis Napoleon Parker." *Modern Drama* 53, no. 3 (2011): 265–86.

Lavery, M. Beatrice. *Presbyterianism through the Ages: Historical Pageant*. Belfast: n.p., 1947.

Lee, J. J. *Ireland, 1912–1985: Politics and Society.* New York: Cambridge Univ. Press, 1989.

LeRoux, Louis N. *Patrick H. Pearse.* Translated by Desmond Ryan. Dublin: Talbot Press, 1932.

Leventhal, A. J. "Dramatic Commentary." *Dublin Magazine* 32 (July–Sept. 1957): 52.

Levitas, Ben. *The Theatre of Nation: Irish Drama and Cultural Nationalism, 1890–1916.* Oxford: Oxford Univ. Press, 2002.

Loftus, Belinda. *Mirrors: William III & Mother Ireland.* Dundrum: Picture Press, 1990.

Lonergan, Patrick. *Theatre and Globalization: Irish Drama in the Celtic Tiger Era.* London: Palgrave Macmillan, 2009.

Lowenthal, David. *The Past Is a Foreign Country.* Cambridge: Cambridge Univ. Press, 1985.

Luckhurst, Mary. "Verbatim Theatre, Media Relations and Ethics." In *Contemporary British and Irish Drama*, edited by Nadine Holdsworth and Mary Luckhurst, 200–222. Oxford: Blackwell, 2008.

MacAloon, John J. *Rite, Drama, Festival, Spectacle: Rehearsals toward a Theory of Cultural Performance.* Philadelphia: Institute for the Study of Human Issues, 1984.

Mac Anna, Tomas. Interview by Karen Carleton. In *Theatre Talk: Voices of Irish Theatre Practitioners*, edited by Lilian Chambers et al., 277–89. Dublin: Carysfort, 2003.

———. Interview by Christopher Murray. "Tomas Mac Anna in Interview about the Later O'Casey Plays at the Abbey Theatre." *Irish University Review* 10, no. 1 (1980): 130–45.

MacAuliffe, M. J. *The History of Aenach Tailtenn and the Ancient Irish Laws.* Ennis: n.p., 1927.

MacCall, Seamus. *And So Began the Irish Nation.* London: Longmans, Green, 1931.

———. *Historical Pageant (Official Guide).* Dublin: Rapid Printing, 1927.

Mac Garry, Milo. "Memories of Sgoil Eanna." *Capuchin Annual* (1930): 35–41.

MacKaye, Percy. *The New Citizenship: A Civic Ritual Devised for Places of Public Meeting in America.* New York: Macmillan, 1915.

MacKenna, Stephen. "Pageants." *Freeman's Journal*, June 23, 1909, 1, 6.

MacKillop, James. *Myths and Legends of the Celts.* London: Penguin, 2006.

MacLíammóir, Micheál. *All for Hecuba: An Irish Theatrical Autobiography.* 2nd ed. Dublin: Progress House, 1961.

———. *Enter a Goldfish: Memoirs of an Irish Actor, Young and Old.* London: Thames and Hudson, 1977.

———. *Theatre in Ireland.* Rev. ed. Dublin: At the Sign of the Three Candles, 1964.

MacNamara, Gerard. *Thompson in Tír-na-n-Og.* In *The Alternative Dramatic Revival in Ireland, 1897–1913,* by Karen Vandevelde, 315–29. Dublin: Maunsel, 2005.

Malone, Andrew E. *The Irish Drama.* 1929. Reprint, New York: Benjamin Blom, 1965.

Mathews, P. J. *Revival: The Abbey Theatre, Sinn Féin, the Gaelic League and the Co-operative Movement.* Cork: Cork Univ. Press, 2004.

Maume, Patrick. *Daniel Patrick Moran.* Dundalk: published for the Historical Association of Ireland by Dundalgan Press, 1995.

———. "Standish James O'Grady: Between Imperial Romance and Irish Revival." *Eire/Ireland* 39, nos. 1–2 (2004): 11–35.

McBride, Ian. *History and Memory in Modern Ireland.* Cambridge: Cambridge Univ. Press, 2001.

———. *The Siege of Derry in Ulster Protestant Mythology.* Dublin: Four Courts, 1997.

McBride, Lawrence W., ed. *Images, Icons, and the Irish Nationalist Imagination.* Dublin: Four Courts, 1999.

———. "Young Readers and the Learning and Teaching of Irish History." In *Reading Irish Histories: Texts, Contexts, and Memory in Modern Ireland,* edited by Lawrence W. McBride, 80–117. Dublin: Four Courts, 2003.

McBrinn, Joseph. "The 1904 Feis na nGleann: Craftwork, Folk Life and National Identity." *Folk Life-Journal of Ethnological Studies* 45, no. 1 (2006): 24–39.

———. "The Crafts in Twentieth Century Ulster: From Partition to the Festival of Britain." *Ulster Folklife* 51 (2005): 54–85.

———. "The Princess Taise Banner at the 1904 Feis na nGleann." *Ulster Folklore* 50 (2004): 71–98.

McGarry, Fearghal. "1916 and Irish Republicanism: Between Myth and History." In *Towards Commemoration: Ireland in War and Revolution, 1912–1923,* edited by John Horne and Edward Madigan, 46–53. Dublin: Royal Irish Academy, 2013.

————. *The Rising: Ireland—Easter 1916*. Oxford: Oxford Univ. Press, 2010.

McGuinness, Frank. Interview by Dominic Cavendish. In *Faber Playwrights at the National Theatre*, 101–18. London: Faber and Faber, 2005.

McIntosh, Gillian. *The Force of Culture: Unionist Identities in Twentieth-Century Ireland*. Cork: Cork Univ. Press, 1999.

McMahon, Timothy G. "The Gaelic Summer Colleges." In *Reading Irish Histories*, edited by Lawrence W. McBride, 118–39. Dublin: Four Courts, 2003.

————. *Grand Opportunity: The Gaelic Revival and Irish Society, 1893–1910*. Syracuse, NY: Syracuse Univ. Press, 2008.

McMullan, Anna. "Reclaiming Performance: The Contemporary Irish Independent Theatre Sector." In *The State of Play: Irish Theatre in the Nineties*, edited by Eberhart Bort, 29–38. Düsseldorf: Wissenschaftlicher Verlag Trier, 2006.

McNulty, Eugene. *The Ulster Literary Theatre and the Northern Revival*. Cork: Cork Univ. Press, 2008.

Meehan, Ciara. *The Cosgrave Party: A History of Cumann Na NGaedheal, 1923–33*. Dublin: Royal Irish Academy, 2010.

Milligan, Alice. *Hero Lays*. Dublin: Maunsel, 1908.

Moran, James. *Staging the Easter Rising*. Cork: Cork Univ. Press, 2004.

Moran, Seán Farrell. *Patrick Pearse and the Politics of Redemption: The Mind of the Easter Rising, 1916*. Washington, DC: Catholic Univ. of America Press, 1994.

Morash, Christopher. *A History of Irish Theatre, 1601–2000*. Cambridge: Cambridge Univ. Press, 2002.

Morris, Catherine. *Alice Milligan and the Irish Cultural Revival*. Dublin: Four Courts, 2012.

Morrow, H. L. "The Battle of Scarva." *The Bell* 2, no. 4 (1937): 15–21.

Mullins, Gerry. *Dublin's No. 1 Nazi: The Life of Adolf Mahr*. Dublin: Liberties Press, 2007.

Murphy, James H. *Abject Loyalty: Nationalism and Monarchy in Ireland during the Reign of Queen Victoria*. Washington, DC: Catholic Univ. of America Press, 2001.

————. *Nos Autem: Castleknock College and Its Contribution*. Dublin: Gill and Macmillan, 1996.

Murray, Christopher. "The History Play Today." In *Cultural Contexts and Literary Idioms in Contemporary Irish Literature*, edited by Michael Kenneally. Gerrards Cross: Colin Smythe, 1988.

———. *Twentieth-Century Irish Drama: Mirror Up to Nation.* New York: Manchester Univ. Press, 1997.

Nally, T. H. *The Aonach Tailteann and the Tailteann Games: Their Origin, History and Development.* Dublin: Talbot Press, 1924.

———. *Finn Varra Maa (The Irish Santa Claus): An Irish Fairy Pantomime in Four Acts.* Dublin: Talbot Press, 1917.

Nic Shiubhlaigh, Maire. *The Splendid Years.* As told to Edward Kenny. Dublin: Duffy, 1955.

Ní Dhonnchadha, Máirín, and Theo Dorgan, eds. *Revising the Rising.* Derry: Field Day, 1991.

Nora, Pierre. *Realms of Memory: Rethinking the French Past.* Edited by Pierre Nora and Lawrence D. Kritzman. New York: Columbia Univ. Press, 1996.

O'Braonain, Cathaoir. "Poets of the Insurrection II: Patrick H. Pearse." *Studies: An Irish Quarterly Review* 5, no. 19 (1916): 339–50.

O'Brien, J. P. *An Tostal.* Dublin: Fogra Failte, 1953.

Ó Broin, León. *Revolutionary Underground: The Story of the Irish Republican Brotherhood, 1858–1924.* Totowa, NJ: Rowman and Littlefield, 1976.

O'Casey, Sean. *Behind the Green Curtains.* New York: St. Martin's Press, 1961.

———. *The Green Crow.* New York: George Braziller, 1956.

———. *The Letters of Sean O'Casey, 1910–1941.* Edited by David Krause. 4 vols. New York: Macmillan / Washington, DC: Catholic Univ. of America Press, 1975–92.

O Cleirgh, Nellie, and Cecilia Saunders Gallagher. "A Political Prisoner in Kilmainham Jail: The Diary of Cecilia Saunders Gallagher." *Dublin Historical Record* 56, no. 1 (2003): 4–17.

Ó Conchubhair, Brian. "*An Gúm*, the Free State and the Politics of the Irish Language." In *Ireland, Design and Visual Culture: Negotiating Modernity, 1922–1992,* edited by Linda King and Elaine Sisson, 93–113. Cork: Cork Univ. Press, 2011.

O'Dwyer, Rory. "Eucharistic Congress." *History Ireland* (Nov.–Dec. 2007): 46.

———. *The Eucharistic Congress, Dublin, 1932.* Dublin: Nonsuch, 2009.

Ó Giolláin, Diarmuid. "The Pattern." In *Irish Popular Culture,* edited by Kerby Miller and James Donnelly, 201–21. Dublin: Irish Academic Press, 1999.

O'Grady, Standish. *Hugh Roe O'Donnell: A Sixteenth Century Irish Historical Play.* Belfast: Nelson & Knox, 1902.

————. *The Masque of Finn*. Dublin: Sealy, Bryers & Walker, 1907.

O'Halpin, Eunan. "The Army in Independent Ireland." In *A Military History of Ireland*, edited by Thomas Bartlett and Keith Jeffrey, 407–30. Cambridge: Cambridge Univ. Press, 1996.

————. *Defending Ireland: The Irish State and Its Enemies since 1922*. Oxford: Oxford Univ. Press, 1999.

————. "Politics and the State, 1922–32." In *A New History of Ireland*, edited by Jacqueline R. Hill, 7:86–126. Oxford: Oxford Univ. Press, 2003.

O'Kane, Finola. "Nurturing a Revolution: Patrick Pearse's School Garden at St Enda's." *Garden History* 28, no. 1 (2000): 78.

O'Leary, Philip. "'The Dead Generations': Irish History in the Gaelic Revival." *Proceedings of the Harvard Celtic Colloquium* 10 (1990): 88–145.

————. *Gaelic Prose in the Irish Free State, 1922–1939*. University Park: Pennsylvania State Univ. Press, 2004.

————. *The Prose Literature of the Gaelic Revival, 1881–1921: Ideology and Innovation*. University Park: Pennsylvania State Univ. Press, 1994.

O Mahony, Sean. *Frongoch: University of Revolution*. Killiney, Co. Dublin: FDR Teoranta, 1987.

O'Toole, Fintan. "The Irish for Ho, Ho, Ho." In *The Ex-Isle of Erin: Images of a Global Ireland*. Dublin: New Island Books, 1997.

Owens, Gary. "Nationalism without Words: Symbolism and Ritual Behaviour in the Real 'Monster Meetings' of 1843–45." In *Irish Popular Culture*, edited by Kerby Miller and James Donnelly, 242–69. Dublin: Irish Academic Press, 1999.

Owens, Rosemary Cullen. *Smashing Times: A History of the Irish Women's Suffrage Movement, 1889–1922*. Dublin: Attic Press, 1984.

Parker, Louis Napoleon. "Historical Pageants." *Journal of the Royal Society of Arts* 54 (1905): 145.

————. *Several of My Lives*. London: Chapman and Hall, 1928.

Parker, Michael. "Reckonings: The Political Contexts for Northern Irish Literature, 1965–68." *Irish Studies Review* 10, no. 2 (2002): 133–58.

Pearse, Patrick. *Macghníomhartha Chúchulainn*. In *Na scríbhinní liteartha le Pádraig Mac Piarais: Scríbhinní i nGaeilge*, edited by Séamas Ó Buachalla, 142–55. Dublin: Mercier, 1979.

————. *Na scríbhinní liteartha le Pádraig Mac Piarais: Scríbhinní i nGaeilge*. Edited by Séamas Ó Buachalla. Dublin: Mercier, 1979.

————. *The Story of a Success*. Dublin: Maunsel, 1917.

Pearse, Patrick, Róisín Ní Ghairbhí, and Eugene McNulty. *Patrick Pearse: Collected Plays*. Dublin: Irish Academic Press, 2012.

Phillips, Walter Alison. *Revolution in Ireland, 1906–1923*. London: Longmans, 1926.

Porter, Raymond J. *P. H. Pearse*. New York: Twayne, 1973.

Proceedings of the Irish Race Congress. Dublin: Fine Ghaedheal Central Secretariat, 1922.

Quinn, Bernadette. "Changing Festival Places: Insights from Galway." *Social and Cultural Geography* 6, no. 2 (2005): 237–52.

———. "Shaping Tourism Places: Agency and Interconnections in Festival Settings." In *Irish Tourism: Image, Culture, and Identity*, edited by Michael Cronin and Barbara O'Connor, 61–80. Clevedon: Channel View Publications, 2003. http://public.eblib.com/EBLPublic/PublicView.do?ptiID=204114.

Ray, R. J. "A Notable Pageant." *Journal of the Ivernian Society* 3–4 (1910–12): 27–38.

Reynolds, Paige. *Modernism, Drama, and the Audience for Irish Spectacle*. Cambridge: Cambridge Univ. Press, 2007.

Roche, Anthony. "Stage Representations of the Rising." In *1916 in 1966: Commemorating the Easter Rising*, edited by Mary E. Daly and Margaret O'Callaghan, 303–22. Dublin: Royal Irish Academy, 2007.

Rolston, Bill. *Politics and Painting: Murals and Conflict in Northern Ireland*. Rutherford, NJ: Fairleigh Dickinson Univ. Press, 1991.

Ronan, Rev. Myles V. "Religious Life in Old Dublin." *Dublin Historical Record* 2, no. 2 (1939): 46–54.

Rowley, Richard. *The Pageant of St. Patrick*. Belfast: United Diocese of Down and Connor and Dromore, 1932.

Ryan, Deborah Sugg. "Performing Irish-American Heritage: The Irish Historic Pageant, New York, 1913." In *Ireland's Heritages: Critical Perspectives on Memory and Identity*, edited by Mark McCarthy, 105–20. Aldershot: Ashgate, 2005.

Ryan, Desmond. *The Man Called Pearse*. Dublin: Maunsel, 1919.

Ryan, Philip B. *The Lost Theatres of Dublin*. Westbury, Wiltshire: Badger, 1998.

———. *Noel Purcell: A Biography*. Dublin: Poolbeg, 1972.

Sauerzweig, Major [Christian]. "Army School of Music." In *The Call to Arms: A Historical Record of Ireland's Defence Forces*, 57–62. Dublin: Abbey, 1945.

Sheehy, Jeanne. *The Rediscovery of Ireland's Past: The Celtic Revival, 1830–1930.* London: Thames and Hudson, 1980.

Sheehy-Skeffington, Francis. *The Prodigal Daughter.* Dublin: Manico, 1914.

Siggins, Brian. *The Great White Fair: The Herbert Park Exhibition of 1907.* Dublin: Nonsuch, 2007.

Signal Fires: 26th Battalion, Easter Week, 1943. N.p., 1943.

Sisson, Elaine. *Pearse's Patriots: St Enda's and the Cult of Boyhood.* Cork: Cork Univ. Press, 2004.

Springhall, John. *Youth, Empire, and Society: British Youth Movements, 1883–1940.* London: Croom Helm, 1977.

St. Vincent's College, Castleknock, Centenary Record, 1835–1935. Dublin: At the Sign of the Three Candles, 1935.

Stafford, Sean. "Taibhdhearc Na Gaillimhe." *Galway Archaeological and Historical Society* 54 (2002): 183–214.

Stoker, Bram. "The Great White Fair in Dublin." *World's Work* 9, no. 54 (1907): 570–79.

Sweeney, Bernadette. *Performing the Body in Irish Theatre.* London: Palgrave Macmillan, 2008.

Synge, J. M. *The Collected Letters of John Millington Synge.* Vol. 1, *1871–1907.* Edited by Ann Saddlemyer. Oxford: Clarendon Press, 1983.

Szabo, Carmen. *The Story of Barabbas, the Company.* Dublin: Carysfort, 2012.

Tailteann Games: Irish Race Olympic. Dublin: Hely's, 1922.

Tattoo: An Illustrated Souvenir Record of the Great Military Tattoo and Exhibition. Dublin: Parkside, 1946.

Taylor, Diane. *The Archive and the Repertoire: Performing Cultural Memory in the Americas.* Durham, NC: Duke Univ. Press, 2003.

Thuente, Mary Helen. "The Folklore of Irish Nationalism." In *Perspectives on Irish Nationalism,* edited by Thomas E. Hachey and Lawrence John McCaffrey, 42–60. Lexington: Univ. Press of Kentucky, 1989.

Trotter, Mary. *Ireland's National Theaters: Political Performance and the Origins of the Irish Dramatic Movement.* Syracuse, NY: Syracuse Univ. Press, 2001.

Turner, Victor. *The Anthropology of Performance.* New York: Performing Arts Journal, 1988.

Turner, Victor, and Edith L. B. Turner. *Image and Pilgrimage in Christian Culture: Anthropological Perspectives.* New York: Columbia Univ. Press, 1978.

Turpin, John. "Visual Culture and Catholicism in the Irish Free State, 1922–1949." *Journal of Ecclesiastical History* 57, no. 1 (2006): 55–77.

A Twelfth Century Pageant Play: Portraying Scenes of Irish History. Dublin: Hodges, Figgis, 1907.

Tymoczko, Maria, ed. "Tableaux Vivants in Ireland at the Turn of the Century." *Nineteenth Century Theatre* 23 (1995): 90–110.

Valiulis, Maryann Gialanella. *Almost a Rebellion: The Irish Army Mutiny of 1924.* Dublin: Tower, 1985.

Vandevelde, Karen. *The Alternative Dramatic Revival in Ireland, 1897–1913.* Dublin: Maunsel, 2005.

Walker, Brian. *Dancing to History's Tune: History, Myth and Politics in Ireland.* Belfast: Institute for Irish Studies, 1996.

Walker, Joseph C. "An Historical Essay on the Irish Stage." *Transactions of the Royal Irish Academy* 2 (1788): 75–90.

Walsh, Brendan. *Boy Republic: Patrick Pearse and the Weapon of Education.* Dublin: History Press Ireland, 2013.

Walsh, J. J. *Recollections of a Rebel.* Tralee: Kerryman, 1944.

Walsh, Oonagh. *Anglican Women in Dublin: Philanthropy, Politics, and Education in the Early Twentieth Century.* Dublin: Univ. College Dublin Press, 2005.

Warner, Michael. *Publics and Counterpublics.* New York: Zone, 2005.

Welch, Robert. *The Abbey Theatre, 1899–1999: Form and Pressure.* Oxford: Oxford Univ. Press, 1999.

Wills, Clair. *Dublin, 1916: The Siege of the GPO.* Cambridge, MA: Harvard Univ. Press, 2009.

———. *That Neutral Island: A Cultural History of Ireland during the Second World War.* Cambridge, MA: Harvard Univ. Press, 2007.

Withington, Robert. *English Pageantry, an Historical Outline.* New York: B. Blom, 1963.

———. "Louis Napoleon Parker." *New England Quarterly* 12, no. 3 (1939): 510–20.

Wright, Patrick. *On Living in an Old Country: The National Past in Contemporary Britain.* London: Verso, 1985.

Yeats, William Butler. "The Reform of the Theatre." *Samhain* 3 (Sept. 1903).

———. "Windlestraws." *Samhain* 1 (Oct. 1901): 3–10.

Zuelow, Eric. *Making Ireland Irish: Tourism and National Identity since the Irish Civil War.* Syracuse, NY: Syracuse Univ. Press, 2009.

Index

Italic page numbers denote illustrations.